DEATH IN FLORENCE

By the Same Author
The Artist, The Philosopher and The Warrior
Napoleon in Egypt: The Greatest Story
The Medici: Godfathers of the Renaissance
Dr Strangelove's Game: A History of Economic Genius
Mendeleyev's Dream
Philosophers in 90 Minutes
The Big Idea: Scientists Who Changed the World

DEATH IN FLORENCE

The Medici, Savonarola, and the Battle for the Soul of a Renaissance City

✝

PAUL STRATHERN

PEGASUS BOOKS
NEW YORK LONDON

DEATH IN FLORENCE

Pegasus Books Ltd
148 W 37th Street, 13th Floor
New York, NY 10018

First Pegasus Books paperback edition October 2016
First Pegasus Books hardcover edition August 2015

ISBN: 978-1-68177-230-1

10 9 8 7 6 5 4 3 2

Printed in the United States of America
Distributed by W. W. Norton & Company, Inc.

To my brother Mark

'The role of individuals is equally important in . . . wars and revolutions, these are historic periods where normal rules do not apply. When traditional ways of doing things no longer offer useful guidance . . . and revolutionary leaders have to fall back on instinct and charisma. Boldness, persuasiveness, and personal judgement can make the difference between triumph and disaster.'

Anatole Kaletsky

'To attribute foreseeable necessity to the catastrophe . . . would be to give it a meaning it did not have.'

Golo Mann

Contents

List of Illustrations

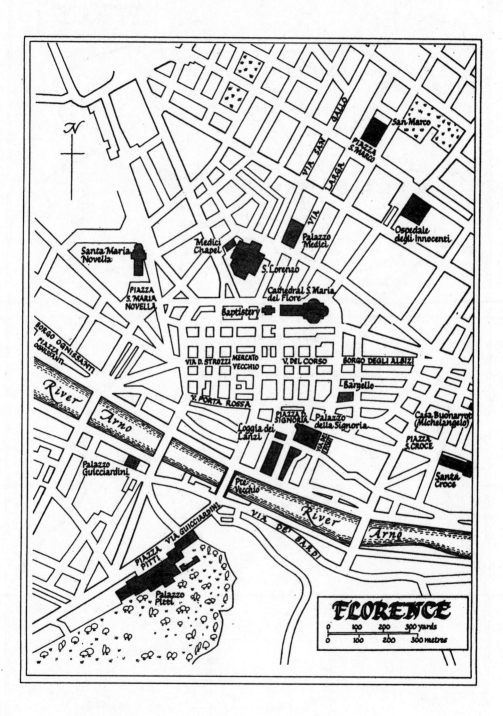

The Medici Family Tree

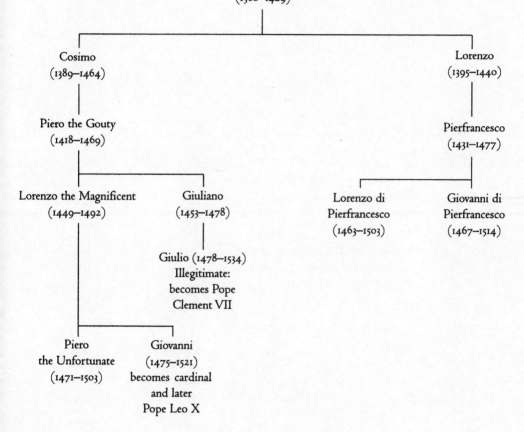

Giovanni di Bicci
(1360–1429)

Cosimo
(1389–1464)

Lorenzo
(1395–1440)

Piero the Gouty
(1418–1469)

Pierfrancesco
(1431–1477)

Lorenzo the Magnificent
(1449–1492)

Giuliano
(1453–1478)

Lorenzo di
Pierfrancesco
(1463–1503)

Giovanni di
Pierfrancesco
(1467–1514)

Giulio (1478–1534)
Illegitimate:
becomes Pope
Clement VII

Piero
the Unfortunate
(1471–1503)

Giovanni
(1475–1521)
becomes cardinal
and later
Pope Leo X

Leading Dramatis Personae and Main Factions

Alexander VI – notoriously corrupt Borgia Pope who became Savonarola's sworn enemy

Alfonso, Duke of Calabria – son and heir of King Ferrante I of Naples. Would later become Alfonso II of Naples

Anne of France – acted as Regent during the youth of Charles VIII

Arrabbiati – the most powerful anti-Savonarola faction

Bigi – faction supporting return of Piero de' Medici

Sandro Botticelli – renowned painter and friend of Lorenzo the Magnificent

Fra Pacifico Burlamacchi – wrote early biography of Savonarola, much of it heard from Savonarola himself

Piero di Gino Capponi – leading Florentine citizen who famously defied Charles VIII

Cardinal Caraffi of Naples – friend of Alexander VI who nonetheless supported Savonarola

'Ser Ceccone' (real name Francesco de Ser Barone) – Savonarola's chief civil interrogator

Charles VIII – the young King of France who invaded Italy

Compagnacci – fanatically anti-Savonarola group led by Doffo Spini

Commines (Commynes) – leading adviser of Charles VIII who kept a diary

Cardinal della Rovere – sworn enemy of Alexander VI, who encouraged Charles VIII to set up a council to depose him

Bartolomeo Cerretani – contemporary Florentine chronicler

Domenico da Pescia – the Dominican monk who was Savonarola's closest and most loyal supporter, who followed his master to the end

Lucrezia Donati – 'the most beautiful woman in Florence', to whom the young Lorenzo the Magnificent addressed love poems

Ferrante I – King of Naples who received Lorenzo the Magnificent

Marsilio Ficino – celebrated Platonist and close friend of Medici family

Francesco da Puglia – a Franciscan monk from Santa Croce and a bitter enemy of Savonarola who issued the challenge for the ordeal by fire

Battista Guarino – the celebrated humanist scholar whose lectures Savonarola attended at the University of Ferrara

Francesco Guicciardini – contemporary historian of Florence and Italy

Fra Leonardo da Fivizzano – Augustinian monk at Santo Spirito who preached in Florence against Savonarola when he was at the height of his power

Giovanni della Vecchia – 'the Captain of the Square', responsible for keeping the peace in the Piazza della Signoria, and later at San Marco

Giovanni Manetti – the *Arrabbiati* responsible for stirring up the crowd at the ordeal by fire, who later demanded permission to inspect Savonarola

Niccolò Machiavelli – contemporary historian of Florence and Italy

Fra Malatesta (Sacramoro) – the *Arrabbiati* spy in San Marco

Domenico Mazzinghi – pro-Savonarolan *gonfaloniere* who later argued in favour of the ordeal by fire

Fra Mariano da Genazzano – the Augustinian who was Florence's favourite preacher before his 'contest' with Savonarola

Cosimo de' Medici – the man who built up the Medici bank, grandfather of Lorenzo the Magnificent

Giovanni de' Medici – second son of Lorenzo the Magnificent, who became a young cardinal

Giovanni di Pierfrancesco de' Medici – taken into the Palazzo Medici by his uncle Lorenzo the Magnificent as a youth when his father Pierfrancesco died.

Giuliano de' Medici – Lorenzo the Magnificent's younger brother, who was murdered

Lorenzo de' Medici ('Lorenzo the Magnificent') – effective ruler of Florence until 1492

Lorenzo di Pierfrancesco de' Medici – son of Pierfrancesco de' Medici. Taken into the Palazzo Medici as a youth when his father died

Lucrezia (neé Tornabuoni) de' Medici – Lorenzo the Magnificent's influential mother

Fra Ludovico da Ferrara – despatched to Florence by Alexander VI to investigate Savonarola

Fra Silvestro Maruffi – monk at San Marco prone to visions who would follow Savonarola to the end

Pierfrancesco de' Medici – cousin of Piero de' Medici and grandson of Giovanni di Bicci, the founder of the Medici bank

Piero de' Medici – first son of Lorenzo the Magnificent who took over his rule of Florence in 1492

Dietisalvi Neroni – long-term business associate of Cosimo de' Medici, who grew jealous of Piero de' Medici

Clarice (neé Orsini) de' Medici – Lorenzo the Magnificent's Roman bride

Pico della Mirandola – charismatic Renaissance philosopher, befriended by Lorenzo the Magnificent, his biography was written by his nephew, Francesco Pico della Mirandola

Piero Parenti – Florentine diarist during this period

Piagnoni – Savonarola's supporters, mainly drawn from amongst the poor, but extending into all sections of Florentine society

Angelo Poliziano – renowned poet and member of Lorenzo the Magnificent's circle

Bishop Remolino – finally despatched by Alexander VI to conduct Savonarola's 'examination'

Bernardo Rucellai – leading Florentine citizen sent by Lorenzo the Magnificent on delegation to persuade Savonarola to tone down his sermons; later turned against Peiro de' Medici ('the Unfortunate')

Girolamo Rucellai – moderating voice at the Pratica called to debate the ordeal by fire

Marcuccio Salviati – commander of the pro-Savonarolan troops at the ordeal by fire

Girolamo Savonarola – the Dominican friar who stood against all that the Medici represented

Michele Savonarola – Girolamo's grandfather and a formative influence. Despite being a pioneering physician, he remained a strict medievalist.

Niccolò Savonarola – Girolamo's unsuccessful father

Galeazzo Maria Sforza – nephew of Ludovico Sforza, and rightful heir to the Dukedom of Milan

Ludovico 'il Moro' Sforza – uncle of Galeazzo Maria Sforza, who acted as ruler of Milan during his nephew's minority

Paolantonio Soderini – leading citizen and supporter of Savonarola

Doffo Spini – the headstrong leader of the *Compagnacci* extreme anti-Savonarola faction

Giovanni Tornabuoni – Lorenzo the Magnificent's uncle, manager of the Rome branch of the Medici bank

Fra Mariano Ughi – the second Dominican who volunteered for the ordeal by fire

Francesco Valori – sent by Lorenzo the Magnificent on a delegation to warn Savonarola to tone down his sermons; later pro-Savonarolan *gonfaloniere*

Simonetta Vespucci – celebrated at the age of 17 as the most beautiful woman in Florence. Lorenzo the Magnificent's brother Giuliano is said to have pined for her love

Acknowledgements

MY THANKS TO Ellah Alfrey, formerly at Jonathan Cape, who commissioned this work. Also to Alex Bowler, who is my present editor at Jonathan Cape and has proved invaluable in his help, as well as being meticulous in his suggestions, guidance and general editing of this work. His advice has improved this book no end. The copy-editing of Mandy Greenfield was painstaking in the extreme, and proved a major contribution.

I would also like to thank the staff I encountered at the various libraries and institutions in Britain and Italy where I did my research for this work, all of whom (with two notable exceptions) were not only courteous and considerate but also extremely helpful with their advice. As ever, the staff in the Humanities 2 Reading Room at the British Library were exceptional.

Once again, I must also thank my agent Julian Alexander, who did so much to get this project off the ground, and has continued over so many years to be both a helpful and reassuring friend. Thanks also to Richard Foreman for great company and ever-encouraging publicity.

Prologue: 'The needle of the Italian compass'

IN THE FIRST week of April 1492 Lorenzo the Magnificent, the forty-three-year-old ruler of Renaissance Florence, lay seriously ill in his villa at Careggi, in the countryside a couple of miles north of the city walls. Lorenzo, a charismatic figure in a charismatic age, had powerful but curiously ugly features, which appeared to lend his personality an almost animal magnetism. His intellectual brilliance and physical daring also contributed to his attraction. Amongst other accomplishments he was a distinguished poet, a champion jouster and a prolific lover of beautiful women (and, on occasion, similar men).

Yet for two months now Lorenzo's powerful frame had been racked with incapacitating pain, a manifestation of the congenital gout and chronic arthritis that had stricken so many amongst the recent generations of the Medici banking family. However, for Lorenzo the worst was yet to come: his beloved friend, the poet Angelo Poliziano, watched as he succumbed to:

> a fever [that] gradually passed into his body, spreading not into his arteries or veins, like others do, but into his frame, his vital organs, his muscles, his bones too, and their marrow. But since it spread subtly and invisibly, with utmost stealth, it was hardly noticed at first. But then it gave clean evidence of itself . . . it so speedily weakened the man and wore him down that because not only his strength had ebbed away and been consumed, but his entire body, he was wasted away to nothing.

By this stage Lorenzo was being attended by the celebrated Lazaro da Ticino 'a very creative physician', who had arrived from Milan. According to Poliziano: 'in order not to leave any method untested, he tried a highly expensive remedy which involved grinding pearls and precious stones of all sorts'. This was a traditional remedy deriving from classical times, which almost certainly arrived in Europe from China, where such concoctions were thought to be ingredients of the fabled 'elixir of life'. Lazaro da Ticino had been despatched to attend Lorenzo the Magnificent by Ludovico 'il Moro' Sforza, the de facto ruler of Florence's powerful northern neighbour, Milan. Ludovico Sforza was probably nicknamed 'il Moro' (the Moor) on account of his dark features; yet there was also a distinctly dark side to his character. A braggart, given to rash gestures, he was deeply superstitious, yet liked to regard himself and his court as highly cultured. In fact, he was a tyrant, of paranoid tendencies, who ruled from behind the high, dark walls of the imposing Castello Sforza, which looked down over the rooftops of his capital city. Some ten years previously, when intelligence had reached Lorenzo the Magnificent that Ludovico 'il Moro' Sforza might be wavering in his vital support for militarily weak Florence, Lorenzo had launched a charm offensive, part of which involved despatching Leonardo da Vinci to Milan. Ludovico Sforza had been deeply flattered; the alliance with Florence had been reinforced, and the Milanese ruler came to regard Lorenzo the Magnificent as his valued personal friend.

During the twenty-three years of his reign Lorenzo had gained the admiration and affection of rulers all over Italy. Late fifteenth-century Italy was split into five major powers – Milan, Venice, the papacy, Florence and Naples – and several minor city states, which tended to ally themselves with their nearest powerful neighbour. The balance of power between the major territories was constantly threatened by the covert shifting of allegiances. Militarily weak Florence had clung to its status as a major power largely through Lorenzo the Magnificent's diplomatic skill, and his tactical astuteness in perpetuating the idea of the city as the centre of Italian culture. Here the Renaissance had first come to fruition, financed by the patronage of its great banking families, with Florentine artists and architects regarded as the finest in Europe, the pride of Italian civilisation. Even so, Florence remained vulnerable to brute military force, requiring a constant diplomatic effort to keep its neighbouring states at bay.

As a consequence, Ludovico Sforza of Milan was not the only powerful Italian leader with whom Lorenzo the Magnificent maintained constant diplomatic dealings, and whom he succeeded in making his personal friend. Perhaps his most surprising alliance was with the ageing King Ferrante of Naples, a man notorious for his treachery, who in his earlier years had delighted in showing visitors his 'museum of mummies', consisting of the embalmed bodies of his enemies. Yet when Ferrante had hatched a plot to assassinate Lorenzo and sent the Neapolitan army to invade virtually defenceless Florence, Lorenzo had been willing to risk his life by dashing to Naples to confront Ferrante personally. The sheer bravado of the twenty-nine-year-old Lorenzo's gesture had so won the admiration of Ferrante that he too declared himself Lorenzo's firm friend. Likewise Pope Innocent VIII, a slippery character of part-Greek descent, of whom it was said the he 'begat eight boys and just as many girls, so that Rome might justly call him Father'. Lorenzo cemented an alliance with Innocent VIII by arranging for the pope's eldest son, Franceschetto Cybo, to marry his daughter Maddalena de' Medici.

Lorenzo certainly lived up to his soubriquet.* Even his contemporary Niccolò Machiavelli, ever the sardonic and incisive observer of political affairs, was dazzled:

> Lorenzo was loved by fortune and by God in the highest degree, and as a result all his enterprises came to a successful conclusion . . . His way of life, his prudence and his fortune were known and admired by princes far beyond the borders of Italy.

---

* 'Il Magnifico' was in fact a courtesy title, frequently used to address leaders, heads of important families and even those in charge of successful commercial enterprises. For instance, when the manager of the Medici bank in Rome wrote to the head of the Medici bank in Florence, he would address him as 'magnifico'. In English, the loose contemporary equivalent would have been 'my lord', as often appears in Shakespeare's plays. However, in the case of Lorenzo the Magnificent the title seems to have taken on a more formal, admirable quality. Many of the citizens of Florence and elsewhere had begun to know him as 'il Magnifico' long before his death. In such fashion, this title had become conventionalised in the familiar medieval manner. During this era nicknames assigned on account of personal characteristics often took on a more permanent aspect — much as Lorenzo's father had been called Piero the Gouty, and earlier kings of France had gone down in history as Louis the Quarreller or Charles the Mad.

This last was no exaggeration. Machiavelli names the Sultan of Turkey and the King of Hungary as Lorenzo's friends, and in the grounds of Lorenzo's villa of Poggio a Caiano he kept a pet giraffe 'so gentle it [would] take an apple from a child's hand', which had been sent as a gift by the Sultan of Babylon. But as Machiavelli makes plain, Lorenzo was no saint: 'His great virtues may not have been flawed by serious vices, but he did however involve himself in the affairs of Venus to an astonishing degree, as well as delighting in facetious gossip, pungent wit and childish games more than was fitting for a man of his position.' Yet such apparently frivolous traits may well have contributed to his charm and aided his more serious endeavours, as Machiavelli understood: 'His reputation for prudence grew with every year, for he was winning and eloquent in discussion, of sympathetic wisdom when it came to resolving issues, as well as being quick of impulse when action was necessary.' Thus was the man who had guided Italy through such treacherous political waters that Innocent VIII would famously refer to him as 'the needle of the Italian compass'.

Despite all this, in Florence Lorenzo's position was rather more contentious. The city was theoretically a democratic republic, a matter of great pride to its citizens. At this time, when the separate territories that made up Italy were ruled for the most part by absolute rulers – a king, a pope, an oligarchy, hereditary dukes, petty tyrants, and so forth – only in the republic of Florence did citizens have a say in their government. In times of crisis, all male members of the population over the age of fourteen would be summoned by the tolling of a bell to assemble in the main square for a *parlamento*. Here they would vote in a *balià*, an emergency committe that had full power to deal with the crisis as it saw fit.

Under more normal circumstances, the city was ruled by the *gonfaloniere* (literally 'standard-bearer') and his eight-man council, the Signoria, each of whom was regularly selected by lot from special leather bags into which were placed the names of members of the guilds. When selected, the new *gonfaloniere* and his Signoria would take up residence in the Palazzo della Signoria, the imposing medieval palace with its tall castellated campanile, which to this day dominates the centre of Florence. Here they would don their ceremonial red robes and be wined, dined and entertained at public expense through their two-month period in office, their opinions and discussions being beyond outside influence. The comparative brevity of their tenure, as well as their isolation, was intended to prevent the city falling under the permanent power of any faction or tyrant.

The same system of selection by lot was used to choose the members of the various councils that advised the Signoria. Unfortunately, the conditions and complexities of the system by which the names placed in the leather bags were chosen had, over the years, proved open to manipulation. The leading families of Florence had long since succeeded in influencing the selection for all powerful posts, and finally even these competing families had succumbed to the single overwhelming influence wielded by the huge wealth of the Medici family. Such corruption was grudgingly tolerated by the citizens of the republic because Lorenzo himself was popular, or at least managed to maintain a façade of popularity by lavish spending on entertainments for the citizenry. But with Lorenzo now ill and incapacitated, how much longer would this state of affairs last?

The prospect of change was not exclusive to Florence at this moment of history. As Lorenzo lay dying, Western civilisation itself was undergoing a profound transformation. Later that very year Christopher Columbus would make landfall in the New World, an event that would soon lead Europeans to realise that much of the world remained to be discovered. Indeed, some four years previously the Portuguese navigator Bartholomew Diaz had rounded the southern tip of Africa into the Indian Ocean, opening up passage to a largely unknown Eastern world. At the same time, many thinkers in western Europe were becoming aware that much of their life within this world extended to wider mental horizons that remained unexplored: a profound evolution in human self-consciousness was taking place. The medieval vision of the world, where knowledge was largely accepted on authority from such sources as Aristotle and the Bible, was beginning to give way to the new vision of humanism. During the medieval era, the world and our life within it had been regarded as a mere preparation for the eternal life of the hereafter, when our souls were judged – assigned to heaven, purgatory or hell – in accordance with how we had behaved during this brief life of the flesh. Now a Renaissance was taking place: a rebirth of knowledge from the pagan classical era was giving humanity a greater confidence in itself and its powers. New ways of painting, as well as advances in architecture and knowledge of all kinds, were encouraging humanity in a more realistic view of the world, transforming both our self-belief and our self-understanding. Instead of the essentially spiritual outlook of medievalism, the new humanism regarded life and the world from a more human perspective.

In Florence, the Renaissance was approaching its zenith, with the city's leading artists recognised as the most advanced in Italy, producing works that continue to this day to be regarded as pinnacles of human achievement. By 1492, Botticelli had already painted his masterpieces *Spring* (*Primavera*) and *The Birth of Venus*, and had worked on the Sistine Chapel in Rome. Leonardo da Vinci had left for Milan, where he had already sketched detailed plans for a manned flying machine and would soon begin painting *The Last Supper*. Meanwhile the precocious seventeen-year-old Michelangelo had begun sculpting his first masterwork, *The Battle of the Centaurs*, which had been commissioned by Lorenzo the Magnificent himself.

Lorenzo was by now well practised in the policy of using Florentine artists in the pursuance of his political aims. Although his despatch of Botticelli to Rome, and of Leonardo to Milan, had been prompted by specific strategic concerns, Lorenzo the Magnificent also regarded the artists he sent abroad as serving a wider purpose, acting as general cultural ambassadors for their native city. For him, art always had both a higher and a lower purpose, even at home. Prior to using his artists as instruments of foreign policy, he had employed them in Florence to contribute to the flamboyant celebrations that he laid on to maintain his popularity with the people of the city, as well as to mark historic events. In this way, Botticelli had been commissioned to paint an exemplary public mural depicting the hanging bodies of those apprehended after the failed Pazzi conspiracy to murder Lorenzo and overthrow Medici rule; on a lighter note, Leonardo had been responsible for spectacular firework displays and ice sculptures that had provided centrepieces for Lorenzo's popular celebrations.

Despite such diversions, a curious atmosphere of foreboding had begun to pervade the city. Its people seemed to sense something hollow at the heart of the new way of life that was coming into being around them. They were not yet fully at ease with the art, knowledge and self-confident celebrations of the Renaissance era. The human soul, which for the long centuries of the medieval era had been the moral focus of every individual's life, was suffering from unwonted neglect. The old spiritual certainties were in danger of being overwhelmed, and with the approach of 1500 many citizens became gripped by a mounting sense of apprehension. It would soon be one and a half millennia since the birth of Christ, and whispers began to spread of a coming apocalypse, heralding the end of the world and the Second Coming of Christ. Amidst this pervasive undercurrent of metaphysical angst, many began turning to a fiery young monk from Ferrara called Savonarola, who had begun preaching the Lenten sermons in the Church of San Marco.

At first glance, Girolamo Savonarola presented an unprepossessing figure: 'the little friar', as he often called himself with deceptive humility. He was indeed short, and thin, intense in manner, and spoke with the heavy accent of his native Ferrara, which lay seventy miles north across the Apennine mountains and was regarded as something of a provincial backwater by the Florentines. Savonarola was not given to social graces, and his portrait by Fra Bartolommeo depicts a cowled, plain-faced man with hollow ascetic cheeks, a hooked nose and thick, sensual lips. Apparently there was nothing particularly remarkable about his appearance apart from his eyes, which were said to have glinted with a burning intensity beneath his dark, heavy eyebrows.

When Savonarola spoke, he had the knack of investing his words with all the power of his driven personality. His sermons were charged with the Holy Spirit with which he felt himself to be filled. He raged with an Old Testament fury, and his words were filled with prophecies of doom. Here, with a vengeance, was a return to the old certainties of times gone by. Savonarola impressed upon the citizens of Florence how they should be devoting themselves to the life of the spirit, not wasting their substance on the sensuality and baubles of the worldly life. All such things were nothing but a wicked delusion, foisted upon them by evil rulers.

In early April 1492, as Lorenzo the Magnificent lay dying in his country villa at Careggi, he unexpectedly sent word to none other than Savonarola, asking the friar to visit him. According to a contemporary report, Lorenzo is said to have justified this request 'using these very words: "Go for the Father [Savonarola], for I have never found one save him who was an honest friar."'

Lorenzo recognised Savonarola for what he was, just as Savonarola did Lorenzo. Ironically, it was Lorenzo himself who had been responsible for inviting Savonarola to Florence. Lorenzo's invitation had perhaps inevitably involved ulterior political motives, and these concerned the plans he had laid for the continuation of Medici power after his death. Lorenzo intended his eldest son Piero to succeed him in taking over the reins of power in Florence, but he had ambitions in a different direction for Giovanni, his highly intelligent second son. Giovanni had been brought up amidst the humanistic atmosphere of the poets and scholars of Lorenzo's circle, with the poet Poliziano even acting as his tutor. But now Lorenzo wanted Giovanni to enter the Church, in order to advance the Medici family name in this new sphere. It was thought that Savonarola's sermons might act as a corrective to Giovanni's liberal education and inspire in him a suitably religious attitude.

Descriptions of what took place when Savonarola visited the dying Lorenzo's bedside vary slightly, although one thing is certain – this unlikely visit definitely took place. Another undisputed fact is that Savonarola stood his ground and refused to be swayed by the sight of his dying ruler, behaving towards him with some severity, and even making certain demands of Lorenzo before he gave him his blessing. These demands are said to have been as follows. Initially, Savonarola asked Lorenzo whether he repented of his sins and believed in the one true God – to which Lorenzo replied that he did. Next, Savonarola demanded that if Lorenzo's soul was to be saved, he would have to renounce his ill-gotten wealth 'and restore what has wrongfully been taken'. To this, Lorenzo replied, 'Father, I will do so, or I will cause my heirs to do it if I cannot.' Finally, Savonarola demanded that Lorenzo should restore to the people of Florence their liberty, which could only be guaranteed by a truly republican government. To this last demand Lorenzo refused to reply, finally turning his face away.

Whether Savonarola actually made these precise demands is not certain – yet most sources agree that he did make three demands, and that they were similar to those cited above. When Lorenzo refused to reply to Savonarola's final demand, the priest is said to have stood in silence before him for some time, until at last he gave Lorenzo his blessing and departed.

The following day, 8 April 1492, Lorenzo the Magnificent died, and his body was carried back to Florence, where it was laid out in the Church of San Lorenzo. It was said that every citizen of Florence had deep feelings concerning the passing of this man who had ruled them for the past twenty-three years – though the precise nature of these feelings was varied. Many loved him, certainly; equally certainly, others secretly hoped that his passing might hasten a return to the old ways of more republican government. The grief-stricken Poliziano wrote:

> Lightning flies from heaven down
> To rob us of our laurel crown* . . .
> Now silence rings us all around,
> Now we are deaf to all thy sound.

Savonarola felt that his moment of destiny was now approaching.

What took place in fifteenth-century Florence has been seen as a clash of wills between a benign enlightened ruler and a religious fanatic, between secular pluralism with all its internal self-contradictions and the repressive extremism demanded by a thorough-going spirituality. Yet as the story unfolds, it soon becomes clear that this black-and-white picture is in fact a gross oversimplification. In describing the turbulent events that characterised these times, the nuances and subtleties that underlay this struggle will be revealed. Even so, the struggle was intense and the stakes were the highest. Not for nothing is this a story of death in Florence.

The Medici ruled for themselves and the preservation of their own power. By 1492, their interests had little to do with the people over whom they held sway. All knew this, but only Savonarola was willing to stand up and preach against such corruption – wherever he saw it. Savonarola was a fundamentalist: in the city that had celebrated the first glories of the new age of the Renaissance, he sought to return to the basic principles of early Christianity and establish a 'City of God'. This was to be a simple, pure, God-fearing republic – where all that was required were the necessities for living

---

* Poliziano uses the Latin word *laurus*, as in the laurel wreath with which poets were crowned in classical times, but this is also intended as a loose pun on Lorenzo.

a life dedicated to the Almighty, before whom all stood in equality. All distinctions of rank and class, all luxuries, baubles and distractions, all licentious and frivolous enjoyment were to be renounced.

Although Savonarola was essentially medieval in outlook, paradoxically his disparaging of the old corrupt powers pointed the way towards an egalitarianism that was quintessentially modern. Savonarola's envisaged republic would prove to be the most democratic and open rule the city had ever known. By a paradox that this narrative will attempt to illuminate, it was also one of the most repressive and inhuman in the city's history. Both sides of this struggle for power were riven by such paradoxes.

All this took place 500 years ago, against the backdrop of the city that gave birth to the Renaissance, the moment that was to transform Western civilisation and provide the first inklings of our modern world. Yet this clash between the secular and the religious has continued to reverberate down the centuries – first in Europe, then in America, and now finally throughout the world the struggle continues. It is nothing less than the fight for the soul of humanity, a struggle over the direction that humanity should take, the way we should live our lives, what we are, and what we should become. This is a struggle that will become all the more pressing and relevant as we exhaust the resources and despoil the environment of the planet that we inhabit, as we face the choice – for perhaps the first time in our progressive civilisation – of how we are to limit our way of living. Five centuries ago in Florence this coming battle was played out for the first time in recognisable modern terms.

I

A Prince in All but Name

Lorenzo de' Medici was born on 1 January 1449 at the Palazzo Medici in Florence. During this time his sixty-year-old grandfather Cosimo de' Medici, head of the Medici bank, was de facto ruler of the city. Cosimo was an extremely astute businessman and had increased the fortunes of the Medici bank to the point where it had branches in all major Italian cities, as well as branches as far afield as London and Bruges, with agents operating in Spain and North Africa, the Levant and the Black Sea. As a result the Medici had soon amassed a fortune which dwarfed that of the older leading Florentine bankers and powerful political families.

Originally the Medici had been against taking power, but it had been virtually forced upon them when they had come to realise that without power they would not be able to protect their fortune. In 1433 the jealousy and resentment of certain influential Florentine political factions, led by the ancient Albizzi family, had resulted in Cosimo's imprisonment on the charge of interfering in state affairs, with the intention of taking over the state. This amounted to treason, a charge that incurred the death penalty, which Cosimo had only been able to escape by means of bribery and outside intervention. Even so, he had been sentenced to exile for ten years. Yet after a year of inept rule, hampered by lack of funds, the *gonfaloniere* and his ruling Signoria had invited Cosimo back to Florence to put his considerable talents and extreme wealth at the disposal of the city. From this moment on, Medici rule over Florence was consolidated. The *gonfaloniere* and the Signoria continued to be selected by lot as before, but Cosimo established an efficient political machine which covertly ensured that all men selected to positions of political power were Medici supporters.

The seat of government may officially have remained the Palazzo della Signoria, but this only operated in consultation with the Palazzo Medici, where all the important decisions were taken by Cosimo. Indicatively, from now on all ambassadors and visiting foreign dignitaries called at the Medici residence.

By the time of Lorenzo's birth, the ageing Cosimo had begun to delegate much of his power to his son Piero, Lorenzo's father. Piero de' Medici was a meticulous, if not overly talented, banker, who had exhibited a sophisticated taste in the arts and had become a highly discriminating patron. Unfortunately, he was chronically afflicted with the congenital Medici curse, to the point where he would soon become known as Piero the Gouty. This debilitating disease meant that for increasing spells his legs were too painfully infirm to support him, and he would have to be carried about on a litter. The constant pain also had a marked effect on his character, punctuating his natural charm with increasing bouts of irascibility. Such a quality did not endear him to others, especially in a society where political influence relied so heavily upon warm human contact.

However, the major influence on the young Lorenzo would undoubtedly be his mother, Lucrezia, an intelligent and resilient woman in an age when females for the most part had little opportunity to assert themselves beyond the restricted domestic sphere. Lucrezia came from an old and distinguished Florentine family, the Tornabuoni, and although her arranged marriage to a Medici was undoubtedly contracted for political reasons, she appears from her extant letters to have been genuinely fond of her husband, worrying over his health and betraying her concern that he should not 'give way to melancholy'. Yet these letters are not the only evidence of her writing, for Lucrezia de' Medici was also a talented poet and hymnist. Although the conventional religiosity of her verse is of little modern interest, such piety did not stifle the warmth of her sympathetic personality. Her verse appears to have been the outlet for a wider creative sensibility, which was used to some effect in guiding her husband's discriminating patronage of such leading early Renaissance figures as the architect Michelozzi, who had designed the groundbreaking Palazzo Medici; the sculptor Donatello, whose innovative realistic sculptures included the first free-standing nude since classical times; and the troubled artist Fra Filippo Lippi, whose

colourful larger-than-life portraits echoed his own larger-than-life personality. All three of these artists Lucrezia came to regard as personal friends.
The Medici were amongst the first patrons to recognise that artists were
now becoming something more than mere craftsmen, and the family did
their best to accommodate the increasingly difficult temperaments and
wayward behaviour of these emergent genius-figures. Lucrezia was also
known to have influenced her husband on more important political matters
– for instance, it would be she who persuaded Piero to allow certain
members of the Strozzi family to return from the banishment they had
suffered for opposing Cosimo. This would prove a particularly astute move.

Of similar impact was Lucrezia's formative influence upon the youthful
Lorenzo, who quickly began displaying precocious brilliance in a variety
of fields, ranging from classical literature to horse-riding. He was also said
to have had an exceptional singing voice, accompanying himself on the
lyre.* In 1459, the self-confident ten-year-old Lorenzo would play a leading
role in the great pageant put on to entertain the new pope, Pius II, when
he visited Florence, though he would not have been aware of the ulterior
motive behind all the 'theatrical performances, combats of wild beasts,
races and balls . . . given in honour of the illustrious guest'. In fact, Cosimo
was attempting to persuade Pius II to reinstate the Medici bank as handlers
of the lucrative papal account.

Lorenzo and his younger brother Giuliano were tutored by leading
members of the humanist intellectual circle that gathered at the Palazzo
Medici. The brothers first learned Latin from the scholar Gentile Becchi,
who would later be rewarded with the bishopric of Arezzo. Lorenzo was
four years older than Giuliano, and as they grew up the two brothers became
increasingly close. Lucrezia, in a letter to her husband, evokes a touching
scene in which the nine-year-old 'Lorenzo is learning [Latin] verses which
his master . . . gave him and then teaches them to Giuliano'. The boys were
taught Greek and Aristotelian philosophy by Johannes Argyropoulos, the
leading Byzantine scholar who had left Constantinople prior to its fall to

---

* Several first-hand sources attest to this talent. However, the mature Lorenzo was known to
have a flattened nose, with no sense of smell, and a curiously high-pitched nasal voice. This
discrepancy has been ascribed to a riding accident, perhaps in the course of jousting, which
may have occurred some time during his teenage years.

the Ottoman Turks in 1453. Aristotelian philosophy was very much the backbone of the old medieval learning, whilst the new humanism turned instead to his predecessors Socrates and Plato, whose philosophy was taught to Lorenzo by Marsilio Ficino. The most knowledgeable Platonic scholar of his age, Ficino had been employed by Cosimo de' Medici to translate the entire works of Plato from the original Greek into more accessible Latin, a task that would occupy most of his life. Ficino appears to have been a curious, but sympathetic character: a tiny, limping hunchback with a distinct stutter and a somewhat volatile temperament, he nonetheless doted on the young Lorenzo. In turn, Lorenzo quickly established a deep rapport with his middle-aged tutor, and throughout his life would continue to debate philosophical ideas with Ficino. Even at this early stage Ficino took it upon himself to provide Lorenzo with philosophical advice: 'by imitating the deeds of Socrates we are taught better how to attain courage than by the art displayed by Aristotle in his writings on morality . . . I beg you to prefer learning from reality instead of from description, as you would prefer a living thing from a dead.'

Surprisingly, it was Ficino who would encourage Lorenzo to write his verse in the local Tuscan dialect of Italian, rather than scholarly Latin. This dialect was now in the process of becoming the predominant Italian language amongst the many dialects spoken throughout the peninsula, in part because it had been used by Dante in his *Divina Commedia* (*Divine Comedy*), which was already becoming recognised by many as the finest work of poetry since the classical era.

However, right from the start Lorenzo's poetry would exhibit a curious schizophrenic tendency. On the one hand, it would be infused with the seriousness and intensity of feeling exhibited by his mother's verse, whilst on other occasions it would be characterised by a bawdy wit and levity suitable for the public carnivals in which it appeared. Indeed, Lorenzo's verse exhibited the same duality that seemed to permeate his entire character. The precocious young scholar who wrote flawless poetry was also the boisterous player of *calcio storico*, the rough-house early version of football in which Florentine boys used to let off steam. Likewise, the intense youth who participated in the high-minded debates on Platonic idealism at the Palazzo Medici was also the rascal who delighted in roaming the streets at night with his pals chanting bawdy verses, or in winter throwing snowballs up at the windows of the local girls. And as Machiavelli noted, this childish element would remain a part of his character throughout his life: 'to see him pass in a moment from his serious self to his exuberant self was to see in him two quite distinct personalities joined as if by some impossible bond'.

This perennial childishness seems to have been a psychological reaction: the serious side of his character would be forced from an early age to assume a maturity well beyond his years. In 1464, when Lorenzo was just fifteen, Cosimo de' Medici died and Lorenzo's father took over as ruler of Florence. The gout-ridden 46-year-old Piero de' Medici suspected that he had not long to live, and quickly began coaching Lorenzo for his future role as ruler of Florence. Within a year, Lorenzo was being sent on his first mission to represent Florence in Milan at the wedding of Ippolita Maria Sforza, daughter of Francesco Sforza, the Duke of Milan, to Alfonso, the son and heir of King Ferrante I of Naples. The bedridden Piero sent a number of letters to his sixteen-year-old son, issuing a constant stream of advice and detailed instructions: 'act as a man, not as a boy', 'follow the advice of Pigello [manager of the Milan branch of the Medici bank]' and, above all, 'do not stint money, but do thyself honour' and 'if thou givest dinners or other entertainments do not let there be any stint in money or whatever else is needful to do thyself honour'.

Piero need not have worried, for Lorenzo was soon exercising both diplomacy and charm and, where necessary, perspicacity – undertaking missions to Venice, Naples, Ferrara, and finally Rome in the spring of 1466. This last was a mission of the utmost importance, for Lorenzo was expected to persuade Pope Paul II to grant to the Medici bank the monopoly on operating and distribution rights for the highly lucrative Tolfa alum mines owned by the papacy.

At the time alum was the mineral salt used to fix vivid dyes on cloth, making it an essential ingredient in the thriving textile industries of Florence and Venice, as well as those in the Low Countries and England. At the height of their trading, the mines at Tolfa some thirty miles north-west of Rome accounted for almost 3,500 tons of alum each year. This was sold for the equivalent of around 150,000 florins – that is, around half the value of the entire papal dues accumulating from all over Christendom, which at the time arrived from dioceses stretching from Greenland to Cyprus, from Poland to the Azores. In effect, the papacy would claim the equivalent of half the total alum-sale revenue; and after costs the operator would expect to recover around 50,000 florins. This was another colossal sum, when the total assets of the Medici bank at its height under Cosimo de' Medici had probably been less than 200,000 florins.*

However, relations between the papacy and the Medici had now taken a sudden turn for the worse. Paul II was a Venetian, and when Venice had recently gone to war with Florence, the pope had transferred the operating rights of the alum mines to a Venetian concern, as well as withdrawing the papal account from the Medici bank. This had plunged the Medici bank into crisis, seriously endangering Piero's rule in Florence: without the constant flow of money required to maintain widespread patronage, Medici political power could not be guaranteed.

It was impossible to overemphasise the importance of Lorenzo's mission, and Piero once again felt the need to stress in his correspondence the significance of his son's behaviour: 'Put an end to all playing on instruments, or singing or dancing ... be old beyond thy years for the times require it.' From the sound of this, Lorenzo's previous missions had not been completely without lapse into what Machiavelli referred to as 'his exuberant self'. Piero had already issued Lorenzo with the most specific instructions on how to present the Medici case to Pope Paul II. Lorenzo was to argue that only the Medici bank had sufficient expertise to organise high production from the mines, while at the same time having the necessary financial resources and contacts to outfit galleys to carry the alum on the long voyage to London and Bruges. Shipwreck, and the constant threat of Barbary pirates, meant inevitable losses, which only the Medici bank could afford to cover; no Venetian operators had funds that could enable them to survive such losses. Lorenzo evidently behaved himself in Rome: his charm, Piero's arguments and Paul II's greed eventually won

---

* To place such sums into perspective: a moderately successful merchant in Florence could support a large household, including his entire family and servants, for 200 florins a year. Meanwhile a worker at one of the many dyeing mills in Florence could expect to earn the equivalent of 15 florins a year at most.

the day, and in April 1466 the Medici bank was finally granted the alum monopoly.

Yet Piero had also sent his son to Rome on another matter of some importance – namely, to learn the day-to-day running of the family business. In between his diplomatic duties, he was instructed to call upon his uncle, Giovanni Tornabuoni, the manager of the important Rome branch of the Medici bank, so that he could be instructed in the art and technicalities of Renaissance banking.

Banking in its modern form had to all intents and purposes been invented by the Italians some two centuries previously. Even in the fifteenth century it remained very much an Italian concern, especially with the recent introduction of double-entry bookkeeping, which enabled a banker to carry out a swift check on the overall balance between credit and debit in his accounts. He could thus determine at a glance whether it was prudent to make a further outlay, or whether the bank was dangerously at risk if a certain debtor defaulted – a situation that was not always readily apparent with more primitive bookkeeping methods. However, banking still suffered from an ancient drawback. Strictly speaking, the lending and borrowing of money fell under the biblical edict against 'usury': officially banks could not charge interest on any money loaned, nor could depositors receive interest on any money banked. This difficulty was largely circumvented by financial sleight of hand. If money (or its equivalent in the form of gold plate, jewellery, and so forth) was deposited, the bank would pay an annual 'gift' to the depositor of around 15 per cent of the deposit's worth.

Another source of income that eluded the ban on usury was 'exchange'. The main Italian commercial centres, such as Milan, Venice and Florence, each had their own different currencies, which had no constant equivalence. For instance, at this period the Florentine florin could be worth anything between 10 and 20 per cent less than the Venetian ducat. Other countries in Europe also had their own currencies, and their exchange rates could fluctuate by similar amounts. This enabled bankers covertly to receive and dispense interest under the guise of 'exchange'. Such was particularly the case with the papal bankers, who were responsible for collecting papal revenues in far-flung regions throughout Christendom and remitting equivalent sums to Rome. Yet the fact remained that in theological terms the practice of banking still involved the sin of usury. Indeed, it was Cosimo de' Medici's increasing anxiety over this matter as his years advanced, and he faced the prospect of death and the Last Judgement, that had played a large part in prompting him to build and renovate so many churches. In this way, Cosimo hoped to absolve himself from the sin of usury. Ironically, it had been this archetypically medieval concern over the ultimate fate of his soul which had prompted the patronage that ushered in the new humanist age of the Renaissance.

By contrast, Cosimo's grandson Lorenzo appears to have been as little concerned with such matters as he was with banking as a whole. The young Lorenzo prided himself on having the mind of a poet and the mental steeliness of a warrior; he enjoyed debating philosophy and discussing the latest humanist ideas. Such a mind was not given to studying the intricacies of account ledgers. Despite the best efforts of his Uncle Giovanni at the bank in Rome, Lorenzo absorbed little or nothing of the processes by which the Medici had made their fortune. Later, when asked about banking, he would confess (or perhaps boast): 'I know nothing about such matters.'

However, if Lorenzo returned home from Rome, after his successful negotiations with the pope over the alum monopoly, expecting a hero's welcome from his father, he was in for a shock. He found Florence divided and his father locked in a struggle for his political life.

Piero de' Medici's unwillingness to travel beyond his native city and the Medici villas in its immediate environs was not only on account of his debilitating illness. Since taking over from his father, Piero had become increasingly aware of the precariousness of his position. By the end of Cosimo's long life, many of the leading Florentine families had begun to tire of the Medici ascendancy, wishing instead for a return to the more apparently republican ways of former times, when they had been able to exercise their own influence over the affairs of the city. The ever-astute Cosimo had certainly realised this, declaring: 'I know the fickle ways of our citizens. Within fifty years we Medici will be chased out of Florence.'

Despite Cosimo's perspicacity, at the end of his life he had made two uncharacteristic mistakes. Firstly, he had left no will clarifying family ownership of the Medici bank. This meant that when he died, his son Piero inherited only 50 per cent of the Medici holding in the bank. The other half was inherited by his cousin Pierfrancesco de' Medici, who took no part in the running of the bank or indeed in running the city. As a result, Piero had large outgoings in the form of patronage to maintain Medici control; and when, as sometimes happened, the bank required a sudden injection of liquidity, it was Piero who advanced the money. Meanwhile, Pierfrancesco simply accumulated more and more assets. He would soon have much greater wealth than the ruling branch of the Medici family, yet he made sure that he was in no way seen as being associated with their rule, despite the fact that he lived next door to the Palazzo Medici. Many in Florence began to wonder how much longer this could continue.

Cosimo's second mistake was to advise his son Piero that when it came to running the Medici bank he should follow the advice of Dietisalvi Neroni, Cosimo's long-term business associate, who had gained a considerable fortune through his association with the Medici. However, unbeknown to Piero, Neroni had become jealous of the power wielded by the Medici and had covertly switched his allegiance. Machiavelli, who was not only a profound judge of human nature, but also knew the devious ways of Florentine politics, described how:

> Messer Dietisalvi [Neroni], inspired more by his own ambition than by his love for Piero or the benefits he had in former times received from Cosimo, thought it would be easy for him to ruin Piero's credit, and to deprive him of the power he had inherited from his father. He therefore gave advice to Piero, in a manner which made him appear entirely honest and reasonable, but which in practice was intended to bring about his ruin.

Neroni began leading Piero through the Medici bank's *libri segreti* (private account ledgers), pointing out to him that — contrary to appearances — the bank was in a distinctly parlous state. During his last years Cosimo had spent vast sums patronising the costly building and renovation of churches; at the same time, he had also quietly loaned considerable sums to a number of leading Florentine figures who had got into difficulties during the recent downturn in the wool trade. On top of this, the bank had several large outstanding loans abroad, leaving a number of its branches in a perilous financial position. Owing to mismanagement, the Bruges branch was close to collapse, and things were if anything even worse at the London branch, where credit advanced to King Edward IV and his various nobles in order to finance the Wars of the Roses amounted to almost 80,000 florins. Word had it that Edward IV was neither willing nor able to repay his debts. Having acquainted Piero with 'the disorder in his affairs and how much money was absolutely necessary to save his own credit', Neroni suggested 'that the most honourable way to remedy his difficulties was to call in the debts due to his father by both foreigners and citizens'. As Machiavelli pointed out, 'such counsel seemed good and honest to Piero, who wished to remedy his affairs with his own means'.

At the end of 1464, just months after taking over from his father, Piero decided to call in the Medici bank's loans. This proved a catastrophic error. As a result, many merchants faced bankruptcy and anti-Medici sentiment began to spread amongst the influential families. Yet whilst the fortunes of the Medici bank had suffered, others had prospered – in particular, the ancient bank headed by Luca Pitti, who had begun to build himself a vast ostentatious palazzo in the Oltrarno district across the river from the main centre of the city. Although Pitti's palazzo remained unfinished, it was evident that this grandiose residence was intended to dwarf all others in Florence, particularly the Palazzo Medici. The changing fortunes of the Medici meant that instead of petitioning at the Palazzo Medici, many now sought patronage at the Palazzo Pitti. The city was beginning to polarise into two opposing camps: the Party of the Hill (the Pitti faction, centred on its palazzo in the hilly Oltrarno) and the Party of the Plain (centred on the less resplendent Palazzo Medici on the flat ground north of the city centre).

The Party of the Hill was backed by several powerful families, including the Acciaiuoli, the Soderini and more covertly the Neroni, all of whom had secretly nursed a grudge against the Medici since their rise to pre-eminence. (Indicatively, the members of the Strozzi family, who had been allowed by Piero to return from exile, refrained from joining.) In May 1465 400 citizens more or less closely associated with the Party of the Hill signed a petition calling for a return to the old republican method of elections and an end to the Medici manipulation of the names placed in the leather bags from which were chosen the new *gonfaloniere* and his Signoria, as well as other leading appointments in the government. This petition was even signed by Pierfrancesco de' Medici, who was married to an Acciaiuoli. Piero de' Medici ignored the petition, biding his time. Then, in March 1466, while the young Lorenzo was away in Rome, news came through that the Medici's great ally, Francesco Sforza, Duke of Milan, had died and been succeeded by his twenty-three-year-old son, the unpredictable Galeazzo Maria Sforza. Piero realised that, in case of trouble, he could no longer be certain of support from Milan.

Meanwhile Luca Pitti and the Party of the Hill had already made secret plans for the overthrow of Piero de' Medici, securing the support of Borso d'Este, Duke of Ferrara, who was on the point of despatching 1,300 cavalry across the Apennine mountains into Florentine territory. Such was the situation when Lorenzo returned from his mission to Rome in the summer of 1466.

In the midst of a sweltering August, Piero became stricken with a particularly virulent attack of gout and was carried out of the city on a litter to recover amidst the cooler air of his villa at Careggi, accompanied by Lorenzo. Only now did Piero learn the full extent of the plotters' plans to overthrow him. Realising the seriousness of the situation, he sent word to Milan, in the forlorn hope that Galeazzo Maria Sforza might come to his aid; then on the morning of 27 August, he prepared for his servants to carry him back to Florence at once, despatching Lorenzo ahead with orders to make ready for his arrival and the defence of the Palazzo Medici. As Lorenzo galloped down the road to Florence he was hailed by some peasants working in the fields and warned that a group of armed men was waiting down the road at the villa of Archbishop Neroni, the brother of Dietisalvi. Lorenzo realised that these men were planning to ambush Piero and assassinate him. He quickly galloped back to warn his father and together they took a cross-country track, enabling them to enter the city undetected through another gate.

By afternoon Piero de' Medici was installed in the Palazzo Medici, summoning his supporters throughout the city. At the same time the unexpected news reached Florence that Galeazzo Maria Sforza had despatched 1,500 cavalry from Milan. When the conspirators who had gathered at the

Palazzo Pitti learned that Piero had returned to Florence, they were spurred into precipitate action. Acciaiuoli, Soderini and Neroni rode off to rally their men. Pitti, finding himself left alone and defenceless in his half-built palazzo, suddenly became suspicious of his fellow conspirators and panicked. Clambering onto his horse he rode pell-mell over the Ponte Vecchio, across the Arno and through the streets to the Palazzo Medici, where he abjectly pledged his alliegance to Piero. Unaware of how deeply Pitti had been involved in the plot to kill him, Piero graciously pardoned him, but made sure that Pitti remained in the Palazzo Medici.*

By now the city was in uproar. Piero sent word next door to the residence of his cousin Pierfrancesco de' Medici, saying that he needed 10,000 ducats† at once, in order to secure the city and provide for the approaching Milanese troops. Surprisingly, Pierfrancesco responded by giving him the money. His motives remain unclear. He certainly favoured a return to a more open republican government, but may have feared that the overthrow of his cousin would result in the demise of the Medici bank, and with it his own fortune. On the other hand, he may simply have feared for his life, with so many armed Medici supporters gathering at the neighbouring palazzo. On receiving the money, Piero despatched men throughout the city to buy up all the supplies of bread and wine. When the frightened citizenry had heard what was happening, many of them had begun flocking to the Palazzo Medici, where the supplies obtained by Piero's men were freely distributed amongst them. The sight of this apparent popular rally of support for the Medici, along with news of the approaching troops from Milan, duly had their effect. The bands of armed men who had been riding through the streets attempting to drum up support for the conspirators now began to melt away through the side alleys. The Duke of Ferrara, hearing that his arrival would not be greeted by the expected popular uprising against the Medici, ordered his troops to turn about and retreat from Florentine territory before they

---

* As a result of Luca Pitti's cowardly behaviour he would become an object of derision. Even the craftsmen working on his palace downed tools in disgust. His palace remained uncompleted in his lifetime, and he was despised throughout the city until his death four years later.
† Florentine florins and Venetian ducats were the most widely used currencies in Italy at the time. Exchange rates between the two fluctuated slightly over the years, but around this period 5 ducats was usually worth around 6 florins.

became involved in any engagement with the Duke of Milan's forces. The Medici had won the day, during the course of which Lorenzo had saved his father's life.

The leading conspirators amongst the Acciaiuoli, Neroni and Soderini families were soon rounded up, tried and sentenced to death. Once again Piero was minded to exercise compassion and commuted their sentences to permanent exile. This proved a serious mistake, as the conspirators gathered in Venice, where an army was raised to attack Florence. Fortunately Piero was able to rely upon the support of Milan, and also hired the crack *condottiere** Federigo da Montefeltro with his mercenary army. Low-key hostilities would continue for a year before peace was declared and Florence was once again safe.

Having achieved success in diplomacy, the seventeen-year-old Lorenzo was now learning the lessons and perils of statecraft at first hand at his father's side. Preparation, decisive action (both personal and in winning over the people), together with good fortune, appeared to be the key factors: this was a lesson he would never forget.

Despite his deep involvement in matters of state, Lorenzo still found time to indulge his 'exuberant' side. He wrote increasingly assured and eloquent poetry, and in the manner of the time began addressing poems to a beautiful woman with whom he had fallen in love. The object of his poems was Lucrezia Donati, who was generally accounted the most beautiful woman in Florence. Sources differ as to Lucrezia's age, some putting this as low as twelve, others insisting that she was already married (at the time, such claims need not necessarily have been mutually exclusive). However, in the tradition of Dante and Beatrice, Petrarch and Laura, this was a chaste poetic love affair – platonic in fact, if not in tone:

> When I see her heavenly smile,
> The love that lights her eyes
> Fires Cupid's dart into my heart.

---

* *condottiere*: literally 'conductor' (i.e. leader or general) of his own army of mercenary soldiers, which he would contract or hire out under his leadership to whichever city-state was willing to pay best for their services. When the contract expired, he was free to offer his services elsewhere.

As Lorenzo's early English biographer William Roscoe so aptly put it, 'Lucretia [*sic*] was the mistress of the poet, and not of the man.' Such public declaration of love to a woman who was possibly betrothed, if not actually married, might have been acceptable in poetic terms; had there been any sexual involvement, this would have involved outrage, scandal and vengeance. The teenage Lorenzo was in fact rehearsing more mature emotions, in much the same way as jousters of this era practised for actual combat. Indeed, when a public joust was held at this time in the Piazza Santa Croce, according to tradition the queen of the tournament was the most beautiful woman in the city, and Lucrezia Donati was duly appointed. One by one the contestants rode up to her place on the dais, making their obeisance with lowered lance, before riding against each other. In this contest Lorenzo not only saluted Lucrezia before the applauding crowds lining the piazza, but also carried her standard and wore her device on his armour; this would indeed be a test of Lorenzo's mettle, for he was competing with some experienced veterans. The tournament, and Lorenzo's part in it, would feature in an epic written by the Florentine poet Luigi Pulci, a member of the intellectual circle at the Palazzo Medici. Pulci's *The Joust of Lorenzo de' Medici* would take its place as one of the most popular heroic ballads of its day. Even so, in the interests of veracity, Pulci felt bound to mention that at one stage Lorenzo fell off his horse, though with poetic legerdemain he would manage to transform this incident into an example of Lorenzo's valour. Lorenzo himself was under no such illusion about his role in the tournament, recording modestly in his journal: 'Although neither my years nor my blows were very great, the first prize was awarded to me, a silver helmet with Mars as its crest.'

If Lorenzo was crowned in the customary fashion – on bended knee, as the queen of the tournament placed the helmet on his head – this would have been the closest he came to actual physical contact with Lucrezia Donati. Such jousts were all about display: no blood was spilled, there was little danger, and enthusiasm was all. Here Lorenzo would have learned another important lesson: the people of Florence were easily distracted from their troubles by the staging of such events, even though they recognised that his victory and his wearing of Lucrezia Donati's device as an indication of his love for her were no more than a charade.

In fact, by this time Lorenzo was actually betrothed to someone else, as a prelude to an arranged marriage. His mother had journeyed to Rome to inspect the prospective bride, Clarice Orsini, a member of one of Rome's most distinguished and powerful aristocratic families, whose long pedigree included numerous cardinals and even two popes. Fortuitously, Lorenzo had seen Clarice during his trip to Rome, though without realising that she would soon be selected as his wife. This union was to be above all else political, as was indicated by the somewhat matter-of-fact tone adopted by Lorenzo's mother Lucrezia, when she wrote from Rome to Piero, describing the woman they wished to secure as Lorenzo's future bride. After mentioning Clarice Orsini's 'good height', 'nice complexion' and 'gentle manners', Lorenzo's mother went on to record: 'Her throat is fairly elegant, but it seems to me a little meagre . . . Her bosom . . . appeared to me of good proportions. She does not carry her head proudly like our girls, but pokes it a little forward.' Despite this dispassionate description, Lorenzo's mother knew that the choice of an aristocratic Roman bride for Lorenzo was a significant and ambitious departure from tradition. Previously, the Medici had married into leading Florentine families such as her own; by marrying an Orsini they were asserting their right to aristocratic status, as well as gaining a foothold in the Roman hierarchy. Here was a public indication that the Medici wished to establish themselves as the permanent aristocratic rulers of Florence. As Machiavelli would perceptively remark: 'he who does not want his fellow citizens as relatives wants them as slaves'.

The precise details of the Medici family ambitions were a closely guarded secret, traditionally passed on from father to son on his deathbed, a custom established by Cosimo de' Medici's father Giovanni di Bicci, the founder of the Medici bank. Giovanni di Bicci, in his wisdom, had advised Cosimo to remain modest, and not to interfere in politics. Cosimo had initially followed his father's advice, but had soon understood that political power was the only way to protect his family and his fortune. Even so it was Cosimo, suspecting that the citizens of Florence would soon tire of the Medici, who had advised his son Piero to find an aristocratic Roman bride for young Lorenzo. If the Medici were driven from Florence, they would still have the highest connections in Rome.

In June 1469 Clarice Orsini travelled to Florence and was duly married to Lorenzo de' Medici. The church bells rang out, and for three days the city of Florence was given over to public feasting and various Medici-funded celebrations. The festivities were largely organised by Lorenzo himself, for by now his father was too ill to move, and it soon became clear that he was dying. Less than five months later, on 2 December, the church bells of Florence pealed for the death of the city's ruler.

Lorenzo recorded in a journal written some years later:

On the second day after [my father's] death, although I was still a young man, being twenty-one years of age,* the principal men of the City and the State came to us in our house to console us and to encourage me to take care of the City and of the State, as my father and grandfather had done. This was against all my youthful instincts, and considering the great responsibility and danger involved, I accepted with reluctance. I did this solely to protect my friends and posses-sions, for it fares ill in Florence for anyone who is rich and does not control the State.

Lorenzo's mistake about his age was forgivable, but in the light of the evidence his insistence upon his 'reluctance' to take office was pure window-dressing. Between 1 and 4 December (that is, in the days *before* the Floren-tine delegation asked him to take power), Lorenzo wrote no fewer than three letters to Galeazzo Maria Sforza, Duke of Milan, preparing the Medici family's most powerful ally for the transition in Florence, as well as soliciting his continued support for the city and the Medici cause. Wary of Galeazzo Maria Sforza's violent and unstable personality, Lorenzo made sure he did this in the most flattering and fawning fashion:

I would like to declare myself as the most devoted servant of Your Excellency, and to recall the ancient devotion of our house and myself in particular toward Your Illustrious Lordship . . . while certain of having here the support of many good friends, it seems to me it

---

* Lorenzo was in fact twenty at the time, and most translations give this figure — yet the Italian version copied by Roscoe from a (now lost) original document, which he claimed was in Lorenzo's hand, quite plainly stated '*cioè di anni 21*'.

would do little good without the favour and aid of Your Illustrious Lordship.

Although Lorenzo wrote in his journal that the death of his father 'was greatly mourned by the entire city', and spoke to Galeazzo Maria Sforza of 'the great support of many good friends' in Florence, this too was disingenuous. True, the city leaders had offered him the post of unofficial ruler, but they had certainly been pressed into doing so by the Medici faction. And in truth the passing of Piero had not been mourned by many outside this powerful and well-organised faction. Indeed, this Medici 'succession' would prove no foregone conclusion.

Seizing on what was perceived to be a groundswell of anti-Medici sentiment, supporters of the Party of the Hill faction staged an uprising in the city of Prato some ten miles north-west of Florence. But to their chagrin this was followed by no popular uprising in Florence itself, and when the rebels heard that Lorenzo had ordered a swift military response, with the backing of the *gonfaloniere* and his Signoria, they quickly surrendered.

At the start of his reign, Lorenzo confided to the Milanese ambassador that he wished to rule the city 'in as civil a way as one can, as far as possible within the constitution'. Yet he now realised that if he was to remain in control of the city and protect the Medici wealth, he would have to take measures that tightened his hold over the electoral process, ensuring that those who were elected to powerful posts in the government always remained favourable to his rule. To this end, encouraged by Medici money, the Medici faction now evolved into an even more efficient and coercive party machine. The Council of One Hundred had been established by Cosimo de' Medici just over a decade previously for the purpose of selecting suitable names to be placed in the leather bags from which were drawn the new *gonfaloniere*, his eight-man ruling Signoria and all senior posts in the government. The new Medici party machine now ensured that the Council of One Hundred was packed with even more Medici men. All this may have remained 'within the constitution', but it hardly encouraged the spirit of republican democracy upon which the city prided itself.

In 1471 Pope Paul II died and was succeeded by Pope Sixtus IV. Lorenzo de' Medici travelled to Rome to represent Florence at the coronation of the new pope and was graciously received as the ruler of Florence. However, Lorenzo was also present as the representative of the Medici commercial concerns, and this role he fulfilled with some success. Paul II had not only renewed the Medici bank's monopoly operation of the Tolfa alum mines, but also reinstated the Medici as the papal bankers. To confirm this new relationship, the pope allowed Lorenzo to purchase a number of exquisite gems from his collection. Although Lorenzo is remembered as a great patron of the arts, in reality his personal preference seems to have been for gems, jewellery, cameos and the like.

Some commentators have seen this proclivity as an indication that Lorenzo privately concurred with his grandfather's opinion that the Medici would inevitably be driven from power within a few years. In case of an unexpected coup, such precious items could be quickly and easily transportable. There may have been some truth in this assessment, at least early in Lorenzo's reign. However, his later treatment of his jewel collection suggests that, as the years went by, his premonitions became very much the opposite – tending indeed to the most grandiose fantasies concerning the future of the Medici family. Far from treating his jewels as assets that could be sold in time of need, he 'desecrated' them by claiming them as permanent Medici property: cameos, vases and even jewels were engraved with his name, usually in the form of 'LAU.R.MED'. This marque has attracted much speculation. The first three letters were evidently the Latinised Lorenzo, and the last three Medici – but what of the R? Could this have stood for 'king': *rex* in Latin, *re* in Italian? Lorenzo appeared to be dreaming that future Medici would become kings, of Florence or elsewhere, and by these marques he wished to claim his place as first in such a royal line.

Having consolidated his position at home, and formed an alliance with the pope that complemented his alliance with Milan, Lorenzo seemed to be in full control of his situation. But it was now that he made a major blunder. Fresh alum deposits had recently been discovered at Volterra, forty miles south-west of Florence. Volterra lay in Florentine territory and was subject to Florentine rule: tribute was paid, and a Florentine governor was installed, but otherwise the city largely ran itself. Perhaps inevitably, a dispute now arose, between a group backed by the governor and one backed by the local council, as to who should be granted the mining contract for the alum. In 1471 this was sent for arbitration to Florence, where Lorenzo unsurprisingly decided in favour of the governor, whom he had appointed. When this news reached Volterra, the city erupted in a riot, several Florentines were killed and the governor was fortunate to escape with his life.

Against the advice of the Signoria, Lorenzo decided that firm action should be taken. Only recently, Prato had fallen with surprising ease to the Party of the Hill dissidents, and he knew that several Tuscan cities were growing impatient of Florentine rule. Once again, Florence hired the *condottiere* Federigo da Montefeltro and his army, which Lorenzo ordered to march on Volterra. Here Montefeltro found the gates barred, and embarked upon a siege. On 16 June 1472, after twenty-five days, Volterra surrendered, whereupon Montefeltro's mercenary troops went on the rampage – looting, raping and murdering the defenceless citizens. As soon as Lorenzo heard what had happened he rode post-haste to Volterra, where he made a heartfelt apology to the citizens, at the same time distributing alms in an attempt to alleviate their distress. But the harm had been done. It was he who had ordered in the troops, and he would for ever be blamed for the atrocity they had committed.

Although Lorenzo was practised in diplomacy from an early age, it was evident that he still had lessons to learn. Within months it was discovered that the alum mine at Volterra was far from matching the rich deposits at Tolfa. In the end it produced only limited quantities of low-grade alum, and mining was soon abandoned. Had Lorenzo not acted so precipitately, all this might have come to light earlier and the threat been defused. As it was, he now had to fortify the local garrison in order to maintain Florentine rule and prevent the city from switching its allegiance to nearby Siena.

As if to underline this irony, the Medici bank now began to suffer its own setbacks in the alum trade. One Florentine galley, and then another, was lost carrying alum on the long sea voyage around Spain to Bruges. Then the Venetians and the Genoese broke the papal monopoly and began shipping in Turkish alum to Bruges, seriously undercutting the alum reserves held in the Medici warehouses. Eventually the situation would become so dire that the Medici bank, which still had to pay papal dues on all alum that was mined at Tolfa, was actually making a loss on alum trading.

Meanwhile life at the Palazzo Medici continued as before, with its patronage of the Renaissance entering a golden age. Amongst the many and varied cultural figures associated with the Palazzo Medici during this period was the artist Sandro Botticelli, who was just thirty years old when he completed *The Adoration of the Magi* in 1475. Apart from being a masterpiece in its own right, this painting is also a monument to the Medici family. Although ostensibly depicting the three wise men and their entourage bearing their traditional gifts to the infant Christ, it also served as a family portrait depicting three generations of the Medici family. There are recognisable portraits of Cosimo, Piero and Lorenzo, along with his younger brother Giuliano; also included are likenesses of several influential Medici supporters and leading members of the Medici intellectual circle. As well as these, the picture included a strikingly assertive self-portrait of Botticelli himself at the edge of the crowd, one of the first indications of the emergent importance of the Renaissance artist, both in his own eyes and in those of his patrons.

Other leading artists in the Medici circle around this time included the ageing Michelozzo Michelozzi, who was now commissioned to create a tomb for Piero. Lorenzo also did his best to secure commissions, and smooth over controversies, for one of his more difficult geniuses, the young Leonardo da Vinci, whose ever-active mind leapt from project to project, from art to invention, frequently losing interest in the work for which he had been paid before he got round to completing it.

However, the figure to whom Lorenzo was most closely drawn was Angelo Poliziano, whom Lorenzo soon recognised as an even more accomplished poet than himself. Poliziano was born in 1454 in the town of Montepulciano, at the very southern limits of Tuscan territory, where his father was the Florentine-appointed governor. At the same time as the attempt to assassinate Piero de' Medici in 1466, the citizens of Montepulciano had staged an anti-Florentine uprising, during which Poliziano's father had been murdered. The twelve-year-old Poliziano was then brought up in Florence, where he quickly displayed precocious brilliance, writing Latin poetry at the age of thirteen and Greek verse four years later. This brought him to the attention of Lorenzo, and some time later he was invited to take up residence at the Palazzo Medici. By now Lorenzo had two sons,

Piero and Giovanni, and Poliziano became their tutor, along with the Platonic scholar Ficino. Lorenzo seems to have been particularly drawn to Poliziano's combination of profound scholarship and sheer *joie de vivre*, and their affectionately shared ebullience led some to suspect that for a time they were even lovers. Lorenzo's sexual omnivorousness had not abated with his marriage. Poliziano also composed an epic featuring Lorenzo's beloved younger brother Giuliano, who had originally been encouraged by Lorenzo to take an equal role in ruling the city, but preferred to remain out of the limelight and now acted more in an advisory capacity. Although Giuliano resembled his brother in his discriminating patronage and zest for life, he struck his contemporaries as lovable, rather than powerfully charismatic like his brother. As distant from his older brother, Giuliano was strikingly handsome, and attempted to emulate Lorenzo in the pursuit of women; but he was unfitted for the role of ruthless womaniser, and would frequently fall in love with women who rejected his advances. As a consequence, he was often plunged into a love-lorn state. In order to bolster Giuliano's pride, Poliziano composed a companion poem to Pulci's *The Joust of Lorenzo de' Medici*, calling it *The Joust of Giuliano de' Medici*. Although this poem did in fact describe an actual joust similar to the one won by his brother six years previously, Poliziano's embellishments upon the event were intended as a private joke amongst the Medici circle. These related how the most beautiful woman in Florence, a title now held by the seventeen-year-old Simonetta Vespucci, fell in love with Giuliano, but failed to win his affection, 'because none could melt the ice within his breast'.

Some time around 1476, Lorenzo's cousin Pierfrancesco de' Medici, the non-active half-owner of the Medici bank who was related by marriage to the Acciaiuoli family, had died. Lorenzo immediately took Pierfranceso's thirteen-year-old-son Lorenzo di Pierfrancesco de' Medici and his younger brother Giovanni to live with him in the Palazzo Medici, where they too were educated by Ficino and Poliziano.* However, Lorenzo's motives for this were not entirely philanthropic. In becoming guardian of his cousin's

---

* Lorenzo di Pierfrancesco de' Medici's full name includes the first name of his father, and I have used this form throughout to distinguish him from his cousin, the ruler of Florence, whose full name – including that of his father – would in fact have been Lorenzo di Piero de' Medici.

sons, he was intending to nullify the influence of the opposing Acciaiuoli family; at the same time he also became 'guardian' of their inheritance, which included their father's half-share of the Medici bank, a sum that by this stage was far greater than that held by Lorenzo, who had sold off part of his assets to finance the Medici party machine.

By now the market for alum had become so glutted, and the price fallen so low, that in order to cut their losses the Medici bank had reduced to a mere trickle the quantity of alum leaving the Tolfa mines. Consequently this so reduced the amount paid in papal dues that Sixtus IV became suspicious and ordered an audit of the Medici accounts. Such distrust in Medici banking practice was unprecedented, and Lorenzo was deeply affronted. In a retaliatory move he refused to allow Francesco Salviati, the new papally appointed Archbishop of Pisa, to take up his office in the city, on the grounds that the pope should have consulted him before making such an appointment in Florentine territory.

The relationship deteriorated further when Sixtus IV, who was constantly short of cash, approached the Medici bank for a loan of 40,000 florins, with which he wished to purchase the lordship of Imola for his 'nephew' Girolamo Riario (who was widely suspected of being his son). Imola's strategic position in the Romagna meant that it controlled Florence's eastern trade route across the Apennine mountains to the Adriatic, and Lorenzo's suspicions were immediately aroused. He politely refused the pope his loan, and advised all other Florentine bankers to do the same.

Although the Medici bank had experienced a decline during the five years since Lorenzo had succeeded his father in 1469, other banks in Florence had continued to prosper – in particular that run by the ancient Pazzi family, whose wealth now surpassed that of the Medici. The Pazzi family saw their opportunity to displace the Medici as the papal bankers, and willingly loaned Sixtus IV his 40,000 florins. Lorenzo was incensed; at the same time he also saw the serious implications of the Pazzi's move. Acting as the papal bankers would add to their already considerable wealth, which could only pose a threat to Medici power. Indeed, it was well known that the Pazzi family were becoming increasingly resentful of the Medici's pre-eminent position in Florence.

Lorenzo vowed to strike back at the Pazzi at the first opportunity, which was not long in coming. In March 1477, the death was announced of the rich father of a woman who had married into the Pazzi family, whereupon his daughter claimed the large inheritance, which would then have passed into the Pazzi family, further adding to their wealth and power. Instead of allowing this inheritance to fall to the Pazzi, Lorenzo chose to intervene: he ruled that the inheritance should pass instead to the woman's cousin, as he was the closest male relative. This was a judgement that nullified centuries-old tradition, at the same time setting a precedent that would have severe implications for every family in Florence, but Lorenzo refused to be dissuaded from his decision. According to Machiavelli, 'Lorenzo, heady with youth and power, was determined to decide on everything and show Florence that all policy came from him.' Even his closest circle was beginning to have qualms about Lorenzo's attitude, which the Pazzi inheritance seemed to have brought to a head. Once more, in the words of Machiavelli, 'With regard to this business, Giuliano de' Medici again and again expressed his misgivings, telling his brother that by wanting to take over too much he was liable to lose everything.' Giuliano's misgivings were soon to be fulfilled.

Just over a year later, on Sunday 26 April 1478, Lorenzo was attending Mass at Florence Cathedral when a commotion broke out amongst the congregation. At the same time, two priests standing near the altar beside Lorenzo withdrew daggers from beneath their robes and attempted to stab him. One stabbed him in the neck, but he broke free of the mêlée and, supported by friends, managed to reach the safety of the sacristy, where he boarded himself in. Only later did Lorenzo learn that in the midst of the congregation his brother Giuliano had been stabbed to death.

Meanwhile there was an attempt by Francesco Salviati, the recently appointed Archbishop of Pisa, to seize the Florentine seat of government, the Palazzo della Signoria, but this too was foiled. Upon hearing of the assassination attempts, the city erupted in turmoil, but Medici supporters were quick to rally the citizens to their cause, spreading word that this was an attempt by foreign enemies to take over Florence. Still clad in his ecclesiastical robes, the Archbishop of Pisa was flung out of a high window of the Palazzo della Signoria with a noose around his neck. Below, the crowd in the piazza jeered as he danced in his death-throes on the end of the rope. Eventually the bloodstained Lorenzo appeared at a high window of the Palazzo Medici and reassured the alarmed citizens gathered below that he was still their leader and would resist all foreign attempts to take over their city. Lorenzo's dramatic speech was received with heartfelt patriotic cheers, and the mob dispersed, hell-bent on revenge.

Only gradually, during the course of the day, did Lorenzo manage to piece together what had in fact happened. In a well-planned bid to overthrow the Medici, the Pazzi family had mounted an assassination attempt and a simultaneous coup, which had covertly been backed by Sixtus IV. The Medici's enemies had united in the plot – one of the priests who had attempted to stab him came from Volterra, while Giuliano's assassin was a leading member of the Pazzi family, and the coup itself was financed by Pazzi money. In retaliation, many genuine (or even suspected) Pazzi sympathisers were dragged from their houses and torn to pieces by the mob. The Volterran priest was caught and castrated, before being hanged.

Over the following week, Lorenzo ordered all leading members of the Pazzi family who had survived to be killed, thrown into prison or banished into exile. All Pazzi property and possessions were to be seized, and Medici agents were ordered in the name of the republic to attempt to sequester all assets of the Pazzi bank throughout Europe.

Yet despite this apparent victory, Lorenzo soon became aware of the extent and continuing determination of his enemies. Not only had the Pazzi been backed by Sixtus IV, but they had also been assured of the support of the pope's close ally King Ferrante I of Naples. Even Florence's trusted *condottiere* Federigo da Montefeltro had secretly been standing by in his nearby territory at Urbino, ready to move into Florentine territory to enforce the Pazzi takeover.

The pope was livid at the failure of the coup, and was especially outraged at the treatment of the Archbishop of Pisa, whilst dressed in his robes of office no less. Such an act was an offence against the Holy Church, and for this he excommunicated the entire population of Florence. These may have been mere words, but they were soon backed by action. War was declared on Florence, and papal troops, Montefeltro's troops, as well as King Ferrante's troops were launched into Florentine territory. Worse still, Florence could no longer even rely upon her usual ally Milan, as Lorenzo's friend Duke Galeazzo Maria Sforza had been assassinated two years previously. Florence was defenceless, and threatened on all sides.

It was now that Lorenzo showed his true mettle. The headstrong impetuousness that had been his failing in his dealings with Volterra and early handling of the Pazzi opposition now proved the saving of himself and his city. Acting on impulse, Lorenzo suddenly rode out of Florence without telling anyone of his intentions. Only when it was too late to stop him did he write to the Signoria, informing them somewhat disingenuously: 'Therefore, with the blessing of Your Excellencies of the Signoria, I have decided to go openly to Naples.' He then boarded a galley at Pisa and sailed down the coast, disembarking at Naples – where he planned to present himself before King Ferrante and intercede personally on behalf of Florence.

This was an act of truly foolhardy courage. The fifty-six-year-old King Ferrante was a merciless tyrant of mixed Spanish and Moorish descent whose upbringing had 'embittered and darkened his nature, and it is certain that he was equalled in ferocity by none among the princes of his time'. Ominously for Lorenzo, Ferrante retained his unique way of dealing with his enemies: 'He liked to have his opponents near him ... dead and embalmed, dressed in the costume which they wore in their lifetime.' But to widespread astonishment, Lorenzo's gamble paid off. King Ferrante welcomed Lorenzo de' Medici to his court, charmed by the daring young man who now proceeded to do all in his power to win over the king and the people of Naples. The galley slaves who had rowed Lorenzo's ship from Pisa to Naples were granted their freedom, clothed in becoming outfits to replace their rags, and awarded with ten florins each to speed them on their way. Dowries were dispensed to families too poor to marry off their daughters, so that they could make good marriages. Setting himself up at the local residence of the Medici bank, Lorenzo began a round of lavish entertaining for the leading families of the city.

All this involved funds that neither he nor the Medici bank possessed. Years later, the Medici family would order all documents from these years to be destroyed, but one survived. This disclosed that at some unspecified date Lorenzo de' Medici had embezzled no fewer than 74,948 florins from the Florentine exchequer, diverting it into his own personal account 'without the sanction of any law and without authority'. This colossal amount almost certainly dates from this period, and seems to have been used for two purposes. First and foremost, it funded Lorenzo's lavish behaviour in Naples; and second, in the opinion of Raymond de Roover, the foremost authority on the Medici bank: 'It is likely, therefore, that bankruptcy after the Pazzi conspiracy was diverted only by dipping into the public treasury.'

On 13 March 1480 Lorenzo de' Medici returned to Florence from Naples as a conquering hero. Not only had he persuaded King Ferrante to sign a peace treaty with Florence, but in the interests of Italian unity even Sixtus IV had joined this alliance. Florence was saved, although its citizens remained unaware of precisely how, and precisely how much, they themselves had contributed to this near-miraculous turn of events.

Well understanding the fickleness of his popularity, Lorenzo decided the time was ripe for him to make a number of changes to the city's consti-tution, which would consolidate his power, though in a largely covert manner. Just five weeks after his triumphant return from Naples, under the guise of reforming the constitution and the tax system in order to make them more just and efficient, Lorenzo suggested to the Council of One Hundred that they allow their powers to be superseded by a more streamlined Council of Seventy. Despite considerable opposition to this move, the Council of One Hundred eventually passed this constitutional 'reform' by a single vote. The Renaissance historian Lauro Martines justi-fiably asks, 'Were bribes paid out, favours promised, or heads banged in private and in the corridors? We are unlikely ever to know.' Lorenzo now appointed a large majority of ambitious citizens who were sympathetic to the Medici cause to sit on his new Council of Seventy. He had staged what 'was tantamount . . . to a constitutional *coup d'état.*' However, there were more than a few – even amongst the Medici faction and members of the Council of Seventy – who remained uneasy about jettisoning the last vestiges of democratic process. Indeed, over the coming years even the Council of Seventy would not always prove reliable in supporting Lorenzo's intended policy. Lorenzo would then find it necessary to attend their meet-ings in person, his intimidating presence – and the fact that he could see for himself who was for, and who was against, his proposed measure – being enough to sway the vote.

Lorenzo could not afford to lose control of his brainchild: the powers of the Council of Seventy were formidable indeed. Its members were to remain in office for five years (this would later be extended to life). They would choose each new *gonfaloniere* and his Signoria. And they would also be the main 'advisory' council to the *gonfaloniere* and the Signoria with regard to the passing of laws, as well as on foreign-policy matters and internal affairs, especially in the criminal and financial sphere. The Council of Seventy had to all intents and purposes superseded the *gonfaloniere* as ruler of the city, with elections for this post (and indeed all senior posts in the government) being reduced to little more than a merry-go-round of Medici puppets, with Lorenzo himself in complete control. Even so, the elections were duly held, and the results duly recorded, as if everything was above board: it may have been a charade, but the appearance of democratic constitutional rule had to be maintained.

Lorenzo's dash to Naples had been viewed by all as a valiant action, unprecedented in the treacherous world of contemporary Italian politics, and from now on the man who had selflessly risked his life in this noble fashion would become known throughout the land as Lorenzo the Magnificent. In the coming years he would play a leading role in keeping the peace in Italy; and his cultural influence would help spread the Renaissance through the Italian states. From now on, Florence's great artists would be loaned out to exercise their talents in the service of Italian leaders, acting as cultural ambassadors, promoting the good name of their native city and establishing it as the cultural centre of Italy, the paragon of European civilisation. Thus, in 1481 Lorenzo despatched Botticelli to Rome to appease Sixtus IV; and a year later, Leonardo da Vinci would be sent to Milan to win over the new ruler, Ludovico 'il Moro' Sforza. Meanwhile back home Lorenzo maintained civil peace and his own popularity with a calendar of spectacular events and festivals. The settings for these were designed by his finest artists, and the pageants performed at them were scripted by his most talented poets. He even put his talent to use on these occasions, composing humorous bawdy ballads. We now only have the words of these ballads, and snatches of the music that accompanied them; but it is not too difficult to imagine the knowing gestures of the actors as they sang

2

'Blind wic[ked]

GIROLAMO SAVONAROLA HAIL[ed from the] city state of Ferrara, whose [...] and its hinterland south of Ver[...] 1452, making him just three years you[nger than Lorenzo's birth, more or less] cent. He too had been exposed to ge[...] of his paternal grandfather Michele Sa[vonarola...] at the flamboyant court of the d'Es[te...] Michele was one of the leading p[...] numerous works, including *The Pract[ice...]* comprehensive study that claimed t[...] extant at that period. He also made [...] that was way ahead of its time. In the [...] Savonarola could well be regarded as [...] Ironically, in real life he was very n[...] remained strictly a man of the era in [...] the late 1300s. In this respect, M[...] medievalist, and 'certain of the min[...] have the quality of being written by [...] doctor of the d'Este court, being as [...] moralising'. Such was the dominant p[...] would devote himself to educating the [...] in his eager pupil all the rigid prin[...] Italy was already passing into histor[y...] case in Ferrara, which was ruled by th[e...] scion of one of Europe's most aristo[cratic...]

their roles. Here, for instance, is a p
Peasants':

> We've all got cucumbers, and
> They may look old and kno
> But they're great for opening
> Use both hands to pluck 'er
> The top, peeling back the sl
> Open wide your mouths and

The citizens may have delighted a
to them it was they who were actua
city of Florence in May 1482, when an
arrived to take up a post at the mon

the arts would during this period become second only to the Medici.*

At the age of seven Savonarola would witness a formative historical event, when the new pope, Pius II, passed through Ferrara on his triumphal procession across northern Italy. (It was earlier on this very journey that the pope had been entertained in Florence by a pageant featuring the ten-year-old Lorenzo de' Medici.) Pius II was accompanied by:

> a *cortège* of incredible pomp, with ten cardinals, sixty bishops and many secular princes in his train ... At Ferrara the Pope made his entrance under a canopy of gold brocade; the streets through which he passed were carpeted with cloth and sprinkled with flowers; rich tapestries hung from the windows, and the city echoed with music and song. On reaching the cathedral, Guarino [a renowned humanist scholar] read him a long Latin oration, crammed with learned allusions and praise of the Holy Father. For a whole week Pius II was detained in Ferrara by a succession of festivities.

During his visit the worldly Pius II's penchant for fine dining and entertainment by courtesans would certainly have been indulged by his generous host. Although this would have taken place amidst circumstances of the strictest privacy, gossip concerning such events would have spread amongst families who retained close court connections, such as the Savonarolas. Even after the retirement of Michele Savonarola, his son Niccolò continued to hold an unspecified minor post at the d'Este court.

Pius II may have been flattered by the magnificent welcome accorded him in Ferrara, but he had few illusions about his host, recording in his memoirs: 'Borso was a man of fine physique and more than average height with beautiful hair and pleasing countenance. He was eloquent and garrulous and listened to himself talking as if he pleased himself more than his hearers. His talk was full of blandishments mingled with lies.' Borso was a homosexual and his frivolous squandering had hardly endeared him to Michele

---

* The d'Este were a widespread aristocratic family, branches of which had already provided a thirteenth-century German king, as well as rulers of Bavaria and Carinthia. Later they would produce the Elector of Hanover, who in the eighteenth century became King George I of Great Britain.

Savonarola, who secretly voiced the opinion that 'the giving of robes, horses, possessions and money to buffoons and unworthy men diminishes the love of the people'. Such opinions were best kept to oneself, as anyone who had attended Borso's court knew only too well, for beneath the *castello* were:

> subterranean dungeons guarded by seven gratings from the light of day. They were full of immured victims, and the clanking of chains and groans of human beings in pain could be heard from their depths, mingling with the strains of music and ceaseless revelry going on above, the ringing of silver plate, the clatter of majolica dishes, and clinking of Venetian glass.

Despite the need for secrecy, Michele Savonarola's views on such matters would certainly have been passed on to his grandson, who was said to have been taken to court only once, by his father, and to have sworn never to repeat the experience.

Michele Savonarola would die around 1468, when his grandson was sixteen.* By now young Girolamo Savonarola was exhibiting the precocious mental brilliance that his grandfather had doubtless detected at an early age, causing him to be singled out from his six siblings. By this time he had already learned by heart entire books of the Bible, and had absorbed as the Holy Writ the oft-repeated maxims of his ascetic grandfather, such as 'That which God has ordered, the Popes and their Vicars cannot rule otherwise.' Such sentiments were not unusual at the time; there was indeed a widespread understanding throughout the secular educated classes in Italy that the Church was corrupt, and many discerning Italians maintained a sincere religious belief that remained separate and personal, paying little more than lip-service (and unavoidable financial contributions) to the hierarchy that claimed to represent their religion on Earth.

However, Michele Savonarola had not seen life this way, and had instilled in his grandson a more unaccommodating attitude. As a result, young Girolamo was filled with outrage at what he saw, and such laxity and corruption only served to spur him to a more urgent conception of life.

---

* Some sources claim this event took place in 1466, others that it was even earlier. At any event, its effect on his youthful grandson was profound.

Either religion meant saving one's soul – the most overriding and vital task on Earth – or it meant nothing at all.

But Girolamo's grandfather had also instructed him in philosophy – and here he learned to embrace Aristotelianism, rather than the fashionable new Platonism so favoured by the humanists. Savonarola took to heart the ideas of Aristotle as interpreted by St Thomas Aquinas, which over the years had become the orthodoxy of medieval scholasticism. This applied some Ancient Greek philosophy and Aristotelian logic to the Bible in order to explain the doctrine and mysteries of the Christian religion. It was an attempt to give religious belief and theology a more philosophical foundation, though over the years this had ossified into something of a rigid orthodoxy. Religious and philosophical argument had to proceed by appealing to the authority of the Bible or Aristotle. The recently rediscovered works of Plato, which had come to western Europe after the fall of Constantinople, as well as the classical works of Ancient Greece and Rome now so favoured by the humanists, were dismissed as pagan heresies.

All this the young Savonarola had taken to heart, and he spent many hours in precocious reading on such matters. During his adolescent years, it was said of him that 'he was in the habit of speaking little with others, and was always withdrawn and solitary'. Despite this, it seems that at some stage following his grandfather's death Savonarola did in fact embark upon a course of liberal studies under Battista Guarino at the University of Ferrara. Savonarola's father Niccolò persuaded him to embark upon this course so that he could obtain a Master of Arts degree, as a prerequisite for studying medicine. Niccolò placed great hopes in his son's future, which he believed would bring the boy fame and fortune like that of his grandfather Michele. But Niccolò also had other motives for persuading his son to try and emulate his famous grandfather. Niccolò had come into a generous inheritance from his father, and in order to supplement his income as a minor functionary at the d'Este court he had used his inheritance to finance a sideline as a banker. Possibly in the attempt to raise his status at court, he had stood surety for loans to various courtiers who had then defaulted. Niccolò Savonarola was desperate for money, and the pressure he exerted on Girolamo to enter the university must have been considerable: when he became a successful doctor he would be expected to provide for the entire family, as well as help his father maintain appearances at court.

Girolamo's studies under Guarino gave him a wide knowledge of humanism and the classical philosophers from whom it derived its ideas. As a result, when Savonarola later attacked humanism so vehemently, his adversaries would often be surprised at how well informed he was about their ideas and the attitude that they encouraged. Indeed, at some stage Savonarola himself even succumbed to the excitement of this new outlook on life, going so far as to learn how to play the lute and write poetry. Yet even here, amidst the melancholy so natural to any young poet, he often focused on the deeper concerns imbued in him by his grandfather:

> In the sadness of my heart I spoke
> With the ancient Mother who never changes,*
> And weeping, her eyes modestly lowered,
> She led me to her beggar's cave.

With his verse exhibiting such Freudian undertones, it comes as no surprise that around this time the young poet fell in love. The object of his intense affections was a girl called Laodamia, an illegitimate daughter of the distinguished Strozzi family, then in exile from Florence, whose house was next door to the Savonarola family home. A narrow alleyway separated the two houses, making it possible to converse between them from the opened windows of the overhanging upper storeys, and it seems that Savonarola and Laodamia got to know each other in this way. Soon he was serenading his inamorata with his lute. However, Savonarola evidently misjudged the situation, for when he asked Laodamia to marry him she scornfully turned down his proposal, telling him that no Strozzi would ever stoop to marry a mere Savonarola. Stung by this rejection, Savonarola at once retorted that no legitimate male Savonarola would ever condescend to marry a Strozzi bastard.

This story only came to light some three centuries later, amongst the

* That is, the eternal Mother Church, as distinct from the corrupted contemporary Church.

papers of Fra Benedetto of Florence, Savonarola's colleague and early biographer. Even so, the story was dismissed as a legend. However, subsequent research has revealed that the Savonarola house in Ferrara did indeed stand next door to the Strozzi mansion; and that according to the records, Roberto Strozzi had an illegitimate daughter called Laodamia, who lived in Ferrara at the time. Fra Benedetto received most of his information at first hand from Savonarola himself, indicating that this incident must have lodged in Savonarola's mind long after he foreswore the ways of the world. Such a sexual rejection, especially with its social overtones, may well have been formative. Some years after this incident, Savonarola would write that even before he took holy orders he had 'not had desire for a woman'. Given his passion for truth-telling, Savonarola must consciously have believed this at the time. Yet according to Fra Benedetto's account, in his later years Savonarola would recall the story of his rejection by Laodamia. The sexual and social implications of this incident may have become all the stronger as a result of this memory being repressed during the intervening years. His detestation of 'lustfulness [and the] lusts of the flesh' and his hatred of class privilege would become integral to his religious drive.

Such inclinations were now to be reinforced in the raw. In 1471 Duke Borso d'Este fell mortally ill, either as a result of his dissipation or by poisoning. As he lay at death's door in his residence at Belfiore, forty miles north of Ferrara, civil war broke out in the city between his younger brother Ercole and his nephew Niccolò, who – in the absence of any declared succession – both claimed to be his rightful heir. Niccolò took over the *castello*, appealing to Milan and Mantua to back his claim; meanwhile Ercole called on nearby Venice for support. Opposing groups of supporters took to the streets, and the result was what Savonarola would later refer to as 'the bloody Saturnalia of Ferrara'. Desperately barricaded into their house on one of the main streets leading to the *castello*, the Savonarola family could only watch terrified as:

the partisans, intoxicated by the fumes of blood, fought a veritable war of extermination. The wives and daughters of the leaders of the opposing factions were dragged from their homes to be publicly dishonoured by the lowest plebs. People were pitched from the roofs of their houses where they had fled for refuge to be hacked to pieces in the streets below. Dwellings were set on fire and the inhabitants, prevented from coming out by their beleaguerers, perished in the smoke and flames.

The mob supporting Ercole eventually prevailed; yet according to one source, the aftermath was almost as bad: 'Caleffini reports that the bodies of two hundred of the leading citizens, after being stripped and mutilated, were nailed to the eaves of the ducal palace.' The young and impressionable Savonarola could hardly have avoided this grotesque sight, which was less than half a mile down the road from his house and the nearby university.

Soon after this, Savonarola obtained his Master of Arts degree and began to study medicine. The intimate involvement with the flesh required of such studies must soon have begun to repel him, awakening in him an intense spiritual yearning. He was disgusted by all he saw around him, and abhorred the sordid world in which he found himself. As he would write in a poem entitled 'On the Ruin of the World':

> Now those who live from theft are all content,
> And those who feed the most on others' blood . . .

He goes on to rail against those who mock Our Lord in Heaven, and how Rome is so filled with vice that it can never return to the days of its great past, and how 'usury is now called philosophy'.

Amidst all his castigating it is possible to detect a growing sense of the injustice of it all. The rich clambered over the poor in an attempt to gain more riches; instead of compassion and theology, men concentrated their minds on making money. Instead of discovering God, they discovered how to make a fortune by means of usury. It is difficult to avoid seeing his father's role in all this: prompted by avarice, Niccolò had lost the family fortune by resorting to usury. And because of this, Savonarola had been forced to go against all his inclinations and study medicine – until early in 1474 things finally came to a crisis. To celebrate the May holiday, Savonarola walked the forty miles to Faenza. Away from his Bible and his medical books, crossing the humid terrain of the Po delta, pacing along the road between the flat green fields, he was alone with his nagging thoughts. Having reached Faenza, he explored the streets amidst the throng of the May Day crowds. But the sight of such blatant godless enjoyment amidst the market stalls, street hawkers and puppet booths drove him to seek sanctuary in the Church of Santo Agostino, where a friar was delivering the day's sermon, his distant voice echoing through the dim stillness. His text was taken from Genesis, where God speaks to Abraham, telling him: 'Get thee out of thy country, and from thy kindred, and from thy father's house . . .' As Savonarola would later recount in his own sermons, he at once recognised that this was the voice of God speaking directly to him. From that day on he knew that he would have to leave his home, abandon his family and forsake everything to follow God. He returned to Ferrara firm in the conviction that he would renounce the world and become a priest.

Yet it would be almost a year before Savonarola could bring himself to act upon this resolution. He had no wish to provoke a hysterical scene, in which he would have been confronted by the tears and entreaties of the various members of his family, for 'truly this would have broken my heart, and I should have renounced my purpose'. Instead, he waited until 24 April the following year, choosing to slip away from his home whilst the family were in the midst of the St George's Day celebrations. Hastily he set off to walk the thirty miles to Bologna, where he made his way to the Dominican monastery, rapped on the door and asked to be taken in as a novitiate monk. The following day the twenty-three-year-old wrote a long letter addressed 'To the noble and illustrious man Niccolò Savonarola, a most excellent parent'. In this he attempted to comfort his family, who were 'doubtless suffering greatly because of my departure, and especially because I departed secretly from you'. He went on:

> I thus beg you, my dear father, to put an end to your weeping and spare me any further sadness and pain than I suffer already. However, you must understand that I do not suffer because of regret at what I have done, for I would not undo this even if such a choice would make me greater than Caesar himself, but instead my suffering is

because I too am flesh and blood, just like you, and our senses quarrel with our reason. I must constantly battle to prevent the Devil from leaping onto my shoulders, and all the more so when I feel for you.

And why had he chosen such a life? After cataloguing 'the great wretchedness of the world, the evil of men, rapes, adulteries' and so on, he sums up his reason for taking holy orders: 'I did this because of the blind wickedness of the people of Italy.'

Either Savonarola had fled from this 'blind wickedness', or his intention was to do something about it. Despite fleeing from his family, the former course of action ran contrary to his nature. Thus from the very outset it would seem that his aim was more than merely the saving of his own soul. Indeed, in a second letter, addressed to his family (the first had been very badly received by his father), he ends by haughtily informing them that they should 'rejoice that God made me a doctor of souls, rather than a doctor of bodies'. He would cure the spiritual ills of the world rather than its physical ailments.

Other evidence tends to contradict this somewhat exalted view of himself. When he first entered the monastery he is said to have done so not with the intention of becoming a priest, but instead to serve out a penance for his sins. He wished to be assigned only the humblest tasks: to become the monastery drudge, sewing the brothers' clothes, digging the garden, working in humility and peace. As he put it, he had no intention of 'exchanging the Aristotelianism of the world for that of the monastery'. Yet it is not necessary to choose between such contradictory evidence. Far from it. Such contradictions hint at the deep conflicts that remained unresolved in his complex and driven character. Only intense pride craves such extreme humiliation; only an intellectual dreams of losing himself in mindless drudgery. Such a drudge would have been regarded as an almost subhuman serf; worse still, sewing was considered women's work. A monk, for all his chastity, remained nonetheless a man in the Italy of this period, and was proud to be regarded as such. In his letter to his father, Savonarola specifically contrasted 'a strong man who spurns transitory things to follow truth' with the 'passion of a simple woman'. In view of his constant strictures against women, it is worth bearing in mind that Savonarola's view of the female sex was for the most part informed by the passionate and angry misogyny of the Old Testament prophets, as well as the prejudices of his time and his country – along with his experiences of Laodamia and of his mother Elena, of whom little is known during this period beyond one salient, undermining fact. On the night before he fled the family home, his mother heard him strumming on his lute, whose melancholy tones caused her to pause from what she was doing. In a flash of intuition she realised what was going to happen and said to him: 'My son, what you are playing today is a sign that you are parting from us.' It had been a 'simple woman' who had seen through him.

In fact, we know little of Savonarola's early life in the monastery; as his biographer Roberto Ridolfi put it, 'the silence which enveloped him through these seven long years seems symbolic of the silence in which as a young man he entered the cloister, intent upon building, in humility and contemplation, his new life'. The Dominican order had been founded in 1216 by St Dominic, a scholarly Spanish monk who gave up his possessions to aid the poor. He established the Dominicans as a preaching order of mendicant friars, who took a vow of poverty and depended upon charity for their livelihood. Much like its founder, the order tended to attract men of high intellectual calibre who sought to preach and alleviate the sufferings of the poor. It also produced many lecturers in the universities, and was later put in charge of the Inquisition (which accounts for why the inquisitors were known as 'Hounds of God': in Latin *domini canes*). However, more generally they were known as the 'Black Friars', on account of the distinctive hooded black cloaks, which they wore over their white woollen habits.

Savonarola would later look back on his novitiate year in the Dominican monastery at Bologna as the happiest in his life, 'where I found liberty, and did all that I wanted, because I wanted nothing else, desired nothing else, than to do all that I was told or commanded to do'. He welcomed the self-denial that was required of the monks, and rejoiced in the further abstinence he was able to impose upon himself. From the outset, Savonarola was excused the usual lessons in Latin because he had already learned this at university. Instead, he spent much of his time studying the great medieval philosopher St Thomas Aquinas, whose interpretations of Aristotelian thought had by now become his favourite reading. Savonarola probably took his vows in May 1476, and thereupon immersed himself in the monastic life. His zeal for abstinence and self-denial soon became apparent to all. So too did his enthusiasm for the customary course of theological studies at the celebrated Dominican *Studium generale* in Bologna. This was one of the most distinguished theological colleges in Italy, with many eminent scholars amongst its teaching staff. Savonarola soon began to shine amongst his fellow pupils. Indeed, such was his exemplary aptitude for both the ascetic and the theological aspects of monastic life that within a few years he was considered ready for a teaching post. In 1479, just four years after leaving home, the twenty-seven-year-old Savonarola returned to Ferrara, where he took up a post as teaching master for the novices at the local Dominican monastery. By now his father had been forced to sell their home to the next-door Strozzi, and the young priest is said to have seen little of his family during this time.

Meanwhile, Italy had entered yet another volatile political period. Three years previously, in 1476, Duke Galeazzo Maria Sforza of Milan had been assassinated in church. In the same year, Niccolò d'Este led an armed invasion of Ferrara in another attempt to wrest the dukedom from his uncle, but this was defeated and Niccolò was beheaded (before his head was sewn on again and he was buried in the family vault). Just two years later, news of the Pazzi family's attempted assassination of Lorenzo de' Medici, backed by Sixtus IV and King Ferrante of Naples, rocked Italy. The fact that his would-be assassin was a priest, and the murder was backed by the pope himself, merely gave public confirmation to what so many had privately known: the Church hierarchy, especially in its upper echelons, had become all but irredeemably corrupt. In his poem 'On the Ruin of the World' Savonarola had written despairingly:

> The sceptre has fallen into the hands of a pirate;
> Saint Peter is overthrown;
> Here lust and greed are everywhere . . .*

---

*The sceptre of course represented the papacy, which traced its lineage back to St Peter; Sixtus IV was widely said to have made his fortune as a pirate in his younger days, using this to enable his rapid advance in the Church hierarchy.

Even so, Savonarola remained unwavering in his faith – as, for the most part, did the pope's flock throughout Christendom. The new Duke Ercole of Ferrara was particularly renowned for his church-going, unfailingly attending Mass and Vespers every day. He also lavished considerable sums on the building of churches and religious institutions in Ferrara, making the Renaissance a golden age for the city. The great historian Jacob Burckhardt was in no doubt as to Ferrara's eminence:

> If the rapid increase of the population be a measure of prosperity actually attained, it is certainly a fact of importance that in the year 1497, notwithstanding the wonderful extension of the capital, no houses were to be let. Ferrara is the first really modern city in Europe; large and well-built quarters sprang up at the bidding of the ruler: here, by the concentration of the official classes and the active promotion of trade, was formed for the first time a true capital.

The population of Ferrara rose to around 25,000 during this period; by comparison the population of London was around 50,000, and that of Florence probably around 90,000. Even so, the architecture of Ferrara certainly rivalled that of its Tuscan counterpart – when Savonarola first arrived in Florence he would be no overawed provincial, despite being regarded as such by many Florentines.*

But in 1482 Ferrara was once again directly disturbed by the volatility of the Italian political scene. In the aftermath of the failed Pazzi conspiracy, and Lorenzo's courageous dash to Naples, which had secured a peace treaty with King Ferrante, Sixtus IV had been forced to join this treaty. This new alliance, and Christianity as a whole, now faced peril. The threat came from the distant East. Since taking Constantinople in 1453, Sultan Mehmet the Conqueror had gradually expanded the Ottoman Empire across Greece and the Balkans, eventually reaching the Adriatic shore oppo-

---

* In 1570 Ferrrara would be struck by a devastating earthquake, which demolished many of its fine buildings, a disaster from which it would not recover. Never again would it bear comparison with Florence. When Charles Dickens visited Ferrara in 1846 he wrote of its 'long silent streets and the dismantled palaces, where ivy waves in lieu of banners, where rank weeds are creeping up the long-untrodden stairs'.

site Italy. In August 1480, Ottoman forces had landed in the heel of Italy, taking the port of Otranto. 12,000 of the inhabitants were slaughtered, a similar number shipped into slavery; 800 remaining inhabitants were then beheaded for refusing to convert to Islam, their skulls piled into a pyramid. Christendom itself had stood in danger, and Sixtus IV had rallied Italy for the defence of the faith. Then in May 1481 Mehmet the Conqueror had died, most of the Ottoman forces had been withdrawn and Otranto was retaken.

With the passing of the Ottoman threat, Sixtus IV thought better of launching another attack on Florence, which would only have brought Ferrante I of Naples into the field against him. Instead, he decided to move against Ferrara, which had long been claimed as a papal possession. Venice had supported Ercole d'Este in his claim to the dukedom, and Ferrara continued to rely for its protection on its powerful northern neigh- bour. But Sixtus IV now secretly induced Venice to switch to an alliegance with the papacy, promising the Venetians the valuable Ferrarese salt-pans of the Po delta if they aided his 'nephew' Girolamo Riario in taking Ferrara. Sixtus IV intended that Ferrara should be added to the papal territory already ruled by Riario. Consequently, in the spring of 1482 Ferrara found itself under threat, with Venetian forces poised to cross the Po and mount an invasion.

At the time, Savonarola was not in fact present in Ferrara. He had been selected as representative for Ferrara at the Chapter General of the Domini- cans of Lombardy – an indication of his growing regard within the order. The Chapter General was the annual congress that debated the theological policy of the order, and was being held at Reggio, sixty miles west of Ferrara, attracting clerical and lay delegates from far and wide, as well as a number of leading philosophical and literary figures. Here Savonarola listened to the debates conducted by distinguished Dominican theologians. As part of these debates, Savonarola himself delivered a passionate attack on the corruption of the Church, which was heard by the precocious nineteen- year-old philosopher Pico della Mirandola, who was so impressed by Savonarola's evident intellectual powers and deep theological learning that he sought him out afterwards. The two established a rapport that was as immediate as it was unlikely.

Count Giovanni Pico della Mirandola, to give him his full title, was a prodigy of impeccable aristocratic descent, with links to the d'Este family, the Sforzas of Milan and the distinguished House of Gonzaga, which ruled nearby Mantua. Pico had spent his early years in the tiny independent city state of Mirandola, which was ruled by his family and was under the protection of Ferrara, whose capital city lay just thirty miles to the east. Pico's appearance was very much the polar opposite of the raw-featured Savonarola in his plain monk's robes. Indeed, Pico was something of a peacock, who dressed in fashionable Renaissance-style attire, his long auburn locks flowing over his shoulders, his delicate face exhibiting an almost feminine sensitivity and beauty. His astonishing learning had by now begun to attract widespread attention: he had already mastered Latin and Ancient Greek, and had launched into studies of Hebrew and Arabic. Later he would be one of the few men in Europe who could understand Aramaic and Babylonian texts in Chaldean script. Yet Pico's intellectual achievements were more than just an exhibition of dazzling brilliance. His studies were driven by a deep theological-philosophical impulse – a pressing need to understand the religions from which Christianity had sprung, combined with a dedicated quest for the common philosophical ideas that enlightened these religions. Indeed, what drew Savonarola and Pico della Mirandola together more than anything was probably their shared deep understanding of the ancient Judaic texts that formed the Old Testament, and thus informed the Christianity of the New Testament. Savonarola may even have seen Pico some three years previously, when the then sixteen-year-old philosopher had taken part in a public theological debate in Ferrara, which had attracted much attention at the time. Pico had also attended lectures given at the University of Ferrara by Battista Guarino, where he too had found Guarino's humanist ideas unsatisfactory. However, Pico's reservations had not been through any dislike for humanism – far from it – but more on account of the narrowness of the classical ideas upon which Guarino's humanism was based. For Pico, these took no account of the earlier and wider sources that had initially informed classical learning.

Although Pico and Savonarola cannot have realised it at the time, their meeting in 1482 at the Chapter General of the Dominicans of Lombardy in Reggio was to have far-reaching effects for both of them. Despite the fact that this encounter between the nineteen-year-old aristocrat-scholar and the twenty-nine-year-old friar can only have been fleeting, there is no denying that it produced a meeting of minds. Their interpretation of the Christian faith, to say nothing of their individual philosophical outlooks, may have been widely disparate, but they certainly respected one another. Perhaps for the first time, each found himself encountering a man of his own generation who was his intellectual equal.

There was, however, to be a more immediate consequence of Savonarola's attendance at the Chapter General in Reggio. And this too would prove momentous. As many had feared, in May Venetian troops eventually invaded Ferrarese territory, and it appeared too dangerous for Savonarola to make his way back to the Dominican monastery in his home town. In consequence, he was posted as a lecturer on biblical exegesis at the monastery of San Marco in Florence. In May 1482 Savonarola set out to walk the ninety miles south across the pass over the Apennine mountains to the city ruled by Lorenzo the Magnificent. Clad in his hooded black cloak, his bare feet shod in sandals, he carried with him his sole worldly possessions: a well-worn breviary, its margins filled with his many annotations beside the hymns and prayers for the daily services, and the Bible that he had inherited from his grandfather Michele.

3

Lorenzo's Florence

SAVONAROLA WOULD HAVE entered Florence in 1482 by the Porta San Gallo, the northernmost gate in the city walls, and less than half a mile down the main Via Larga he would have come to the monastery of San Marco.* After pulling the bell beside the gate in the wall, he would have been admitted to the enclosed precincts.

The monastery of San Marco, which stood just two blocks north of the Palazzo Medici, had been founded in the thirteenth century. However, it had been completely renovated and considerably expanded by Lorenzo the Magnificent's grandfather Cosimo de' Medici just thirty years previously. Cosimo had used his favourite architect Michelozzo Michelozzi, and incorporated the work of the resident monk Fra Angelico, one of the great early Renaissance artists. Michelozzi would be responsible for some of the finest early Renaissance architecture in Florence, including the renovation of the Palazzo della Signoria and the design of the Medici villa at Careggi. For his part, Fra Angelico's ethereal paintings would heavily influence Michelangelo, whose depiction of God's finger passing on life to Adam in the Sistine Chapel was directly inspired by the artist-monk. The work of Fra Angelico and Michelozzi came together at San Marco in the delightful shaded San Antonio cloister, whose delicate pillars and colourful frescoes enclosed a tranquil green garden in the midst of the monastery.

Cosimo de' Medici had undertaken the renovation of San Marco late in his life, intending it as absolution for the sin of usury, which had enabled

---

* In fact, this is called the convent of San Marco, but as in English this term mostly refers to closed religious communities of women, in order to avoid confusion I have throughout used the usual English term for a building that houses a community of monks.

him to accumulate his fortune as a banker. Yet there had also been a less manifest reason for Cosimo's benevolence, one that explained why in particular he chose to lavish his wealth on San Marco, rather than other similarly prestigious monasteries in the city. Before the 1433 coup which had removed Cosimo from power in Florence, almost costing him his life, he had managed in the nick of time to transfer secretly to San Marco a large quantity of the funds held in the Medici bank in Florence. After Cosimo's banishment into exile, his enemies had raided all Medici premises, as well as those of known supporters, but had been unable to discover the whereabouts of these funds, which had been held on trust, without a word, by the monks at San Marco.

In consequence, Cosimo had spared no expense on the rebuilding of San Marco, which eventually cost 30,000 florins – an unprecedented sum at the time. The monastery had been furnished with a library, together with many hundreds of religious manuscripts, intended for public use – the first lending library in Europe. Instead of the usual communal dormitory, each monk was assigned his own cell, many of which contained frescoes painted by Fra Angelico and his assistants. These were mainly portrayals of angels and biblical scenes. A special double cell, sumptuously frescoed, had been created for Cosimo's personal use, to which he would often retire for periods of contemplation. However, he had taken a more active role in the creation of the gardens across the street from San Marco: as a man who delighted in retiring to the countryside, he had done his best to create a pastoral space here within the walls of the city. These gardens would in turn become a favourite spot of Lorenzo the Magnificent, who began decorating the shady spaces with pieces of ancient classical sculpture. It was here, as he walked along the paths between the beds of greenery and marble relics, that according to legend Savonarola would first catch sight of Lorenzo the Magnificent from the window of his cell across the street.

The monastery of San Marco was hardly the kind of religious institution to which Savonarola aspired, or indeed to which he had been accustomed. The Florentine Dominicans no longer lived in poverty, or depended upon the charity of their congregation. The cells of the individual monks were for the most part well furnished, and indeed the librarian and the prior lived in some luxury, with meals served privately in their cells, where on occasion they would entertain leading citizens with sumptuous meals served on dishes and plates bearing the Medici crest. All the food for the monastery was supplied by Lorenzo the Magnificent – with olives, wine, bread, fish, fruit, oil and eggs provided in abundance. By special dispensation from Lorenzo, all such produce for the monastery was imported into the city free of the usual customs charges. Even the monks' robes and silk vestments were specially tailored by Lorenzo's appointed haberdashers – the very ones who also ran up the costumes for his carnivals and popular entertainments.

Savonarola saw these entertainments, when they were laid on for the high days and holy days, and quickly decided that they were not to his taste. Instead, we gather from remarks in his later sermons that he began taking long walks through the streets of the city. In those days one could walk from the Porta San Gallo, in the northern walls, right across the city to the southernmost Porta Romana at the limits of the Oltrarno district in half an hour, and Savonarola had soon explored all the various districts and neighbourhoods in between. He insisted that he was not overawed by the large piazzas, palaces and churches that he saw in the centre of the city – he was used to such buildings in his native Ferrara. But Florence's larger population, and the commercial success of its leading families, produced greater contrasts between the palazzi of the rich and the back-street tenements and narrow lanes of the slums occupied by the poor. These crowded dwellings mainly housed the families of the many dyers and cloth workers employed as day-workers in the textile industry for which the city was famous throughout Europe. Here, in the mean alleyways, Savonarola encountered the destitute: the haggard beggars who tugged at his sleeves and the blind with their pitiful cries. His regime of self-denial and abstinence had taught him what it was like to starve, yet as he would recount in his later sermons, he soon became heart-rendingly aware of the contrast between his Dominican 'poverty' and this genuine poverty, which he came across amongst the inhabitants of the squalid teeming slum districts. Worse still, he found that these people actually resented his presence when he walked amongst them in his distinctive black robes – the Dominicans were seen as 'Lorenzo's men', their friars regarded as his spies, Lorenzo's eyes and ears amongst the public. In Ferrara, the Dominican Black Friars had been regarded as friends of the poor.

Yet there was an even more fundamental difference between the numerous poor of Florence and those of Ferrara. In Ferrara the poor had grown resigned to their lot. The d'Este ruled as tyrants, with every aspect of the administration under their strict control. There was no veneer of democratic government. But here in Florence things were different. The democratic process by which Lorenzo maintained power may have become a sham, but there was no denying that its *ethos* remained amongst the people. They still regarded themselves as equal citizens; quietly, they talked politics. Unlike in Ferrara, where dissenting voices were quickly despatched to the dungeons of the *castello*, the people of Florence were not afraid of airing their views, though for the most part only covertly and amongst themselves, especially in the case of the poor. Indeed, there remained a widespread feeling that one day things could change. As the little Black Friar passed alone through the back streets, he would have been aware of the odd catcall or insult called out behind his back.

Meanwhile Lorenzo the Magnificent had more pressing things to do than stroll amongst the statuary in his garden under the beady eye of a Ferrarese friar. In fact, he was attempting to deal with the very situation that had brought Savonarola to San Marco, namely the war between Venice and Ferrara. By the midsummer of 1482 this had escalated to the point where it threatened Florence's eastern trade route acoss the Apennines to the Adriatic Sea. But the situation was not entirely one-sided. Duke Ercole of Ferrara was married to Leonora d'Aragona, the eldest daughter of King Ferrante of Naples, and when the Venetians had invaded the duke's terri-tory he had immediately called upon his father-in-law to come to his rescue. Knowing of Lorenzo the Magnificent's constant attempts to maintain the balance of power in Italy, Duke Ercole also appealed for aid to Florence. Lorenzo responded positively, calling in his ally Milan, at the same time joining forces with his friend King Ferrante of Naples.

The troops of the allies were placed under the command of Alfonso, Duke of Calabria, the son of King Ferrante. In a subtle move, Alfonso now requested formal permission from Sixtus IV to march his troops north from Naples across papal territory towards Ferrara. Sixtus IV refused permis-sion, thus bringing into the open his secret support for Venice. Alfonso advanced into papal territory nonetheless, but was then defeated by the pope's forces. In response to this setback, King Ferrante immediately played on Sixtus IV's unpopularity amongst the Roman nobility by inciting the Orsini and other noble families to rise up against him. In order to guard Sixtus IV, Girolamo Riario and the pope's forces had to return from the papal territories to Rome itself. Meanwhile, Lorenzo directed his mercenary commander Duke Federigo of Urbino to march east to prevent the Venetians from overrunning all the territory ruled by Ferrara, whose troops were hampered by the untimely illness of Duke Ercole.

In September 1482 news reached Florence of the unexpected death of Duke Federigo of Urbino. Once again, it looked as if the Venetians were going to prevail. Girolamo Riario, who remained unable to fulfil his side of the secret pact with the Venetians by providing papal forces, sent word of this latest development to his 'uncle' Sixtus IV, who immediately realised the danger. If the Venetians took over Ferrara completely, and there was no military pact between them and his nephew, there would be nothing to stop them expanding to take over the papal territories ruled by Riario. In a lightning volte-face, Sixtus IV at once ordered the Venetians to halt their invasion, declaring that it had no just cause. The Venetians pressed forward nonetheless, and when news of this reached Rome the pope became so enraged that he excommunicated the entire Venetian Republic. But still the Venetians continued to advance, until finally by November 1482 they were laying siege to the city of Ferrara itself. At this stage Sixtus IV succumbed to a fever, his condition exacerbated by an incapacitating attack of gout.

In an effort to remedy the situation before it was too late, Lorenzo called a conference of the anti-Venetian allies at Cremona. Besides Lorenzo, the conference was attended by Alfonso of Calabria, Ludovico 'il Moro' Sforza of Milan, Ercole of Ferrara and the pope's respresentative in the form of Girolamo Riario. It was soon agreed that Ludovico Sforza should launch his Milanese troops in a diversionary attack on Venetian territory, while Alfonso of Calabria led his remnant troops north in an attempt to relieve Ferrara before it fell into Venetian hands. These moves soon persuaded the Venetians to withdraw, and all parties now agreed that peace negotiations should be opened. But with the prospect of negotiating territorial gains, the fragile pact between the allies fell apart. Girolamo Riario persuaded

Alfonso of Calabria to back his claim to add Ferrarese territory to the papal territories that he now ruled, but unbeknown to these plotters, Ludovico Sforza had entered into a secret agreement with the Venetians. When news reached Rome that peace negotiations were to open, Sixtus IV immediately understood that things had now slipped beyond his control. He was liable to lose everything he had set out to gain, while his enemies stood to gain everything at his expense. According to the diplomatic representative for Ferrara, the pope was beside himself with fury: 'He uses the most terrible language in the world, and says that he has been deceived and betrayed.' Such were the difficulties faced by Lorenzo the Magnificent in his attempt to maintain the balance of power in Italy. All he could do was prevail upon the interested parties to conclude a reasonably balanced peace, in the hope that this would last.

Peace terms were finally agreed on 7 August 1484. Despite Lorenzo's best efforts, these inevitably reflected the underhand pacts between the stronger of the negotiating allies. Although Venice had finished the war in retreat, it actually increased its territory at the expense of Ferrara, as did its covert ally, Milan; meanwhile Naples regained lost territory. At the same time Girolamo Riario gained nothing, and Duke Ercole of Ferrara had to be content with retaining just the city of Ferrara and a reduced surrounding territory. Sixtus IV, whose machinations had been responsible for the war, had not only lost any immediate prospect of adding to Riario's papal territories, but was now distrusted by all – former allies and present allies alike. When news of the outcome of the peace negotiations reached Rome a few days later, the pope's reaction was decidedly mixed. At a public audience with his cardinals he expressed, seemingly without qualm, his regret over the turn of events. 'With great expense to ourselves have we carried on the war to save Ferrara, and to please the majesty of the King [of Naples] and the other allies, so we were ready to continue.' Yet when the ambassadors had withdrawn, his anger was such that he succumbed once more to his fever. He particularly blamed Ludovico Sforza of Milan for his 'treachery', since just a few months previously Sixtus IV had made his brother a cardinal, in the expectation of tying Milan to his cause. During the evening of 12 August Sixtus IV suffered a severe relapse and, in the words of the papal historian F. Ludwig von Pastor, drawing on a report by the Ferrarese ambassador: 'That same night Sixtus died, denouncing the conditions of the peace with his last breath, declaring that Ludovico Sforza was a traitor.' As his contemporary Machiavelli drily remarked in his history of the period: 'Thus at last this pope left Italy in peace, having spent his life ensuring that it was constantly at war.'

News of these historic events soon reached the thirty-two-year-old Savonarola in his monastic cell at San Marco in Florence. The death of Sixtus IV, whom he had so long despised, inspired Savonarola to write another of his impassioned poems about the Church, appealing to the Lord even as the cardinals gathered in Rome to elect another pope:

> Jesus, highest good and sweet comfort,
> Of all hearts that suffer,
> Look upon Rome with perfect love . . .
> Save thy Holy Roman Church
> From the devil who tears it apart.

Savonarola still entertained hopes that the Church might yet return to its original state, 'that peace she knew when she was poor'. Such hopes appeared patently unrealistic. Italy was now moving inexorably away from the simple poverty and timeless way of life that had been the lot of most people during the previous medieval era: an existence that, amongst many levels of society, retained a recognisable rapport with the earliest days of Christianity — in Judaea, in the Levant, and later amongst the slaves of Ancient Rome. But now, despite the wars and political uncertainties that racked Italy as the fifteenth century drew to a close, the transformations brought about by the Renaissance were entering a new phase. Classical knowledge and pre-Christian ideas had by this stage begun to stimulate an entirely new spirit of enquiry and consequent originality. New discoveries were being made in fields ranging from architectural technique to mathematics and pictorial perspective. Nowhere was this more apparent than in Florence, where the man who epitomised this phase of the Renaissance more than any other was the artist Botticelli. After being loaned by Lorenzo the Magnificent to Sixtus IV and completing the first frescoes to adorn the pope's new Sistine Chapel, Botticelli had returned to Florence in 1482, the very year in which Savonarola had taken up residence at San Marco.

Botticelli once more renewed his contact with the intellectual circle associated with the Palazzo Medici, where he was particularly influenced by the Platonic idealism of the philosopher Ficino and the humanism of the poet Poliziano. As a result, Botticelli's work underwent a spectacular tranformation. Instead of religious scenes, he began to depict pagan subjects from classical mythology. Typical of these was his *Pallas and the Centaur*, which depicts the goddess Pallas Athena grasping the hair of the mythical half-man half-horse, apparently restraining the repentant centaur. The scene is illustrative of how the Renaissance was beginning to emerge from its slavish mimicking of classical learning into an originality of its own. There is no classical legend involving Pallas Athena and a centaur, but Botticelli has used these two figures to suggest an encounter between wisdom (Pallas Athena) and lust (in the form of the half-man half-beast). It was intended to be an allegory depicting rational restraint overcoming animal sensuality.

This painting was commissioned by Lorenzo the Magnificent in 1482 as a gift to his nineteen-year-old cousin and ward, Lorenzo di Pierfrancesco de' Medici, on the occasion of his marriage to Semiramide, daughter of Jacopo IV d'Appiano, Lord of Piombino. As was customary, this marriage had been arranged by Lorenzo, largely for political reasons. The city of Piombino occupied a strategic location on the coast seventy miles southwest of Florence, and its alliance to Naples during the war against Florence after the Pazzi conspiracy had represented a serious threat; with this marriage it would be permanently allied to Florence. As Jacopo IV was also a *condottiere*, it meant that his army would prove a useful addition to Florentine forces. On top of this, Jacopo IV's territory included the island of Elba, which at the time contained the only iron-ore deposits being mined in the entire Italian peninsula. Medici control of this monopoly would represent a considerable income. The subject matter of Lorenzo's wedding gift to his young cousin was intended as an exemplar of the benefits of marriage and the wisdom of restraint – a subtle hint that it was time for him to curb the wild behaviour in which he seems to have indulged.

Lorenzo di Pierfrancesco must have taken the hint and amended his ways, for his former tutors Ficino and Poliziano – who almost certainly suggested the painting's subject matter to Botticelli – now both spoke highly of him. The enigmatic hunchbacked Ficino, in a characteristically florid Platonic turn of phrase, wrote of how Lorenzo di Pierfrancesco's 'mind and the radiance of his manners and letters [shine] like the sun among the stars'. Poliziano was equally gushing, speaking in a poem of how Lorenzo di Pierfrancesco was lacking in 'neither gravity, nor winning grace of countenance, nor the high honour of a lofty head, nor capacious genius equal to civil affairs, nor a tongue that can minister the ample riches of your mind'. Such fulsome flattery may not have been utterly sincere, but it does indicate that Lorenzo di Pierfrancesco was held in the highest regard by the man who employed these two silver-tongued intellectuals – namely, Lorenzo the Magnificent himself. Indeed, Lorenzo was so impressed by his young cousin that when he was just nineteen he began sending him on diplomatic missions, much as he himself had been sent by his father. As far as this aspect of Lorenzo di Pierfrancesco's life was concerned, Botticelli's painting was evidently intended to serve much the same purpose as Piero the Gouty's earnest letters warning his son about his 'exuberance'.

The diplomatic tasks entrusted to the young Lorenzo di Pierfrancesco were of some importance, including as they did missions to the pope and Venice. The messages he delivered may have been written by Lorenzo the Magnificent, but under the circumstances Lorenzo di Pierfrancesco's presence would have been deemed of considerable significance: he would to all intents and purposes have been regarded as a stand-in for Lorenzo the Magnificent's firstborn son and heir Piero, who was just thirteen years old. And two years later Lorenzo di Pierfrancesco travelled all the way to France to represent Florence at the coronation of the nine-year-old Charles VIII at Rheims on 30 May 1484 – an event that was to prove of great significance to Italy over the coming years. France was the most powerful nation in Europe, and Lorenzo the Magnificent had long since realised how vital it was that France should be discouraged from taking any active part in the politics of weak and divided Italy.

Despite all this, it is possible with hindsight to recognise that Lorenzo the Magnificent may also have had other, less honourable financial motives for keeping his cousin away from Florence, although these would prove to no avail. On 4 August 1484 Lorenzo di Pierfrancesco finally came of age and claimed the inheritance that had been left to him and his brother Giovanni by his father, money that had been entrusted for safekeeping to Lorenzo the Magnificent. Initially Lorenzo simply refused to pass on this inheritance, but it soon became clear that most – if not all – of it had already been spent. The cash value of this inheritance is difficult to ascertain, though it would certainly have been considerable. Lorenzo the Magnificent is said to have held the money in 'thirteen leather bags', though precisely how much these contained is disputed. He certainly dipped into them during the aftermath of the Pazzi conspiracy, when the city was threatened by war and he made his celebrated dash to Naples. According to de Roover, the meticulous expert on Medici financial affairs:

> Between May and September, 1478, Lorenzo de' Medici, being in desperate straits, at different times took a total of 53,643 florins in coin which belonged to Giovanni and Lorenzo, the minor sons of Pierfrancesco de' Medici, whose guardian he was.

Others suggest that a further 20,000 florins were removed later. However, the two brothers claimed that together they were owed 105,880 florins, including interest, and applied to the city authorities for legal arbitration on this matter. That Lorenzo the Magnificent's power in Florence was far from absolute is reflected in the verdict that the legal arbitrators handed down some two years later in 1486 – doubtless after much profound discussion and much covert pressure from the Medici faction. The verdict went against Lorenzo, but by this time the sum that he owed had been whittled down to 61,400 florins. His justification for this reduced sum was that his cousins, being shareholders in the Medici bank, were liable for at least some of the money needed to shore up the bank so that it could manage the large debts that it had recently been forced to absorb. These had been incurred when the London branch had been forced to close down, and when the assets of the Rome branch had been seized by Sixtus IV after the failure of the Pazzi conspiracy (when the pope had also reneged on his large overdraft at the Medici bank).

In the event, Lorenzo the Magnificent simply did not have 61,400 florins with which to pay off his cousins, and instead was forced to hand over to them the Medici villa at Cafaggiolo, and further much-treasured ancestral land, property and farms in the Mugello valley, across the mountains to the north of Florence, the original homeland of the Medici. This judgement provoked considerable acrimony between the two branches of the Medici family.

Despite Lorenzo the Magnificent's apparent lack of liquid funds, he continued to live as lavishly as ever. His celebrated circle of poets, philosophers and artists continued to be maintained (and entertained) at the Palazzo Medici, exquisite items were added to his famed collection of jewels, and the populace of Florence went on being placated with extravagant entertainments and festivals. Much of this must certainly have come from public funds, though as mentioned earlier the details of the city's financial transactions for this period were all later destroyed by the Medici family. What we do know is that Lorenzo by now had complete control of the financial affairs of the city, and of its exchequer, which had been placed in the hands of his close friend and associate Antonio Miniati, a man who incurred much hatred throughout the city. Finance was one of Lorenzo the Magnificent's chief weapons against wealthy citizens who sought to oppose him. The amount of tax to be paid by each citizen was assessed by a panel of taxation officers, who took account of registered property, a reckoning of possessions, as well as declared income. Inevitably any such estimate was open to abuse, and enemies of the Medici were liable to be bankrupted by swingeing taxes, or forced into exile to avoid losing all their wealth.

As Lorenzo the Magnificent pleaded near-bankruptcy, he did not have to pay tax during these later years of his reign. In reality, by this stage his financial affairs had become so identified with those of the city that there was a considerable 'overlap' between the two. And although Lorenzo certainly benefited from this state of affairs, it is also undeniable that the citizens of Florence benefited from his stewardship of the city. Lorenzo, through his leadership and sheer force of personality, gave much to Florence. Its citizens may not have been entirely free, but the independence of Florence itself resulted largely from Lorenzo's astute statesmanship. The assessment of the city some years later by the Florentine historian Francesco Guicciardini, who lived through these times, holds largely true for the coming years:

> The city was in perfect peace, the citizens who made up the administration were united and the government was so powerful that none

dared speak against it. The people were entertained daily with all manner of festivals, spectacles and novelties. The city had abundant supplies of all its needs, whilst its trades and commercial activities brought great prosperity. Men of intellect and talent were able to engage in literature, the arts and the sciences, which were all encouraged, such that their efforts were not only recognised but also well rewarded. While the city remained peaceful at home, it was held in the highest esteem abroad because she had a government and a leader of the highest authority, because her territory was expanded, and because she had the full support of pope Innocent VIII,* as well as being allied with Naples and Milan, by which means she maintained the balance of power in Italy.

Such a picture may appear somewhat idyllic in the light of the preceding descriptions – of the Ferrara war and poverty in the Florentine slums – but it had more than an element of truth. These were years of some prosperity for Florence, whose overseas trade had once again spread to the limits of Europe, and beyond. As we have seen, several decades previously Cosimo de' Medici's Florentine galleys had plied the sea route through the Straits of Gibraltar across the Bay of Biscay to Bruges and London, carrying the dyed cloth for which the city was famous, as well as alum and oriental spices. These spices had been shipped from the eastern Mediterranean; and despite stiff competition from Venice and Genoa, Medici agents had penetrated Egypt as well as other trading centres throughout the Levant. But with the Medici bank in decline, such opportunities were now being exploited by other Florentine merchants and banking families. Not least amongst these, in the coming years, would be Lorenzo di Pierfrancesco and his brother Giovanni, who would establish a number of successful international trading enterprises.

The divergence between the two branches of the Medici family was now evident to all. Yet for the time being, Lorenzo di Pierfrancesco and his brother would eschew any direct competition or conflict with their cousin. Lorenzo the Magnificent and his side of the family would be concerned

---

* He had succeeded the duplicitous, warmongering Sixtus IV.

with political power, while Lorenzo di Pierfrancesco and his family would pursue commercial wealth. The di Pierfrancesco brothers were soon establishing ventures in Spain and then Flanders, and such was the success of their enterprises that for a brief time the brothers left Florence altogether and took up residence in Bruges. Here they branched into the lucrative oriental spice market, a move quickly followed by other Florentine merchants. Indeed, such was Florence's commercial penetration of the East during these years that word of the city spread along the Silk Road as far afield as China, where it was assumed that Florence, with all its wealth and culture, was the capital of Europe. Nearer to home, in 1487 the Sultan of Egypt sent an ambassador to Florence, who brought with him greetings from various rulers, as well as an assembled menagerie of rare and exotic animals. The people of Florence were accustomed to the sight of lions: these were the city's mascots, kept in a cage behind the Palazzo della Signoria on a street still known as Via dei Leoni. On the other hand, they were filled with genuine wonder at the sight of the tall, long-limbed animal they called *cameleopardo*, on account of it having the head of a camel and the spotted furry coat of a leopard. This was the giraffe that would end up in the grounds of Lorenzo's country villa at Poggio a Caiano, which now became his favourite country residence after the loss of Cafaggiolo to Lorenzo di Pierfrancesco.

There may have been a rift between the two branches of the Medici family, but Lorenzo di Pierfrancesco and his brother continued to occupy their town residence attached to the Palazzo Medici on the Via Larga, and they also continued to mix with members of Lorenzo the Magnificent's intellectual circle. Evidence of this can be seen in the fact that Lorenzo di Pierfrancesco continued to commission work from artists attached to the Palazzo Medici, especially 'Lorenzo's artist', Botticelli. A direct consequence of this was one of Botticelli's most magnificent and most mysterious works – namely his *Primavera (Spring)*.* This painting suggests, as much as any other of the period, the happy state of the Renaissance city as

---

* The precise date when *Primavera* was painted remains in dispute. Many favour the earlier date of 1482, immediately after Botticelli had returned from Rome, and some even favour 1477 when Lorenzo di Pierfrancesco would have been just fourteen. However, even if *Primavera* was not painted at the later date that I have favoured, other works confirm that the interaction between the intellectual circle of the Palazzo Medici and Lorenzo di Pierfrancesco next door continued after the rift between Lorenzo the Magnificent and his cousin.

described earlier by Guicciardini. The painting depicts a group of delicate classical figures in the shade of a woodland clearing. The golden apples hanging from the high branches of the trees identify this as the Garden of the Hesperides, the blessed isle inhabited by nymphs at the western edge of the world. The central figure is Venus, whose apparent pregnancy may symbolise fecundity. To the left of her the Three Graces, symbolising Joy, Beauty and Creativity, dance in their diaphanous robes whilst above their heads blindfolded Cupid is pulling back his bow, about to pierce one of them with his arrow – of love, or lust. To the left of them stands Mercury, the messenger of the gods with his phallic sword at his waist, while to the right of Venus stands Flora, the goddess of spring, her blonde hair crowned with flowers, resplendent in her flowered dress, in the act of scattering flowers that blend into the flowers amongst the grass at her feet.

Primavera has prompted all manner of interpretation through the centuries. Some have identified it as a scene from classical myth; others have read it as an ingenious political allegory; while many contemporaries hinted at personal identifications (Lorenzo di Pierfrancesco as Mercury, his wife Semiramide as the apparently pregnant Venus). At the same time, it is undoubtedly infused by the philosophy of Ficino, with the figures as embodiments of Platonic ideas; paradoxically, it is also characterised by the realistic humanism of Poliziano's poetry. Unlike so much of the painting that had preceded it, *Primavera* depicts an unmistakably secular, even pagan scene. Here is a touching humanity completely devoid of religious overtones, in no evident Christian setting.

In the event, Botticelli seems to have intended no precise allegory or 'meaning' in his *Primavera*, seeing it more as a starting point: an object of aesthetic contemplation and philosophical reflection. Its very mystery may be seen as the mystery of what was happening to human consciousness (and self-consciousness) at this point of profound and subtle transformation in our evolution. These are the elements of our burgeoning humanity: inspired by the philosophical and poetical suggestions of Lorenzo de Medici's trusted intellectual circle and realised by Botticelli.

Of the figures within the Florentine cultural community, Ficino was enjoying an unprecedented ascendancy. His expert knowledge of Plato had now begun to attract widespread attention. No less a figure than Pico della

Mirandola had already opened a correspondence with him. Pico's quest to understand the early religious ideas that had inspired Christianity had extended beyond Judaism to include the ideas of the Ancient Greek philosophers. Scholasticism, the official philosophic backing of medieval Christianity, may have been deeply imbued with many of the ideas of Aristotle, but Pico now sought to discover Christianity's links with Platonic idealism. In pursuit of this quest Pico arrived in Florence in 1484, expressly in order to study under Ficino, who quickly introduced him to the intellectual circle at the Palazzo Medici. Here he was rapturously received. According to Poliziano:

> He was a man, or rather a hero, on whom nature had lavished all the endowments both of body and mind ... Of a perspicacious mind, a wonderful memory, indefatigable in study ... Intimately conversant with every department of philosophy, improved and invigorated by the knowledge of various languages, and of every honourable science.

For his part, Pico was similarly impressed by Lorenzo the Magnificent. He would go on to dedicate his *Apology* to Lorenzo, and upon reading Lorenzo's poetry he judged it superior to that of Dante – its humanism more reflective of the age than Dante's religious subjects.*

Ficino was deeply grateful that such a distinguished scholar as Pico della Mirandola should champion his Platonism in the face of the vehement criticism it was receiving from some orthodox Aristotelians. A number of these theologians had even gone so far as to suggest that Ficino's ideas were heresy, though this was largely on account of his dabbling in certain hermetic ideas that he had found in later Platonic texts. Despite Ficino's adherence to Plato's philosophy, he remained deeply religious, and he would regard Pico della Mirandola's ability to convince devout humanist adherents of classical philosophy that they belonged in the Christian fold with such admiration that he called him a 'fisher of men'.

However, this great and enthusiastic meeting of minds at the Palazzo

---

* In all fairness, this was not mere flattery. Pico's assessment was shared by a number of intellectuals of the time.

Medici was based upon a profound misunderstanding. Pico della Mirandola, with his elegant manners and deep philosophical learning, may have
appeared as the embodiment of the new humanism, but this was a misreading
of his intellectual stance. Although Pico was willing to embrace Platonism,
this did not mean that he rejected orthodox scholastic Aristotelianism. On
the contrary, the aim of his philosophical quest was *inclusive* – he wished
to discover true religion as it manifested itself in all these different sources.
This becomes clear in a letter that he wrote as early as 1485 to the Venetian scholar Ermolao Barbaro, in which he explained that when he travelled to Florence to study with Ficino he went 'not as a deserter' from
Aristotle, 'but as a spy'. In fact, the Latin word he used for 'spy' was *explorator*,
whose English connotations come closer to conveying what he actually
meant. Pico della Mirandola certainly had no hostile intent in coming to
study with Ficino, though the possibility of deception remains. The fact
is that the Medici court accepted him as a fellow humanist. This would
seem to indicate either a secrecy that was alien to Pico's flamboyant nature,
or that he was simply content to go along with Lorenzo the Magnificent,
Poliziano, Ficino and the others in their erroneous assumption, because
this better enabled him to understand their thinking. For there can be no
doubt that, certainly at this stage, the assumption made by Lorenzo and
his circle was erroneous. This can be seen from the other company that
Pico kept during his residence in Florence. Besides becoming a favourite
of the liberal intellectual circle at the Palazzo Medici, it is known that
Pico also renewed his contact with Savonarola. Regarding his visits to the
austere cell at the monastery of San Marco, the twenty-one-year-old Pico
would later write of how he spent his time 'piously philosophising' with
the earnest thirty-two-year-old monk. The worldly philosopher and the
ascetic theologian – in so many ways such opposites – indubitably continued
to have one thing in common: the exceptional depth of their theological
knowledge.

They also had another, somewhat surprising, element in common: their
extensive knowledge of unorthodox philosophical thinking. Pico della
Mirandola was already beginning to show an interest in esoteric learning
– such as the Kabbala (a mystical branch of Judaism) and Zoroastrianism
(the early monotheistic religion of Persian fire worshippers). Although

Savonarola's religious interests are unlikely to have extended to such exotica, we know that his learning was not confined to orthodox Christianity. It was probably around this time that Savonarola completed his *Compendium totius philosophae* (A Brief Summary of all Philosophies), which would not be published until after his death. We now know that parts of this work, some of which elaborated an aspect of unorthodox religious thought, were lost, or possibly destroyed by overzealous followers who wished to eradicate all hint of heretical thinking from his works. Still, despite Savonarola's early years of humanist education with Guarino at the University of Ferrara — an experience shared by Pico — there can be no doubt that by this stage Pico's knowledge of unorthodox thinkers and philosophers was far greater than that of Savonarola. Yet as we shall see, Savonarola's informed discussions and critiques of such thinkers would later play an integral part in Pico's beliefs. For the time being, it seems, Savonarola and Pico merely exchanged their views and agreed to differ; for though Savonarola studied such matters, he remained deeply opposed to unorthodox thinking of any sort.

By this stage, Savonarola was already establishing something of a reputation for himself within San Marco, such that soon after his arrival he had been made master of the novices. His intellect, as well as his exemplary asceticism and fervour, had inspired a devoted following amongst those who attended his theological instruction — a following that included both the novices in his charge and his fellow monks. Despite this, the indications are that Savonarola was undergoing something of a spiritual crisis during this period. One of his fellow monks recounts how he would arrive to give his morning lessons with his eyes swollen from the weeping that had overcome him during the night-long vigils and hours of fervent meditation that he imposed upon himself. Regardless of Savonarola's evidently distressed psychological state, 'His teachings ... raised men's hearts above all human things.' It seemed to his listeners 'that from the time of the early Christian fathers no one equalled him in the teaching of the sacred books'. This comparison to the early days of Christianity would seem to be no accident: Savonarola's stated aim was to return the Church to the physical poverty and utter spiritual devotion of its origins.

Part of Savonarola's duties involved delivering the occasional sermon at predecessor Sixtus IV. Not only had Innocent VIII been the first pope openly to acknowledge his own children, but he had also institutionalised the selling of holy offices. Savonarola may have lamented the papacy of Sixtus IV, but with the elevation of Innocent VIII to the papal throne he recognised that things had in reality gone from bad to worse. As he wrote in a poem at the time: 'When I did see that haughty woman * enter Rome' it reduced him to a state of 'constant weeping'.

Savonarola also told the citizens of San Gimignano that God had sent prophets to warn mankind of what was about to happen – the coming of 'the antichrist, war, plague or famine'. Despite being so specific, he insisted, 'I do not warn you about this because I am a prophet, but because I can tell from reading the Bible that such a scourge of the Church is coming.' Although he was undoubtedly performing the task of a prophet, he was not yet sure enough of himself to take on the mantle publicly.

After finishing his Lenten sermons at San Gimignano, Savonarola returned to Florence, where some months later he learned that he had been appointed a master of studies at the great *Studium generale* in Bologna. He would be returning to the very place where he had first studied theology; but now, just ten years later, he himself would be amongst the distinguished theologians of the teaching staff.

---

* This was Simony personified, as Savonarola made plain by writing in the margin in his own hand: 'the ambition for ecclesiastical honours'.

words and her pitiful plight. Addressing her as 'Most honourable and most beloved Mother', he explained that he could not send her the money for which she was asking because his vow of poverty meant that he had none. Instead he sent her all he could: a five-page letter that took him many days to compose. This was a curious blend of a sermon and advice on how to become a saint, complete with biblical references ranging from Psalms to Corinthians:

> I want your faith to be such that you could watch [your children] die and be martyred without shedding a tear for them, as that most holy Hebrew woman did when seven of her saintly children were killed and tortured in front of her and she never cried, but instead comforted them in their death.

Parts of this tract can be read as an exhortation to himself and, when read in this light, its attitude towards its recipient appears utterly heartless and selfish. However, it is in fact a call to place one's life completely in the hands of God. 'It is better, therefore, to tolerate patiently our brief tribulations so as to have eternal joy and peace and glory everlasting.' This last advice is certainly intended for his mother, rather than for himself. Yet it is not hypocrisy: Savonarola had come to see his own life as something more than striving for 'eternal joy and peace'. His revelation at the convent had convinced him that he was intended to become a prophet. This would soon become evident in his sermons. Savonarola's initial Lenten sermons at San Gimignano had proved so popular that he was invited back to deliver the 1486 Lenten sermons. For many years it was thought that the contents of these too had been lost; but in 1935, whilst searching through the Florentine archives, the Italian scholar Roberto Ridolfi came across some notes written in medieval Latin. On inspection, it became clear that these were Savonarola's rough drafts for his 1486 Lenten sermons. In these, he elaborated upon his 'revelation', when he had learned of 'at least seven' reasons why 'a scourge of the Church is imminent', including the presence of evil 'shepherds' in the Church, the corruption of the Church, and simony (the selling of Church posts for money). This last was an obvious reference to the new pope, Innocent VIII, who had proved every bit as corrupt as his

4

Securing the Medici Dynasty

WHEN LORENZO THE Magnificent learned that Innocent VIII
had been elected the new pope, he at once launched a diplomatic offensive designed to win him over to his cause. But
what precisely was his cause? Undoubtedly, Lorenzo wished to maintain
the balance of power in Italy, so that Florence and her thriving trade could
continue to prosper without threat from her powerful neighbours. An
alliance with the pope, a major spiritual and political force throughout the
land, was essential to this end. But it soon became clear that Lorenzo the
Magnificent had ulterior motives for becoming the pope's ally and friend:
he wanted to secure the Medici dynasty, and was intent upon doing this
in the most spectacular fashion.

Lorenzo the Magnificent's oldest son Piero was thirteen years old in
1484, and was seen as Lorenzo's natural successor to power in Florence.
He was a difficult, somewhat arrogant child, who had many of his father's
more dashing physical attributes, but as yet had demonstrated little of
Lorenzo's intellect or judgement. Despite being educated by the likes of
Poliziano and Ficino, Piero showed more interest in hunting than in learning
or affairs of state. In an attempt to rectify this, Lorenzo despatched his
son, accompanied by Poliziano, at the head of the Florentine delegation
to Rome to congratulate the new pope on his succession.

Innocent VIII was a suave, mild-mannered and somewhat devious character, who had only been elected as a compromise, when neither the powerful
and notorious Cardinal Rodrigo Borgia, nor his sworn enemy the well-
connected Cardinal Giuliano della Rovere, had been able to muster sufficient votes for themselves. Lorenzo knew that having diplomatic dealings

Levantine trading ventures. The London branch had never recovered from the 80,000 florins owed by Edward IV and his nobles. The closure of the highly lucrative Bruges branch had in part been due to the extravagance and financial legerdemain of the trusted long-term manager Tommaso Portinari. In order to establish the prestige of the Medici bank (and its manager), Portinari had spent almost 10,000 florins buying and renovating the Hôtel Bladelin, which was (and remains to this day) one of the finest medieval residences in Bruges. Later, he had invested Medici bank assets in a joint side-venture in the wool trade, which was skilfully contracted so that he personally received a large share of the profits, while the bank (and Lorenzo) was responsible for any losses. Lorenzo, in his somewhat lackadaisical attitude towards the family banking business, had not noticed this, until it was pointed out to him too late. Meanwhile the wily and inept Portinari had delivered his masterstroke, investing — contrary to all strict and explicit instructions — in a hazardous Portuguese expedition to the Guinea coast of West Africa. When this failed, Portinari destroyed all the evidence he could lay his hands on, so that, as the Medici financial historian de Roover put it with masterly understatement: 'Not much is known about this profitless venture.' Although Lorenzo had competent advisers at the Medici bank in Florence, as well as his uncle in Rome, the overall affairs of the bank remained largely unsupervised. After his father Piero the Gouty's initial ill-advised mistake in calling in the bank's debts, Piero had applied his considerable commercial talents to steering the bank through the difficult period of his five brief years at the helm. On the other hand, his attentions were constantly directed elsewhere, and chicanery such as that of Portinari was almost bound to have occurred. Indeed, Portinari was not the only manager to become involved in underhand deals, which for the most part went undetected until they were beyond remedy.

Lorenzo does not seem to have realised quite how deeply Portinari was involved in working against Medici interests. After the closing of the Bruges branch, the ageing Portinari was left facing large personal debts. Lorenzo felt that these were at least in part the responsibility of the Medici, and thus conferred diplomatic status upon the banker so that he could return home to Florence without constraint from his creditors. A of this venerable assembly. In fact, the boy was not even eleven: in his effort to persuade Innocent VIII, Lorenzo added two years to his son's age. If Giovanni became a cardinal, this meant that by the time any other young candidates entered the College of Cardinals, he would be well established: a senior, experienced and well-connected operator within the group. A pope-maker, no less – well positioned at some later stage to become pope himself. But Innocent VIII would not be persuaded; such an appointment was liable to call his entire programme of simony into question, by reducing it to an absolute mockery. Lorenzo was irritated and disappointed; Innocent VIII assured him that he should bide his time, but Lorenzo was determined to persist in his campaign by more covert means.

Meanwhile, in order to secure the Medici succession in Florence as far as he could, Lorenzo arranged in 1488 for his seventeen-year-old son and heir Piero to marry into another branch of his mother's aristocratic Roman family, the Orsini. The father of Piero's bride Alfonsina Orsini had died fighting for King Ferrante of Naples, who had thereupon taken her under his wing. Her marriage to Piero de' Medici was to reinforce a strategic alliance: it would serve the multiple purpose of strengthening the Medici's claim to aristocratic status, as well as allying Florence with Naples, and further cementing their links with the powerful Orsini in Rome. With the Medici backed by such powerful friends, any enemies would be forced to think twice before attempting to take over Florence.

Besides attempting to secure the Medici family succession, Lorenzo had also done his best to secure the Medici intellectual heritage. To this end, he had appointed his grandfather's favourite intellectual, Marsilio Ficino, as a canon of Florence Cathedral, a sinecure that enabled the hunchbacked classicist to continue with his philosophical works unhindered by financial worries. Ficino's attempt to reconcile Platonism with accepted Christian belief had by now led him to write a number of commentaries on Plato, which can be seen as original works in their own right. Notable amongst these was his commentary on Plato's *Symposium*, the celebrated work in which the Ancient Greek philosopher describes a banquet where Socrates and others explore the nature of love, from its ideal aspects to more scurrilous homoerotic examples. Plato asserted that love, with its attraction to the form of beauty, led us to the philosophical quest for few years later Portinari died, but in a final twist his son refused to accept his inheritance — for as he did not have diplomatic status, this would have left him open to prosecution by agents despatched to recover his father's large debts.

Thus, partly through mismanagement, and partly through Lorenzo the Magnificent's neglect, the Medici bank was now entering what appeared to be a period of terminal decline. The income derived by the Medici from this source continued to dwindle, but Lorenzo saw no reason to reverse this state of affairs. On the contrary: a family with ambitions to become one of the royal houses of Europe would not wish to be seen as mere bankers. And by the mid-1480s Lorenzo's income was no longer dependent upon currency transactions or financing commercial enterprises. He had identified himself so totally with Florence that he had come to regard its exchequer as his own — both as his income, and to dispense with as he saw fit in the city's interests. To his mind, Florence's interests were now inseparable from Medici interests: when one flourished, so did the other.

However, there remained certain technical differences. Although the purchase of benefices for young Giovanni de' Medici may have been subsidised by the Florentine exchequer, through Miniati's financial sleight of hand the rich incomes provided by these benefices went directly to their Medici owner — a subtle distinction of which the people of Florence remained ignorant. It was now that Lorenzo the Magnificent chanced his most daring request of his new friend Innocent VIII. In 1484 he broached the subject of his son Giovanni being made a cardinal. Even with the advent of institution-alised simony, such a request was unprecedented. The College of Cardinals was the most important and influential body in the Church, second only in power and prestige to the pope himself. Indeed, it was the College of Cardinals that was responsible for electing the new pope — in the secret conclave held in the Vatican after the death of the incumbent. Here, isolated from outside influences, the different factions would bargain for votes, occasionally joining in prayer for divine guidance. Those who supported the victorious candidate could expect favours and rewards, as well as the possibility of exerting influence upon papal policy. Lorenzo the Magnificent was now suggesting that his eleven-year-old son Giovanni be made a member wisdom. (It is not difficult to recognise how such ideas affected Botticelli, and how he embodied them in works like *Primavera*.) Ficino's commentary on Plato's *Symposium* is called *De Amore* (*About Love*), and takes the form of a similar banquet at one of Lorenzo the Magnificent's villas, which is attended by members of the Palazzo Medici intellectual circle. In this work, Ficino also discusses homerotic love, a subject that was certainly not foreign to Lorenzo the Magnificent, Poliziano and others present. On a more elevated plane, it elaborates Neoplatonic ideas of how life is created by love, the world is sustained by love, and how creation attains its highest wisdom and returns to its ideal by means of love of beauty. However, in this and other similar works Ficino had been influenced by the Neoplatonic philosophy of Plotinus and its hermetic aspects, as well as by thinkers of an even more metaphysical and magical inclination. Ficino was drawn by temperament to such esoteric ideas and wished to believe what they said. (The arrival of Pico to study with him in Florence was attributed by Ficino to the astrological omens on the day in question.)

Pico della Mirandola was for his part also attracted to the more esoteric and metaphysical aspects of Ficino's teaching. This chimed with Pico's attempt to draw together all regions and philosophies, in the search for a universal truth that underlay them. This attempt at reconciling disparate philosophies and religions would come to be known as syncretism.*

Interestingly, it took a mind as perceptive as that of Savonarola to surmise with some degree of accuracy the direction of Pico's thought during the period after he arrived in Florence in 1484. Years later, referring to the occasions when Pico visited him in his cell at the monastery of San Marco and they spent their time 'piously philosophising' together, Savonarola would recall his impressions of Pico in a sermon:

> He was wont to be conversant with me and to break to me the secrets
> of his heart: in which I perceived that he was by private inspiration

---

* This derives from the Greek words *syn*, meaning 'together', and *kretismos* meaning 'Cretans', referring to the habit of the Ancient Cretans, who habitually fought each other, but came together (*syncretismos*) when faced with a common enemy. Syncretism would not become a recognised philosophy until the seventeenth century, when it attempted to reconcile the Protestant and Catholic religions. Pico della Mirandola would be seen as one of syncretism's leading modern forerunners.

all his hours of obsessive study, was well practised. Pico was certainly bisexual. He seems at some point to have become more than poetically involved with Poliziano (whose effusive description of him as 'a hero on whom nature had lavished all the endowments both of body and mind' may well date from this period), and there are indications that Pico may also have formed a similar attachment to the bisexual Lorenzo the Magnificent. However, despite Pico's slightly effeminate appearance, there was no denying that there was a strong heterosexual element to his nature, and it was this that would get him into trouble.

Some time early in 1486, Pico became romantically involved with a young woman called Margherita, the wife of an ageing grocer from Arezzo. When the grocer died, Margherita was compelled by the family of her former husband to marry a local tax official, Giuliano Mariotto de' Medici, a distant relative of Lorenzo the Magnificent. Upon hearing of this, some time in May 1486, Pico set out on his horse for Arezzo, in the foothills of the Apennines forty miles south-east of Florence, accompanied by twenty mounted armed men. They met up with Margherita, who was waiting at the city gate, and rode off with her. The local authorities at once sent a detachment of the city's armed guards in hot pursuit. When they caught up with Pico and his men there was a violent fracas, during which fifteen men were said to have been killed. (This must have been a particularly hot-headed encounter: the carefully choreographed battles of the period in Italy often resulted in fewer casualties than this, before one of the opposing mercenary armies decided to flee the field.)

Pico and his secretary, along with Margherita, managed to escape from this bloody encounter, but their pursuers caught up with them at the village of Marciano in the hills twenty miles to the north of Arezzo, where they were detained and the two men were later imprisoned. When news of this incident reached Florence, it proved a considerable embarrassment to Lorenzo the Magnificent. He had no wish to abandon his close friend Pico in his time of need, even though he was evidently in the wrong; yet at the same time the honour of the Medici family was at stake and had to be seen to be protected. Lorenzo reached a verdict that demonstrated to the full his diplomatic skills. He ordered that Margherita should be returned to her husband forthwith, as it was impossible to believe that any wife would be unfaithful to her Medici husband; in which case, there was no further reason to detain Pico, who was to be released. The entire incident was blamed on the machinations of Pico's secretary, whose fate remains unclear. Lorenzo's friends at the Palazzo Medici appear to have regarded the whole thing as something of a joke, which was commemorated by Ficino, who wrote a poetic *Apologus* in which the affair was likened to a classical scene in which a nymph was raped by one of the gods.

But this embarrassment caused by Pico della Mirandola to Lorenzo the Magnificent was as nothing compared with what was to follow. And this would prove no laughing matter, either to Lorenzo or to the intellectuals at the Palazzo Medici. It is no exaggeration to claim that the ensuing events in Pico's life would be instrumental in transforming the intellectual climate of the Renaissance, and would later lead to its eclipse in the city of Florence.

5

Pico's Challenge

PICO'S SYNCRETISM, TO say nothing of his unprecedented intellectual ambitions, now reached their apotheosis in the form of 900 theses which he drew up, claiming that they dealt with, and answered, all questions in philosophy and theology. These were taken from Ancient Egyptian, Greek, Latin and Hebrew sources, and were intended as the central axioms for a new universal knowledge, as well as a system of belief that incorporated the truth of all faiths. This was to be the foundation of the one true religion, no less.

Pico's *Nine Hundred Theses* contained many deep insights into the human condition, which remain of interest to this day. Take, for instance, his assertion: 'Because no one's opinions are quite what he wills them to be, no one's beliefs are quite what he wills them to be.' The implication here is that elements of our deepest beliefs arise from beyond our conscious, willing mind. In other words, we are something more than simply rational beings. This insight, and the questions it raises, would echo through the centuries, achieving a particular relevance in the modern era with the writings of Freud on the unconscious, as well as contemporary attempts to define consciousness. Others among Pico's theses have a similar prescience: 'When the soul acts, it can be certain of nothing but itself.' This uncannily anticipates the celebrated conclusion that was reached one and a half centuries later by the French philosopher René Descartes – his 'I think, therefore I am', which many see as the starting point of modern philosophy. Indeed, Pico's entire project bears a striking similarity to Descartes' philosophic aim, which sought the undeniable foundation upon which human knowledge rested, as well as seeking to establish the proper method for scientific thinking.

Pico's *Nine Hundred Theses* were in many ways the nearest the Renaissance came to producing an original philosophy. Renaissance art, literature and thought would be characterised by humanism. Yet humanism was not in itself a coherent philosophy, more an attitude that pervaded all the arts and humanities.* Philosophically speaking, the Renaissance was a period of rediscovery of classical thinkers such as Plato, some forgotten works of Aristotle, Lucretius, Plotinus and the like, which awoke a new enthusiasm for such secular thought. This may have released Renaissance thinkers from the strictures of a stale and hidebound Scholasticism, yet in doing so it overwhelmed their imagination and originality, to such an extent that they would produce little new philosophic thought of their own.

Many of the works of these ancient philosophers had reached Italy around the time of the fall of Constantinople in 1453, when fleeing scholars had salvaged all they could from the extensive libraries and archives of the doomed Byzantine Empire. But these libraries also harboured manuscripts and ancient scrolls relating to the darker side of Byzantine learning – works dealing with the hermetic arts, astrology, alchemy, magic and the like. And these too would represent part of the world that the new humanism sought to understand. Indeed, the darker and the clearer sides of Byzantine thought were often inextricably mixed. Astronomy was still permeated with the 'meaning' imposed upon it by astrology, whilst alchemy had yet to give birth to the science of a chemistry cleansed of all attempts to transform base metals into actual or spiritual gold. Pico was influenced by such sources, and was clearly intrigued by the Jewish mysticism of the Kabbala, as plainly stated in his *Nine Hundred Theses*: 'No science affords better evidence of Christ's divinity than magic and Kabbalistic practices.' Aided by the clear vision of hindsight, it is easy to spot the muddle of rational and metaphysical categories here. This indeed is a prime example of the confused thinking that preceded (and helped give birth to) the consequent Age of Reason. In this example of Pico's theses, 'science' and empirical evidence are both invoked – but not in the search for physical truth. Instead, they

---

* Our term 'humanities', as in the academic classification, dates from this period. The human-ities embraced the study of secular (that is, human) learning and literature, especially classical literature, and natural philosophy (that is, science) – as distinct from divinity, which studied divine knowledge, or theology.

are summoned to provide evidence for metaphysical truth, for 'Christ's divinity'. In a further conceptual confusion, the 'science' that is deemed best suited to this search is not that conducted by means of secular reasoning, but that of magic and mystical practices. Western thought would have to evolve for more than two centuries before it learned how to disentangle such antithetical categories and pursuits.

At the same time Pico's brave, if misguided, attempt to incorporate hermetic and mystical thinking into the search for divine truth was leading him into dangerous territory. His other theses may have been unorthodox, but those invoking Kabbalistic mysticism were undoubtedly heretical. However, Pico refused to see it this way – either through political naivety or simply blind hubris, it is difficult to tell which. This supreme confidence is reflected in the other title that he appended to his *Nine Hundred Theses*, which characterised them as *Conclusiones*. Far from being tentative hypotheses or proposals, as a liberal interpretation of the word 'theses' might have allowed, Pico saw his theses as conclusive. And he was prepared to defend them as such. In order to do this he decided to travel to Rome, where he would publish his *Nine Hundred Theses*, with the aim of achieving their widespread distribution amongst the scholars of the day. These would be invited to travel to Rome, at Pico's expense, and he would then hold a public debate, defending his *Nine Hundred Theses* against all arguments. Some time in the spring of 1486 Pico set out on his journey to Rome.*

His arrival in the Eternal City was greeted with considerable suspicion by the Church, despite the fact that Pico had announced he would 'maintain nothing to be true that was not approved by the Catholic Church and her chief Pastor, Innocent VIII'. Pico duly circulated copies of his *Nine Hundred Theses*, and by November 1486 claimed in a letter to a friend that these were 'on public display in all the universities of Italy'. But news soon reached the Vatican concerning the controversial nature of Pico's work. Innocent VIII may have been a venal man, but as pope he was mindful of the authority of the Church. And Pico's behaviour was nothing less than a challenge to this authority. Innocent VIII forbade Pico's proposed public

---

* A number of sources claim that Pico's amorous incident at Arezzo took place whilst he was on his way to Rome, and the dates of this incident and his departure for Rome would appear to be close, despite their disparate intentions.

bank, so that it could be transmitted to Rome. It was no longer so easy to disguise what was happening to taxpayers' money, and many were beginning to become suspicious of Miniati's activities.

Eventually Innocent VIII relented, and in March 1489 Giovanni's name was added to the list of cardinals. Yet even Innocent VIII was aware that such an appointment would be viewed as a scandal, and he made Lorenzo the Magnificent swear, on pain of excommunication, that this appointment would not be made public for another three years. Only then would Giovanni's promotion be finalised. Lorenzo wrote to the Florentine ambassador in Rome, telling of his joy: 'This is the greatest honour that has ever befallen our house.' Even so, Giovanni's cardinalate still remained very much in the balance. During the autumn of 1490 news reached Florence from Rome that the overweight Innocent VIII had suffered an apoplectic fit. If the pope died before the formal confirmation of Giovanni's appointment, then all was lost. Fortunately he recovered from this fit, but a chastened Lorenzo made sure that he kept in close contact with Innocent VIII, corresponding regularly with Rome.

Earlier in 1490, in another letter to the Florentine ambassador at the papal court, Lorenzo had written with news that he expected to be conveyed to Innocent VIII:

> The Count della Mirandola is here leading a most saintly life, like a monk. He ... observes all fasts and absolute chastity: has but a small retinue and lives quite simply with only what is necessary. To me he appears an example to other men. He is anxious to be absolved from what little contumacy is still attributed to him by the Holy Father and to have a Brief by which His Holiness accepts him as a son and as a good Christian ... Do all you can to obtain this Brief in such a form that it may content his conscience.

But Innocent VIII would not relent. In truth, since the scandal over Pico della Mirandola, Lorenzo himself had become increasingly concerned about his own orthodoxy, and was worried that his circle of humanist intellectuals might themselves have begun to embrace heretical ideas. Ficino's Platonism and Poliziano's interpretations of Botticelli's pagan paintings began to appear increasingly suspect. And this was not all. Lorenzo now began to see himself as responsible for the increasingly lax attitude towards religion that had begun to prevail amongst the citizens of Florence – an attitude that had to a large extent been encouraged by the joyous and irreverent festivals which he himself had provided for them. Such matters were starting to prey on his mind.

Then there was the pressing matter of young Giovanni's education. If he was to fulfil his role in the Church with any seriousness, he would now have to become conversant with a far stricter theology than prevailed at the Palazzo Medici amongst his tutors such as Ficino and Poliziano. Lorenzo had communicated with Rome, requesting that Innocent VIII be approached for advice on this matter, telling him, 'I much wish to know how to order Messer Giovanni's future life.' He also spoke of these matters with Pico della Mirandola. However, Pico was in no position to advise his friend. After his condemnation by the pope, he too was looking to the Church for guidance and was desperate for the pardon that the pope continued to withhold. Still Lorenzo put the question to him. What should he do? In his misery, Pico's mind turned to thoughts of the one man whose erudition and spirituality had impressed him above all others – namely, Savonarola. Here was the man who could solve Lorenzo's problems. This was a man whose orthodoxy was beyond question; this was surely the man to infuse Florence with a new enthusiasm for religion. Lorenzo the Magnificent was immediately convinced by Pico's argument – to such an extent that he even placed the whole matter of Savonarola's invitation in Pico's hands, telling him: 'So that you may be assured that I desire to serve you sincerely and faithfully, Your Lordship shall write the letter in whatever form you please, and my chancellor will write it out and seal it with our seal.' A letter requesting the recall of Savonarola to the monastery of San Marco in Florence was duly despatched to the Vicar General of the Dominican order.

After leaving Florence some two years previously, Savonarola had travelled to Bologna, where he had taken up his new post as master of studies at his alma mater, the *Studium generale*. He would remain here for several months, before being posted back to his home town of Ferrara, where he took to visiting his mother, and the rift between them appears to have been healed. However, there was to be no softening of his attitude towards the rest of the world. His earlier revelation in Florence 'that a scourge of the Church was at hand' and his subsequent delivery of Lenten sermons at San Gimignano prophesying this scourge (yet at the same time insisting 'I am [not] a prophet'), had transformed his entire being. Judging from remarks he made during his later sermons, it was around now that he first began to have inklings that before him lay a larger destiny, which he had to fulfil.

Ferrara seems to have served as little more than a home base for Savonarola; he spent almost two years travelling 'to various cities all over the place', as he put it in one of the letters he wrote back to his mother. Savonarola was now fulfilling his intended role as a monk in the preaching order of Dominicans, and it is known that he preached throughout much of Lombardy and northern Italy, travelling to places as far afield as Brescia, Piacenza and even Genoa. The last-named would have involved a journey of more than 130 miles, across the high passes of the Apennine mountains whose peaks rise to well over 6,000 feet in this region, and it is known that Savonarola always travelled on foot, refusing the comparative comfort of travel by donkey or mule, to which he would have been entitled. Hiking barefoot in leather sandals in all weathers may well have appealed to his ascetic nature, but how was it fulfilling the increasing sense of destiny that he felt within him? Savonarola would later claim that he continued to preach during this period in the sensational prophetic manner he had first tried out at San Gimignano, often using Old Testament subjects: 'In this way I preached in Brescia and in many other places throughout Lombardy, frequently on the same topics.' In a letter to his mother he even went so far as to claim that his sermons had such a great effect that 'when it is time for me to leave both men and women are wont to burst into tears and set great store by what I say to them'. However, although contemporary local chroniclers in the cities he visited were in the habit of recording anything out of the ordinary, ranging from the weddings of the local ruling family to simple gossip, no mention was made of Savonarola's sensational sermons. Possibly this was because he did not remain in one particular spot, which would have enabled him to drive home his message and inspire a devoted following. Only one source supports Savonarola's claim to have made such a great impression with his sermons, and this is his contemporary and early biographer Pacifico Burlamacchi, who learned much of his information from Savonarola himself and those close to him. Burlamacchi refers to a single occasion in Brescia when Savonarola delivered an Advent sermon on St Andrew's Day, 30 November 1489. Taking the Book of Revelation as his theme, he delivered a prophetic sermon during which 'he spoke with a voice of thunder; reproving the people for their sins, denouncing the whole of Italy, and threatening all with the terrors of God's wrath'. In the course of his sermon, he referred to the four and twenty elders of the Apocalypse seated around the throne of God, whom the Bible described as clothed in white raiment with gold crowns upon their heads. Savonarola recounted how in a vision he had seen one of these elders rise to prophesy that the citizens of Brescia:

> would fall a prey to raging foes; they would see rivers of blood in the streets; wives would be torn from their husbands, virgins ravished, children murdered before their mothers' eyes; all would be terror and fire, and bloodshed.

Standing in the pulpit above the aghast faces of the congregation, Savonarola brought his sermon to a close with 'a general exhortation to repentance, inasmuch as the Lord would have mercy on the just'.

The people of Brescia would have cause to remember Savonarola's words when twenty-three years later their city was sacked by an invading French army and around 10,000 of its inhabitants were slaughtered amidst scenes of the same hideous cruelty that Savonarola had described.*

Savonarola's travels through northern Italy may have enabled him to hone his preaching skills, but his mother soon became pained by his frequent absences from Ferrara, and wrote telling him so. Savonarola replied to one of her letters:

> You must not be upset that I am so far away from you . . . because

---

* The years following Savonarola's apocalyptic prediction were particularly turbulent in Italy, and many cities in northern Italy beside Brescia would have fulfilled such a prophecy.

I am doing all this for the good of many souls – preaching, exhorting, hearing confession, reading and counselling. It is for this reason that I am constantly travelling from place to place wherever my superiors send me. For this reason you should take comfort from the fact that one of your children has been chosen by God to undertake such work. If I remained continually in Ferrara, I would not be able to do such good work as I manage to do outside it. Hardly ever does a genuinely religious person work fruitfully in his own country. This is the reason why we are so frequently told in the Scriptures that we must leave our own country, for the preaching and counsel of a local man is never appreciated as much as that of a stranger. This is why Our Saviour says that a prophet has no honour in his own country. Therefore, because God has deigned to elect me from my sinful state to such a high office, you should be content that I labour in the vineyard of Christ so far from my own country.

It is evident from these words that his sense of his own destiny as a prophet had by this stage become firmly fixed in his mind – indeed, central to his sense of his own identity. And it was now that news reached Savonarola of his call to return to Florence. Savonarola was ordered to take up residence as a teaching master at his old monastery of San Marco. Here at last he would have a more permanent base, and a permanent congregation on which he could exercise his powers to some lasting effect. We know that some time around late May 1490, Savonarola set out from Bologna on the fifty-mile journey south along the Savena valley towards the pass across the high Apennines to Florence.

According to an illuminating tale recorded by Burlamacchi, Savonarola only reached the village of Pianoro, some ten miles down the road, before he was overcome with exhaustion. Despite his earnest, youthful appearance, Savonarola was by now no longer a young man – indeed he was less than three years from his fortieth birthday (a ripe old age in an era when the evidence of the monastery registers suggests that a monk was very lucky to live beyond fifty). Yet still he obstinately refused to modify his ascetic ways, even whilst travelling; as a result, his frugal diet proved inadequate for the physical task of trudging up the long trail into the mountains, and he finally collapsed. The unconscious monk, devoid of possessions other than his breviary and the worn Bible he had inherited from his grandfather Michele, was found lying at the roadside by an anonymous traveller who gave him food and drink. After a night's rest at a wayside tavern, Savonarola continued on his way, accompanied by the kind stranger. Some time later they approached Florence, with the dome and towers of the city visible beyond the walls, and the traveller accompanied him right up to the Porta San Gallo, where he took his leave of Savonarola and bade him: 'Go and do the task which God has assigned to you in Florence.' Savonarola never discovered the name of his Good Samaritan, but he would remember his charity and his benediction for the rest of his life.

This tale has all the ingredients of mythology, yet it may well contain a grain of truth. It certainly has psychological veracity: we know from remarks made in his later sermons that Savonarola felt he had specifically been guided back to Florence by God, so that he could embark upon a new life and fufil the destiny that he was convinced now lay before him.

6

The Return of Savonarola

SAVONAROLA TOOK UP the post of teaching master at the monastery of San Marco probably some time in early June 1490, delivering lectures on logic to novices and other members of the community. However, he also took to giving extra lectures on Sundays after Vespers, beneath a damask rose-tree in the monastery gardens. In these informal, almost intimate lectures to his fellow friars he began explaining passages from the Bible, resorting to the quiet, intense manner that had always attracted listeners during his more personal teaching. The beauty of the gardens on those long summer evenings, combined with the atmosphere of intense spirituality, soon began to attract devout listeners from beyond the monastic community. He also began receiving regular visits in his cell from Pico della Mirandola, who was now eager to receive religious instruction from Savonarola. As Savonarola would later confess, during their previous meetings he had done all he could to dissuade Pico from pursuing his ambition to create a universal philosophy. Instead, he had tried his best to convince Pico that he should follow his true calling and devote his life to Christianity and the one true God, without further delay. Savonarola had warned him that:

for this delaye I threatened him ... he wolde be punished yf he forsook that purpose which our Lorde had put in his mynde, and certainly I prayed to God my selfe (I will not lye therefore) that he might be some what beaten: to compell him to take that waye whiche God had from above shewed hyme.

Now Pico had indeed been 'some what beaten' and was a changed man. He had given away his villa and his estate near Mirandola to his nephew Gianfrancesco, who would later repay this gift by writing the first biography of his uncle. According to Gianfrancesco, during the period around the summer of 1490 Pico conceived the idea of following in the footsteps of St Francis of Assisi, travelling barefoot through the towns and cities of Italy. He was preparing to join the same order as Savonarola, the Dominicans, and devote his life to preaching, but could not yet bring himself to renounce the world entirely, despite the frequent urgings of Savonarola.

All the indications are that Pico and Savonarola spent many hours discussing philosophy. Although Savonarola was undeniably seeking to influence Pico, there are indications that Pico also influenced Savonarola in the course of these discussions. Savonarola was engaged in his lectures on logic, and it was around this time that he conceived of his 'Division of all the Sciences'. This is the nearest he came to providing a purely philosophical underpinning to his belief. Savonarola separated philosophy into two aspects: the rational, and the positive. Positive philosophy included the real and the practical, embracing the moral (ethics, economics*, politics) and the mechanical (the arts). Rational philosophy, on the other hand, embraced logic and the speculative, which included physics, mathematics and metaphysics. Physics was inseparable from matter, mathematics was abstracted from matter, but metaphysics was absolutely free from material constraint, and was thus the queen of the sciences; it strove to discover the highest truth, and in doing so it elevated the human spirit. And as far as Savonarola was concerned, the only metaphysics was theology — Christian theology, as derived from the Bible.

Savonarola's philosophy was neither original nor particularly clear. For him, philosophy was not important — even so, it certainly illuminated the nature of his faith. The spiritual quest of metaphysics was quite separate from ethics, economics and politics. Yet these latter belonged to the real world, and as such could not be ignored. Savonarola's regard for his congregations would always involve a deeply compassionate element. Besides being metaphysical, his message was also moral, and as such included ethics, economics and politics. These were not subjects that were open to free

---

* Economics as such had not yet come into being: Savonarola's concern was more with the social effects of commercial activity.

discusssion during this period: the Church laid down the law on ethics, and economic life was strictly regulated by the powerful guilds, whilst politics was a matter for rulers. But Savonarola saw these as subsumed by morality, and thus in the realm of real and practical philosophical debate. Society, which included ethics, economics and politics, was moral or it was nothing. And as such, contemporary society was due for a change.

In the light of how many long hours Savonarola and Pico spent discussing philosophy, it is worth comparing their different philosophies. Pico had wished to build a universal philosophy-cum-religion upon 900 basic axioms: these would include all belief systems and all manner of thought, and yet would retain an outlook that was essentially humanistic. It left humanity free to choose what it wished to become, yet urged the use of reason to achieve 'the higher realms of the divine'. By contrast, Savonarola's basic axioms were contained in the Bible, and faith alone (aided by the reason of metaphysics, the queen of the sciences) could aspire to the divine. Once Savonarola had convinced Pico that it was right for him to abandon his 900 theses and his reliance upon arguments derived from all religions, the way was open for him to embrace an analogous mode of thought using the Bible and faith. Yet although Pico discarded his philosophy, he did not discard his intellectual powers. His traumatic clash with the pope may have rendered him a changed man, but it had not broken him. He never lost his compelling personal qualities and his supreme ability to reason: he could still discuss philosophy with his intellectual equal, Savonarola. This much was confirmed by Savonarola himself, who was hardly a man to be impressed by such qualities: yet years later, on Pico's death, the austere friar would pronounce him 'a man in whom God had heped many great gifts and singular graces, who is an inestymable loss to the church'.

Savonarola's first sermon on his return to Florence was delivered on 1 August 1490 in the church at San Marco, just two months after his arrival. He had, it seems, already gained a certain hearsay reputation as a result of his apocalyptic sermons delivered in northern Italy; and this, together with the growing audience for his evening talks in the monastery gardens, ensured an unusually large crowd at San Marco that Sunday. According to Burlamacchi, who might even have been present, some were left standing, while others clung to the iron gratings, peering into the body of the church.

Savonarola did not disappoint the spilling congregation beneath the delicate frescoes and long, echoing nave. He returned to his favourite topic, the Apocalypse, and for the first time in Florence articulated what would become his famous prophecies regarding the Church: its reform, how it would be scourged, and the imminence of these events. In later years he would fondly recall the effect of his sermon with the words: 'I am the hailstorm that shall smash the heads of those who do not take cover.' Such was the popularity of this, and of Savonarola's ensuing sermons, that when he was chosen by the prior of San Marco to give the Lenten sermons for the following year, it was decided that he should deliver them in Florence's main church, the Cathedral of Santa Maria del Fiore (the Duomo).

By now, word had reached Lorenzo the Magnificent of the disturbing tenor of Savonarola's preaching. The man brought to Florence to assist the spiritual life of Lorenzo and his son Giovanni, to inspire a new orthodoxy within the court and the populace, had started making subversive prophecies concerning the Church. As a result Lorenzo sent word to Savonarola, by way of a group of leading citizens, that in the forthcoming Lenten sermons it would be best if 'he did not speak much about future events'. But this was not the way to deal with Savonarola: threats only incited him to obstinacy, and worse. He saw them as attempts to compromise his integrity, an element that was central to his faith, his personality, indeed his very being.

Yet Lorenzo the Magnificent was not the only one alarmed by Savonarola's attitude, and Savonarola himself admitted that he was approached 'by all kinds of people' who warned him against being so reckless. Some of these were young monks at San Marco, amongst whom he had begun to gather a devoted following. Unlike the deputation from Lorenzo, these were not threats, but friendly advice from those he knew to be sympathetic to his cause, and Savonarola decided to take heed of their warning. He set about preparing a series of sermons on more orthodox themes, which he would deliver in a less sensational manner. But he soon found 'I was unable to do this, because everything that I read or studied was so boring, and when I tried to preach in any other manner than the one I was used to, I even bored myself.' He would recall how he had heard a voice encouraging him to return to his former way of preaching: 'You fool, do you not understand that it is the will of God that you should preach in this way?' This 'voice' soon persuaded him.

As result, when Savonarola next stepped up to the lectern in the cathedral, he delivered what even he would characterise as 'a terrifying sermon'. His voice rang out beneath Brunelleschi's great dome as he spoke of the coming of 'a time such as none has ever heard of before'. He launched into a long and explicit tirade against the city's evils, denouncing sodomites 'who hide not what they are', murderers 'who are filled with evil', gamblers and blasphemers, all of whom were 'abhorred by God'. He denounced banking as 'usury', explained how the rich 'will suffer great affliction' and condemned 'the unjust taxes which are grinding down the poor'. He warned them that 'the time is nigh when you will be struck down with the sword'. The city would no longer be known as Florence, but as 'the great den of iniquity'.

The large audience for Savonarola's Lenten sermons of 1491 included all elements of the city's population, but especially the poor, who began to know him as 'the preacher for those in despair'. According to his biographer Ridolfi, 'as a result of this Lenten preaching, Savonarola started to become master, if not of Florence itself, at least of the people of the city'.

In accord with Florentine tradition, the preacher of the Lenten sermons at the cathedral delivered a private sermon for the *gonfaloniere* and his eight-man Signoria at the Palazzo della Signoria on the Wednesday after Easter, which this year fell on 6 April. In practice, this would also have been attended by a number of other senior government officials, advisers and counsellors: even so, it would have been a small gathering compared with a sermon in San Marco or the cathedral. We do not know precisely how Savonarola spoke, but his notes for the sermon survive, giving a good indication. He must have found the prospect of preaching in this more intimate atmosphere intimidating. Beginning a little ineptly and provocatively, he compared himself to Christ in the house of the Pharisee, 'which forces me to be somewhat more subtle and sophisticated than in Church'. Despite this, he soon launched into a rather more explicit confrontation:

Everything that is good and everything that is evil in this city depends upon the man who rules it. He is the one responsible for all that is wrong with this city, for if he acted in the proper manner the entire city would be sanctified. Tyrants never change their ways, and this is because they are arrogant, they thrive on flattery, and refuse to return what they have stolen from the people. They leave everything in the hands of corrupt ministers, listen only to false praise, pay no attention to the poor and only care about those who are wealthy. They require the poor and the peasants to labour ceaselessly for them without being paid proper wages. They expect their ministers to condone this, they corrupt the voters, employ criminal tax-collectors, and thus make it even worse for the poor.

One can but imagine the expressions of outrage on the faces of his distinguished listeners. For many years now, during the years of the Medici ascendancy, the leading citizens who governed Florence had grown unaccustomed to hearing such downright democratic criticism. Savonarola was venturing into dangerous political territory, yet such was his ever-increasing self-confidence that he now went even further. He delivered his final Lenten sermons in the cathedral to a packed congregation, his harsh voice with its homely Ferrarese intonations ringing out over the sea of rapt upturned faces. They were hardly able to believe what they were hearing, but Savonarola could now see beginning to unfold before him the destiny of which he had dreamed. Filled with the Holy Spirit, he felt empowered to inform the gathered citizens of Florence, 'I believe that Christ speaks through my mouth.'

Word of these latest outrages soon reached Lorenzo the Magnificent, and he was strongly advised to banish Savonarola. But he decided against such a drastic step. There were several reasons for this. According to the contemporary historian Guicciardini, Lorenzo retained 'a certain respect for Fra Girolamo, whom he considered to be genuinely holy'. At the same time, there were other, more worldly reasons for Lorenzo's lack of decisive action. Just three years previously a preacher named Fra Bernardino da Feltre had begun to gain a similar popular following in Florence. Fra Bernadino's simple innocent sermons, with their homilies on the sanctity of the poor, had evoked widespread sympathy amongst the deprived sections of the population. In this way, he had gained an almost saintly reputation, but his otherworldly manner had not prevented him from making several very worldly observations. He had begun to attack the bankers of Florence for charging such high interest on their loans to the poor that entire families were often plunged into penury for life. As a remedy for this he had suggested the establishment of a *Monte della Pietà* (in effect, a 'bank for the people'). Fra Bernardino's direct honesty had caused the people of Florence to see their rulers through new eyes, and they had not liked what they saw. Lorenzo the Magnificent had quickly sensed how the tide of public opinion was turning against him. Not only amongst the poor, but also amongst the more educated classes, there was a growing dissatisfaction with the Medici regime and the taxes that not only kept the poor in their place, but could also be applied punitively in order to ruin any factions that might be contemplating opposition to Medici rule. Lorenzo had promptly banished Fra Bernardino into exile, but this had proved a highly unpopular move, resulting in widespread dissatisfaction and grumblings, which had taken some time and considerable expense (in the form of bribes and entertainments) to dissipate. Lorenzo was not going to make the same mistake again – especially in light of the irony that he had been responsible for inviting Savonarola back to Florence in the first place. Such a decision would have made him a laughing stock, and would have struck at the very heart of his reputation for decisive action. The great protector of Florence against its enemies could not be seen as a ditherer who went back on his word.

Instead, Lorenzo decided that he would attempt to destroy Savonarola using a more subtle method. He would undermine his reputation as a public speaker by demonstrating that he was not only a dangerous rabble-rouser, but also blasphemous. How could any mere friar claim to speak with the voice of Christ? If Savonarola could be exposed as a charlatan, his following amongst the poor would soon evaporate. More important still, his growing following amongst the humanists would also be destroyed.

As far as this last point was concerned, Lorenzo was at least in part working against himself. His increasing inclination towards religion was grating with his humanist beliefs; he too was attracted to Savonarola's piety. Indeed, Lorenzo's latest writing was a religious verse drama about St John and St Paul. Similarly, his close friend Pico had long since succumbed to

Savonarola's siren song, and now even Poliziano was attending his sermons
and was on the verge of being won over. The poet would later describe
Savonarola as 'a man eminent both in learning and in sanctity and a superb
preacher of heavenly doctrine'. Poliziano's personality was both emotional
and intellectual, and he seems to have responded to what he saw as the
poetic intensity in Savonarola's style of preaching. Yet paradoxically it was
the friar's very lack of style that appealed to the poor. Savonarola appears
to have been all things to all men. Where Pico had recognised a great intellect, Poliziano recognised the ringing phrases of a poet — and meanwhile
the downtrodden were inspired to recognise a man who had their cause at
heart. Even the ardent Platonist Ficino was impressed, though at this stage
he still had reservations. There appeared to be little place in Savonarola's
creed for much of the pagan philosophy of Plato, which saw the world as
the mere play of shadows cast by the distant brilliance of the abstract
ideas whose radiance constituted the ultimate reality. Such ethereal Platonic
idealism would have been of little consolation to the poor. Yet curiously,
Savonarola was in fact inspired by Plato, almost certainly through the influence of Ficino's writings, a fact that would not have escaped Ficino when
he read Savonarola's words:

> The ultimate aim of man is beatitude. This does not consist, as the
> natural philosophers would have us believe, in the contemplations of
> speculative science. Nay, beatitude is the pure vision of God. In this
> life we are only capable of seeing a distant image, a faint shadow of
> the beatitude. Only in the next life can we enjoy this vision in all its
> radiant reality.

Pico, Poliziano and Ficino would all have recognised Savonarola's philosophical reference. Likewise, the power and clarity of this image would
have been easily understood by the less educated amongst his congregation. Savonarola's words seemed to fill some emptiness that lay at the heart
of the society he was addressing. For all the surface aesthetic changes which
the Renaissance had brought to the city — architecture, frescoes, festivals,
humanism and its discovery of the pagan classical world — this transformation had brought with it a certain spiritual malaise; at the same time,

perhaps inevitably, it had also awoken dormant fears. It was this malaise, and these fears, that Savonarola addressed.

Lorenzo the Magnificent, increasingly racked by gout, sensed that he was now dying. The mortal man faced with death responded to the absolutism of Savonarola's call to faith. But the man who had ruled Florence so successfully for more than two decades knew that Savonarola posed a political threat – to the stability of the city and all that it stood for as the leading cultural centre in Italy, as well as to his own rule, the Medici family and all that they stood to achieve in future generations.

Lorenzo's plan to undermine Savonarola was an ambitious and subtle one, which could only have been achieved by one man: Fra Mariano da Genazzano, the superior of the local Augustinian order. Where Savonarola harked back to a past era, Fra Mariano was very much a man of the coming age – a preacher of considerable sophistication and intellect.

Despite Savonarola's growing popularity, Fra Mariano held, and jealously guarded, the title of the most celebrated preacher in Florence. Some twenty years previously the monastery housing the Augustinians had burned down, whereupon Lorenzo the Magnificent had commissioned Brunelleschi to design a new residence for them just outside the city's northern Porta San Gallo. The result was a resplendent building with cells for 100 monks and a Renaissance-style church. Lorenzo was particularly drawn to Fra Mariano, and had taken to visiting him at his monastery, where they would discuss the cultural and theological issues of the day. Fra Mariano was well versed in the new Renaissance learning, and saw no contradiction between his role as a monk and his love of pagan classical poetry and philosophy. When Lorenzo retired to one of his country villas during the long, hot summer months, he was in the habit of inviting Fra Mariano to stay with him, and here the Augustinian monk made a favourable impression on Lorenzo's intellectual companions. Poliziano's opinion of Fra Mariano was typical:

> I have met Fra Mariano repeatedly at the villa and entered into confidential talks with him. I never knew a man at once more attractive and more cautious. He neither repels by immoderate severity nor deceives and leads astray by exaggerated indulgence. Many preachers

think themselves masters of men's life and death. While they are abusing their power they always look gloomy and weary men by setting up as judges of morals. But here is a man of moderation. In the pulpit he is a severe censor; but when he descends from it he indulges in winning friendly discourse . . . I and my friend Pico have much conversation with him and nothing refreshes us after our literary labours as [sic] relaxation in his company. Lorenzo de' Medici, who understands men so well, shows how highly he esteems him . . . preferring a conversation with him to any other recreation.

Poliziano was equally impressed by his style of preaching, writing to a friend of Fra Mariano's 'musical voice, his precisely chosen words, his grand sentences. Then I become aware of his telling metaphors, the way he pauses for effect, and the enchantment of his harmonious cadences'. Fra Mariano's sermons, with their wealth of classical and philosophical allusion, may have owed much to Ficino's erudite expositions before Lorenzo and his circle, but there was no denying that he was above all else an actor. Besides his graceful flourishes and gestures, he was not above resorting to more histrionic groans and trembling cries to stir the emotions of his less-educated listeners. He too had his following amongst the poor.

Even some of the monks from San Marco went to hear Fra Mariano's sermons. Savonarola's admirer and defender Domenico Benivieni could not refrain from telling Savonarola: 'Father, there is no denying that your doctrine is true, useful and necessary, but your way of delivering it lacks grace, especially when it is so frequently compared to that of Fra Mariano.' To this, Savonarola is said to have replied bluntly, 'Such verbal elegance must soon make way for simple preaching of sound doctrine.'

Fra Mariano had become aware of Savonarola's growing reputation, and in the spring of 1491 he visited him at San Marco, evidently with the aim of sizing up his rival. He left, assuring Savonarola of his friendship. Around this time Lorenzo the Magnificent suggested to Fra Mariano that he should take on his upstart competitor, and deliver a devastating sermon that would demonstrate the hollowness of his rival's claims and prophecies, at the same time so humiliating Savonarola that he would be eclipsed once and for all in the public mind. Fra Mariano readily agreed to this, telling Lorenzo that he would deliver his sermon at the Church of Santo Spirito, the priory church of the San Gallo monastery, on Ascension Day, Thursday 12 May 1491. This was the first major date in the religious calendar after Easter, falling forty days later; it allowed sufficient time for the controversy over Savonarola's Lenten sermons to have died down, and also made it look as if Fra Mariano's sermon was not some hasty personal response to San Marco's 'preacher for those in despair'.

Word of this coming attack was soon passed on to Savonarola, who merely responded by predicting, 'I shall wax, and he shall wane.' By Ascension Day news of this 'joust' had spread through Florence, and the crowds that gathered at the San Gallo monastery more than filled its sizeable church.* Poliziano and Pico della Mirandola were also amongst the congregation, together with Lorenzo the Magnificent himself – all of whom were now fully aware of the import of what was taking place. Savonarola's contemporary biographer and friend, Fra Placido Cinozzi, has left an eyewitness account of what happened. Fra Mariano took as his text Jesus' reply to his disciples, when they asked him to tell them what would come to pass in the future: 'It is not for you to know the time, or the seasons.' He went on to elaborate that it was sheer nonsense for anyone to pretend to have knowledge of future events, and then launched into a passionate personal attack on Savonarola, labelling him as a false prophet who was responsible for spreading subversive sedition, with the aim of stirring the people of Florence to rebellion. But Fra Mariano had evidently misinterpreted what Lorenzo the Magnificent wished of him, for he soon became so carried away with himself that he began mimicking Savonarola's brusque gestures and provincial accent, before unleashing a stream of intemperate insults against Savonarola, calling him a worm, a snake, a clown who was ignorant of the Bible, and an inept priest who was not even capable of conducting a Mass in proper Latin. By the end of his sermon, Fra Mariano was all but incoherent with rage and vitriolic condemnation. Lorenzo, Poliziano and Pico were horrified at such an inappropriate and vulgar display, and the congregation was deeply shocked. This was not the kind of behaviour Florentines wished to see in church. Even those who had championed Fra Mariano against Savonarola now began to have second thoughts.

* Neither the San Gallo Augustinian monastery nor the attached church of Santo Spirito exists any longer, for reasons that will become clear in a later chapter.

Just three days later, on the following Sunday, Savonarola gave his reply in a sermon delivered at the cathedral. Fra Mariano had played into his rival's hands, and Savonarola intended to take full advantage of this. Using the selfsame text as Fra Mariano had chosen, he proceeded to elucidate its true meaning, disposing one by one of what he claimed were Fra Mariano's specious arguments against him. He then began a personal attack on Fra Mariano, but unlike his rival's attack, this was neither intemperate nor insulting. Instead, 'in the most gentle manner', he reminded Fra Mariano how just a few days previously he had called at San Marco expressly to see him. Savonarola reminded him how during the course of their meeting Fra Mariano had congratulated him on his sermons, praising their biblical erudition, and assuring him that they would do much good in Florence. Having prepared the ground, Savonarola then began asking some devastating questions: 'Who was it who made you change your mind? Who was it who suggested that you should attack me?' All present knew precisely to whom Savonarola was alluding. Not only had his sermon rebutted Fra Mariano, but it had also implicated Lorenzo the Magnificent.

The people of Florence had witnessed the crushing defeat of their celebrated preacher; and Fra Mariano, unable to bear the humiliation, packed his bags and left for Rome, now a lifelong and dangerous enemy of Savonarola who would use all his influence in the Vatican to wreak his revenge. Pico, who had been worried by the turn of events, called upon Savonarola in his cell at San Marco and warned him, 'You will not fare well, if you continue jousting in this fashion.'

7
Cat and Mouse

UCH WAS SAVONAROLA's popularity amongst his fellow friars at San
Marco that in July 1491 they elected him prior of the monastery. As
the Medici family had been responsible for the rebuilding of San
Marco, and continued to be its benefactors (to the extent that they even
referred to it as 'our' monastery), it was customary for any newly elected
friar to pay a courtesy visit to the Palazzo Medici, a short walk down the
Via Larga. However, when Savonarola's fellow monks urged him to fulfil
this obligation, he demanded of them: 'Who made me prior – God or
Lorenzo?' When they replied, 'God', Savonarola declared, 'Thus it is the
Lord God who I will thank', and then returned to his cell to continue
with his habitual regime of prayer and fasting.

When word of Savonarola's refusal reached the Palazzo Medici, Lorenzo
remarked irritatedly, 'A foreign monk has come to live in my house and he
does not even deign to come and see me.' Lorenzo's illness was giving him
increasing pain, and this time he decided against any confrontation with
Savonarola. Instead, he chose to take a conciliatory course of action which
would give the new prior the chance to make amends without either of
them losing face before the people of Florence. Lorenzo began attending
the church of San Marco on Sundays to hear Mass, and afterwards he
would walk in the garden, or in the cloisters, in the hope of encountering
Savonarola, engaging him in conversation and exerting his famous charm
upon the new prior. On earlier occasions when Lorenzo had strolled in
the monastery gardens after Mass he had been joined by the previous prior,
along with several of the more senior monks, who were still pleased to
join the man they regarded as their benefactor. When Savonarola's fellow

monks came to inform him of what Lorenzo was doing, he said to them, 'Is he asking for me?' When they replied that he was not, Savonarola told them, 'Then let him walk as he pleases.'

This made Lorenzo even more determined to gain the confidence of the man whose holiness he viewed with increasing respect, yet whose opposition he knew it was politically dangerous to tolerate. By this stage Lorenzo's illness was causing him to lose his grasp of affairs and cloud his judgement – a fact that became evident in the way he now misjudged Savonarola. Lorenzo ordered gifts to be sent to San Marco, but these were simply returned to the Palazzo Medici. In a public allusion from the pulpit to this turn of events, Savonarola likened a true preacher to a loyal watchdog who is not distracted when a thief throws him a bone or a lump of meat; instead, he ignores these gifts and continues barking.

As a last resort, Lorenzo ordered his chancellor, Piero da Bibbiena, to deposit anonymously gold coins to the value of 300 florins in the alms chest of San Marco. This chest was the chief source of public financial support for the monastery, and would accumulate a collection of largely copper coins, plus the occasional silver one, through the week. When Savonarola was informed of this hugely generous anonymous gift, he knew at once that it came from Lorenzo. He decreed that the silver and bronze coins deposited by the good citizens of the city should be set aside as usual for the running costs of the monastery. However, the gold coins were to be taken to the brotherhood of St Martin, who distributed alms amongst the deserving poor. When Bibbiena heard of what Savonarola had done, he reported back to Lorenzo, declaring, 'This is a slippery customer we are dealing with.'

It was evident that Savonarola was unwilling to make any accommodation with Lorenzo's authority. There would be no compromise on his behalf, and Lorenzo was forced to the realisation that although he respected Savonarola, he could not allow him any further concessions. It was time to assert his authority. Lorenzo could still have banished Savonarola without further ado, as he had Fra Bernardino three years previously; and he was certainly capable of savage reprisal when he felt his political power was under threat. A decade or so earlier, Lorenzo had become suspicious that a pilgrim begging for food at the gate of his country villa was in fact a hired assassin. The pilgrim had been arrested and interrogated, the soles of his feet held over a fire until the fat dribbled, spitting in the flames. When still no confession was forthcoming, the pilgrim was made to walk on his charred, bloodied feet over coarse salt, an excruciating ordeal that resulted in his death. As Machiavelli, who lived through these events, would later write in his characteristically sardonic fashion of Lorenzo, 'all his enemies met with an unhappy end'.

Yet once again Lorenzo hesitated from taking an absolute and final step against Savonarola: he would exercise his authority indirectly. Some days later, five of Florence's leading citizens arrived at San Marco and demanded to see Savonarola. This delegation consisted of members of some of the most respected families in the city: Guidantonio Vespucci, Paolantonio Soderini, Francesco Valori, Domenico Bonsi and Bernardo Rucellai.

The ensuing meeting took place in the sacristy, and was reported by a number of contemporary sources, each of whom left a remarkably similar account of Savonarola's sensational behaviour. To begin with, the citizens explained to Savonarola that they had come of their own accord to warn him against persisting in his current behaviour, which was putting both himself and his monastery in some danger. But Savonarola soon cut them short, interjecting: 'I know that you have not come of your own free will, but have been sent by Lorenzo. Bid him to do penance for his sins, for the Lord is no respecter of persons, and does not even spare the princes of this earth from his judgement.' The citizens then repeated their warning, insisting that if he continued to behave in this fashion he was liable to be banished from Florence.

Savonarola replied: 'Only people like you, who have wives and children, are afraid of banishment. I have no such fear, for if I did have to leave, this city would become no more than a speck of dust to me, compared with the rest of the world. I am not frightened, let him do as he pleases. But let him realise this: although I am a mere stranger to this city, and Lorenzo is the most powerful man in Florence, it is I who will remain here, and he who will depart. He will be gone, long before me.'

The citizens were amazed; they realised that Savonarola was in fact predicting that Lorenzo was going to die. Collating the contemporary reports, Savonarola's biographer Pasquale Villari described what happened next: '[Savonarola] began to speak about the city of Florence and the political state of Italy, displaying a depth of knowledge in these matters which astonished his listeners. It was then that he predicted, in front of the many witnesses who were present in the sacristy of San Marco, that great changes would soon take place in Italy. He then specifically prophesied that Lorenzo the Magnificent, Pope Innocent VIII and King Ferrante of Naples would all soon die.' Whispers of these sensational prophecies soon began to spread around Florence.*

Lorenzo the Magnificent was aware of the vital power slipping from his grasp. Physically he was reduced, and as a consequence he could no longer stand centre-stage politically. Yet he was not one to make excuses for his misfortunes. As he had written on an earlier occasion:

> So great was the persecution I endured at that time, from both Fortune and from men. Even so, I am inclined by nature to rise above such things, to mention them but briefly, in order to avoid the charge of being proud and vain, since reporting one's own serious dangers cannot be done without the presumption of vainglory.

Congenital gout was reducing his charismatic physical presence to a shell. The champion jouster and insatiable lover, filled with such inspirational physical and intellectual *joie de vivre*, who had so enchanted Poliziano and Pico della Mirandola, whose charm had won over King Ferrante of Naples and Innocent VIII, was now a crabbed, irritable and weak forty-two-year-old invalid, his mind clouded with pain. A ghost of his former self, he would spend hours on end shivering in his cloak by the fire, attempting to melt the icy crystalline needles of pain in his joints. By this stage he had become desperate, willing to resort to all manner of quack remedies. Even his famous collection of jewels was brought to bear on the problem. The physician Petrus Bonus Avogarius wrote advising him:

* Ridolfi even goes so far as to claim: 'With such words he prophesied that Lorenzo would soon die, and to those closest to him he even went so far as to predict the very date.' The latter claim was certainly made around this time, but after the event. This was typical of the mythologising that grew up around Savonarola's name, even during his lifetime. The celebrated claims regarding Italy, together with the deaths of Lorenzo, Innocent VIII and King Ferrante, are more definitely verifiable, and their grounds will be examined later.

To prevent the return of these pains, you must get a stone called sapphire, and have it set in gold, so that it should touch the skin. This must be worn on the third finger of the left hand. If this is done the pains in the joints, or gouty pains, will cease, because that stone has occult virtues, and the specific one of preventing evil humours going to the joints.

Lorenzo's jewels remained his pride and joy — it was, after all, on them that he had left evidence of his deepest, most secret ambition: LAU.R.MED, Lorenzo de' Medici — king, or the father of future kings. This was his prediction, far more likely than the prophecies of some ranting priest. His oldest son Piero would succeed him as ruler of Florence. All this had been settled with the leading Medici lieutenants — the likes of Soderini, Vespucci and Valori, who could be relied upon to do his bidding. Lorenzo himself had only been invited by the Signoria to take over the reins of power out of respect for his father Piero, but during the twenty-two years of Lorenzo's rule things had changed: from now on the succession would be a Medici right.

At the same time, the Medici family would extend its power beyond Florence and into the Church, by means of Giovanni's rich benefices and his coming cardinalate. But Innocent VIII had driven a hard bargain for the cardinalate, leaving Lorenzo's finances under strain and only adding to his overall debt.

A portion of this debt had been to cover the education of Giovanni, who in 1490 had been sent to study at the celebrated university that Lorenzo had recently re-established at Pisa. It had quickly become clear to Lorenzo that Giovanni should not be exposed to Savonarola's inflammatory sermons, and he hoped that a scholastic university education would give him a more suitable theological grounding. However, Giovanni's education had proved rather more costly than his father had anticipated. Although he had shown high intelligence, combined with a certain indolence, the chubby, likeable teenager had at the same time inherited his father's inclination towards hedonistic extravagance. As a result, the cash-strapped Lorenzo had been obliged to order the Medici bank to cover Giovanni's debts in Pisa. According to some sources, these amounted to the astonishing sum of 7,000 florins.

As if all this were not enough, some time towards the end of 1491 Lorenzo had received a request from Innocent VIII for the equivalent of 10,000 florins as a 'final' down payment on Giovanni's cardinalate, which was due to be confirmed and made public in a few months' time. Lorenzo knew that he could not refuse this 'request' if he wished the pope to confirm Giovanni's appointment. He had been forced once again to turn to Miniati and his underhand manipulations of the Florentine exchequer. This was a desperate last resort, as the latest financial reform undertaken by Lorenzo – with the connivance of Miniati – had provoked considerable unrest. During the previous year there had arisen a problem over the coinage circulating in Florence. The city's role as a centre of trade, especially in commodities such as wool, alum and fine cloth, had resulted in a large number of foreign coins entering circulation. These coins mostly originated from nearby cities that issued their own currency, such as Bologna, Siena or Lucca, and were similar to the Florentine *quattrini* (or pennies), for which they were frequently exchanged. The foreign coins were known as 'black *quattrini*'. In order to resolve this anomaly, Lorenzo set up a committee, which decided to call in the 'black *quattrini*' and replace the old Florentine *quattrini* with similar new 'white *quattrini*', which were worth 25 per cent more. The old coins would be melted down, and only the 'white *quattrini*' would be accepted for payment of taxes, duties and other contributions to the city exchequer. This caused little complaint amongst the citizens, until it was discovered that instead of melting down the old Florentine *quattrini*, the authorities were reintroducing these selfsame coins as equivalent to 'white *quattrini*', thus making 25 per cent on any transaction involving these old coins (which could not then be used to pay taxes, and thus effectively reverted to their old call-in rate).

To exacerbate the problem, Lorenzo's sudden unexpected need for the equivalent of 10,000 florins to pay Innocent VIII led him to a rash embezzlement, which would not be exposed until after his death. This involved the public fund known as the *Monte delle Doti*, a public deposit account that had been established in 1424 by Cosimo de' Medici for the provision of dowries for the daughters of the poor, who would otherwise not have been able to get married. Anyone paying into this fund received a 5 per cent interest on their savings, which could all be withdrawn after an agreed number of years to become a daughter's dowry. The establishment of the *Monte delle Doti* (Dowry Fund) had proved a highly popular move, and it had soon accumulated a considerable sum, as payments into the fund greatly exceeded withdrawals. Thus when the Florentine exchequer found itself short of assets, instead of repayments it would issue the citizen with shares in the Dowry Fund, which also rose by 5 per cent annually and could be withdrawn at a future date to provide a dowry. This enforced form of saving was not popular, but was tolerated. Even this measure only made small inroads into the Dowry Fund, which had continued to increase over the years.

However, by 1485 a downturn in trade had cut the tax revenue, leaving the Florentine exchequer heavily indebted. In an effort to rescue the city's finances, and his own, Lorenzo had ordered Miniati to expropriate a sizeable sum from the Dowry Fund. (The precise figure remains unclear, owing to the Medici family's subsequent destruction of all ledgers relating to these years, but this too may be a candidate for at least part of the 74,948 florins later demanded from the Medici family in compensation for money taken by Lorenzo 'without the sanction of any law and without authority'.) In order to cover this embezzlement, Lorenzo had issued Miniati with orders to explain that, owing to the harshness of the economic downturn, only one-fifth of anyone's savings could be withdrawn from the Dowry Fund at one time, but in compensation the interest on the remaining savings would be increased to 7 per cent. Inevitably this restriction proved highly unpopular. For three generations the poorer families of Florence had taken to depositing their meagre savings in the Dowry Fund. Indeed, over the decades the fund had proved so popular that by now a majority of the population had stakes in it. In mitigation for Lorenzo, this raid on the Dowry Fund may well have been his only hope for restoring the city's finances. Had the city gone bankrupt, this would probably have meant the end of Medici rule; yet as far as the populace was concerned, the city's bankruptcy would also have resulted in considerable hardship – starvation even – and the inevitable civil strife would have torn it apart. Under such circumstances, Florence would inevitably have lost its independence to one of the other major powers in Italy.

Lorenzo would certainly have been mindful of such dangers, lending an altruistic, or at least pragmatic, element to this appropriation. On the other hand, he almost certainly used some of this appropriation to cover his own expenses. Yet the distinction between Medici expenses (often for civil entertainments and such) and the city's exchequer had by now become hopelessly blurred. This makes it difficult to assess the rights and wrongs of the preceding restriction on Dowry Fund payouts. As it was, Lorenzo's embezzlement may well have played a significant role in saving the city, and more. During the ensuing years there was a boom in trade from which Florence was well placed, financially, to benefit.

However, there would seem to be no mitigating circumstances with regard to Lorenzo's later dealings with the Dowry Fund. Faced with Innocent VIII's request for 10,000 florins before Giovanni could be confirmed as a cardinal, Lorenzo once again turned to Miniati, and this time the Dowry Fund was ransacked to the tune of 10,000 florins purely for Lorenzo's use, leaving it seriously depleted. To cover this, it was announced that the interest accruing to deposits would be reduced from 7 to 3 per cent. Not unnaturally, this move too proved highly unpopular.

Savonarola tapped into this unpopularity when he preached during the period, and was well aware of what he was doing. Indeed, some later commentators go so far as to claim that he specifically mentioned this appropriation from the Dowry Fund during his Lenten sermons in 1492, 'accusing Lorenzo of stealing the dowries of poor girls to line his own pocket'. Savonarola kept himself well informed about what was taking place in Florence, and would certainly have heard the rumours about Lorenzo dipping into the Dowry Fund that began circulating at this time. Whether he took the inflammatory step of actually mentioning this is less clear. However, we do know from the Latin notes that Savonarola made for his 1492 Lenten sermons that he certainly denounced Lorenzo in more general terms: 'These great men, as if unaware that they are just men like anyone else, want to be praised and blessed by everyone. But he who preaches the truth must attack these vices . . .' Did he elaborate on this theme when he actually spoke? Either way, Savonarola's congregation would have known in their own minds, from their own experience, a good part of what these 'vices' involved.

At long last, in March 1492, the news came through from Rome, confirming the sixteen-year-old Giovanni's appointment as a cardinal. This event was marked by a solemn ceremony on 10 March in the Badia (the eleventh-century abbey) at Fiesole, outside Florence, during which Giovanni received his cardinal's red hat. The following day Cardinal Giovanni, accompanied by his older brother Piero, entered Florence in a grand procession. A contemporary chronicler described the scene:

> the whole city, nay, the whole territory, was gathered together, as one man, from which it may be judged how earnestly this dignity had been desired for one of the citizens of Florence.

Following the celebration of high Mass in the cathedral, Cardinal Giovanni proceeded with all due ceremony through the streets to visit the Signoria, where he received gifts of more than ceremonial value, which the contemporary diarist Luca Landucci detailed as:

> 30 loads of gifts carried by porters. These included silver plate, bowls, jugs, and dishes, and all kinds of silver utensils which can possibly be of use to a great lord. So everyone said, all this must have cost over 20 thousand florins, though this hardly seems possible to me. But this is what people were saying, so I wrote it down. There is no doubt that it was an expensive magnificent gift. Praise be to God!

Rumour may indeed have exaggerated the value of the gift, but its sheer size must have been impressive, and there is no denying that this was seen by the watching citizens of Florence as Cardinal Giovanni proceeded across the centre of the city from the Palazzo della Signoria to the Palazzo Medici on the Via Larga. All this would seem to indicate that although rumours of Lorenzo's financial chicanery fomented a certain unrest in the city, which was further augmented by Savonarola's sermons, the Medici still remained to a certain extent popular as rulers. The chubby young Giovanni was undoubtedly likeable, and the citizenry spontaneously responded to him and his great parade, as well as to the honour that he brought to the city.

However, by the time of Giovanni's installation as a cardinal, Lorenzo had become too incapacitated with gout to attend any of the ceremonies, let alone appear in reflected glory at his son's side as he paraded through the streets. Yet he certainly saw Giovanni when he arrived back at the Palazzo Medici that day. Here the new cardinal presided over a ceremonial banquet in the main hall attended by sixty guests, consisting of foreign ambassadors and leading citizens. Whether Lorenzo actually put in an appearance at this banquet remains uncertain. Some suggest that at one stage he came, or was at least assisted, into the hall, where his crippled body and gaunt features shocked the guests. They had not realised that he was so ill, and only now understood that he was dying. Other reports suggest that Lorenzo had himself carried on a litter onto a balcony overlooking the hall, where – unseen – he gazed down at his son, who in the eyes of his proud father had assumed a new maturity with his office and seemed 'to have changed since yesterday'. Despite this, Lorenzo remained worried about his son's character; and next day, after Cardinal Giovanni had set off to take up his post in Rome, Lorenzo began writing a letter of advice to his son. The composing of this long letter must have taken considerable effort for Lorenzo, but he was determined that the Medici legacy should prosper, so that one day the family would fulfil his dream. Like father, like son: just as Lorenzo's father Piero, when he was incapacitated with gout, had worried about Lorenzo's 'exuberance' when he had sent him abroad to represent him at the courts of Italy, so in turn Lorenzo had worried about the behaviour of his oldest son Piero, and would now worry about his son Giovanni's 'extravagance':

> I recommend that on feast days you should celebrate less than others, rather than more . . . In keeping with your position, be sparing when wearing jewels and fine silks. Far better to have a few fine antiques and learned books . . . Eat plain food and take regular exercise, for those who wear the habit are prone to illness if they are not mindful of their health.

After this homely advice, evidently so necessary in Giovanni's case, his father moved on to more serious matters. It is clear that Lorenzo shared at least some of Savonarola's views of the Church, for he refers to Rome as a 'sink of all iniquities' where Giovanni will be regarded with great envy by 'enemies that had striven to prevent your appointment, who will do their best to denigrate little by little, your public reputation, attempting to drag you down into the very ditch into which they themselves have fallen'. But unlike Savonarola, Lorenzo believed that the city had its redeeming features, containing 'many good and learned men who lead exemplary lives', and he advised his son to behave likewise. Moving on to more practical matters, he advised Giovanni to:

> be sure that your conversation with all people avoids giving offence . . . As this is your first visit to Rome, I think it would be much better for you to use your ears more than your tongue . . . devote yourself entirely to the interests of the Church, and in doing so you will not find it difficult to aid the cause of Florence and that of our house . . . Remain close to the pope, but ask of him as few favours as possible.

Despite advice on such weighty matters, the anxious Lorenzo could not refrain from returning to his original theme, admonishing the lazy Giovanni that whatever else he did: 'One rule above all others I urge you to observe most rigorously: *Get up early in the morning.*'

There is nothing exceptional in this advice from father to son, yet it is its very lack of originality or insight that makes it interesting. Lorenzo's mind may have been dulled by pain when he was writing (or, more likely, dictating) this letter, but the fact remains that he was one of the finest intellects of his time, he felt that he was nearing death, and he was passing on his final advice to the young man he believed to be his most talented son. (Of Piero and Giovanni, Lorenzo had said: 'one is foolish, one is clever'.) Lorenzo was passing on the fruits of a lifetime of statesmanship, the wisdom gained by 'the needle of the Italian compass', no less. Yet his most insistent advice to Giovanni was with regard to his behaviour, his personality. Lorenzo had perhaps tried to follow the commonplace wisdom that he passed on; it had probably been the guidance passed on to him by his own father. Yet for the most part he had surpassed this advice, if not simply contravened it. His greatness as a statesman, and his flaws, had come about through his seemingly rash decisions, his impulsiveness, his belief in his own brilliance: the dash to

King Ferrante in Naples, the catastrophe at Ferrara, his decision to raid the Dowry Fund in order to further the Medici cause, his insistence on giving refuge to his friend Pico after he had fallen foul of Innocent VIII, his gesture in allowing Pico to write in his name to Savonarola inviting him back to Florence. Lorenzo knew that Giovanni too was possessed of such qualities – the precocious young cardinal well understood how to conduct himself, knew how to charm others, how to win over the crowd. He needed little advice here. What he had to be protected from was the one flaw that might destroy these qualities: sloth. Get up early in the morning – and the rest would follow. How Lorenzo must have been aware of the irony of this, now that he (never the sluggard) was confined to his bed.

Writing this letter to Giovanni had been a heroic effort. By now Lorenzo had become so ill that he was unable to conduct the business of running the state. The Milanese ambassador, representative of Florence's most powerful ally, was forced to wait a fortnight for an audience with him. His personal physician Piero Leoni had exhausted all the remedies he knew, and it was at this stage that the Milanese ambassador conveyed to his master Ludovico Sforza of Milan the gravity of Lorenzo's condition, causing him to order the famous physician Lazaro da Ticino to travel to Florence at once to treat his friend. Despite such measures, the physician Leoni still insisted that there was no cause for alarm. Lorenzo may have been ill, but his complaint was far from being fatal, so he assured Lorenzo's oldest son Piero, who was becoming highly agitated at his father's incapacity and Leoni's unwillingness to inflict any further painful remedies on the old man. Part of Piero's agitation appears to have been caused by the prospect of taking over the reins of power. Now just twenty years old, he had developed into an arrogant young man, but growing up under the shadow of his father's dominant personality had left him with deep inner uncertainties as to his own abilities.

On 21 March, some days after Lorenzo completed his letter to his son Cardinal Giovanni, he was carried on a litter from Florence to his villa at Careggi, in the countryside a couple of miles north of the city walls. This seemed to many an ominous sign: it was here that both Lorenzo's grandfather and his father had retired to die.

On 5 April 1492 news reached the Medici villa at Careggi that two of the city's famous lions had mauled each other to death in their cage. This was taken as an extremely bad omen by all who heard of it. These mascots were the living emblem of the city's heraldic symbol, the lion. The significance appeared obvious: evil events lay in store for Florence. The Florentine apothecary Luca Landucci, who kept a diary covering these years, would record the event that took place in the city that night:

> 5th April. At about 3 at night (11 p.m.)* the lantern on top of the dome of Florence Cathedral was struck by a thunderbolt and was split almost in two. As a result, one of the marble niches and many other pieces of marble on the side by the door leading to the *Servi* [that is, on the north of the building], were broken off in a miraculous way. No one had ever seen lightning have such an effect before ... Many pieces of marble fell around the building, outside the door leading to the *Servi*; one piece even fell on the paving-stones of the street, split the stone, and buried itself underground.

Amidst such a climate, even the great humanist Lorenzo the Magnificent found himself succumbing to the old superstitions. When he heard news of the lightning bolt striking the cathedral, he immediately demanded to know which side of the cathedral the shattered marble had fallen. As soon as he was told that it had fallen on the north side, he is said to have declared: 'That is the side facing this house. It means that I shall die.'

Another commonly reported story connected with the lightning incident concerns Savonarola, whose biographer Ridolfi reports: 'That night Savonarola was not able to sleep, and stayed up late trying without success to prepare the sermon he was to deliver next day.' Savonarola had then experienced a striking vision of how the world was to be scourged by God. Next morning he had included this vision of God's scourge in his sermon, and the congregation had immediately associated it with the thunderbolt. However, Savonarola's original texts in his *Compendio di Rivelazioni* ('Compendiom of Revelations') make it clear that he had this vision 'on the night before the last of my Advent sermons'. This would place

* The hours of the Florentine day were counted from the ringing of the Angelus bell at sunset, which at this time of year would have been around 8 p.m. our time.

Savonarola's vision just before Christmas 1492, around nine months later, giving it no reinforcing coincidence with the thunderbolt.

Despite Leoni's protestations to the contrary, it was now evident to all in attendance on Lorenzo the Magnificent that he was dying. The celebrated physician Lazaro da Ticino, recently arrived from Milan, took over from the ineffective Leoni, administering his elixirs of ground pearls and the like. At some point Lorenzo called in Piero, and in accordance with the family tradition passed on to him the secret of the Medici ambitions. The enormity of these ambitions must have seemed staggering at the time: the plans laid for them to become royalty and ascend to the papal throne. These were indeed unprecedented aspirations — yet, astonishingly, all of them would take place within fifty years. Such momentous events do not happen by accident: the precise details of how they would come about must have been relayed during this deathbed exchange.

Lorenzo was also to have another fateful encounter on his deathbed. Amazingly, this would prove to be of even greater significance to the city of Florence in the immediate future. This meeting would be the only known face-to-face encounter between Lorenzo the Magnificent and Savonarola.

Precisely how and why Lorenzo invited Savonarola to his bedside at Careggio is not known. All we do know is that he extended this personal invitation to the man he regarded as the only 'honest friar', and that Pico della Mirandola may well have encouraged him in this. Exactly how and why Savonarola accepted this invitation is also unclear. It seems likely that Pico della Mirandola, or maybe Poliziano, acted as messenger. Both are known to have been at Careggio during these last days, and either could easily have travelled across the fields to the city walls and in to San Marco. Either one's known admiration for Savonarola could well have proved the deciding factor that persuaded him to visit Lorenzo.

There are several contemporary accounts of this personal encounter between Savonarola and Lorenzo the Magnificent. The most vivid is that of Poliziano:

> Pico arrived to see Lorenzo and sat down beside his bed, while I sank to my knees nearby so that I could hear what Lorenzo was saying, for his voice was by now so frail that it could hardly be heard

... Pico had only just left when Savonarola came into the bedroom. He exhorted Lorenzo to keep the faith (to which Lorenzo replied that he held firmly to his belief), he must live a blameless life from now on (Lorenzo replied resolutely that he would be sure to do this), he must endure death, if this should now prove unavoidable, with due equanimity. To which Lorenzo replied, 'Nothing would be more pleasant, if God has decreed that this must happen.' Just as Savonarola was leaving, Lorenzo called to him, 'Father, give us your benediction before you depart.' After simultaneously bowing his head and composing his features in an attitude of suitable piety, he gave the responses to the preacher's words and prayers, replying each time correctly and from memory, not at all disturbed by all the weeping and wailing of his family and close friends which could no longer be contained.

Poliziano's description was written down just over a month later, on 18 May, in a long letter to his friend Jacopo Antiquari in Milan. There is no doubt that Poliziano was deeply distressed during his attendance at Lorenzo's bedside on these last days. He speaks of 'turning away from [Lorenzo] and trying to hide my emotions', and how on occasion he would 'rush to the nearby inner chamber where I could give vent to my grief without restraint'. Poliziano's emotional state may account for his version of Savonarola's three demands differing in detail from the version described in the Prologue at the opening of this book, which came down to us from Savonarola's followers (who probably heard the story from Savonarola himself). As we have seen, according to this version Savonarola asked Lorenzo whether he repented of his sins and believed in the one true God – to which Lorenzo replied that he did. Next, he demanded that if Lorenzo's soul was to be saved, he would have to renounce his ill-gotten wealth 'and restore what has wrongfully been taken'. To this, Lorenzo replied, 'Father, I will do so, or I will cause my heirs to do it if I cannot.' Finally, Savonarola demanded that he should restore to the people of Florence their liberty, which Savonarola believed could only be guaranteed by a truly republican government. To this last demand Lorenzo refused to reply, finally turning his face away. This version of events would seem to be more appropriate to the characters of the two protagonists.

Yet this was not all. Later evidence suggests that there may have been an even more sensational element to the exchange between the two men. This is mentioned in no sources, and would appear on the surface to be utterly unlikely, were it not for the fact that what was agreed on this occasion would play an unmistakable role in ensuing events, its details gradually emerging as these events unfolded. Astonishingly, it would seem that Lorenzo asked Savonarola to back the succession of his son Piero, and to support his rule over Florence. And even more astonishingly, this was precisely what Savonarola must have agreed to do. Lorenzo's reasons for this request are evident; Savonarola's motives were at the time less clear. Yet why did no source mention this pact? Those of Lorenzo's circle who were at his bedside, including Poliziano, may well have connived to keep this agreement secret – understanding that if it came out, Savonarola would certainly repudiate it, leading him to a more vigorous opposition to Medici rule. Yet why should Savonarola agree to support the continuance of Medici rule, when his preachings had been so opposed to it? Ironically, his motive was his wish to increase his power, and that of his monastery, within the city. As prior of San Marco, Savonarola was beginning to understand that not everything could be accomplished by straightforward preaching, even when this was reinforced with prophetic visions. If he was to achieve his aims, there would have to be a political element to his strategy: the achieving of power could not be done by spiritual means alone. For the time being, power remained inextricably linked with politics, and without power he would achieve nothing.

This was the first clear indication of Savonarola's conscious ruthlessness in his pursuit of his theological ambitions. It is possible to view this as unscrupulous, hypocritical or simply pragmatic. Previously Savonarola's will to impose himself, and his theological vision, on the people of Florence had not strayed from the path of determined righteousness – at least not in his own eyes, and not in any conscious form. Even so, this ruthlessness had certainly expressed itself in an unconscious form. Savonarola was not aware of what drove him to his prophetic visions; he neither questioned them, nor their motive. Here there was no unscrupulousness, no hypocrisy: he believed in what he experienced in his mind and saw before his mind's eye. There seems little doubt that he did indeed 'see' his visions, and was utterly sure of their 'prophecies'. Convinced that they were not his doing, he felt that they came from outside him, and they came with such force – so where else could they have come from, but from God?

Now, in pursuance of God's will, he was prepared to sacrifice even his integrity. If he was required to seek accommodation with the Devil, this too he would do. Like Lorenzo the Magnificent, he too had his secret long-term agenda. And for the time being it so happened that these two agendas were the same: focusing on the need for a Medici to succeed as ruler of Florence.

8

The End of an Era

LORENZO THE MAGNIFICENT died on the night of 8 April 1492 at the age of forty-three. All those around him at the Villa Careggi were distraught. During that night and the following days all manner of omens were said to have been witnessed in and around Florence. Poliziano mentions some of them:

On the night of Lorenzo's death, an unusually large and bright star was observed in the night sky above the villa [Careggi] in which he lay dying. This fell from the sky and was extinguished at the very time when it was subsequently learned that he had died. As well as this, for three consecutive nights torches were witnessed racing down the hills around Fiesole, all night long. These torches ended up over the sanctuary where the Medici family are buried; here they flickered for a while and then vanished.

Almost all contemporary sources refered to these omens. Guicciardini recorded how 'people heard wolves howling, and a woman became possessed in Santa Maria Novella and cried out that a bull with horns of fire would burn down the entire city'. And even the level-headed Machiavelli spoke of how 'there were many signs from the Heavens that this death would lead to the greatest calamities'. Lorenzo's late eighteenth-century biographer William Roscoe remarks perceptively:

Besides these incidents, founded perhaps on some casual occurrence, and only rendered extraordinary by the workings of a heated imagination, many others of a similar kind are related by contemporary authors, which, whilst they exemplify that credulity which characterises the human race in every age, may at least serve to shew that the event to which they were supposed to allude, was conceived to be of such magnitude as to occasion deviation from the ordinary course of nature.

The people of Florence – from the humble cloth-dyers of the slum quarters to the proud intellectuals of the Palazzo Medici – seem to have been particularly susceptible to such 'events' (as Savonarola was becoming aware). However, we can be sure that another of the 'events' described at this time did in fact take place, though in aptly ambiguous circumstances. When Lorenzo's personal physician Piero Leoni learned of the death of his master he became deeply troubled, blaming himself for what had happened. Despite all his renowned medical expertise, he had been unable to do anything to prevent this catastrophe. So great was his anguish that he fled from Careggio, hiding himself away in the remote village of San Gervasio, up in the hills some thirty miles west of Florence, and here he committed suicide by throwing himself down a well. However, whispers soon began to circulate that Leoni's demise was not all that it seemed, and some time later these rumours would surface in a work by the well-known Neapolitan humanist poet Giacopo Sannazaro, which openly stated that Leoni had been murdered on orders from Piero de' Medici. Apparently the suspicious Piero had become convinced that Leoni's seeming ineffectiveness was part of a plot to kill Lorenzo, and even got it into his head that Leoni had poisoned his father. If this was so, it was an ominous indication of the character of Florence's new ruler.

Historians of such repute as Guicciardini and Machiavelli, as well as the diarist Landucci, all seem to have recognised – even at the time it happened – that Lorenzo the Magnificent's passing marked the end of an era. Landucci, who ran a small apothecary's shop and was in many respects no more than a chronicler of events, certainly recognised at once the historical significance of what had taken place, writing in his entry recording Lorenzo's death:

In the eyes of the world, this man was the most illustrious, the most healthy, the most statesmanlike, and the most renowned among men. Everyone declared that he ruled Italy; and truly he was possessed of great wisdom and all his undertakings prospered. He had succeeded in doing what no citizen had been able to do for many years: that is, getting his son made a cardinal; which was not only an honour for his house, but for the whole city.

This passage is interesting on several counts. If even the small-time apothecary was aware that history was being made, and that an era had passed, then a large section of the population must have been aware of this too. Thus a sizeable portion of the citizenry of Florence would now have been mentally prepared for change, and perhaps even expecting it.

At one in the morning, just hours after Lorenzo the Magnificent had died, his body was borne aloft and carried down the road to Florence in a solemn procession accompanied by lighted flares. On reaching the city walls, the Porta San Gallo was opened and the body borne to the monastery of San Marco, where next day the citizens of Florence would file past to pay their last respects. Although the Medici considered San Marco 'our house', as prior of this monastery Savonarola must certainly have been consulted in advance about this — further evidence, it would seem, of a certain reconciliation between Savonarola and the Medici. Lorenzo's body lay in state for a day and a half, and during the afternoon of 10 April it was carried on the short journey to the Church of San Lorenzo, the traditional burial place of the Medici. This funeral procession advanced down the Via Larga, past the Palazzo Medici and around the corner to San Lorenzo, with the draped coffin followed by the *gonfaloniere*, the Signoria and all the foreign ambassadors. Poliziano, Pico della Mirandola and Ficino would all have been present, as would the painters Botticelli and Michelangelo, as well as Lorenzo's supporters amongst the leading families, such as the Soderini, Vespucci, Rucellai and Valori, and less savoury figures like his financial fixer Miniati. Amongst the crowds would have been Landucci, Machiavelli and the nine-year-old Guicciardini. The people of Florence lined the streets, watching in silence as the sombre tolling church bells rang out over the city rooftops. However, what they actually thought as the coffin of 'il Magnifico' passed in front of them remained a secret behind their silent, staring faces. How many of them genuinely mourned Lorenzo's passing? How many were secretly relieved to see the last of the 'tyrant' who had been so publicly decried and condemned by Savonarola? According to some sources, the entire city mourned the passing of Lorenzo the Magnificent, much as his death was mourned by the pope, as well as by rulers throughout Italy and beyond; according to others, only his immediate family, his intellectual circle and the grateful members of the Medici mafia were genuinely moved.

Contrary to the rosy report of Guicciardini, a view supported by Machiavelli, that 'the people of Florence were living in great prosperity until 1492', there are indications that some citizens had begun to suffer from a decline in the wool trade. This had become inevitable when the English, for so long the suppliers of wool to Florence, had begun to process and dye their own wool at source. The rich banking families, the merchants and small traders such as Landucci may all have benefited from the wave of 'great prosperity', but this had not filtered down to the precariously employed wool-combers and wool-dyers – the so-called *ciompi*.*

Even the surface prosperity alluded to by Guicciardini and Machiavelli remains problematic. It certainly existed: this was a major period of the Renaissance, with considerable spending on painting, sculpture and architecture (whilst Lorenzo was not alone in his spending on jewels and rare manuscripts). Yet this must somehow be squared with the assessment of de Roover, the major economic historian of the Medici bank:

> It is now generally accepted that the last decades of the fifteenth century were not a period of great prosperity, but witnessed a depression which was both lasting and profound. It played havoc with the Florentine economy and was certainly in part responsible for the straits of the Medici Bank.

Yet how is it possible to reconcile this assessment with the fact that a number of merchant families – most notably that of Lorenzo di Pierfrancesco

* Or 'the clompers' – so named after the sound that their distinctive wooden clogs made on the stone-slabbed streets, especially when they trudged off to work in the stillness of the dawn.

de Medici and his brother Giovanni – made their fortunes during just this period? Admittedly, this other branch of the Medici family accumulated much of its wealth through overseas trade, with Spain and the Low Countries. Yet some merchants undeniably prospered through internal trade with Milan, Rome, Naples and Venice.

One way to resolve these apparently opposing views of the Florentine economy is to accept that, in their different ways, both were true. The gap between rich and poor widened considerably during these years. An indication of this can be seen in the large numbers of the poor who began turning to religion – the trend so perceptively utilised by Savonarola. Well before the death of Lorenzo the Magnificent, an increasing number of Florentines seem to have been filled with a sense of apprehension about the future and turned to the Church for guidance. This came to a climax in the weeks during his final illness. On 5 April 1492, three days before Lorenzo's death, Landucci recorded that in the cathedral during Lent 'a sermon is preached every day now, with 15 thousand people listening'.

These were not sermons by Savonarola, though. He was at this time preaching at the smaller Church of San Lorenzo, where – without actually breaking his covert pact with the Medici – his sermons nonetheless remained highly inflammatory, to say the least, and became the talking point of many in Florence. Just three days after Lorenzo's funeral had taken place in the very church where Savonarola was preaching, a letter written by Niccolò Guicciardini, an older relative of the historian, told how 'Each morning in his sermon Savonarola insists upon repeating how all mankind shall suffer the scourge of God . . . and this very morning I am told he said that God had passed judgement, so that nothing can now save us.' A week later, on Good Friday, Savonarola described a vision that he experienced – the second of his great visions, which was in its own mysterious way as vivid as the apocalyptic imagery of his bloodthirsty revelation at Brescia. The vision revealed to him:

a black cross which stretched out its arms to cover over the whole of the earth. Upon this cross were inscribed the words 'Crux irae Dei' [The Cross of the Wrath of God]. The sky was pitch black, lit by flickers of lightning. Thunder roared and a great storm of wind and hailstorms killed a host of people. The sky now cleared and from the centre of Jerusalem there appeared a gold cross which rose into the sky illuminating the entire world. Upon this cross were inscribed the words 'Crux Misericordae Dei' [The Cross of the Mercy of God], and all nations flocked to adore it.

Surprisingly, this vision had not come to Savonarola during some fervent night of prayer in the solitude of his monastic cell. Years later, in his written version of his revelations, he would claim that he had seen this vision whilst he was in the midst of delivering his sermon, and merely described it to the congregation as he saw it.* One can but imagine the intensity of this experience and Savonarola's description of it, as well as the effect this must have had on his listeners.

But what did this latest revelation mean? Savonarola refused to be drawn on this topic, and for days afterwards Florence remained rife with speculation. Over two weeks later, a leading citizen wrote in a letter concerning this latest sensation: 'All of Florence is trying to work out what his prophecies are about.' We can only speculate, but it seems evident that Savonarola's revelation was but a further elaboration of his theme concerning the scourge of God, and how this wrath would strike the Church in Rome, whilst all those who remained faithful to the original word that Christ had preached in the City of Jerusalem would receive God's mercy.

The first tyrant whose death Savonarola had predicted, that of Lorenzo the Magnificent, had duly taken place. Then word reached Florence that on 25 July Innocent VIII had died in Rome. The second of Savonarola's three 'prophecies' had come true. Only King Ferrante I of Naples remained alive, and rumour had it that he too was now ill. The murmurs amongst the people of Florence began to grow. How could Savonarola possibly have known that such things would come to pass, unless he was indeed a true prophet, receiving word directly from God?

* Given Savonarola's fanatical adherence to the truth, such a claim is highly unlikely to have been a lie. Indeed, modern neuroscience would tend to support Savonarola's claim. During such 'visions', localised brain activity indicates that the person undergoing this mental state does actually 'see' what he claims to see. Similarly, when a subject claims to hear 'voices' speaking to him, appropriate brain activity indicates that he is speaking the truth. In neither of these cases does the subject feel that he is in any way responsible for these mental effects, which appear to him to emanate from a powerful outside source.

The answer to this lies in the original report of the prophecy that he made in mid-1491 in the sacristy of San Marco to the delegation sent to him by Lorenzo the Magnificent, a prophecy that was overheard by a number of onlookers. Villari's collation of their firsthand reports decribes how Savonarola 'began to speak about the city of Florence and the political state of Italy, displaying a depth of knowledge in these matters which astonished his listeners'. In this sense, Savonarola was undoubtedly a very worldly monk, who kept himself well abreast of the latest political developments in Florence, throughout Italy and beyond. In the absence of newspapers, for the most part word of events passed from city to city by way of regular diplomatic reports, as well as news from visiting merchants and travellers. A good number of such travellers were educated monks, passing between monasteries. Dominicans would regularly have arrived at, or passed through, the monastery of San Marco in Florence, bringing with them informed opinion of the latest developments in the cities through which they had journeyed. Under such circumstances, Savonarola would certainly have been aware that Innocent VIII was seriously ailing, that the degenerate seventy-one-year-old King Ferrante of Naples was also not long for this world, and of course he already knew that Lorenzo the Magnificent had been striken with a possibly terminal bout of his congenital affliction. Indeed, many of the more informed members of Savonarola's congregation would have found little exceptional in his 'prophecy' concerning these three tyrants. Others in Florence, more credulous and less informed, would certainly have found such 'revelations' about the fate of the great men of their time sensational.

But there was a further factor at work here, which had already won over many of the more informed listeners to his sermons – including exceptional intellectuals like Pico della Mirandola, Poliziano and even, to a certain extent, the dedicated Platonist Ficino.

It is Michelangelo who hints at Savonarola's true power. The teenage Michelangelo had honed his sculpting skills in the garden set up by Lorenzo the Magnificent close by the monastery of San Marco. Here Michelangelo had spent many long hours painstakingly copying the fragments of classical sculpture collected by Lorenzo. In the midst of his labours he would hear Savonarola preaching to his novices and fellow friars beneath the damask rose-tree in the monastery garden across the street, an experience that he would never forget. Michelangelo's character had been imbued with a profound spirituality from his earliest years, and he soon found himself listening intently to what Savonarola was saying. But more than this, Michelangelo found himself so enchanted by the manner in which the friar spoke that more than sixty years later he would confide to his favourite pupil Ascanio Condivi that 'he could still hear [Savonarola's] living voice ringing out in his mind'.

There can be no doubt that by the time Savonarola returned to Florence and became prior of San Marco he had become an exceptional preacher. He had learned how to project his voice so that it resonated in precisely the most effective manner through any church interior, from the chapel of San Marco to the vast echoing space beneath the dome of Florence Cathedral. He had also learned to tone down his thick Ferrarese vowels, which pronounced the soft Tuscan 'g' as if it was a 'z' (similar to the Venetian dialect, which is spoken and can be seen on signs in the city to this day). Referring in a sermon to the Bargello (the palace of justice) as the 'Barzello' would only have evoked smirks all round in church, and would have been mimicked amongst the people to ridicule him. No, the siren song that would remain in Michelangelo's mind for ever, and which so entranced the fine minds of the intellectuals and so swayed the common people, must long since have ironed out such risible flaws. This would have been a conscious process undertaken by Savonarola, which must have been carried out during his preaching tours of northern Italy after he first departed from Florence, when his sermons had proved such a failure that he had determined to give up preaching altogether. During his later preaching tours through the cities of northern Italy – all of which had their own highly distinctive dialect and accents – he must have had to adapt his voice so that it was both comprehensible and lacking any quaint colloquialisms or comic idiosyncrasies. This he could have done by trying out various different accents and assessing their effects.

In those peripatetic years, Savonarola would not have known that he was to return one day to Florence, but he would have been aware that the Florentine dialect was in the process of becoming accepted throughout Italy as the national language. Dante may have played his part in instigating this in the previous century by writing his *Divine Comedy* in Tuscan dialect, but the process had been assisted by his two great literary contemporaries Boccaccio and Petrarch, who had also chosen to write in the Tuscan dialect of their native region rather than in the more usual scholarly Latin. *The Divine Comedy*, Boccaccio's racy tales and Petrarch's love sonnets had spanned the entire gamut of literature, with their works proving so popular to readers of all tastes that the educated classes throughout Italy had soon become proficient in this Tuscan dialect. By the following century it would have been more or less comprehensible throughout northern Italy, where Savonarola (in common with other travelling preachers who delivered sermons to lay congregations) chose to preach in this version of Italian so that he had a better chance of being understood by as many as possible amongst his audiences. This combination of circumstances had meant that by the time Savonarola returned to Florence three years later he would have been fluent, and fully at ease, in the Tuscan dialect, the growing Italian language.

Another point to be borne in mind was that the sermon was invariably the main feature of a contemporary service, especially in Lent and at Advent, when there would be a series of them, delivered as often as not on a daily basis. Such sermons could draw large crowds and could last anything up to two or three hours. All this involved much more than orthodox preaching. In order to keep his audience attentive for such an extended period, the preacher would be required to put on a lively performance. This would often involve rousing rhetorical questions – which he would then proceed to answer himself. Certain sections of society, certain individuals or even particular members of the congregation who were present in the rows of pews, were liable to be singled out. Social types or modes of behaviour would be held up to scorn – often involving mimicry, to comic effect. Local events would be commented upon, and favourite devices such as irony (usually heavy), parody and forthright humour were frequently employed. As was polemic, often extended and rising to passionate invective flights or descending to plain harangues. But such methods were usually employed as a mere device to warm up the congregation, to involve all its disparate individuals. Then would come the most frequent and effective oratorical device: the invocation of mortal fear, which would be exploited to its ultimate degree – fear of death, fear of God's wrath, fear of hell-fire and all its torments.

Savonarola had become particularly adept at such methods after he had discovered during his Lenten sermons at San Gimignano, six years previously, how apocalyptic revelations could electrify his audience. Initially, he had implied that such revelations were taken from the Bible: the Old Testament prophets and the Book of Revelation. Later he would elaborate upon these, still claiming that they had the backing of the Bible, maintaining that this was the source of his words, even as his imagination extended beyond this source. Only when he became intoxicated with his own powers, to the extent that he began having his own revelations, did Savonarola begin to depart altogether from textural authority and orthodoxy. And it was only then that he had the first inkling that the power he exercised over his congregation from the pulpit could also be extended beyond the church in which he preached.

Savonarola wished to free his congregation from the corruption that had by now permeated the Church at every level. He wished to return to the simple spirituality of the original Christianity that had been preached by Jesus himself. The austere dedication required for such a life could easily be imposed within the confines of a monastery; it could even be observed by those believers amongst the poor who took his words to heart. And within the sanctified confines of the church, with its harrowing crucifixes, holy scenes and exemplary statues of the saints, many would be inspired to change their lives. But after the service the congregation would stream out into the bright sunlight of the city piazzas and streets, which remained unchanged in all their worldly glory. Friends would be greeted, news and gossip exchanged. Life would return to secular normality: family closeness and squabbles, the hard daily drudge of earning one's bread, the little joys and grim disappointments of everyday existence, life ground down by taxes, harsh laws and political masters. If Christ's words were to be fulfilled in any permanent and meaningful sense, Savonarola knew that his power would have to be extended beyond the confines of the church buildings and out into the streets of Florence.

Just as Lorenzo the Magnificent had planned, he was duly succeeded by his eldest son, the twenty-year-old Piero de' Medici. Opinions differ as to Piero and his abilities. Some have regarded him as inept, while others have seen him as talented, but inexperienced. He was a handsome young man, both physically and intellectually gifted. He loved hunting and jousting, but his favourite pastime was the rough-house football known as *calcio storico*, which took place in the large piazza in front of the church of Santa Croce and was not for the faint-hearted. Much like his father, Piero was well educated, with tutors of the calibre of Poliziano and Ficino, and he also wrote verse, though not as well as his father. In fact, throughout his teenage years he strove hard to emulate Lorenzo. So why did his father secretly concede that of his two sons 'one is foolish, the other is clever' – the former relating to Piero?

During Lorenzo's twenty-three-year reign the Medici had gradually come into their own as Florence's first family, with all traditional pretence of modesty cast aside. Lorenzo had not been slow to notice that Piero's privileged status as his son and heir had encouraged a certain arrogance in his character. This had sometimes led Piero to act impetuously or take rash decisions, in imitation of his father's fabled and courageous decisiveness (which would certainly have been labelled rash or impetuous, had it failed). It was perhaps inevitable that Piero should have felt an underlying uncertainty concerning his own talents, and a wish to excel in the eyes of his father – or perhaps even outshine him. His arrogance and rashness were merely symptoms of these ambitions and uncertainties.

Lorenzo had done his best to curb these flaws in his son, carefully grooming him to take over the reins of power. He had made sure that Piero cultivated the friendship of leading men amongst the Florentine families, such as Paolantonio Soderini, Bernardo Rucellai and Francesco Valori, many of whom were related to the Medici by marriage, and who had proved so loyal during his reign. Lorenzo had also encouraged Piero to listen to their advice. The continuation of Medici rule depended largely upon its popularity with a majority of the powerful leading families, to say nothing of the fickle support of the people. Unfortunately, Piero's arrogance had not done much to encourage his popularity. This in itself would not have been too harmful had it not been for his aristocratic wife, Alfonsina Orsini. Lorenzo had married Piero to Alfonsina in order to strengthen the Medici alliance with Rome, as well as with King Ferrante of Naples, who had been her mentor. But Alfonsina was a snobbish young woman, and thought that in marrying a Medici she had married beneath her. Worse still, she considered Florence a dull provincial city, lacking the aristocratic and papal residences of Rome, devoid of the ostentatious riches and culture of the city that held sway over the entire realm of Christendom.*

Like his father, Piero very much regarded himself as his own man, and as such he wished to establish his own style of rule, rather than merely follow in Lorenzo's footsteps. Yet at the same time he also shared his father's impatience with the petty details of the day-to-day administration of the city and the need to supervise the workings of the Signoria. As a result he retained his father's counsellor Piero da Bibbiena for this purpose, and also kept on the ageing Giovanni Tornabuoni as manager of the ailing Medici bank. Yet in order to put his own stamp upon the administration of the city, at the same time he began promoting a number of new figures – some of whom were deserving and genuinely talented, whilst others were merely friends. Inevitably, these new appointments displaced a number of influential figures, who were often related to the powerful families that supported the Medici. Consequently, Piero began to fall out with the likes of Paolantonio Soderini and Bernardo Rucellai and would soon begin ignoring their recommendations, eventually dismissing them altogether as his advisers.

Lorenzo's skilful political stewardship had ensured that advisers such as Paolantonio Soderini and Bernardo Rucellai were married into the Medici family, thus commanding the loyalty of the powerful families to which they belonged. Hence, the dismissal of Soderini and Rucellai left them in something of a quandary. They could hardly now ally themselves with those leading families who bitterly, if covertly, continued to oppose Medici rule. Yet it soon became clear that there was a solution to this problem of divided loyalties. The brothers Lorenzo and Giovanni di Pierfrancesco de'

---

* In the eyes of history, the very opposite is of course the case. By now the Renaissance was at its height in Florence, whereas Rome was still largely medieval in its culture. In the Holy City, the Renaissance was only just beginning – and even this was to a large extent due to imported Florentine artists.

Medici had by this time returned to Florence after their years in the Low Countries and Spain building up their business, whose main commodity was the lucrative transportation of grain. Not only were they considerably richer than the senior branch of the Medici family, but in order to protect their fortune they had followed in the footsteps of their relatives and begun building up a political power-base of their own. This was inevitably allied to the power-base established by the senior branch of the family. However, Piero de' Medici made little secret of his increasing jealously of Lorenzo and Giovanni, whom he regarded as mere upstarts, causing relationships between the two sides of the family to cool. This disaffection was particularly accentuated by the dismissal of Soderini and Rucellai. Unable and unwilling to break their ties with the Medici, Soderini and Rucellai let it be known that their loyalties now inclined towards the other branch of the Medici family, headed by Lorenzo di Pierfrancesco, who had already served his time in several senior elected posts in the city administration, where he had proved himself to be a highly organised and talented politician.

As a result, some began to question why the descendants of Cosimo de' Medici's branch of the family should simply accede to the rule of the city by right, especially if another member of the family proved himself better equipped to fulfil this role. Yet such talk gained little support within the Medici faction as a whole. These adherents rightly understood that if rule by the son and heir of one branch of the Medici family was questioned, it might not be long before the entire structure of Medici rule came under question. Why, in a city that so prided itself upon being a democratic republic, should one particular family take precedence?

9

Noah's Ark

IT IS JUST possible that such behind-the-scenes machinations might even have led to the early downfall of Piero de' Medici, especially if the people had turned against him. Yet they did not; and one of the main reasons for this must be accorded to Savonarola, who kept his secret deathbed agreement with Lorenzo and refrained from preaching against Piero. Savonarola had sensed his own growing power from the pulpit, and had even been willing to compromise with Lorenzo in the hope of gaining some political influence beyond San Marco. But at this stage any conscious idea of how to impose his beliefs upon the city of Florence as a whole almost certainly remained beyond his conception. After all, how on earth could such a thing have been done? He may secretly have wished to achieve this, have longed for it, even have dreamed of it – but such a thing was simply not possible. It would have involved something akin to turning the entire city into a monastery. Yet there is no doubt that some impossible dream along these lines was beginning to evolve in Savonarola's mind. How consciously, how practically, it is impossible to tell – but the evidence is incontrovertible. For it was now, during his Advent sermons delivered in December 1492, that his preaching began to focus upon an entirely new topic. Amidst his usual condemnation of the irredeemable evil that threatened to engulf the world, he began preaching his first sermons on Noah's Ark. Here was the vessel that had in biblical times carried the survivors of God's Flood, and would do so again when once more God submerged the entire world of his original creation because it had become so corrupted that it was beyond redemption. This was something more than the apocalyptic warnings and injunctions to the faithful to adhere to the original teachings of Jesus in the City of Jerusalem. For the first time, Savonarola was suggesting a positive practical idea for salvation on this Earth. Or so it would seem.

In fact, we do not know the precise nature of these sermons, for according to his biographer Villari, the printed version that has come down to us:

> is so ill-assembled and filled with errors that it no longer contains even the slightest hint of Savonarola's characteristic style, because whoever took down these notes was unable to keep up with the preacher's words. It seems that all he could manage was to jot down the occasional rough and fragmentary indication of what Savonarola actually said. This was later translated into a coarse form of dog-Latin.

However, according to Villari, who not only had an unrivalled knowledge of Savonarola, but also seems to have had access to other sources:

> Savonarola spoke in his sermons of a mystical Ark, where all who wished to escape and survive the Flood which was soon to overwhelm the world could take refuge. In the literal sense, this was the Ark of Noah which featured in the Book of Genesis. However, in the allegorical sense it could also be seen as the coming together of the righteous who would be saved. Savonarola then elaborated upon this theme, explaining that the length of the Ark represented Faith, its breadth was Charity, and its height was Hope.

Savonarola's 'strange allegory' then took on even more practical dimensions, as he explained how this Ark was to be constructed out of ten planks. Unusually for Savonarola, here he was contradicting the Bible, where God explicitly states, 'The length of the ark shall be three hundred cubits,* the breadth of it fifty cubits, and the height of it thirty cubits.' A clue to Savonarola's motive here can perhaps be gleaned from the fact that in Roman times the city of Florence was originally divided into *decumani*, or

---

* A cubit is usually reckoned to have been at least one and a half feet, making Noah's Ark around 150 yards long.

ten districts. Yet Savonarola evidently went out of his way to ensure that this interpretation was not widely recognised, for 'each day he would give a different interpretation of the ten planks out of which the ark was to be constructed'.

This curious melange of the practical, the metaphorical, the biblical and the spiritual would have a different emphasis to each section of his congregation. Indeed, its very mixture would have reinforced its powerful message. Even so, it was but a short step from the more spiritual aspects of the Ark to its practical manifestation, with its ten planks. Savonarola was clearly dreaming aloud here, letting his imagination roam, even if he still had no conception of how his Ark could be built. At the same time, he was certainly not making a political statement: this much he made clear. Piero de' Medici and the authorities would not have felt threatened by his sermons, which merely encouraged the citizens to live a more deeply committed Christian life. Savonarola's promise of support for Piero remained intact.

Such an argument may appear far-fetched, but its force is confirmed by Savonarola's attitude towards the rest of Italy in these sermons, a political theme that he returned to again and again. Indeed, Florence appears to have been the only major power in the land that escaped his censure during the course of these sermons. Delivering his regular Advent sermons had certainly taken a heavy toll on Savonarola's physical, mental and imaginative powers, and it was now, at the end of 1492, that the prolonged strain of this ordeal caused him to experience the third of his major 'revelations'.* Alone and sleepless in his cell during the long, cold winter night, Savonarola racked his brains, seeking inspiration for the final Advent sermon that he was due to deliver the next day. But nothing came to him. Then suddenly he had a vision of a hand brandishing a sword, which was inscribed with the words 'Gladius Domini super terram, cito et velociter' ('The sword of God above the Earth, striking and swift'). Later, he heard a great booming voice, which proclaimed itself as the voice of the Lord and announced to him:

---

* This was the revelation mentioned earlier, which was wrongly thought to have preceded the death of Lorenzo the Magnificent, allegedly causing the congregation to see the thunderbolt that struck the cathedral as miraculous evidence of God's scourge, as mentioned by Savonarola.

The time is nigh when I shall unsheath my sword. Repent before my wrath is vented upon you. For when the day of my judgement comes you may seek to hide but you will find no refuge.

As Savonarola's vision continued, he saw that amidst the roar of thunder the hand in the sky turned the sword towards the Earth, as if to smite it, whilst the air was filled with flames, burning arrows and other omens, which indicated that the Earth was soon to be overwhelmed by war, famine and plague.

The sword in the sky, signifying God's imminent wrath, was to become a central preoccupation with Savonarola, and a regular feature of his visions. Such were the horrific scenes that Savonarola witnessed in this 'revelation' that he refrained from revealing all of them in his sermon next day. Three years later, when he came to write his 'Compendium of Revelations', he would confess his reason for withholding what he had seen. He feared that telling of such outlandish things would merely make him a subject of ridicule amongst the people of Florence. Once again the full text of this sermon has not come down to us, but contemporary sources concur that, far from turning him into a laughing stock, this sermon in fact terrified a large section of his congregation, who had never before heard of such things as he predicted. All the indications are that this was the occasion when Savonarola warned that Italy was to be invaded by a new Cyrus,* whose conquering army would cross the mountains, sweeping all before it. Because this invasion would be fulfilling God's will, this army led by 'Cyrus' would prove invincible, and 'he shall take cities and fortresses with great ease'. In support of his chilling prophecy, Savonarola quoted the words of the Lord as they had been inscribed by the Old Testament prophet in the Book of Isaiah: 'I will go before thee and make the crooked places straight: I will break in pieces the gates of brass, and cut in sunder the bars of iron.'

However, not all were terrified by Savonarola's words. Despite the

---

* Cyrus the Great, who appears several times in the Old Testament, was the sixth-century BC King of the Persians who set free the Israelites from their captivity in Babylon, allowing them to return to their homeland to rebuild the Temple of Jerusalem. As such, Cyrus had long been seen in the Judaeo-Christian tradition as an unwitting instrument of God.

precautions that Savonarola had taken, many came away from his sermon convinced that this time he had gone too far: he had revealed himself to be nothing more than a deranged publicity-seeker. His claims to prophecy, far from revealing him to be a saint, were no more than hallucinations, the symptoms of incipient mental illness or simply imaginative ravings. But such opinions were in the minority, and over time this sermon would come to be seen as perhaps the most significant evidence supporting Savonarola's assertion to be a prophet. Here, undeniably, he claimed to see the future. And it would soon become clear what he had in mind. The westward expansion of the Ottoman Empire remained a constant threat to western Europe, from Hungary to the Balkans. It had only been twelve years since Ottoman troops had actually landed on the Italian mainland and occupied Otranto in the heel of Italy for two years, before withdrawing: it seemed only a matter of time before they would return. Indeed, in one of his sermons Savonarola seemed to welcome this prospect:

O Lord, we have become despised by all nations: the Turks are masters of Constantinople, we have lost Asia, we have lost Greece, and we pay tribute to the Infidel.* O Lord God, Thou hast punished us in the manner of an angry father, Thou hast banished us from Thy presence. Make haste with the punishment and the scourge, so that we may be returned to Thee. *Effunde iras tuas in gentes* ['Unleash Thy wrath upon our people'].

Savonarola found himself uncomfortable in his new position as prior of San Marco. During his earlier years at the monastery, the lax and often luxurious existence indulged in by the more senior members of the community, who belonged to important Florentine families and were often personal friends of Lorenzo, had brought him close to despair. But now that he had been elected prior, and Lorenzo was dead, he was determined that all

* The Asia referred to here is the orginal territory given that name – the province of the Roman Empire that occupied the bulk of western Anatolia (modern Turkey), including the entire Aegean coast. The tribute was that paid to the Turks by the Venetians and the Genoese so that they could continue their lucrative trade with the Levant.

this should change, and that San Marco should return to the austerity intended by the founder of the Dominican order. At the end of the twelfth century, St Dominic had travelled the highways and byways barefoot, preaching the original gospel of Jesus and living off the meagre charity provided by his listeners. After founding his order, he had insisted that its friars follow his example, taking strict vows of poverty, chastity and obedience. Yet despite taking these vows, Savonarola now found himself at San Marco, living amidst the many luxuries and beautiful frescoes donated over the years by the Medici family and other wealthy patrons. He was distressed by the apparent hypocrisy of his position, and longed for his community to live according to the austerity that he so enthusiastically preached in his sermons.

This preyed on his mind to such an extent that one night it caused him to have a dream.* During the course of this, Savonarola saw living in the afterlife the twenty-eight friars of San Marco who had died during the previous years. To his consternation he saw that all but three of these friars had been damned to spend all eternity in hell for breaking their monastic vows, especially with regard to poverty. During their life in San Marco they had all fallen prey to the desire for luxuries and a life of comfort. This dream confirmed Savonarola's resolve to embark upon his reform of San Marco. Indeed, he decided, it would probably be better for all concerned if the community moved out of San Marco altogether, for it was already becoming too crowded, though such a move would obviously involve protracted negotiations with higher authorities.

Savonarola's reputation for piety had spread, and was already beginning to attract to San Marco a stream of earnest young visitors intent upon returning to the simple Christianity of Jesus that Savonarola advocated in his sermons. These visitors came from far and wide and were not all young men; they included a number of scholars and artists, inspired

---

* This particular incident, along with several others, is usually referred to as one of Savonarola's 'visions'. Circumstances suggest that on this and some other occasions what he experienced was in fact a dream, rather than a waking 'vision'. The latter he would seem to have experienced (that is, seen in his mind) in a waking context whilst he was in a heightened emotional state (such as during a sermon) or when his mind was affected by his regime of excessive self-denial — which involved such mind-altering activities as painful self-chastisement, starvation or sleep deprivation.

by Savonarola's intellect and personality in much the same way as he had attracted Pico della Mirandola and Poliziano. Amongst these was the Jewish scholar Mithridates, who had instructed Pico and Ficino some years previously in the mysteries of the Kabbala. Both Mithridates and Ficino were striving to reconcile their essentially heretical knowledge with the simple Christianity of Jesus.

Amongst the artists, Botticelli appears to have had no qualms about surrendering himself altogether into the hands of Savonarola, although the suggestion by Giorgio Vasari that 'he gave up painting' during this period, in order to devote himself to God, has since been shown to be almost certainly false. Instead, his art now returned to the depiction of religious scenes, especially of a sorrowful nature; and Botticelli's colourful temperament, which had previously celebrated the pagan symbolism of the classical era with such serene beauty, now began to darken, taking on a more profound psychological depth. The case of Michelangelo, the other major artist so attracted to Savonarola and his teachings, is more problematic. Michelangelo's temperament had always had a deep religious strain. This was undoubtedly encouraged by Savonarola's teaching, but there is no evidence that the 'little friar' in any significant way influenced his art – which, although religious in a profound sense, retained a surface muscular sensuality that drew on essentially secular influences such as humanism and classical art.

Savonarola's closest friend amongst the Florentine intellectual community seems to have presented an altogether different case. Where Pico was concerned, all question of heresy was a thing of the past. During the months following his return to Florence under the protection of Lorenzo he appears to have abandoned all thought of creating any further philosophical works. Yet it is now clear that around this time he returned to writing. He had long since renounced any secular beliefs, placing his faith in the hands of Savonarola, who was more than ever impressed by the quality of his friend's spirituality and intellect. Savonarola would even go so far as to claim of Pico that 'in mind alone, he was greater than St Augustine'. This was some compliment, considering that the philosopher and theologian St Augustine was undeniably one of the greatest intellects amongst the saints, and as such had been an object of extreme veneration to Savonarola from his earliest days as a novice.

This superlative respect appears to have been mutual – despite there being such evident differences between Pico and Savonarola with regard to temperament, ambition, social standing and lifestyle. And there can be no doubt that these differences remained evident – especially where the last of these categories was concerned. For even during this most pious and penitent stage of his life, Pico found it impossible to set aside the habits of a lifetime. Ridolfi paraphrases 'a previously undiscovered note' written by Fra Giovanni Sinibaldi, one of Savonarola's most trusted confidants at San Marco during this period:

> From this we learn an extraordinary and unexpected fact which certainly does not accord with the much-vaunted 'life of a saint' which Pico was reported to have lived during this period – namely, the fact that he was living with a concubine.

In such circumstances – historical, linguistic and geographical – the use of the word 'concubine' (*concubina*) would indicate a common-law wife, rather than, as can be the case elsewhere, a mistress, an unaccredited extra wife or simply a 'kept woman'. Pico had evidently abandoned his previous licentious habits, but could not bring himself to forgo the pleasures of the flesh entirely. Yet why should Pico, who was now striving in so many ways to emulate his friend Savonarola, and was discussing theological matters with him on such a regular basis, have chosen to live in sin, especially when he knew all too well Savonarola's horror of fornication? Why didn't Pico simply get married? Nothing is known of his partner, and it is of course possible that in the manner of the period a wide difference in class rendered marriage out of the question. However, there could have been another reason for Pico remaining single, and this appears to be the most likely explanation. Pico had been encouraged by Savonarola to prepare himself for taking up monastic vows and entering the Dominicans as a friar. Pico was at first all for this idea, but would later be less sure if he was fitted for such a life. At any rate, although he blew hot and cold about this life-changing choice, it remained a strong possibility, and any officially documented marriage would have rendered such a vocation out of the question. Ridolfi also makes a rather surprising suggestion, writing that,

'According to Sinibaldi, Savonarola was well aware of this state of affairs and even confided it to Fra Roberto Ubaldini . . . the future chronicler of San Marco.' This all-but-unbelievable circumstance provides a key to a number of ensuing events that might otherwise appear utterly inexplicable.

Although Pico may have renounced his humanist ideas and heretical universal philosophy, Savonarola was determined that his friend should not renounce his formidable intellect. To this end, he encouraged Pico to write a work that would eventually become entitled *Disputationes adversus astrologiam divinatricem* (loosely 'Against Astrological Prediction'). Astrology had become highly popular amongst the humanists, because it attempted to show that human lives were dominated by psychological traits (star signs) whose movements through the night sky could be scientifically mapped in relation to one another (producing 'influences'). All this ran parallel with the burgeoning Renaissance sense of individualism, self-understanding and growing scientific awareness. Unfortunately, this was not psychology but wishful thinking, not self-understanding but self-delusion, not physics but metaphysics. And instead of allowing the soul the freedom to choose its own destiny, so that it could be judged fit for heaven, purgatory or hell, by implication its predestined determinism locked each human being into an inescapable fate no matter how he or she chose to behave. There could be no denying that astrology was incompatible with Christian doctrine (as indeed it was with the central tenets of the humanist outlook).

Savonarola was so keen to promulgate this argument, and encourage Pico to put his intellectual talents to good use in its cause, that he became a source of constant encouragement to his friend. According to Giovanni Nesi, a Platonist friend of Ficino, Savonarola assisted Pico by giving him 'advice and judgement' whilst he was writing *Disputationes*. How far this went is difficult to say, but other informed contemporary sources suggest that Savonarola's role may have extended to the point where he virtually co-authored *Disputationes*. Either way it was a work of some brilliance, which systematically dismantled one by one the foundations upon which this ancient Babylonian science of divination existed. Parts are unmistakably authored by Pico, such as when he reverts to ridicule, pointing out that astrologers – far from being able to prophesy great events – were not even able to forecast the weather. Other more subtle theological points could have been written by either of the putative co-authors. Typical of these was the insistence that by relying upon the movements of zodiacal signs and planets, named after secular images and pagan deities, the astrologers were in fact interceding with false gods. These owed no allegiance to God and operated according to their own movements or whimsical laws, all of which had nothing whatever to do with the Christian orthodoxy of the Ten Commandments of the Old Testament or with the New Testament teachings of Jesus in the Sermon on the Mount. In essence, the astrological universe was a mechanical universe with 'influences', rather than a meaningful universe with a moral purpose.

Despite such evidence of his continuing brilliance, Pico's mind had now undergone a profound categorical transformation. Previously he had sought to synthesise the ideas of various ages and religions into a creative unison, to reconcile all of humanity's experience of the world into one imaginative vision that would be acceptable to all human beings. This 'syncretism' was a positive aspiration, in tune with the Renaissance ethos, and it is not difficult to see it as a metaphor, prescient of the scientific world view that would begin to emerge over the coming centuries, with its universally applicable laws. To a certain extent, *Disputationes* can also be viewed as a scientific work – in that it is a rejection of metaphysics and whimsical associations involving 'influences' and symbols. Unfortunately, in all other aspects it represents a complete reversal of Pico's thought. Rejecting the Renaissance way of thinking, Pico was now returning to the characteristic mindset of the medieval era. Instead of attempting to create a truth by synthesis, he was now reverting to the medieval method of thought championed by Savonarola. The truth was to be found in the correct interpretation of a body of authoritative texts. Incorrect interpretations, or other unorthodoxies, had to be condemned as the antithesis of such truth, as heresies. Authority, as in the word of God, was the only acceptable truth. Pico's great intellect had reverted from the Renaissance to the medieval world, from the freedom of creative imagination to the limitations of orthodoxy.

Savonarola was, of course, most supportive of Pico's wish to take up holy orders, and did his best to dissuade him from his moments of vacillation. Yet even Savonarola knew that such a step would require more than his strong support and Pico's belief in his vocation. The charge of heresy

— the result of Pico's earlier philosophical activities — remained outstanding after Innocent VIII's death. The only way Pico could be pardoned was by order of the new pope, Alexander VI. Concrete evidence of Pico's reform and strict adherence to orthodoxy could certainly have been produced by the publication of his brilliantly argued *Disputationes adversus astrologiam divinatricem*, but Savonarola had his doubts about presenting such a work to the Borgia pope Alexander VI. Not only was the new pope degenerate and unreliable (facts to which Savonarola had already begun making oblique reference in his sermons), but it was also rumoured that the Spanish Borgia family were highly superstitious and deeply committed practitioners of astrology. (This may well explain why *Disputationes* was not in fact published, or even widely distributed in manuscript form, until well after the death of both its putative authors.) No, if Alexander VI was to be persuaded to drop the charge of heresy against Pico, Savonarola realised that some other approach would have to be used.

But for the time being he became preoccupied with another important matter.

10

A Bid for Independence

SAVONAROLA'S WISH TO move his Dominican friars from San Marco into new, more appropriate premises received an unexpected boost sometime around 1493, when a rich patron donated to the monastery a plot of woodlands, containing a wild chestnut forest, on the hillside of Monte Cavo near Careggi. Now it would be possible for Savonarola and his fellow friars to move out of San Marco and set up from scratch a monastery of their own. Savonarola had already thought long and hard about such a project, insisting that he and his fellow friars could live:

> a life of sanctity, erecting a poor and simple monastery, wearing woollen habits that are old and patched, eating and drinking sparingly in the sober manner of the saints, living in poor cells without anything but the bare necessities, maintaining silent contemplation and solitude, cut off from the world.

According to contemporary sources he had even worked out a suitable design for his new priory:

> He intended to build his new monastery in a remote and solitary spot, which would express in every part of its design the spirit of poverty and simplicity. He wished the structure to remain low, close to the ground, with small cells separated by partitions of board or screens made out of plastered wattle, all with their door frames, thresholds and latches made out of wood. None would have iron

bolts or keys. The columns would be constructed out of brick, not stone, and would be devoid of any decoration.

Here at last Savonarola's group of friars, utterly dedicated to their community, living out in the countryside in a simple building devoid of locks or protective iron bars, would be able to devote their lives to the vision of true Christianity that had become Savonarola's ideal. As Savonarola explained to his colleagues:

When we have completed the building of this monastery and men come to the door and ask to speak to any particular friar or father, the gate-keeper will answer them: 'Are you simple people? If you are indeed simple people you may come in. If you are not simple, you must leave us, for there are only simple people here.'

On the surface, Savonarola's motives for building his new priory were entirely pure. This would mark his withdrawal from the world and any attempt at political influence in Florence. But in reality, it was precisely the opposite. Only now does the full nature of Savonarola's agreement with Lorenzo the Magnificent on his deathbed begin to emerge. In return for Savonarola's support for his son Piero, and for refraining from preaching sermons demanding the freedom of the people of Florence from the 'tyranny' of the Medici regime, Savonarola would be guaranteed the support of Piero in his own political struggle for freedom.

Although Savonarola was prior of San Marco, the most prestigious Dominican monastery in Florence, and indeed the whole of Tuscany, he was not Vicar General of the Dominican order in the region. By a quirk of historical fate, the Dominicans of Tuscany belonged to the Congregation of the Lombardy region of northern Italy, which in turn belonged to the Dukedom of Milan. When the Vicar General of the Congregation of Lombardy was informed of Savonarola's plans, which were due to proceed without his permission, the project for a new monastery was immediately vetoed. Instead, Savonarola was told to move his friars into the adjoining building of La Sapienza, an educational establishment attached to San

Marco, at the north-eastern edge of the piazza.* According to some sources, Piero de' Medici supported the Vicar General in this move. Yet this can only have been part of a subterfuge, for Piero de' Medici was in close touch with Savonarola through their mutual close friends Pico and Poliziano, and remained well aware of his plans. At the same time, there is a letter from Savonarola to Piero de' Medici in which he states in the most loyal and respectful terms, 'it is my intention and that of the monastery to do all that Your Lordship [*Vostra Magnificentia*] wishes'.

In Piero de' Medici's attempt to emerge from the dominating shadow of his father and establish himself as his own man, he had decided that Florence should become less dependent upon its powerful northern ally Milan, at the same time strengthening its ties with its other main axis ally, the Kingdom of Naples. The veto of Savonarola's plans by the Vicar General of the Lombardy Congregation presented Piero de' Medici with a perfect opportunity to pursue his new foreign policy. He decided to send a delegation to petition Pope Alexander VI for the Dominican Congregation of Tuscany to be declared independent of the Dominican Congregation of Lombardy, as this link was no more than a historical anomaly, which no longer bore any relevance to contemporary Church administration.

However, following the death of his friend Lorenzo the Magnificent, Ludovico 'il Moro' Sforza of Milan now considered that he was the main arbiter of power in Italy, and as such he should be the one to be consulted with regard to any initiatives affecting the Italian political situation (which at this period very much included the Church administration). Any lessening of Milan's power, as impudently suggested by Piero de' Medici, was out of the question. As it stood, the Dominican Congregation of Lombardy provided Milan with both a useful source of information in Florence and a hold over some of the most influential clerics in the region. Milan would send a delegation to Rome to contest Piero de' Medici's petition to the pope, and this would be backed by the strongest possible diplomatic representations. Ludovico Sforza knew that in Rome there were powerful conservative elements within the Church who had no wish to see any such 'reforms' – especially one involving Savonarola, whose antagonism towards Rome

* This site is now part of the University of Florence.

and everything it stood for was all too plain. Amongst Ludovico Sforza's allies in Rome were the ambassadors from Venice, Bologna and Naples. Also, within the Tuscan Congregation there were many priors who fiercely opposed Savonarola and his new 'message', realising that his 'independence' would have an immediate and radical effect upon the administration of their own monasteries. Specifically, these included the Dominicans of Fiesole, Pisa, Siena and in particular the prior of San Gimignano. As if this body of powerful opinion were not enough, it was decided that the pro-Lombardy delegation should be led by none other than Cardinal Ascanio Sforza, who was not only the brother of Ludovico Sforza of Milan, but also a close personal ally of Alexander VI. Indeed, it was Cardinal Ascanio who had given the casting vote (encouraged by a mule-train of gold and jewellery delivered to his villa) that had ensured Alexander VI the papacy. Piero's delegation faced a difficult – if not impossible – task.

Yet the machinations of politics, and especially the exercise of power, were not all they seemed in fifteenth-century Rome, especially with a pope of Alexander VI's character occupying the throne of St Peter. Florence's entire case was to hinge upon this. In line with Piero de' Medici's new foreign policy, his choice to lead his delegation in Rome was Cardinal Oliviero Caraffa of Naples, the official 'Cardinal Protector' of the Dominican order, though he was hardly a man of influence when compared with his opponents. Piero de' Medici's seventeen-year-old brother Cardinal Giovanni, who had only been a cardinal for just over a year and was still inexperienced in the ways of papal politics, may well have had a hand in this seemingly ineffectual choice; but it may also have been endorsed by Pico and Poliziano, whose wide network of intellectual friends throughout Italy perhaps afforded them a somewhat better vantage from which to judge Cardinal Caraffa's character.

Around 10 May 1493, the Florentine delegation set out from San Marco for Rome to meet up with Cardinal Caraffa. At the insistent request of Savonarola himself, this small delegation included two of the prior's most trusted colleagues: his confidant and San Marco's future historian, Fra Roberto Ubaldini, and Fra Domenico da Pescia, one of Savonarola's earliest and most fervent followers in the monastery. Appearing beside the elegant Cardinal Caraffa in his ceremonial silk scarlet, his two monastic fellow delegates in their threadbare robes would not have seemed the kind of experienced political advisers likely to impress Alexander VI, but Savonarola insisted that he be represented at least in part by men of his own religious conviction.

On arrival in Rome, the delegation from San Marco met up with Cardinal Caraffa, and received further support from Filippo Valori, the sophisticated and knowledgeable Florentine ambassador. Just under a year previously, when the new Cardinal Giovanni de' Medici had first arrived in Rome, he had been accompanied by Valori, who had done his best to instruct him in the protocols, as well as the extracurricular ways, of the papal court. Valori had also attempted to monitor the young cardinal's behaviour, ensuring that he conformed to the advice set down at such length in Lorenzo the Magnificent's final long letter of instructions – above all rising early, living an abstemious life and taking sufficient exercise. This had proved a difficult task, for news of the death of Lorenzo the Magnificent had soon followed Cardinal Giovanni's arrival in Rome, whereupon the likeable and intelligent young Giovanni had quickly found himself invited to dine by one after another of his fellow cardinals, all eager to sound out the policies that the Medici and Florence were liable to pursue under their new ruler, his brother Piero. During the course of these sumptuous repasts, Cardinal Giovanni had developed a particular delectation for Roman cuisine, which was much richer than its Florentine counterpart, a taste that had soon begun to have a deleterious effect on his waistline. However, with regard to other sensual pleasures Cardinal Giovanni had remained remarkably abstinent – indeed, Valori and his informants, in common with other observers, had soon been convinced that he maintained a life of the strictest chastity, an all-but-unique virtue amongst the Roman cardinals of the period. But the attentions of Valori and the other Roman observers had been misdirected. Young Cardinal Giovanni was not in the least interested in women, and may already have begun indulging discreetly in the homosexual practices that would later flourish under his façade of jovial clerical chastity.

Cardinal Giovanni's careful tutelage by ambassador Valori had been reinforced by Lorenzo the Magnificent's advice on how to treat with the pope:

At all times take the advice of His Holiness . . . yet ask as few favours of him as you can. The Pope soon tires of those who bend his ears . . . so when you see him, talk of amusing subjects, but modestly, in order to please him.

All this had served the new cardinal in good stead, and he had been welcomed by the ailing Innocent VIII. However, this happy situation had not lasted for long. With the pope's death in August 1492 the situation in Rome had changed drastically, in a way that even a seasoned member of the College of Cardinals would have found difficult to foresee or even to handle. During the ensuing papal elections, Cardinal Giovanni had eventually been persuaded to favour the most popular candidate, Cardinal della Rovere, a man who was known to be well disposed towards the Medici. Della Rovere also had the backing of the powerful King of France, who had placed 200,000 ducats at his disposal to facilitate votes from 'undecided' cardinals. Unfortunately, Cardinal della Rovere's not altogether scrupulous canvassing for votes amongst his fellow cardinals had been devastatingly sabotaged by the unprecedented magnitude of Cardinal Rodrigo Borgia's bribery. To paraphrase a contemporary annalist of the Church:

[Cardinal] Rodrigo Borgia was proclaimed as pope Alexander VI. The result was unexpected; it was obtained by the rankest simony. Such were the means . . . by which in accordance with the inscrutable counsels of Divine Providence, a man attained to the highest dignity, who in the early days of the Church would not have been admitted even to the lowest rank of the clergy, on account of his immoral life.

Besides simony, his immoral life included a succession of mistresses, some of whose children (including the notorious Cesare and Lucrezia Borgia) would take up residence with him in the Vatican, an unprecedented violation of contemporary papal convention. Quite apart from his scorn for public opinion, the new pope already had a reputation for being ruthless and unforgiving.

When Cardinal Giovanni heard who had won the election, he exclaimed:

'Now we are in the clutches of the wolf, the most rapacious in the world. If we do not flee, he will devour us all.' Cardinal della Rovere had well understood the truth of these words and had immediately fled Rome in fear of his life – first barricading himself in the port of Ostia, and then removing himself into exile to France, where he remained under the protection of the king. For the time being, Cardinal Giovanni had remained in the Holy City, as his father would have wished, in order that he should gain experience of the papal court, but then he too had found it prudent to retire to Florence, where for a while he took up residence with his brother Piero in the family palazzo.

Giovanni remained in Florence and did not make the trip to Rome, which meant that the delegation to put Savonarola's case for the independence of the Tuscan Congregation included just one cardinal, when it could have had two. The presence of two cardinals on the Tuscany delegation, both well connected, could easily have swayed the issue against the Lombardy delegation, which contained just the one cardinal. Indeed, Cardinal Ascanio Sforza may have been the recipient of the vital muletrain of valuables that had confirmed Alexander VI as pope, but he was not quite the powerful force he appeared. As so often happens with collaborators in such enterprises, the benefactor was beginning to have his suspicions about Cardinal Ascanio, who was not only dangerously wealthy, but had now served his purpose.

Upon taking up residence in Rome, the Tuscan delegation began doggedly arguing their case, encouraged by regular supportive letters from Savonarola assuring them that they were following the will of God. However, it soon became clear that the Lombardy delegation were winning Alexander VI to their cause. The pope made it plain that he was finding the entire issue increasingly tiresome, to the point where it looked as if only a miracle could save the Tuscan case. Savonarola's most fervent follower, Fra Domenico da Pescia, certainly seemed to think so. Overcome with zeal by Savonarola's inspirational letters from Florence, he suggested throwing himself at the feet of Alexander VI, and promising to perform a miracle by reviving a man from the dead, thus demonstrating to one and all that God was in favour of the independence of the Tuscan Congregation.

Fortunately, Cardinal Caraffa decided against this radical tactic: raising the dead would have less effect on the bored Alexander VI than raising his spirits. On 22 May, when the time set aside for the daily negotiations had finally expired and the two delegations had duly been escorted from the papal presence, Cardinal Caraffa remained behind with His Holiness. Alexander VI had been rendered exhausted and irritable by the day's proceedings, but Cardinal Caraffa soon managed to raise his spirits, playing on the close connection between his Neapolitan charm and Alexander VI's Spanish ways. They were friends, foreigners amongst these resentful Romans with their outmoded aristocratic customs and pretentious disdain for all such 'foreigners' as themselves. The two men were soon laughing together, at which point Cardinal Caraffa drew from his robes the Brief of Separation, granting independence to the Tuscan Congregation, which he had had the foresight to prepare beforehand. Alexander VI was highly amused by Caraffa's subterfuge, but refused to attach his seal to it, declaring that he was far too tired to undertake any further business that day. Where-upon, with a deft move, Caraffa laughingly slipped the pope's ring from his finger and used it to seal the Brief, thus imbuing it with the papal authority. Alexander VI appears to have taken this as something of a jest, and merely laughed at Caraffa's impudence. But Cardinal Caraffa had plotted this subterfuge down to the last detail. After taking his leave of the pope, he at once passed on the Brief to Fra Domenico da Pescia, who had been ordered to wait outside in the antechamber. Fra Domenico then hastily left the Vatican and at once despatched the Brief to Savonarola in Florence.*

Unaware of what had taken place, the Lombardy delegation now arrived at the Vatican, demanding a private audience with the pope, during which they also presented the pope with a Brief for him to sign, this one with-holding independence from the Tuscan Congregation. During the earlier negotiations it had already been made clear to Alexander VI that Ludovico 'il Moro' Sforza of Milan regarded this matter with some seriousness. If

---

* The seemingly unlikely scene between Cardinal Caraffa and Alexander VI is confirmed by many sources (See the Notes for details). It has been claimed that the laughter and jocular horseplay involved in the removal of the papal signet ring indicate that Cardinal Caraffa may have remained behind with Alexander VI to deliver and share with him a gift from the pope's favourite Tuscan vineyard.

the Tuscan Congregation was granted independence, he would regard this as a personal slight upon his honour – one which would jeopardise relations between Milan and Rome, an alliance upon which it was known the new pope depended to further his political schemes. But by now Alexander VI wished to be rid of the whole affair and merely replied to the Lombardy delegation: 'If you had arrived less than ten minutes earlier, your request would have been granted.' It was all too late: what had been done had been done.

Savonarola was now free to run San Marco as he saw fit, instituting his reforms without the possibility of their being rescinded by any superior authority in the Lombardy Congregation. One of his first reforms was perhaps his most radical, yet it was also most true to the spirit of his order. The dying words of St Dominic to his disciples, the pioneers of the Dominican order, had been unequivocal:

> Have charity, maintain humility, observe voluntary poverty: may my malediction and that of God fall upon whosoever shall bring possessions into this Order.

Although these words were indeed inscribed on the walls of the monastery of San Marco in Florence, their observance had long fallen into abeyance. Around the time when Cosimo de' Medici had completely renovated the monastery, which had been publicly blessed by Pope Eugene IV in 1443, an appendage had been added to its constitution expressly exempting the community of San Marco from the Dominican ban on possessions, thus allowing them to own the various gifts that had been lavished upon them by their grateful benefactor. Besides renovating San Marco itself, Cosimo had also passed on to the monastery considerable properties from the Medici estates outside Florence, thus enabling the friars to work these lands, or live off the agricultural rents accruing to them, rather than remain completely dependent upon public charity. One of Savonarola's first reforms was to divest the monastery of these lands and return them to their previous Medici ownership.

Piero de' Medici was particularly gratified by this move, which he regarded as a payback for supporting Savonarola's cause. These properties would certainly help to augment his ailing income, enabling him the better to weather the uncertain financial state of affairs that had been left by his father. The city's exchequer remained in a parlous state, and Miniati was hard put to divert sufficient funds to Piero, who continued to maintain the lifestyle at the Palazzo Medici that he had come to expect under his father. On top of this, Piero still had the considerable expense of maintaining the Medici political machine, involving the payment of his loyal lieutenants and their 'enforcers'.

An indication of the Florentine administration's financial difficulties, and the extent of the population's poverty, can be seen in the fact that during these years around 30 per cent of the taxable population (that is, almost 10,000 people) were so impoverished that they paid no tax at all, while 50 per cent of the working population paid little more than a florin each. The citizens of Florence were assessed for tax puposes according to the *catasto* – initially a land registry, this soon became extended to a register in which each family in the city was required to list all its properties, income, investments and valuables. The *catasto* was originally carried out every three years, and later at longer intervals, by teams of highly inquisitive official inspectors; however, tax payment assessed in accordance with the *catasto* was enforced annually – though in times of need this could take place two or even three times a year. Another method of raising money by the government was the dreaded *prestanze* – an enforced loan pressed upon taxpaying citizens in a sliding scale according to their assets. Much like a modern government bond, it paid interest and waivers (which could amount to as much as 15 per cent of the full loan), and the initial sum could be redeemed after a certain number of years. Yet during lean economic times the government would frequently be forced to suspend these terms – with interest payments becoming sporadic (at best) and full repayments being delayed for an indefinite period. An indication of the confidence in these bonds can be seen in the fact that bond certificates, which were negotiable, would sometimes be exchanged during these lean times for as little as 30 per cent of the cash value of the initial loan. Even so, it was always in the administration's interest not to act in too high-handed a fashion with regard to such pressed loans. Genuine efforts would be made to pay back as much as the city's coffers could reasonably afford – for the members of the administration came from amongst the very families which were required to pay the most in the *prestanze*.

Savonarola now began to make plans for his new community on the slopes amidst the wild chestnut woods near Fiesole, a pious haven for 'simple people'. Although *semplici* was the actual word that Savonarola himself used, a more apt description would be a monastery for simple living, or living the simple life. In no way were most of the recruits that Savonarola was now attracting to the Dominicans simple in any mental sense; indeed, often the deepest enthusiasm for his cause was amongst highly educated young men – intellectual young idealists who appreciated Savonarola's learning and profound understanding of the message actually imparted by the Bible, which contrasted so acutely with the life lived by corrupt members at all levels of the Church during this period.

His dream of establishing this simple community separate from the world was no passing fad. As late as the following year, on 1 May 1494, Savonarola's close colleague Fra Roberto Ubaldini would write to him from Rome, explaining that he had at last managed to obtain permission from Alexander VI for Savonarola to build such a monastery '*vivae vocis oraculo*' (in other words, on the pope's verbal authority).

It is worth bearing in mind that as long as Piero de' Medici remained ruler of Florence, it was this spiritual aim rather than political power that remained Savonarola's main concern. His priority at this time was establishing a frugal way of life for the Dominicans in his new Tuscan Congregation, rather than inciting unrest amongst the citizens of Florence. The mystical Noah's Ark that would save the community, both sacred and secular, from God's scourge in the form of the coming Flood, now remained little more than a figure of speech, which he had used in his sermons. The enigmatic 'ten planks' for building this Ark also remained part of a growing, not yet fully articulated, dream. With hindsight, it is possible to discern that these two ideas – a salvation achievable only through a simple remote monastic life, as distinct from salvation for all those repentant and downtrodden souls throughout Florence who chose to enter the Ark – were inherently contradictory. A similar and simultaneous salvation would not be possible for both the elite few living a simple life consecrated to God and at the same time the many sufferers who had to continue to labour amidst the secular world. Either the few would have to expand to become the many, or the many would have to be made to emulate the few.

For the time being, Savonarola concentrated on the newly independent Tuscan Congregation, of which he was now the official Vicar General. At San Marco he introduced sweeping reforms that emphasised the simple life, made the Dominicans less reliant upon public charity (especially from the Medici family) and at the same time encouraged the monks to develop their intellectual skills and learn new crafts. The emphasis was on austerity: from now on, the friars would wear plain cloth robes, partake in fasting and prayer vigils, as well as developing a more egalitarian collective spirit. All meals would be communal, consisting of plain food and pure water – private dining in cells with influential secular friends on sumptuous repasts accompanied by fine wines would no longer be permitted. The cells themselves were to be stripped of all unnecessary ornamentation and possessions, such as gold and bejewelled crucifixes, private libraries of valuable or secular books, unnecessary or opulent furnishings. All friars were expected to work, in order to contribute to the cost of their bed and board as well as to the maintenance of the monastery. Each friar was encouraged to develop to the full whatever skills he possessed, whilst others were taught new crafts. Lay brethren and friars were instructed in wood-carving, others became copyists, transcribing sacred manuscripts. Some even became sculptors and architects. More intellectually gifted members of the community studied theology and philosophy, and there is evidence that Savonarola consulted with Pico on which of the foreign and ancient languages these friars should learn. Burlamacchi mentions that these included 'Hebrew, Greek, Latin, Chaldean, Moorish and Turkish', which suggests that Pico may well have been employed as a regular teacher at San Marco, along with Mithridates (who would have taught Hebrew), Poliziano and Ficino (who could have taught Ancient Greek).

Savonarola's purpose in having his friars instructed in such an extensive range of languages was twofold. The ancient languages would enable them to understand the Bible with the aid of earlier, more original texts, thus enhancing their theological insight and enabling them better to understand Savonarola's essential message. His second motive was characteristically sensational. In later sermons, Savonarola revealed that his friars were learning Turkish and Moorish in anticipation of the day when they would be sent on missions to the Ottoman Empire and North Africa to preach the gospel and convert the heathens. Such astonishing optimism can only be regarded as parochial in the extreme – severely limited in both a literal and a historical sense. Although it was evident that Savonarola had by this stage developed a supreme intuition with regard to the political situation in Florence, and even to a certain extent the whole of Italy, his claim that he wished to convert the Islamic world indicates an uncharacteristic ignorance of the wider political and religious situation. It would also seem to run contrary to his prophecy that a new Cyrus would cross the mountains to act as God's scourge and destroy everything in his path. Once again we are faced with a dichotomy that lay buried in Savonarola's vision: on the one hand was the impossible dream, and on the other the apocalyptic revelation that would destroy the world. Was it to be utopian simplicity or revolution?

Meanwhile, on a more practical level, Savonarola began despatching friars from San Marco out into the countryside to preach his new fundamentalist Christianity in the villages and towns of Tuscany. Each of these friars would be accompanied by a lay brother or working novice, who would take on labour to provide for their basic needs. In this way, Savonarola's friars were not discouraged from preaching by any fear that their often unpopular message would provoke the locals into denying them the alms upon which Dominican preachers had previously depended.

However, there were still those within the Congregation opposed to Savonarola's role as Vicar General. At nearby Fiesole four friars chose to depart from the monastery rather than submit to Savonarola's new authority. When the news of the newly formed Congregation reached San Gimignano, some thirty miles to the south, the entire monastic community unilaterally declared that it would remain part of the Lombardy Congregation. Dominican communities even further from Florence presented similar opposition. Here the friars knew Savonarola only by reputation, which laid great emphasis on his wild apocalyptic sermons and his fierce adherence to austerity. Few of these had actually heard him preach, or had had any opportunity to fall under his mesmerising spell.

In an attempt to resolve such difficulties, Savonarola decided to set off from Florence, accompanied by twenty or so of his most loyal friars, for the city of Siena. Although Siena was in fact independent of Florence, it nonetheless fell within the boundary of the new Tuscan Congregation, and Savonarola was determined not to lose control of this important city. His mission was given the full backing of Piero de' Medici, who saw this as an opportunity to extend Florentine influence over Siena, which at the time controlled a territory more than one-third the size of that controlled by Florence. For many years Florence had sought to absorb Siena, and Piero de' Medici realised that this move could mark the initial stage in such a process. If Piero could gain such a prize for Florence, this would certainly stand comparison with the achievements of his father, establishing him as a great ruler in his own right.

By the time Savonarola and his band of friars set out in June 1493 to cover the forty miles on foot to Siena, news of his mission had preceded him. According to an eyewitness report :

A rumour quickly spread throughout the citizenry of Siena that as the [Dominican] monastery of Santo Spirito was at the city walls, Savonarola and his monks had in reality been despatched to take the city for Florence.

Consequently, when Savonarola and his men arrived on 21 June, they received a hostile reception:

As Savonarola proceeded on his way to speak to the Captain of the People, three members of the ruling Signoria of Siena confronted him, giving voice to the most violent threats. Soon many citizens began joining in, while even the women attacked him and yelled all kinds of improprieties at him . . . Indeed, Savonarola was despised, rejected and threatened by the entire population of the city, and I am certain that if he had not departed they would have stoned him.

After being officially ordered out of Siena by the Signoria, and forced to beat a hasty retreat by the angry population, Savonarola and his monks hurried to the safety of the Florentine border. Here, in biblical fashion, Savonarola ceremoniously shook the dust of Siena from his feet.

Later that summer Savonarola and another accompanying band of monks set off for Pisa, another city that fell within the jurisdiction of the newly independent Tuscany Congregation. Pisa had long maintained its independence of Florence, but had been conquered by the republic earlier in the century. Here again his arrival on 20 August was greeted with much suspicion, not least by the Dominican friars of Santa Caterina. Forty of the forty-four friars simply refused to submit to his authority and departed from the city; whereupon Savonarola appointed twenty-two of the friars who were accompanying him to remain behind and take up residence in the depleted monastery.

That year Savonarola gave the Advent sermons in Florence Cathedral, probably preaching on a text from Genesis and Psalm 73. Although his biographer Ridolfi has his doubts about the transcriptions of these sermons, he remarks:

> They contain a few of the usual outbursts against wicked priests and the Court of Rome, but no reference to visions, and none (which is stranger) to the affairs of the city, which . . . is not even mentioned.

Savonarola and Piero de' Medici continued their curious alliance, while Poliziano, Pico della Mirandola and even Botticelli – to name but a few of the Palazzo Medici intellectual circle – seemed to find no contradiction in remaining closely involved on an all-but-daily basis with both Piero and the prior of San Marco.

II

'Italy faced hard times . . . beneath stars hostile to her good'

I N 1493 THE POLITICAL situation in Italy took a sudden and dramatic turn for the worse. The balance of power had still survived, somewhat precariously since the death of Lorenzo the Magnificent. Yet it was now to be upset by the overweening and wholly misguided ambitions of Ludovico 'il Moro' Sforza of Milan. Ludovico was not in fact the rightful Duke of Milan, but was only acting as de facto ruler for his nephew, the young Gian Galeazzo Sforza, who had succeeded his assassinated father at the age of eight. In 1488, at the age of nineteen, Gian Galeazzo had married his cousin Isabella of Naples, the granddaughter of King Ferrante. However, before Gian Galeazzo came of age it became apparent that his uncle Ludovico had no intention of surrendering his power to his nephew, whom he regarded as a weak and simple young man. Instead, when Gian Galeazzo became twenty-one, Ludovico took the novel step of ordering the Milanese mint to begin issuing double-headed currency – with his head on one side, and Gian Galeazzo's on the other. At the same time, he covertly confined Gian Galeazzo and his wife Isabella to their estates at Pavia, just over twenty miles south of Milan in the Po valley. Gian Galeazzo was little concerned by this move, being more interested in hunting and feasting. Isabella, on the other hand, was not prepared to settle for such belittling treatment and turned to her father, the heir to the throne of Naples, to persuade King Ferrante to order the instatement of her husband as the rightful duke. So unconcerned was Gian Galeazzo with taking over his duties as ruler of Milan that he even informed his uncle of his wife's scheming, convincing Ludovico that when Isabella's father Alfonso ascended to the throne of Naples on the death of the aged and ailing King Ferrante, he intended to assert Gian Galeazzo's claim to power. Should Alfonso act upon this threat, Ludovico realised that he was in a vulnerable position. Despite the prevailing uneasy peace amongst the major regional powers, Venice remained Milan's traditional enemy, Florence was simply too weak to come to his assistance and, despite his alliance with Alexander VI, he rightly felt that he could not trust the pope.

In order to counter this threat, Ludovico Sforza then made what he considered to be a diplomatic masterstroke. In 1493, in a wholly unexpected move, he sought help from outside Italy, appealing for support to Charles VIII, the new young King of France, at the time the most powerful nation in Europe. In return for such support, Ludovico Sforza promised that he would support Charles VIII if he chose to enforce his claim to the kingdom of Naples, to which he had a somewhat obscure entitlement by way of his paternal grandmother. This certainly had the effect of cowing Isabella, and Ludovico now saw himself as the heir to Lorenzo the Magnificent as the arbiter of the Italian political scene. He even 'boasted that the Pope was his chaplain, the Signoria of Venice was his chamberlain, and the King of France his courier'.

In a moral parable that Savonarola would recognise, the words of the Old Testament prophet Hosea rang down through the centuries, once again finding their fulfilment: 'For they sow the wind and reap the whirlwind.' What Ludovico Sforza had not realised was that Charles VIII had been waiting for just such an opportunity. Long before ascending to the throne he had dreamed of invading Italy and proving his knightly valour in emulation of the legendary tales to which he had listened so avidly during his childhood.

In reality, the education of Charles VIII had consisted of little else but listening to tales of chivalry. He could not have read them himself, for he could neither read nor write throughout his childhood, and even when he was twenty-one and assumed full royal powers he remained barely literate. Charles VIII had been an odd child, and had grown into an even odder man — both mentally and physically. His body was short and hunched, while he walked with a limp that was accentuated by his oversized feet, both of which were said to have six toes, suggesting the possibility that at least his physical defects were the result of inbreeding amongst the French royal families. Nor did his behaviour indicate normality: his apparent naivety was accentuated by the fact that his mouth constantly gaped open between his fleshy lips, and his habit of muttering to himself made many feel uneasy in his presence. His prodigious sexual appetite was accompanied by an overweening ambition that bordered on megalomania. This was indulged by his family who wished, for their own purposes, to have him out of the way. His dreams of chivalrous adventure were quickly encouraged, and in no time he envisioned his invasion of Naples as but the prelude to a glorious crusading campaign which would see the retaking of Constantinople from the Ottoman Turks, followed by the capture of Jerusalem. Such was the way the young Charles VIII saw himself going down in history. Naive he may have been, but the power of his presence, his ambition and the nation he ruled made all fear him.

However, Charles VIII was aware that it would have been impolitic, and certainly unwise, simply to march into Italy and lay claim to the throne of Naples. This would set a dangerous precedent. There were many outstanding, if more or less justified, claims to the thrones of Europe (not least his own), and taking unprovoked action to depose the long-enthroned King Ferrante of Naples would probably unite most of Italy against him. Such a move was best avoided, as he would have to cross more than 500 miles of Italian territory just to reach Naples, and he needed this territory to be neutral, or at least acquiescent, if he was to maintain his overland supply lines and links with France. Charles VIII, as well as his advisers and family, knew that he needed some justification if he was to put the first stage of his glorious plan into action: for the moment, he would have to bide his time.

Meanwhile, during January 1494 Italy suffered the coldest winter of the century. The Florentine diarist Landucci recorded:

20th January . . . Florence suffered the worst snowstorm that even the oldest living citizens could remember. And amongst other extraordinary things, this was accompanied by such a violent tempest that for the whole day it was not possible to open any shops, or even any doors or windows. The blizzard lasted from the time of the morning Ave Maria until the Ave next morning, without ceasing for a moment throughout the entire twenty-four hours. Neither did the tremendous wind abate, so that there was not a crack or a hole, however small, which did not let a pile of snow into the house. Indeed, there was not one house so sufficiently sealed that it did not become filled with such a quantity of snow that it took days afterwards to clear it out. Along every street there were such piles of snow that in several places neither man nor beast was able to get through. There was so much snow that it took days before it all finally melted away, just like when boys make a snow-lion. It would be impossible to believe this if I had not seen it with my own eyes.

This may well have been the occasion when Michelangelo carved a large lion (the emblem of the city) out of packed snow for Piero de' Medici, just as Leonardo da Vinci had carved ice-sculptures for his father. Lorenzo the Magnificent had been particularly impressed by the youthful Michelangelo's precocious sculptural talent and had invited him to live at the Palazzo Medici. Piero was just three years older than Michelangelo and they knew each other well, despite being such disparate characters. Piero's preference for dashing physical pursuits such as hunting and fencing, and his enjoyment of the good life, contrasted with Michelangelo's intense personality, his obsessive sculpting and his frugal habits. Even so, Michelangelo remained attached to the difficult Piero, who would often treat the young sculptor with some arrogance; despite such patronising behaviour, Piero for his part retained a regard for his father's highly accomplished protégé, and ensured that the ambitious eighteen-year-old Michelangelo continued to receive commissions from wealthy patrons, especially the Church.

The other artist who remained deeply attached to Piero was Botticelli, who had painted a number of colourful and lively portraits of Piero as a young man. But Botticelli was also beginning to feel the strain of divided loyalties, becoming increasingly pained by the contrast between life at the Palazzo Medici and the simple life he wished to follow in accord with Savonarola's preaching. This inner conflict had by now begun to affect his work. Instead of vivid, colourful celebrations of humanism, such as *Primavera* and *The Birth of Venus*, he had turned to more sorrowful religious subjects.

It was Lorenzo di Pierfrancesco who suggested that Botticelli should work on a topic deeply in keeping with his spiritual preoccupations, and commissioned him to produce a series of drawings illustrating scenes from Dante's *Divine Comedy*. This was a project to which Botticelli would return again and again over the years, and his vivid renderings of the tortures undergone by those souls condemned for eternity to inhabit the Inferno give us an insight into his troubled state of mind. His illustration for the ring of hell inhabited by 'a horde of shades' who in life had indulged in 'perverse vices [that] damage and corrupt the natural powers of the body' is particularly apt. These are the sodomites against whom Savonarola so continually railed in his sermons, and Botticelli may well have believed that this was the fate to which he too would one day be damned throughout eternity. From Dante's words he conjures up a horrific image of a multitude of naked bodies writhing and staggering in pitiful agony across the burning sand beneath the continual rain of falling flakes of fire, an image that consciously echoes the biblical fate of the citizens of Sodom and Gomorrah.

On 29 January 1494, Landucci recorded in his diary: 'We heard that the King of Naples was dead.' The throne of Naples was immediately claimed by his son, who installed himself as King Alfonso II. Charles VIII now had his opportunity to contest this, staking his own claim to the kingdom of Naples. The French king's claim was dismissively rejected by Alfonso II, and Charles VIII began assembling a large French army in preparation for an invasion across the Alps. In order that the French army could reach Naples it would have to march through the territories of Milan, Florence and the Papal States. Ludovico Sforza in Milan was only too happy to welcome Charles VIII; meanwhile Alexander VI and Piero de' Medici prevaricated. Piero de' Medici's foreign policy had been aimed at strengthening Florence's ties with Naples, while at the same time loosening his close dependence upon Milan. This shift in diplomacy had been put into practice in the dispute over the Tuscan Congregation's independence from the Lombardy Congregation, which had also strengthened Piero's links with the pope. Yet Alexander VI remained as untrustworthy as ever. Piero de' Medici realised that if he backed Naples, and the pope decided not to support him, he might well be left on his own, facing the might of the

French army. Yet if he chose not to back Alfonso II, and the pope sided with Naples, with the Venetians joining this alliance, Florence might once again stand in peril, this time from its Italian neighbours – especially if, for any reason, Charles VIII postponed his invasion.

In the spring of 1494 news reached Florence that this was precisely what he had done. Even the mighty French exchequer was unable to bear the cost of such an ambitious campaign as Charles VIII had in mind, whilst on top of this the king had reason to suspect that his position as monarch lay under threat, both because of his own scheming family and because of his general unpopularity amongst the people. On hearing this news, Piero de' Medici pledged Florence to support Alfonso II, an alliance that was soon favoured by Alexander VI. Meanwhile the pope's sworn enemy Cardinal della Rovere, who remained in exile at the French court, did his best to encourage Charles VIII in his ambition to invade Italy – a move that would surely result in the defeat of Alexander VI. Eventually the French king was persuaded: he had been reassured that his position was safe enough at home, and he knew that he had sufficient funds at least to launch the expedition – more funds could be plundered en route, especially from the pope, and perhaps even from Florence.

Florence had traditionally been an ally of France, a policy that had been carefully built up over the previous decades, especially during the reign of Lorenzo the Magnificent. The Signoria was in the habit of frequently sending envoys to the French court to maintain friendly relations with the French king, who had granted many favours to Florence. For example, a good portion of the rich benefices bought by Lorenzo the Magnificent for Piero's younger brother, the future Cardinal Giovanni Medici, had been graciously permitted by the previous French king, Louis XI, and the ensuing regency. It would seem that before Piero had taken his decision to switch alliegance, he had not even bothered to consult his brother, Cardinal Giovanni – who was living with him at the Palazzo Medici, and still relied upon these French benefices for a sizeable part of his income.

Giovanni was not the only one to lose from Piero's decision. During Lorenzo's reign, Piero di Gino Capponi had been appointed ambassador to the French court and had become particularly close to the young Charles VIII, sympathising with the gauche, gnomic, splay-footed child, who was widely derided during his minority, when France had been ruled by the regency of his powerful and intelligent older sister Anne of France.* Charles VIII, for his part, had come to regard ambassador Capponi with deep affection; consequently, Piero's breaking of the Florentine alliance with France was regarded by the touchy French king as an act of deep personal betrayal.

To compromise his brother and Capponi in this way suggests that Piero had taken this foreign-policy decision without even a semblance of democratic consultation. The largely Medici-appointed administration was hardly popular during this period, yet significantly the people of Florence regarded the *gonfaloniere* and the Signoria as blameless for the break with France. As a result, not only were there grumblings amongst the people, but many amongst the leading families – the Capponi in particular – now began turning against Piero, who struck them as arrogant and incompetent. Already he was coming to be regarded by his subjects as an unworthy successor to 'il Magnifico', earning for himself the reputation that led his enemies to refer to him as 'Piero il Fatuo', Piero the Fatuous. Others would refer to him less harshly as 'Piero il Sfortunato', Piero the Unfortunate, which perhaps does more justice to him in the impossible situation that he now faced – forced to choose between France and untrustworthy Italian alliances. The situation in which Florence found itself, combined with the mortal peril facing Italy, would probably have defeated even the most able of leaders.

Even so, many at the time could not help but compare the Florentine leader's qualities with those of his seemingly more gifted cousin, Lorenzo di Pierfrancesco de' Medici. It was evident that Lorenzo di Pierfrancesco was the one possessed of the older Medici values, the astute commercial and political wisdom that had been exhibited so admirably by his great-uncle Cosimo de' Medici. In a recognisably similar fashion, Lorenzo di Pierfrancesco had accumulated a fortune in various commercial ventures, and when he had been voted onto various government committees he had proved himself an able administrator. Like Cosimo de' Medici he conducted himself modestly, making him popular amongst the leading familes.

* Louis XI had ensured that his eldest daughter Anne of France became regent after his death, bestowing upon her what he regarded as the highest compliment by describing her as 'the least deranged woman in France'.

As informed opinion began to turn against Piero de' Medici, certain obvious ideas presented themselves. Yet each had their flaws. For instance, any attempt to overthrow Piero at such a time would have provoked far too great an upheaval, and would certainly have weakened Florence's position in Italy. On the other hand, if Lorenzo di Pierfrancesco were to be elected *gonfaloniere*, and thus take over as official head of state, this would prove equally ineffective, as the *gonfaloniere* only held office for two months. Still, there was no denying that many now looked upon Lorenzo di Pierfrancesco as Piero's natural successor.

Both men were aware of this growing groundswell of public opinion. Lorenzo di Pierfrancesco did his best to play it down: he genuinely had no wish to take over the reins of power. Piero de' Medici, on the other hand, felt that he was being increasingly undermined by his older and more wealthy cousin. This only fuelled his feelings of uncertainty, which led to an increasing high-handedness in his behaviour.

Things came to a head between the two cousins during the season of spring balls that traditionally followed Easter (which in 1494 fell on 30 March). At one particular ball, Piero de' Medici and Lorenzo di Pierfrancesco's younger brother Giovanni found themselves rivals for the attentions of an attractive young woman with whom they had both fallen in love. When Giovanni di Pierfrancesco wished to dance with her, Piero became incensed and publicly slapped his cousin in the face. The traditional response to such an insult would have been a challenge to a duel, but no such option was open to Giovanni as Piero was ruler of the city. Giovanni was thus forced to accept this public insult and withdraw in disgrace. The split in the Medici family was now a matter of gossip throughout the whole city, and Piero realised that he should, like his father, take immediate and decisive action. Instead, mindful of public opinion being against him, he dithered for some days, during which he was informed that Giovanni di Pierfrancesco, along with his brother Lorenzo, was strongly in favour of abandoning the alliance with Naples and instead forming an alliance with Charles VIII. This was certainly true, and Piero de' Medici was probably well aware of it already. However, worse was to come. Charles VIII had previously despatched his close adviser Philippe de Commines as an envoy into Italy to seek out the lie of the land: who was liable to support his invasion, and who would oppose it? Piero had informed Commines that Florence would not grant the French army safe passage across Florentine territory on its way to Naples; but he now learned that Lorenzo di Pierfrancesco had been in contact with Commines. He had sent word through Commines to Charles VIII, claiming that although Piero de' Medici had declared for Naples, promising to defend Florentine territory against the incursion of any French army, an overwhelming majority of the citizens of Florence felt otherwise, and the French army would thus be able to cross Florentine territory with impunity. This assessment of the situation was undoubtedly accurate; but it was also claimed that Lorenzo and Giovanni di Pierfrancesco had written to Charles VIII promising that they would give financial assistance to him and his army in their passage across Tuscany. If true, this was treason, meriting the harshest punishment. In fact, we learn from the diarist Landucci that on 26 April:

> Lorenzo and Giovanni, sons of Piero Francesco de' Medici, were locked up in the Palagio*; and it was said that some wanted them to be executed, but no one could say why. On the 29th they were let out; and on the 14th May they went away, being restricted within certain boundaries.

The time-lapses between the dates, as well as the decision not to go ahead with the death-penalty, indicate some indecision on Piero's behalf, as well as divisions amongst the ruling Signoria. Indeed, on 4 May, in the very midst of these doubtless acrimonious discussions, a vital event took place. As confirmed by Guicciardini and Landucci, a delegation of four French ambassadors travelled through Florence on their way to Rome. Whilst in the city they passed on the news that their king was in the midst of preparations for an invasion of Italy. He requested the support of Florence, or at least safe conduct for his army as it passed across Florentine territory. News soon leaked out that Piero had refused this request,

---

* Almost certainly the Palazzo del Bargello, residence of the *Podestà* (Chief Magistrate). This fortified building, just around the corner from the Palazzo della Signoria, housed the city's courts and became notorious as the city's prison, where torture became a routine method of punishment; executions took place in the inner yard.

despite the attempts of wise and important citizens to dissuade him from this course.

It was just days after this that Lorenzo and Giovanni di Pierfrancesco both 'went away, being restricted within certain boundaries'. In effect, this was not quite so lenient as it might sound: both were rearrested, formally banished from the city (thus being deprived of all their civil rights), and escorted under armed guard to their separate villas, where they were held under strict house-arrest – Lorenzo di Pierfrancesco at Cafaggiolo across the mountains in the Mugello valley, and Giovanni at Castello five miles north of the city.

As the summer months passed, the whole of Italy waited in trepidation – nowhere more so than Florence. The demise of King Ferrante had finally confirmed Savonarola's prophecy concerning the death of the 'three tyrants'. And it looked as if another of his prophecies was on the point of being fulfilled, though not quite in the way Savonarola had foreseen. The prospect of Italy being overrun by the vast and ruthless French army confirmed in the minds of all that this was Savonarola's prophecy concerning the arrival of a new Cyrus from across the mountains. It seemed that the King of France, rather than the Ottoman sultan, was to be the 'scourge of God'.

At the end of August 1494, Charles VIII marched south into the French foothills of the Alps, crossing the ancient Col de Montgenèvre, which rises to 6,000 feet. By the first days of September he was into Italian territory twenty miles east of Turin. His army was reported to consist of more than 40,000 men: 24,000 cavalry and 20,000 infantry, accompanied by a motley host of camp followers consisting of everything from chefs and astrologers to washerwomen and prostitutes.* The soldiers themselves were for the most part tough regular servicemen schooled in the northern-European manner of warfare – where, unlike the encounters between armies in Italy, battles were fought in brutal earnest and people actually got killed. In Italy, by contrast, battles remained largely tactical exercises practised by opposing mercenary armies led by hired *condottiere*, where the

---

* Figures vary concerning the precise number of soldiers in this army, but there can be little doubt that as a mobile mass of humanity, including camp followers, it almost certainly exceeded 50,000.

army that had been manoeuvred into a 'losing' position was usually permitted to flee the field with the minimum of casualties (which frequently resulted from the disorderly haste in which this latter operation was conducted). Such methods enabled the defeated soldiers to continue practising their mercenary trade at a later date, when they might well be hired to fight on the same side as their previous enemies. All this only encouraged wars between Italian states to become self-perpetuating, and played its part in contributing to Italy's constantly divided state during these years.

A disciplined army equipped with superior weaponry such as that of Charles VIII had not crossed the Alps into Italy for more than 700 years, when Hannibal had sought to destroy the mighty Roman Empire. But instead of Hannibal's terrifying elephants, Charles VIII's army was bringing with it the latest artillery, which was not only mobile but so powerful that it was capable of destroying the walls of any city or fortress that stood in its path. The age of medieval conflict, involving lines of archers and long sieges, was now giving way to an entirely new form of warfare.

At the same time as Charles VIII's army was crossing the Alps, Landucci heard in Florence, 'the fleet of the King of France arrived at Genoa, and there was much talk of a battle'. Alfonso II had been prepared for this and had despatched his fleet north from Naples. As the latest despatches began reaching Florence, Landucci recorded in his diary what news passed from mouth to mouth amongst the increasingly anxious citizenry:

11 September. The fleet of the King of Naples was defeated at Rapallo by the combined forces of the King of France and the Genoese. This was not a naval battle, for the Neapolitan fleet rashly landed three thousand soldiers with the aim of taking Rapallo. But they were eventually cut off by the Genoese and French, and were unable to return to their ships. They fled towards the mountains and were all killed or taken prisoner; while the fleet of the King of Naples was disarmed and destroyed.

Ten days later, further news and muddled rumours had covered the 100 or so miles to Florence, increasing the anxiety of its citizens:

21 September. News reached us that the King of France had entered Genoa, and that the Genoese were preparing to receive him with great honour. They have decorated the whole city, and even gone so far as to take down its gates and lay them on the ground, to show how welcome the king is, and to ensure his safety. But it turned out not to be true that the king was going to Genoa, even though its citizens had expected him and had made so many preparations. He was said to have felt he could not trust the Genoese.

If Charles VIII felt distrustful of such allies, how would he feel towards Florence, which had declared against him? In fact, Charles VIII had made no attempt to divert to Genoa. Summer was already giving way to autumn, and he had no time to lose before winter hampered, or perhaps even halted, his march on Naples. On 9 September he had been welcomed at Asti, the gateway to Milanese territory, by Ludovico 'il Moro' Sforza, the very man who had invited him into the country, who would be castigated by Machiavelli as 'the prime mover of Italy's distress'. Now began the period of which Machiavelli would later lament:

> Italy faced hard times . . .
> beneath stars hostile to her good.
> So many mountain passes,
> and so many marshes,
> filled with blood and dead men . . .
> [When] Italy in turmoil opened her gates
> to the Gauls [the French]
> and the barbarians rushed in . . .
> So all Tuscany was in confusion.

12

'I will destroy all flesh'

IN THEIR HOUR of need, the people of Florence turned to Savonarola, who rose to the occasion by delivering a sermon in the cathedral on 21 September 1494, which besides being the feast of St Matthew also happened to be his birthday. He was forty-two years old, and at the height of his powers. His prophecies had come true: now was the time. He was determined to fulfil the role that he was convinced God had entrusted to him.

The people of Florence flocked into the cathedral, the largest congregation ever to have gathered beneath its huge, high dome – cramming the pews, spilling down the aisles and out into the surrounding piazza. Savonarola was now well practised in the art of holding the attention of a large congregation. His tiny cowled figure stood at the raised lectern above the sea of heads gathered before him, gazing over them as if his intense eyes were returning the gaze of his entire hushed audience.

Without reference to notes, Savonarola began preaching, his voice resounding through the high silence of the nave. This was the 'living voice ringing out in his mind', which the aged Michelangelo would still be able to hear some sixty years later. Yet on this occasion Savonarola was not attempting to win over his audience; instead he was intent upon instilling in their hearts the fear of God, the wrath of the Almighty as they had never experienced it before. Previously he had preached on the theme of Noah's Ark, on the building of the craft that would save all true believers. This time he went further, using as his text the ensuing verses of the Book of Genesis, where the angry voice of the Lord thunders down from the heavens, warning the Israelites:

For Behold, I will bring a flood of waters upon the earth, to destroy all flesh in which is the breath of life from under heaven; everything that is on the earth will die.

This was but the beginning, as Savonarola launched into a fiery castigation of the wretched sinners gathered before him. The congregation well knew who these sinners were: previous sermons had railed against gamblers, blasphemers and sodomites – a constant theme. Yet it was noticeable that amidst all his railings and prophecies of doom, no matter how apparently carried away he became, he still kept to his pact with Lorenzo the Magnificent and made no direct attack on Piero de' Medici. In many ways there was now no longer any need for this. The 'scourge of God' had at last arrived, in the form of Charles VIII and his army. Yet even these details were now of little consequence: history was giving way to apocalyptic reality. All that was taking place was unmasked as the will of God:

Lo, the sword has descended. Finally the scourge has fallen upon us and the prophecies have reached their fulfilment. Lo, it is the Lord God himself who leads this army. Such a thing was not prophesied by me, but by God himself. And it is now coming into being. More than that, it is taking place before our very eyes.

Pico della Mirandola, who was amongst the congregation, later confessed to Savonarola that when he heard these words he was barely able to contain himself: he began to quake and his hair stood on end. Others amongst the crammed congregation were even more affected, and soon the majority appeared to be in the grip of mass hysteria. Many openly wept, others cried out in fear at Savonarola's words, whilst still others called out to the heavens, imploring God to have mercy upon them. After Savonarola had finished and the congregation dispersed, 'Everyone walked in awe-struck silence about the city, as though only half alive.'

Piero de' Medici was becoming increasingly uncertain about what action to take, about what action he *could* take. His advisers, and even members of the Signoria, were also divided. Many now secretly wished for an end to the Medici regime. In an undercover bid to stir up the population against Piero, he was informed that Savonarola was now openly preaching against him, calling for his overthrow, in much the same way as the 'little friar' had once called for the overthrow of his father with his sermons denouncing the 'three tyrants'. These slanders were intended to provoke Piero into having Savonarola banished from the city – a move that in all likelihood would have provoked a popular uprising. Yet others, especially amongst the intellectual circle of the Palazzo Medici, assured Piero that Savonarola was doing no such thing: his preaching merely reflected the dangerous situation facing the city, and indeed the whole of Italy, placing this situation in what he saw as its religious context. He had made no direct reference to Piero, or his rule over the city. Here again, Piero de' Medici remained uncertain: he had not been present when Savonarola preached, and was thus not able to judge for himself. He knew of Savonarola's secret agreement with his dying father – a fact known by few others – and still wished to believe his father's view that Savonarola was a man of his word; but his suspicions continued to grow, encouraged by these disloyal factions.

Those loyal members of the Medici circle who felt drawn to Savonarola now found themselves profoundly conflicted. None more so than Poliziano and Botticelli. It must have been some time during the preceeding months that Poliziano suggested to Botticelli that he should create a painting on the subject of the Calumny of Apelles. Significantly, this was not a religious subject, like the other works Botticelli was producing at this period. Poliziano must have intended this work to reassure Piero that, despite their admiration for Savonarola, neither he nor Botticelli had completely abandoned all that his father had stood for: the cultural transformation that we now know as the Renaissance.

The Calumny of Apelles is the most mysterious of all the many enigmatic paintings that Botticelli created. Yet unlike *The Birth of Venus* and *Primavara*, the mystery contains no bright or optimistic philosophical idealism: there is no doubting the darkness that it conveys. The painting is based on a work by Apelles, said to have been the finest painter of the classical world, none of whose works have come down to us. All we have is a verbal description of this work by the second-century-AD Greek writer Lucian. The occasion of the original painting was when jealous rivals had slandered Apelles, telling King Ptolemy that he had taken part in a conspiracy. Apelles' painting was his answer to this calumny, and in Botticelli's version it depicts the naked figure of the young Apelles being dragged by the hair to face the king, who sits on his throne with the dark-robed figures of Ignorance and Suspicion whispering into his furry, donkey-like ears, which are intended to emphasise the king's credulity. The allegorical nature of the painting leaves it open to a wide range of psychological and philosophical interpretations. Apelles can be seen as maligned truth, innocent and vulnerable in his nakedness. Is he intended as the slandered Savonarola? Is the king whose asinine ears cannot escape the whispers of Ignorance and Suspicion meant to represent Piero de' Medici? This would seem the most obvious answer – yet other interpretations abound, not least Botticelli's identification with the naked Apelles. And perhaps this ambiguity was what Botticelli intended. He still did not know himself what to do, what was really going on – in himself, in his divided loyalties or in his threatened city.

Other, highly relevant questions remain about *The Calumny of Apelles*, especially concerning the actual painting itself. Botticelli could certainly not have afforded the time and effort required to produce such a large and complex painting unless it had been commissioned. And here the painting takes on another, even more unexpected aspect. For many years Botticelli's chief patron had been Lorenzo di Pierfrancesco de' Medici. From his distant house-arrest beyond the mountains in the Mugello, did he perhaps convey a message commissioning Botticelli to paint a work suggesting that Lorenzo di Pierfrancesco's alleged antipathy to Piero de' Medici was a slander put about by those who wished to divide the family? Was the painting intended to bring about a reconciliation between the cousins? Florence itself was divided and in danger: this was no time for such divisions within its leading family.

The dark ambiguities embodied in this painting doubtless reflected the emotional atmosphere prevailing within the Palazzo Medici at this period – suspicion, slander, truth abandoned and much more. Besides Poliziano, Ficino and Pico della Mirandola would also have been caught up in this atmosphere, and they too may have added their suggestions to Botticelli. The fact that the painting was intended for Piero de' Medici would seem to be confirmed by Vasari in his celebrated *Lives of the Artists*, where he records that a Latin verse was later inscribed beneath Botticelli's canvas:

> This small picture warns earthly kings
> Not to charge people with false things.
> When the King of Egypt did Apelles hurt,
> Apelles served him like this with just desert.

The painting was never given to Piero de' Medici, perhaps because Poliziano, Pico della Mirandola, Ficino and Botticelli judged the moment not ripe, or were afraid of how Piero might react. Given the tension he was under, might Piero have considered the painting a provocation from the cousin he had grown to hate? Would Poliziano, Botticelli and the others have been willing to risk appearing disloyal to Piero in his hour of need? These are indeed possible explanations. Yet by now, such was the desperate political situation, Piero de' Medici would probably have had no time for such things. Indeed, he may not even have been in Florence when the painting was finally finished. Events were moving fast.

No sooner had Ludovico 'il Moro' Sforza greeted Charles VIII at Asti in September 1494 than he was beset by misgivings. As Guicciardini recorded:

> Although he was responsible for inviting the French into Italy, and knew they were his friendly allies, he now began to have his doubts about the whole enterprise. Considering the faithlessness of princes, and in particular the French, who appeared to have little honour or principle when their own interests were concerned, he began to have his suspicions about the French king . . . and whether Charles VIII might find an excuse to remove him from power.

Specifically, he suspected Charles VIII of wishing to install his young and weak nephew Gian Galeazzo Sforza, the rightful ruler of Milan, in his place – a suspicion that was strengthened when Charles VIII expressed his intention to visit Pavia, where, in accordance with protocol, he wished to be received by Gian Galeazzo. Ludovico did his best to delay Charles

VIII, and the French king eventually arrived in Pavia to find Gian Galeazzo struck down with a mysterious illness. Then, in mid-September, Charles VIII himself fell ill, succumbing to a bout of chicken pox; the main bulk of the French army halted its advance while Charles VIII recovered.

Tuscany was now the immediate hostile territory that stood between the French army and its march south. But Charles VIII had a good idea of what to expect. Philippe de Commines, his highly experienced envoy who had led the earlier French mission to Florence, had been unimpressed by Piero de' Medici, finding him to be 'a young man of little wisdom'. Piero now appeared to prevaricate, and despatched a Florentine mission to Charles VIII, purposely including amongst its members Piero di Gino Capponi, the king's former mentor, in the hope of somehow averting conflict between Florence and the French. But when Capponi appeared before Charles VIII he betrayed Piero. According to Commines, who was present, 'behind his hand Piero Capponi informed us that moves were afoot to turn the city of Florence against Piero'. Commines was convinced that the days of the Medici were numbered and that Florence would prove no impediment to the French advance.

Yet now Charles VIII had other matters on his mind. No sooner had he recovered from his illness than news came through that on 21 October Gian Galeazzo Sforza had died. Guicciardini reported:

> A rumour was circulated that Giovan Galeazzo's death had in fact been caused by excessive copulation; nonetheless it was believed throughout Italy that he had died not from his excesses but from poison. One of the royal doctors, who had been present when Charles visited him, indicated that he had observed evident signs of this. No one doubted that if he had been poisoned, this was the work of his uncle.

Indeed, the very next day Ludovico 'il Moro' Sforza had himself proclaimed the rightful Duke of Milan, despite the fact that Gian Galeazzo had already fathered a young son, who was thus the legitimate heir. Charles VIII now had few illusions concerning the character of his main ally in Italy, and several amongst his court (including Commines) began to have their doubts, suspecting Ludovico's duplicity 'with regard to the entire enterprise'.

This enterprise was already well under way, with the French army approaching the border of Tuscany intent upon securing the strategic port of Pisa. In mid-October Lorenzo di Pierfrancesco and his brother Giovanni managed to elude their house-arrest and made their way to the camp of Charles VIII. Here the French king was again reassured that the people of Florence had no wish to oppose him, and were utterly against Piero de' Medici. This was certainly true, for the most part; yet it was only two years since the death of Lorenzo the Magnificent, and there were some who still remembered his patronage with deep gratitude. Typical amongst these was Michelangelo, who would remember this time to the end of his days, when he recalled how a friend had come to tell him of a strange dream:

> that Lorenzo de' Medici had appeared before him dressed in black garments, all in tatters so that they barely covered his nakedness, and Lorenzo had commanded him to say to his son [Piero] that in a short time he would be driven from his house, and would never return.

Within a few days Michelangelo became so perturbed by this dream that 'he convinced himself that it would come about and departed from Florence for Bologna ... fearful that if this dream came true he would no longer be safe in the city'.

On hearing of the French advance, in a desperate last measure Piero de' Medici began hiring mercenaries to defend the fortresses guarding the northern border of Tuscany; 300 infantrymen and a small detachment of cavalry were despatched under the command of the trusted *condottiere* Paolo Orsini, Piero's brother-in-law. But on 29 October the alarming news reached Florence that the French army had overrun the mountain fortress at Fiviz-zano, slaughtering its entire garrison. The French then began to lay siege to the strategic fortress of Sarzanello, which together with the fortresses on either side of it, at Sarzana and Pietrasanta, commanded the coast road to Pisa and the south of Italy, as well as the main route from Milan to

Florence itself. According to Commines, 'if the place had been well garrisoned, the king's army would have been defeated, for this was barren territory where nothing lived to provide sustenance for the soldiers and it was also covered in deep snow'. But even manned by a skeleton garrison, the fortress of Sarzanello on its high rock proved impregnable to the French soldiers laying siege down below, and it looked as if the French advance was blocked, putting the entire invasion in jeopardy.

Yet it was now that Piero de' Medici embarked upon an enterprise that, as much as any during his often inept and frequently ill-fated rule, would result in confirming the nickname by which he has become known in history – namely, Piero the Unfortunate. It was a move that revealed his true character – demonstrating in equal measure that mixture of indecision and impulsiveness he had developed from living in the shadow of his exceptional father, while striving to outshine him. Instead of resisting the French invasion, he would emulate his father's most famous gesture, when he had travelled alone to Naples to confront King Ferrante and had so impressed him that he had saved Florence. Following precisely his father's actions, Piero de' Medici rode out of Florence without consulting the Signoria, only informing them of what he was doing in a letter despatched to them en route, when it was too late for them to thwart his plans. He would present himself before Charles VIII, intercede on the city's behalf and personally save the day for Florence.

However, Piero's arrival at the French court, where the king and his army had by now been camped out beneath the besieged rock at Sarzanello for three days, evoked no admiration for his brave gesture. On the contrary, Piero was received with ill-disguised disdain by Charles VIII – an attitude that was quickly mirrored by his counsellors and advisers. According to Commines, 'those who had dealings with Piero counted this as nothing, mocking him and paying little attention to him'. This treatment evidently unnerved Piero, precisely as intended: Charles VIII knew that his entire invasion hung in the balance. The French king opened the bargaining by announcing his most extravagant demands:

He told [Piero] that he required the immediate surrender of Sarzanello [as well as its twin fortresses at Sarzana and Pietrasanta].

He also demanded that he be allowed to take possession of Livorno and Pisa.

This would not only secure his route to the south, and deprive the republic of its two major coastal cities, but would also leave the city of Florence cut off and at his mercy. To the secret astonishment of all, Piero de' Medici dispensed with any pretence at negotiation and at once agreed to all the French king's demands, declaring that Charles VIII could occupy these forts and cities for as long as he required. Piero then went even further: when Charles VIII demanded that Florence should loan him money to replenish his dwindling exchequer, Piero agreed to give him a massive 200,000 florins. And when the French King expressed his intention to pass through Florence with his army, Piero went so far as to offer him the use of the Palazzo Medici, which Commines had described as 'the most beautiful house owned by any citizen or merchant that I have ever seen'.

Meanwhile Piero Capponi, who had now been elected *gonfaloniere*, had summoned his Signoria and immediately despatched a delegation in pursuit of Piero de' Medici, with the aim of thwarting his mission to Charles VIII. But this had proved too little too late. Back in Florence, the whole city now waited in trepidation. All shops remained closed, whilst the streets became forlorn, with rubbish uncleared in the gutters. According to the envoy from Mantua: 'All the girls and many of the wives have taken refuge in the convents so that only men and youths and old women are to be seen in the streets.' But Savonarola was determined that the people should be made aware of the meaning of what was taking place. On 1 November, while Piero de' Medici was still away at the French court, he began delivering his All Saints' Day sermon in the cathedral to a packed and fearful congregation:

> Before there was even the slightest rumour of these wars which have come to us from across the mountains, I foretold that great tribulations were to come. You also know that less than two years ago I warned you, '*Ecce gladius Domini super terram, cito et velociter*' [Behold, the sword of the Lord, striking and swift]. This prophecy was given to you not by me, but by the word of God, and now it is being fulfilled.

This was Savonarola's moment of truth, the vindication of all that he had predicted, and he was determined to seize his opportunity. Rousing himself, he went on:

O Italy, because of your lust, your avarice, your pride, your envy, your thieving, your extortion, you will suffer all manner of afflictions and many scourges . . . O Florence, for your sins, your brutality, your avarice, your lust, many trials and tribulations will be heaped upon you . . . O Clergy, who are the principal cause of so many evils, woe unto you!

In the midst of these incantations against Italy, Florence and 'the clergy', he exclaimed: 'O Florence, I have wished this morning to speak to each and every one of you, openly and sincerely, for I can no longer do otherwise.' At last, now that Piero de' Medici was out of Florence, Savonarola felt that he could speak more candidly, without breaking the promise he had made to Lorenzo on his deathbed. Yet significantly, he still did not mention the Medici by name. His message was emotional and forceful, yet he expressed himself only in terms of biblical metaphor. God was smiting Italy, and in particular Florence, for its evil. The people of Florence were being invited – nay, implored – to placate God's wrath by offering up their prayers and repentance. He returned once more to his old theme of the Flood and Noah's Ark. When God unleashed his Flood over the Earth, only those worthy of salvation would be allowed to enter the Ark. Yet what precisely was this Ark, constructed out of ten planks, which curiously echoed Florence's ten ancient districts?

Savonarola had so longed to speak to the people of Florence 'openly and sincerely', yet still his ultimate aim remained unclear – perhaps even to himself. Unconsciously, it seemed, two ideas struggled in his mind: his promise to Lorenzo to refrain from attacking the Medici status quo, and his wish to convert Florence into a spiritual 'Ark'. His voice resonated through the cathedral, filled with passion, invigorated by the openly expressed conviction that God spoke through him. First would come 'God's scourge', yet after this it remained unclear precisely what would happen. He had placed himself in God's hands, and would do his utmost to fulful God's will – as and when it revealed itself.

Savonarola would deliver a long and impassioned sermon in the cathedral on three consecutive days, working himself up to fever pitch on each
occasion. 'During the course of those three days, as he later recalled, he
shouted so vehemently from the pulpit that the vein in his chest almost
burst, and he reached such a point of physical exhaustion that he almost
fell seriously ill.'

Guicciardini and other contemporary sources indicate that this was a
pivotal time. Piero Capponi and the Signoria were at a loss. With Piero
de' Medici out of the city, and the Medici supporters in an increasingly
conflicted state, the authorities were reduced to paralysis. As details of the
deal that Piero de' Medici had made with Charles VIII began reaching
Florence, spreading rapidly through the city, the entire population was soon
on the verge of anarchy. Then the news arrived that the French army was
on the march, on its way to 'occupy' Florence. The structure of civic power
was on the point of crumbling, with the people liable to erupt and destroy
the city in their state of panic, fear and pent-up rage at what was happening.
But, miraculously, Savonarola's sermons appeared to have averted this disastrous disorder. According to the despatch by the Mantuan envoy, 'A
Dominican friar has so terrified all the Florentines that they are wholly
given up to piety.' In the eyes of the people, Savonarola's preaching – the
voice of God – was their only hope.

The Signoria were quick to recognise the effective power that had now
passed into Savonarola's hands. On 4 November, Gonfaloniere Capponi
and the Signoria summoned the Council of Seventy, the body that Lorenzo
the Magnificent had created to maintain Medici power and influence the
Signoria. With Piero de' Medici out of the city, and circumstances as they
were, even the Council of Seventy began voicing anti-Medici sentiments.
Piero Capponi expressed the opinion 'that it is time we stopped being
ruled by children' (a reference not only to the twenty-three-year-old Piero
de' Medici, but also to his younger nineteen-year-old brother Cardinal
Giovanni, whom he still intermittently turned to as his adviser). Capponi
suggested that the only way to save Florence, or at least try to ameliorate
the present dire situation, was to send to Charles VIII a delegation of four
ambassadors as true representatives of the people of Florence. He himself
was willing to serve as one of these ambassadors, but in his opinon the

person best suited to lead this delegation was 'a man of holy life . . . courageous and intelligent, of high ability and great renown' – namely Savonarola.
The Signoria and the Council of Seventy quickly backed Capponi in this
proposal. Savonarola's de facto leadership of the city was now evident to
all.

Despite his chronic exhaustion after three days of passionate sermon-
ising, during which he had often appeared to be on the point of a physical and mental breakdown, Savonarola could not bring himself to turn
down Capponi's request. His motives, as well as those of Capponi, are
open to question here. Was Savonarola simply incapable of suppressing his
lust for power? Was Capponi lining up Savonarola as scapegoat, in case
things went wrong? The possibility of such mixed motives must inevitably
be borne in mind during the ensuing events.

The very next day, Wednesday 5 November, Savonarola and his fellow
ambassadors left the city. Despite the urgency of the situation, as well as
the need to create an impression at the French court, Savonarola insisted
that he would only travel on foot. The others were forced to follow behind
on their horses, which were decked out in the city's livery in the customary
fashion. Such protocol was not only intended to convey the importance
of the ambassadors and the city they represented, but was also to be seen
as a mark of respect for their hosts. Thus the determined friar in his
threadbare robes, carrying only his usual breviary, led the somewhat uncertain Florentine delegation north-west of the city into the Tuscan countryside. It was unclear whether Charles VIII and his army were still in the
region of Sarzanello, or had already set off south to take Pisa. The Florentine mission continued, enquiring on the latest news concerning the French
army at each village through which it passed. It was hardly an auspicious
start.

The whereabouts of the French court was not the only thing of which
the Florentine mission remained in ignorance. No sooner had it left the
city than an advanced French detachment arrived in Florence, proceeding
directly to the Palazzo della Signoria, where it demanded permission to
start making billeting arrangements for the arrival of the French army.
Impotently, the Signoria agreed, and French soldiers began making their
way through the streets, marking chalk crosses on the doors of the houses

that were to billet the French garrison. The town heralds with their trumpets preceded them through the city, announcing that anyone who rubbed off the chalk crosses on their doors would be liable to a draconian fine of 500 florins (more than twice the annual income of many merchants, let alone householders of lesser fortune).

When Piero de' Medici received news of the Florentine delegation approaching the French camp, he at once set off back to Florence, meeting up with Paolo Orsini and his 300 mercenaries on the way. On Saturday 8 November – just three days after Savonarola and his delegation had left – Piero arrived outside the city walls of Florence at the northern Porta San Gallo. Unprecedentedly, he found no official party at the gate to welcome him – an ominous portent. Nonethelesss, possibly out of tact for the citizens' sensibilities, he ordered Orsini and the mercenaries to wait outside the city walls. Piero then rode on through the Porta San Gallo into the city, arriving at the Palazzo Medici to find a crowd of silent, curious onlookers gathered outside. Immediately after dismounting in the protected inner courtyard, Piero ordered that *confetti* (little sweet cakes and sugar-coated almonds) be scattered from the windows down to the waiting crowd below. In a further traditional homecoming gesture, he also ordered long tables to be set out in the street, where wine and bread could be served to the poor. But the sceptical onlookers seemed determined not to be won over, and there were none of the usual grateful loyal cries of 'Palle! Palle! Palle!'*

Next day being Sunday, Piero de' Medici attended Mass, where he soon learned of the situation in the city. Accompanied by a group of armed men, he then proceeded to the Palazzo della Signoria, intending to deliver his official report on his mission. By now the members of the Signoria felt they had the backing of the majority of the population, with many convinced that Piero was personally responsible for the peril in which Florence found itself. Even so, the Signoria remained wary: they knew that

---

* This was the traditional rallying cry of the Medici and their supporters, referring as it did to the *palle* (red balls) that featured on the Medici shield, the emblem that could be seen on the Palazzo Medici and so many other buildings in the city. According to one tradition, these represented the pills that had appeared on the signboard above the original Medici shop, when, as their name suggested, they had first begun as sellers of medicine in the city some three centuries previously.

Orsini and his 300 mercenaries remained camped outside the Porta San Gallo.

By this stage further detachments of French troops had begun arriving in the city by way of the western gate, in order to seek out and chalk the doors of all possible available billets. Although the Signoria were conscious of the deep shame this inflicted upon the city, and aware that many blamed them for allowing it to take place, they soon saw how this French presence could be turned to their advantage. Piero de' Medici would not dare to order Orsini and his mercenaries into the city to defend him if this was liable to lead to a clash with the armed French detachments. Such a move would have put the entire approaching French army against him. This meant that Piero was essentially on his own, and any move the Signoria made against him would help shift the blame for the presence of the French troops and their humiliating activities. By dissociating themselves from Piero de' Medici they could redeem their own ineffectiveness and essential impotence, thus isolating him as the sole scapegoat for all that was happening.

When Piero arrived at the Palazzo della Signoria, accompanied by his small band of armed guards, he was astonished to have the main door slammed in his face. A voice informed him that he could only enter the palazzo alone, without his armed men, by way of the *sportello*, the tiny side gate intended for servants and delivery boys. As Piero stood pondering this direct insult, unsure of what he should do to avoid loss of face, the Signoria took matters into their own hands. From high up in the castellated tower of the palazzo came the deep, resonant toll of the city's famous bell, the *Vacca* (literally, 'the cow', so called because its booming tone resembled the mooing of a cow). The tolling bell resounding over the rooftops of the city was the traditional call to all citizens in time of danger or emergency, summoning them to gather in the wide stone-paved Piazza della Signoria in front of the palazzo. As the people hurried into the square and it began to fill, the mood of the crowd turned. Some began calling out insults at Piero as he stood uncertainly on the raised pavement outside the main door of the palazzo. As such sentiments began gathering momentum, people started throwing objects, refuse and then stones. Piero's armed guard quickly persuaded him to leave, forcing a way for him through the increasingly antagonistic crowd, whereupon they set off back for the safety of the Palazzo Medici.

Meanwhile Piero's younger brother Cardinal Giovanni had begun taking his own measures, riding up and down the Via Larga with an armed entourage, attempting to rally support for the Medici cause with cries of *'Palle! Palle! Palle!'* This drew a number of armed Medici supporters, who began spilling out of the nearby streets. Cardinal Giovanni then led his band of armed men and chanting Medici supporters towards the Piazza della Signoria. Yet as they approached the square they found themselves faced by a much larger hostile mob, and were forced to beat a hasty retreat through the streets back to the Palazzo Medici, where Piero and his men were confronting another armed gathering of opponents. For a while it looked as if there would be violent conflict between the rival groups, with blood shed; but when a crowd of further armed opponents of the Medici arrived on the scene, Giovanni reportedly declared to Piero, 'We're finished!' Whereupon the Medici brothers and their supporters withdrew through the gateway of the Palazzo Medici and barricaded themselves in behind its high walls.

The point had now been reached where the city was on the brink of civil war, and the Signoria followed up their summoning of the people by taking decisive action, publicly issuing a decree 'forbidding anyone on pain of death to aid or abet Piero de' Medici'. This may have been opportunistic, but it was also irrevocable: if the Medici succeeded in retaining power, the Signoria's decree would certainly be regarded as treason, punishable by death or at least permanent exile. But the Signoria's gamble appeared to pay off. According to Landucci, 'In consequence of this [decree], many abandoned Piero and laid down their arms. They dropped off on all sides, so that few remained with him.'

Partly as a result of this decree, the crowd outside the Palazzo Medici began to disperse – few of them wishing to be mistakenly seen 'to aid or abet' the Medici cause, or to become involved in the bloody conflict that now seemed inevitable. As the crowd dispersed, Piero de' Medici, along with his wife and children, rode out of the Palazzo Medici protected by an armed escort and swiftly made his way up the deserted Via Larga, arriving at the Porta San Gallo, which was being held by Orsini and his

men. Many sources claim that this escape took place under cover of dark-
nesss, but Landucci's eyewitness report states how later that same day (that
is, the late afternoon of Sunday 9 November) he observed Cardinal Giovanni:

> The poor young cardinal stayed behind in the house and I saw him
> through a window, kneeling with his hands joined, praying to Heaven
> to have mercy. The sight of him moved me greatly, for he was in
> truth a good and upright character.

Had Cardinal Giovanni been left behind by Piero because he hoped that
the popular Giovanni might yet rally sufficient support for the Medici
cause and reverse the situation? Indeed, the sight of Cardinal Giovanni
praying at the window prompts all manner of questions. What precisely
would Giovanni have been praying for? And why should he have done this
so publicly, at the window of the palazzo for all to see, when surely the
private chapel would have been the more appropriate venue for such an act
of worship? This appearance at the window is not the act of a man praying
for his own safety. Had he been worried on this score, he would surely
have made every effort to join his departing brother and his armed party,
thus demonstrating his loyalty to Piero. No, in all likelihood, if Giovanni's
prayers had any supplicatory object at all, it must have been a plea to God
for the preservation of Medici rule. And the very public nature of this act
must have been intended to elicit sympathy, which it certainly did in the
case of Landucci, whose position as a mere shopkeeper surely rendered
him representative of widespread popular feeling in the city. Giovanni's
public praying was the act of a man hoping to take advantage of his
personal popularity and swing the crowd in his favour.

Yet it must soon have become apparent to Cardinal Giovanni and his
remaining supporters inside the palazzo that the crowd had irrevocably
turned against the Medici. Doubtless the voices of the people outside made
this clear. As a result, Cardinal Giovanni and his supporters made no further
effort to court popularity, and now began a frantic, but thorough, attempt
to rescue their situation in an entirely different manner. Hurriedly they
started scouring all the rooms of the palazzo, collecting up as many portable
valuables as they could carry. Amongst these were the jewels that Lorenzo

the Magnificent had collected so avidly – those precious stones whose very nature was contradictory: easily transportable, in case Cosimo's prediction that the Medici would be driven from Florence came true, yet bearing the marks of Lorenzo's ultimate royal ambition for the family. Along with these jewels, Cardinal Giovanni is said to have collected up some 200,000 ducats: amongst the last remaining assets of the Medici bank in Florence. Other items included various statuettes, gold and silver medallions, as well as valuable books and rare ancient manuscripts from the Medici library.

According to Landucci, some time after Piero de' Medici left, Cardinal Giovanni 'disguised himself as a monk and took his departure also'. This escape must surely have been made under cover of darkness, and with some stealth, considering the value of the treasure involved. Yet not all of this was taken directly up the Via Larga to the safety of the Porta San Gallo. Extraordinarily, it seems that the young Cardinal Giovanni stopped off en route at the monastery of San Marco, where he delivered the rare books and manuscripts from the Medici library, and perhaps some of the more religious treasures as well, to the safekeeping of the monks.

This raises a number of intriguing questions. We know that, at the time, Savonarola was absent on the mission to Charles VIII – yet San Marco would have remained very much in the hands of his supporters. On the other hand, San Marco had long been considered by the Medici as 'our' monastery, and it is possible that some amongst its monks remained ardent, if clandestine, Medici supporters. Yet how could they have received Medici treasures from Cardinal Giovanni, disguised as a Dominican monk though he was, and have managed to conceal them, without other monks loyal to Savonarola being aware of this? A more credible scenario would have involved the disguised Giovanni delivering rare manuscripts and books from the Medici library with the full knowledge of the monks who supported Savonarola. Such a contingency could have been arranged by go-betweens such as Pico or Ficino. This gift could well have been a gesture to Savonarola, who would certainly have welcomed the addition of such items to the monastery collection. Was this by way of being a recompense to Savonarola for keeping his promise to Lorenzo on his deathbed and refraining from attacking Piero, or even directly denouncing Medici rule, in his sermons?

Inevitably, such a theory is purely speculative – yet it seems difficult to account for Cardinal Giovanni's gesture in any other way. Having deposited his gifts at San Marco, he hurried up the Via Larga to the safety of the Porta San Gallo, and Orsini's waiting armed men.

Landucci recorded how around this time the Signoria at last took even more drastic action, once again too little and too late:

> Another proclamation was publicly announced in the Piazza, promising that whoever slew Piero de' Medici would receive a reward of two thousand ducats, and whoever slew the cardinal would receive a thousand ducats.

But the Medici were gone, galloping across the Apennine mountain passes towards the safety of the nearby territory of Bologna. Piero the Unfortunate had been forced into exile, and the rule of the Medici family in Florence was over.

13
Humiliation

WHEN THE NEWS spread through Florence that the Medici had fled the city, a mob descended on the Palazzo Medici bent on pillaging the legendary treasures that it was rumoured to contain. However, they found the palazzo locked and barred by its new occupant, a French nobleman from the court of Charles VIII called 'seigneur de Balsac', who had taken up residence some days beforehand. On orders from Piero de' Medici, he had been instructed to prepare the palazzo for when Charles VIII came to take up Piero's offer of residence. Yet no sooner had the Medici fled than Balsac secured all possible modes of entry and 'began pillaging the contents of the palace, claiming that the Lyons branch of the Medici Bank owed him a great sum of money'. Cardinal Giovanni had only been able to remove from the palace such valuables as he and his men could carry, leaving behind many treasures and works of art for Balsac. These included all manner of exotic items, and Commines recorded that 'among other things he seized an entire unicorn's horn worth six or seven thousand ducats'.*

It seemed that all Medici properties throughout the city were now considered fair game. According to Commines, in no time:

> others were behaving in the same manner as [Balsac]. All that was most valuable had been stored in another house in the city. The

---

* According to Joseph Calmette, the editor of Commines' *Mémoires*, 'it was believed that the horn of this fabulous beast was capable of detecting the presence of poison'. Likewise, its rarity, hardness and phallic symbolism had given rise to the belief that, when ground into a powder, it was a highly efficacious aphrodisiac.

people pillaged this too. The signoria managed to sieze some of the finest jewellery, as well as some twenty thousand ducats which remained in the premises of the local Medici bank, and several fine agate vases, a vast amount of beautifully cut cameos, as fine as any I had seen. They also seized three thousand gold and silver medallions weighing forty pounds: one would not have believed that there were so many fine medallions in the whole of Italy.

In order to protect the Palazzo Medici from the gathering mob, the Signoria sent a guard of armed men, and these together with Balsac and the French soldiers within the palace seem to have kept the would-be pillagers at bay. However, it appears that at one stage a number of Florentine citizens must have broken into the palazzo, starting a fire amongst the registry files, with the aim of destroying documents related to tax details and debts owed. Indeed, to this day 'Black scorch marks are still visible on the papers that survived.' Yet what is so surprising is that so many Medici treasures did in fact survive – other than those deposited at San Marco or removed from Florence altogether by Cardinal Giovanni. Many Medici paintings, both in the palazzo and elsewhere in Florence, including both family portraits and religious scenes (which often incorporated family portraits, such as Botticelli's *Adoration of the Magi*) survive to this day. And the latter would not have been spared on account of their religious content. Far from it: in these first heady hours of liberation nothing was sacred where the Medici were concerned. Even the resplendent San Gallo monastery, reckoned to have been one of the finest early Renaissance works of architecture, was not spared. This may have been designed for the revered Augustinians, whose prior had once been Savonarola's great rival preacher Fra Marianoda Genazzano, and built by none other than Brunelleschi himself, but it had been commissioned by Lorenzo the Magnificent, and that was enough. The building was completely razed to the ground by the mob so that not even a ruin remained – today its former site is a green open space lined by trees just outside the Porta San Gallo, known as the Parterre.

The seizure by the Signoria of the remaining assets hidden in the premises of the local branch of the Medici bank* effectively marked the demise

---

* Put at 20,000 ducats by Commines; other sources suggest the sum of 16,000 florins.

of this once-great financial institution. The precise ledger figures and imbalances remain unknown, since a large amount of the bank's records were destroyed in the fire at the Palazzo Medici. However, de Roover makes it clear that by this stage the ruin of the Medici bank was probably inevitable. Even if there had been no French invasion in 1494 and Piero had not been deposed, 'the Medici bank might have ended even more disgracefully in a financial crash of the first order'. Its entire organisation was already virtually bankrupt. 'Most of its branches had been closed, and those still in existence were gasping for breath.' This was particularly true of its main foreign agency, previously its chief source of income through handling papal dues, accounts with cardinals and the alum monopoly: 'Even the Rome branch, for so long the pillar of the Medici Bank, was giving way because funds were immobilised in loans.' And these loans even directly involved the Medici themselves: 'the debt of the Medici family to the Rome branch exceeded their equity by 11,243 large florins. In addition, Messer Giovanni, the youthful cardinal . . . owed another 7,500 florins.'

Despite the letter Lorenzo the Magnificent had written just before his death to his son Giovanni, expressly advising him to curb his extravagance, this had evidently produced little effect. On the other hand, Cardinal Giovanni's initiative in rescuing from the Palazzo Medici as much of value as could be carried would prove vital in preserving the Medici family's financial status. Lorenzo's fabulous collection of precious jewels and the like would provide for both Piero de' Medici and his family in exile, while Cardinal Giovanni would support himself, and provide further funds, from the rich benefices so prudently accumulated for him by Lorenzo. All this would also help to finance the schemes initiated with the aim of restoring Piero to power in Florence, which he embarked upon from the moment he entered exile.

On 9 November 1494, the very day that Piero de' Medici fled from Florence, Charles VIII entered Pisa. In the hours preceding the French occupation, the citizens of Pisa had risen up in revolt against their governor and his administration, only too pleased to throw off the yoke of their detested Florentine conquerors. The French army was little concerned by these events: Charles VIII was welcomed as the city's saviour and took up residence in the imposing Citadella Nuova by the River Arno. It was here at Pisa that the Florentine delegation led by Savonarola finally caught up with the French army and were immediately granted an audience with the king.

Charles VIII certainly presented an unprepossessing figure: 'small in stature, and excessively ugly', according to Guicciardini, who went on to describe how 'his limbs were so proportioned that he seemed more like a monster than a man'. However, seated on his throne, surrounded by his counsellors and the trappings of his court, even when it was on the move, the gnomic king presented a grand and imposing prospect – Europe's most powerful monarch in all his medieval glory. By contrast, the entry of Savonarola in his sandals and threadbare robes, followed by his three some-what overawed fellow delegates, hardly created an impressive sight. Yet Savonarola was undaunted, and launched into an oration in which he welcomed Charles VIII: 'At last you have arrived, O King! Just as I have been predicting through these last years, thou hast come as the Minister of God, as an emblem of Divine Justice. We welcome thy presence with joyous hearts and smiling faces. You have been sent by God to chastise the tyrants of Italy, and nothing will be able to resist you or defend itself against you.' Having welcomed the all-conquering 'Scourge of God', Savonarola then abruptly changed his tone, warning that although Florence might unintentionally have given him offence, Charles VIII should forgive the city and do no harm to its citizens, for 'although he was sent by God, Heaven was capable of wreaking a terrible revenge even upon its own instru-ment', should the French king allow his army to harm Florence.

Charles VIII had already been briefed by his advisers concerning Savonarola and his gift of prophecy – a subject that particularly appealed to the illiterate young king's superstitious nature (as well as to that of several of his more intellectually endowed advisers). As a result, Charles VIII listened intently to Savonarola's words, most encouraged by his predic-tions concerning the French campaign in Italy. Indeed, so impressed was Charles VIII that when Savonarola's royal audience came to an end, he allowed the other three Florentine ambassadors to withdraw, but insisted that Savonarola remain behind with him for a private audience – during which, according to Commines, they discussed 'what God had revealed to him'. Commines was also impressed: a sophisticated man much practised in the cynicism of diplomacy and the vicissitudes of court life, he nonetheless confessed that with regard to Savonarola, 'for my part, I found him to be a good man'.

The following day Charles VIII decamped with his army and set off down the Arno valley towards Florence, halting at Signa, some eight miles before the city walls. At this point Savonarola went on ahead into Florence, possibly at the behest of Charles VIII, in order to inform the city of the imminent arrival of the French army and assess the situation. With civil government on the point of complete breakdown under the leaderless Signoria, it was vital that order should be restored. The French king wished to make a triumphal entry into Florence, along with his army, and he wished for this parade to be welcomed by the people of the city. If anarchy prevailed, he was liable to send in troops to quell any disturbances, with bloody consequences.

Savonarola arrived in Florence early on Tuesday 11 November and immediately made it known that he would deliver a sermon later that day. People from all over the city crammed into the cathedral to hear the words of the one man they now regarded as their only possible saviour. In his sermon, Savonarola returned to his theme of the Ark, 'the boat of true repentance and salvation, to be launched against the surrounding flood of tribulation'. Yet he also sought to reassure the citizens of Florence that no harm would come to them, if they inflicted no harm on others. In reference to the new state of affairs following the flight of Piero de' Medici, he warned against taking revenge upon those who had been Medici supporters. The citizens of Florence should thank God that such a revolution had taken place with no blood being shed. Likewise, he reassured them that he had Charles VIII's word that if they offered no violence to the French, Charles VIII would see that no harm came to them.

For five days the French army remained encamped beyond the city walls whilst the citizens of Florence waited in trepidation. Then on 16 November, having heard that Charles VIII was planning to enter the city the following day, Savonarola delivered another sermon. He began by 'urging every man to keep his place'. He insisted that the French army must be allowed to enter the city without opposition: they would not stay for long before they continued on their way to Naples. Savonarola went on to explain that a

new government would soon be appointed in place of the Medici administration, and that this too must be accomplished without violence. Such
matters were in good hands: 'Lots of men would like to help administer
the state, but cannot do so because they do not have the aptitude.' Every
citizen 'should be content with his state'.

However, despite Savonarola's pleas for order and restraint, the people
remained fearful and the situation was fraught with the danger of civil
breakdown, followed by anarchy and the prospect of a bloodbath. By now,
further advance parties of French troops had begun arriving in the city,
taking up residence in the billets marked for them. From these they sallied
forth, marking further chalk crosses on the doors of literally hundreds of
houses in every part of the city, even 'including all the Camaldoli', the
western slum district occupied by the very poorest wool-combers, dyers
and fishermen, which lay across the river from the city centre, in the
Oltrarno, crammed between the river bank and the southern city walls.

Piero Capponi had returned to resume his role as *gonfaloniere*, doing his
best to enforce some kind of civil government; but inevitably there were
outbreaks of vengeance against those who had supported the Medici, with
the ever-present danger of French soldiers becoming involved. A typically
muddled and volatile incident was described by Landucci:

Girolamo Tornabuoni had his breastplate torn off by anti-Medici
supporters in Orto Sa' Michele, but when he pleaded for mercy they
spared his life. Giovan Francesco Tornabuoni was badly wounded in
the cheek, and returned home. When this disturbance began, some
of the French who had been billeted in Florence armed themselves
and joined the Medici supporters, yelling *Francia*. I believe they were
informed that this was a matter between citizens only, and that if
they did anything against the *Palagio* [the palazzo i.e. the Signoria],
they would be doing wrong and find themselves in trouble. So they
returned to their lodgings ... The number of soldiers and of the
people going about robbing innocent citizens was constantly increasing.

As Savonarola's biographer, Villari, put it:

There was great cause for alarm; but fortunately several wise and determined citizens pledged their support for the signoria. Chief amongst these was Piero Capponi, who became the right hand of the republic, in much the same way as Savonarola became its heart and soul. As Savonarola preached forgiveness, charity and brotherhood, Capponi sped from place to place, wherever his authority was needed, handing out arms and recruiting men to keep the peace.

Finally, late in the afternoon of Monday 17 November, Charles VIII and his army entered Florence through the south-western San Friano gate. Here the French king, clad in black velvet with a mantle of gold brocade, was greeted with all due ceremony by the assembled Signoria and all the leading citizens on horeseback, dressed in their finest robes, who bowed their heads and formally invited him to enter the city. But from the outset Charles VIII made it perfectly plain that he was here as a conqueror, not as a welcome guest, riding forward into the city with his lance on his hip in the traditional manner of the victor. Despite Savonarola's reassurances, no one knew what the unpredictable French king had in mind for Florence. Indeed, it is now clear that at this stage Charles VIII had not even decided himself.

Despite the extreme humiliation their city was undergoing, many Florentines lined the streets, cheering and calling out *'Viva Francia! Viva Francia!'* as the king and his army passed through the city, crossing the River Arno by way of the Ponte Vecchio, continuing meaningfully past the Palazzo della Signoria and on to the cathedral. Most eyewitnesses agree that the French army consisted of around 10,000 men. The rest of the French forces were camped near Pisa, with a detachment in the Romagna, ready for the march south. According to a report by the Venetian ambassador, the soldiers were led into the city by 'a monster of a man [*omaccione*] with a polished sword like a spit for roast pork, and then four big drums played with both hands and accompanied by two pipes, making an infernal noise, such as one hears at a fair'. Of the 10,000 who entered Florence behind him, 7,000 were Swiss infantrymen, generally regarded as the toughest and most brutal battle-hardened soldiers in Europe at the time.

A Florentine eyewitness was rather more impressed, recalling how they marched past 'with such discipline that only the sound of drums and pipes could be heard'. The Swiss were followed by all manner of mounted archers, infantry with pikes, men-at-arms, 'men from Dalmatia and other strange places'. Despite their cheers, the Florentines were filled with awe and fear at the sight of such soldiers, the like of which they had never seen before. Bartolomeo Cerretani's reaction was typical, seeing them as 'barbarians ... from cold regions that produced men like beasts with their ugly manners and speech'. Amongst these he particularly noted 'Bretons, Scots and all sorts of men who spoke so many tongues they could not even understand one another'. Such was the terrifying babel that now took possession of the city that regarded itself as the most civilised in Europe.

The only exception to this fearsomeness was the king himself. As he reached the cathedral and dismounted, Landucci recorded that 'when he was seen on foot he seemed to the people to be somewhat less imposing, for he was in fact a very small man'. It had taken the procession more than two hours to cover the mile-or-so route from the city gate to the cathedral, and by now it was dark. Inside, the cathedral was lit with candelabra, and the king prayed at the altar before remounting his horse and riding between flares to take up residence at the Palazzo Medici – which Balsac, aided by the Signoria, had decked out in all its glory (or what remained of it). At any rate, Charles VIII was certainly impressed, for later that night he wrote proudly to his brother, the Duc de Bourbon, back in France:

> My brother, today I entered this city of Florence, in which I have been grandly received by the signoria, and have been given such honour as I have never received in a city within my own kingdom ... It is a long time since anyone made such a grand entry into a place like this. And the signoria is totally disposed to do for me whatever thing I order them.

But what would these orders be? Would he instruct his terrifying soldiers to sack Florence? Or would he heed Savonarola's words of warning? Charles VIII had certainly decided upon one thing: he wanted to extract as much

1. Contemporary portrait of Savonarola by his friend Fra Bartolomeo

2a. Portrait bust of Lorenzo de' Medici, probably after a contemporary model, suggesting his powerful and charismatic character

2b. Portrait of Lorenzo de' Medici's eldest son, Piero (known as 'Piero the Unfortunate'), who succeeded his father as ruler of Florence

PIERO DI LORENZO DI PIERO DE MEDICI

FIORENZA

3. A view of early Renaissance Florence, looking eastwards up the Arno Valley.
The prominent domed building in the centre of the picture is Florence Cathedral (the Duomo). To the right of this can be distinguished the Palazzo della Signoria, the tip of whose tower can be seen against the distant city wall.

4a. Rodrigo Borgia,
who became
Pope Alexander VI

4b. Charles VIII,
the young king of France

IOĀN·PICVS·MIRANDVLA·

5a. The philosopher
Pico della Mirandola

5b. The poet Angelo Poliziano

5c. A somewhat flattering portrait
of the Platonist and translator
Marsilio Ficino

6a. Savonarola preaching

6b. Self-portrait of Sandro Botticelli in his prime

7. *The Birth of Venus* by Botticelli

8. One of Botticelli's late troubled images of Dante's Inferno

money as he could from this rich city, so that it could finance his vast and expensive army on the next leg of its march, as far as Rome, where he expected to extract further gold for his coffers from the pope, so that his men would be well fed and well paid for the final leg of their march on Naples.

Whatever Charles VIII decided, he felt confident that his French army now had Florence at his mercy. At the time, the population of Florence is estimated to have been less than 70,000 men, women and children (many having fled into the countryside at the approach of the French army). Billeted in their midst they now had 10,000 of the toughest soldiers in Europe, to say nothing of those who had been sent ahead to organise this billeting, who probably numbered in their hundreds by the time the main body of the French army arrived.

Within a few days Charles VIII and his advisers began setting out their terms to the Signoria, who were horrified to hear that the French king wished them to pay him no less than 150,000 gold florins* – even though this represented a considerable climb-down from the 200,000 florins that Piero de' Medici had been forced to promise. On top of this, Charles VIII expected them to reinstate Piero de' Medici as their ruler, and furthermore he intended to leave behind two French 'commissioners' who would sit in on the meetings of the Signoria. Fearful that Charles VIII might yet decide to sack the city, but determined not to surrender their newly won freedom, the Signoria dug in their heels. There was no question of Piero de' Medici being reinstated, the Signoria resented the idea of the two French 'commissioners' as their virtual rulers, and finally they informed the king that they simply did not have 150,000 florins to give him.

Much hard bargaining ensued over the next few days, but meanwhile the situation in Florence was deteriorating daily. Many citizens had armed themselves, and increasingly violent incidents were taking place throughout the city. These culminated around 21 November, when:

A gang of French soldiers began passing through the streets dragging behind them some Italians tied up with ropes who had been

---

* At the time, a moderately prosperous merchant in Florence could expect to provide for his entire household, including family, relatives and servants, for the equivalent of around 150 florins a year.

taken prisoner during the fighting near the border, making them beg for money to pay their ransom so they could be freed. The French threatened that they would be killed if not enough money was given. The Florentines were so incensed by this barbarous spectacle that some brave young men cut the ropes, allowing the prisoners to escape. The French were enraged, and tried vainly to recapture them. Then a fight began, with the citizens resisting, and soon others poured in from all sides to assist them. The Swiss soldiers heard rumours of this, and imagined that the king's life was in danger. They made a dash for the palazzo, but their passage was blocked in the Borgo Ognissanti. When they tried to force their way through they were met with a fusillade of stones from the windows and had to retreat. The fight went on for an hour before some of the king's officers and many leading citizens managed to quell the disturbance on the orders of the Signoria.

As the contemporary diarist Piero Parenti observed, 'only divine providence stopped things getting out of control'. The situation was defused, but the entire city remained tense over the coming days. According to Landucci, 'and all the while it was being spread about the city that the King had promised his soldiers that they would be allowed to sack the city'.

Eventually a compromise was reached between Charles VIII and the Signoria, in accordance with which a treaty was agreed upon. Rather than surrender its freedom, the Signoria of Florence was willing to give Charles VIII 150,000 florins, but nothing else. On 25 November a ceremony was held for the signing of the treaty: this was attended by Charles VIII and his advisers, along with the Signoria and a cross-section of the city's representatives. The herald began reading out before the assembled delegates the terms of the solemn treaty — but instead of the agreed total of 150,000 florins, the Signoria had deviously inserted the sum of 120,000 florins. On hearing this, Charles VIII leapt to his feet and threatened: 'We will have to sound our trumpets!'

This was the signal that would call his men to arms throughout Florence, to begin the sack of the city. Capponi, who had befriended Charles during

his awkward childhood, became incensed at what he saw as the imperti-
nence of the gauche young king's threat to Florence. Shaking with fury,
he leapt forward and snatched the treaty from the herald's hands. He then
began tearing it up, scattering the pieces of paper about him contemptu-
ously, declaring: 'If you sound your trumpets, we will ring our bells.' This
was Florence's traditional call to arms, summoning all its citizens to defend
their city. Charles VIII was faced with the prospect of a pitched battle
amidst streets with which his soldiers were unfamiliar, where every alleyway
was known to its inhabitants.

The French king at once tried to calm things down, making a joke, 'O
Capponi, Capponi, what a capon* you are!' Somehow this remark defused
the situation, and Charles VIII now relented, accepting the lesser sum of
120,000. Such a spontaneous climb-down has been attributed to various
causes. Capponi's reckless bravery may well have made Charles VIII immediately suspect that this was all part of a plan, that the citizens of Florence
were now all armed and set to ambush his troops. Either this, or his genuine
feeling for his old friend made him abashed at having so upset the normally
equable Capponi.

The 120,000-florin treaty was now signed, but the tension through the
city continued to rise, with each day bringing further stabbings and kidnap-
pings. And still Charles VIII showed no sign of wishing to depart from
Florence, taking his troops with him. How much longer would he refrain
from allowing his troops to sack the city?

As a last resort, the Signoria called upon Savonarola to try and use his
personal influence with Charles VIII. According to a contemporary report,
Savonarola went to the Palazzo Medici and demanded to see the king.
When the guards barred his way, he simply pushed past them. Inside he
found Charles VIII dressed in full armour, preparing to lead his men in a
sack of the city. Savonarola stood before him and raised a brass crucifix,
whereupon Charles VIII's manner changed and he greeted the priest with
full respect. Savonarola addressed him forcefully, insisting:

---

* That is, a castrated chicken. Many have characterised this as a feeble joke by the dim-witted
Charles VIII, yet under the circumstances it would have appeared to be something of a sharp
pun.

It is not me to whom you should be paying respect. You should be giving honour to Him who is King of Kings, He who grants victory to the kings of this world only in accordance with His will and His justice, but punishes those who are unjust. You and all your men will be destroyed by Him unless you cease at once your cruel treatment of the citizens of our poor city . . .

Savonarola pointed out to the young French king that the longer he stayed in Florence, the more he lessened the impetus of his campaign against Naples. Exasperatedly, he told Charles VIII:

Now listen to the voice of God's servant! Continue on your journey without any more delay. Don't try to ruin this city or you'll bring God's anger down on your head.

Savonarola's words evidently had their effect, for on 28 November Charles VIII and his army duly left Florence. Contemporary reports make it clear that there was a widespread belief amongst the citizens of Florence that the city had been saved only by Capponi's bravery and by Savonarola's calming influence, both on his congregation and on Charles VIII.

Savonarola's spirited demeanour during this tense and difficult period is rendered all the more admirable by what we now know of his personal situation at the time. On 15 November, the very day before he delivered his vital sermon before the French occupation calling for calm and 'urging every man to keep his place', he had learned of the death of his mother in Ferrara. Savonarola's closeness to his mother can be gauged even from the few letters that he wrote to her, where in the view of Ridolfi: 'beneath the pious resolution, there is an unmistakable current of great tenderness not to be found elsewhere'. He also refers warmly to his mother in one of his later sermons. Two days after his mother's death, on the very day the French marched into Florence, Savonarola learned of another death, that of his beloved Pico della Mirandola. This meant that in the course of just a few months he had lost both of his closest secular admirers — for on the night of 28–9 September he had learned of the death of his friend, the poet Poliziano. This had come suddenly and unexpectedly, at the very time when Poliziano was encouraging Botticelli with his painting of *The Calumny of Apelles*, with the intention of persuading Piero de' Medici that the whispers concerning Savonarola preaching against him were in fact nothing but slanders. Yet Poliziano would also be the object of slanderous rumours himself, and on his death a scandalous story began to circulate. According to the rumour, Poliziano had succumbed to a fever brought on by his love for a local Greek youth. In the middle of the night he had been possessed by a frenzy, rushed from his house and begun playing a lute beneath the Greek youth's window; he had then been brought back home, only to expire later that night in a delirium. Savonarola had been deeply upset by Poliziano's death, and had understood at once that the scandalous rumour concerning its circumstances was only intended to blacken his friend and expose his recent conversion to Savonarola's teachings as a mere charade.

Now, on the very day the French army was to march into Florence, Pico too lay on his deathbed, having suddenly succumbed to a fatal illness at the age of just thirty-one. For some time Pico had been torn between his natural inclination to the life of a worldly intellectual, sharing a villa outside Florence with his concubine, and his longing to dedicate his life to God by becoming a Dominican monk – a longing heavily encouraged by his friend Savonarola. Yet now that Pico so suddenly and unexpectedly found his life ebbing away, he is said to have bequeathed all his possessions to San Marco and at last begged Savonarola to receive him into his order. According to legend, Savonarola laid out a Dominican habit over the body of the dying Pico, and later he would be placed in his coffin wearing this habit, buried on Savonarola's instigation in San Marco beside the tomb of his friend Poliziano. After Savonarola had delivered his sermon on the following Sunday, 24 November, he gave a brief oration marking the death of his friend, declaring that 'if he had lived longer he would have written works which would have outshone those of any other during the previous eight centuries'. Savonarola went on to say that he had worried about his friend Pico's ultimate fate, fearing that on account of his life he would be condemned to the everlasting torments of hell. However, during the night Pico had appeared to him in a dream, saying that he was instead expiating his sins in purgatory. This remission had been granted on account of his alms-giving to San Marco and the fervent prayers of its Dominican monks who had come to regard him as one of their brethren.

Pico's death would be mourned all over Italy, as had been the earlier death of his friend Poliziano. Curiously, Savonarola had seen to it that Poliziano too had been buried in the robes of a Dominican monk, despite the fact that – according to a contemporary Florentine – he had been 'the object of as much infamy and public vituperation as it is possible for a man to attract'. This public disgrace had been caused not only by the slanderous rumours that had been spread about the manner of his death, but also by his closeness to Piero de' Medici.

However, all this was to have a sensational denouement. In 2008 the cadavers of both Poliziano and Pico della Mirandola were exhumed in order to try and determine the true cause of their deaths. As reported in the *Daily Telegraph*:

> The scientists used biomolecular technology and scanning equipment as well as DNA analysis to find a cause ... they concluded that both men had been poisoned with arsenic, after finding a toxic quantity in their bones. High levels of mercury and lead were also found ... Silvano Vincenti, head of the national cultural committee that organised the exhumation, said the killers came from Pico's closest circle ... 'Combining the results of our analysis with historical documents which have recently come to light, it seems Piero [de' Medici] was the most likely culprit for the assassination order.'

In the end, Piero de' Medici had never been given Botticelli's *Calumny of Apelles*, and had come to believe the calumnies against Savonarola that were being whispered into his ear. These had finally convinced him that his apparent close friends Poliziano and Pico della Mirandola, who were evidently in such sympathy with the prior of San Marco, were in fact plotting against him and would have to be destroyed.

14

A New Government

THE FRENCH ARMY had left Tuscany in ruins – its ports in French hands, its main thoroughfare under French control. As Guicciardini recorded: 'Florence was stripped of Pisa, Leghorn [Livorno], Sarzana and Pietrasanto – places on which our power, safety, authority and reputation depended.' Other cities in Tuscany, such as Arezzo and Montepulciano in the south, had taken the opportunity to cast off Florentine rule: 'so many lands had been lost and practically our whole dominion had been broken up, that the city was greatly weakened, its income and power diminished'. The Medici days were over, and the city would have to reconstitute itself. Guicciardini described how:

> When Charles VIII had departed, the city was left in civic disorganisation and the citizens set about reforming the government. A plan was put forward by several of the most important citizens whose leaders included ... Piero Capponi ... Lorenzo di Pier Francesco [de' Medici] and Bernardo Rucellai. When they had agreed upon this plan, the bells were rung.

On 2 December 1494, just four days after the French had marched out of Florence, the *Vacca* tolled atop the campanile and the citizens flocked to the Piazza della Signoria for a *parlamento*, to hear and vote upon the plans suggested by the 'principal citizens'. The chief proposals were the abolition of the corrupt councils brought in by the Medici to maintain their power, and that all citizens who had been banished since the Medici took full power in 1434, as well as their families and descendants, were to be allowed to return from exile. To each of these proposals the crowd shouted over-whelmingly in favour. It was also communally decided that 'an election should take place as soon as possible. For the present twenty of the noblest and ablest men would be appointed who would do the work of the Signoria and other offices, until the election should be arranged.' In effect, the council of twenty 'noblest and ablest' citizens would decide upon a new constitution that would replace the old corrupt Medici councils. The coming election would then select a new *gonfaloniere* and Signoria, as well as the members of any new councils set up by the twenty citizens. It was also agreed that the election would be carried out entirely openly and in a manner free from the previous corrupt practices, such as rigging the names of those eligible for office and tampering with the leather ballot bags.

By now many exiles were already beginning to return, the Signoria having posted a general amnesty immediately after Piero de' Medici had fled. This inevitably stirred up old conflicts and a wish for revenge, especially against citizens who had openly supported the Medici and benefited from their rule. As Guicciardini describes it:

> Anyone who had held public office during the time of Lorenzo or Piero was terrified. And the same was true of anyone who had ever harmed, or even whose ancestors had harmed, any of the exiles or their forefathers.

As a precautionary measure, Lorenzo di Pierfrancesco de' Medici decided that in order to dissociate himself from the previous regime, he would change his name from Medici to Popolani (that is, 'of the people'). But there were some who were beyond such cosmetic measures. From the very day when news spread that Piero de' Medici had fled the city, the mobs gathered, bent on revenge, and went in search of his chief henchmen. The house of Piero's financial fixer Miniati was ransacked for cash and then burned to the ground, along with that of several other leading Medici supporters. But Miniati himself and his cronies managed to escape and went on the run within the city as best they could. According to Guicciardini, 'although they had hidden in churches and convents, [they] were eventually taken prisoner to the gaol'. Luckily for them they were arrested by the authorities, or they would certainly have been torn limb from limb by the mob. There was a mood for swift and murderous vengeance throughout the city and, in the attempt to assuage this, the authorities gave in to popular feeling. Landucci recorded in his diary:

12th December (Friday). Antonio di Bernardo di Miniato [Miniati] was hanged in the morning, from a window of the *Casa del Capitano;** and his body remained hanging there until 24 in the evening [8 p.m.].

But the mob were in no mood to be so easily appeased and began baying for more executions of Piero's henchmen. The Twenty caved in, and according to Guicciardini:

They decided that Ser Giovanni, the government notary, should suffer the same fate. He was widely hated and a man of little worth. But Savonarola came to his rescue, preaching from his pulpit that the time for justice was over and instead it was now a time for mercy.

Savonarola was now well into his series of Advent sermons, which were being delivered at the cathedral to such vast crowds that 'there were always 13 or 14 thousand people at his sermons', and these were beginning to act on his every word. As early as 6 December, the diarist recorded how Savonarola had:

preached and ordered that alms should be given to the *Poveri Vergognosi†* . . . These were collected the following day, on Sunday. Indeed, so much was given that it was not possible even to estimate its value. These alms consisted of gold and silver, woollen and linen materials, silks and pearls and all manner of other things. Everyone gave so much out of love and charity.

---

* The residence of the *Podestà*, the militia captain in charge of policing and justice for the city. This building, which resembles a smaller version of the nearby Palazzo della Signoria, is better known as the Bargello.

† Literally 'the shamed poor' – that is to say, those who lived in a state of humiliating destitution.

When Savonarola saw how the Twenty had been willing to follow his recommendation of mercy for Ser Giovanni, he began to sense the true extent of his power. The fate of Florence would be decided during the coming free elections and he was now determined to have his say. On 14 December, Savonarola:

> did all he could in the pulpit to convince the people of Florence to adopt a good form of government ... he preached in some detail about matters of State, and that we must love and fear God, and love good government; and that no one should set himself up proudly above the people. He always favoured the people.

By this stage Savonarola had made it clear that 'he did not want any women to attend his sermons'. He was addressing his words to the enfranchised male population who could attend a *parlamento*, and he wanted as many of these as possible to be present. If Landucci's estimate of the numbers attending his sermons at this time is correct, it means that a large majority of those who could vote were now in attendance.

In the last of Savonarola's Advent sermons before Christmas he demanded that Christ should be declared King of Florence. The administration duly ordered the striking of a coin with the Lily of Florence on one side and on the other the words '*Jesus Christus Rex Noster*' (Jesus Christ Our King). From now on, Florence would be the 'City of God'. Yet even at this stage Savonarola's main concern appeared to be with the spiritual governance of the people; although he left no doubt as to his views on civil governance, political matters were ultimately to be left to the voters themselves. The freest elections in Florence that anyone could recall were now set to take place, and with Savonarola's apparent blessing; he went so far as to declare, 'the one form of government that suits us is a civil, collective government', though he did admonish his congregation of voters: 'May real misfortune strike you, if you choose a tyrant to crush and oppress everybody.' Elections had been promised, but what precise form these would take had yet to be worked out. The difficulties here were formidable. As Villari points out, after so many years of corrupt government:

> the people no longer saw themselves as a democratic body, and lacked

all confidence in themselves. This made the organization of any new government exceedingly difficult ... None of the old Republican forms of government were in any way suited to the present situation. As well as lacking the necessary aptitude, the people had no gifted leaders to guide them through the difficult but essential task of forming a new constitution.

The obvious choice of a leader would have been Piero Capponi, but many were of the opinion that although:

Piero Capponi had won immortality by his defiance of Charles VIII and all his powerful court, he lacked the necessary qualities and patience of a statesman. When brave action was required, and he could draw his sword, he was in his element; yet his ability to sit quietly in his cloak and hood listening to endless nit-picking debates over matters of constitution was quite beyond him.

Discussions concerning a new constitution continued at the Palazzo della Signoria, and Savonarola was called in several times for consultation. In his sermons he had let it be known that he was in favour of a Great Council, which would elect the *gonfaloniere* and the Signoria, as well as all senior posts in the administration, would approve all laws and embark upon a reform of the tax system. Membership of this Great Council would be open to all citizens who qualified for elected posts in the administration – by tradition this included any male over twenty-nine years old who paid taxes, or whose family had in the past provided a senior member of the administration. Desite such restrictions, the council's actual membership would consist of 'one-fifth of the male population over twenty-nine' – initially some 3,200 people. In order that the assembly should retain its democratic nature without being too unwieldy, this larger group was divided into three, with each third serving for six months in turn. At the same time, 'to encourage the young and incite older men to virtue', every three years a further sixty men not eligible to vote would be selected for the Great Council. Despite its limitations, this institution introduced by Savonarola would make the government of Florence comparable with an independent city state in Ancient Greece – arguably the first of its kind in a major European city for more than 1,800 years.

If anything, the Great Council was an improvement on its classical counterparts – as found, for instance, in ancient Athens – for it would prove more efficient in its operation. Although such government was far from being democratic in the modern sense, 'it so broadened the number of citizens who could take part in the making of laws and in elections to public offices that it was regarded then as a *governo populare* [populist government]'.

As ever, politics remained an explosive issue. Landucci recorded how during his Advent sermons Savonarola

> went on discoursing about State matters, and great fear was felt lest the citizens should not agree. *Chi la volava lesso e chi arrosto* (One wished it boiled another roast): i.e. everyone had a different opinion, one agreed with the *Frate* [Savonarola], and another was against him; and if it had not been for him there would have been bloodshed.

Even so, the situation remained fraught. On the very Sunday (21 December) when Landucci wrote the preceding entry in his diary, he also directly contradicted himself by recording how at ten o'clock that evening when he was returning home, for no apparent reason, his son 'was stabbed in the face, across the cheek'.

Next day, 22 December, the elections were duly held and a new Great Council was appointed. But there now arose an unforeseen difficulty, which had not been covered by the new constitution. Before the Great Council could begin what would doubtless be a lengthy process of wrangling over the selection of a new Signoria, the stop-gap Council of Twenty claimed that it remained their right as de facto rulers to appoint a new Signoria at once, so that the city could return to some semblance of proper government.

The Twenty included many leading figures who been publicly outspoken in their opposition to the rule of Piero de' Medici, such as Piero Capponi, Bernardo Rucellai, Francesco Valori and Guidantonio Vespucci. Normally no man could be appointed to such office until he had reached the age of forty, but an exception was made in the case of the thirty-one-year-old Lorenzo di Pierfrancesco Popolani, on account of his leading role in the opposition to his cousin, and also because of the exceptional skills and foresight he had shown in the building of his business empire. The Twenty duly went ahead and elected a new Signoria, and on 1 January 1495 Landucci happily recorded:

> The new Signoria entered into office, and it was a great joy to see the whole Piazza [della Signoria] filled with citizens, quite different from other times, as a new thing, thanking God who had given this impartial government to Florence, and delivered us from subjection. And all this had been done at the instigation of the *Frate*.

Yet despite the Twenty including several figures who had been united in their public opposition to Piero de' Medici's rule, and all being enthusiastic proponents of the city's new democratic form of government, its membership was riven with factions. Piero Capponi, aware that he was not favoured as a leader, had manoeuvred the situation to ensure that his main rival, Paolantonio Soderini, did not get elected to the Twenty. Likewise, the Great Council quickly began to separate into groups, each bent on pursuing their own interests, with voting patterns soon reflecting the differing social and economic aims of its members.

However, this embryo parliament was as nothing compared with the power that Savonarola now held: his sermons had attracted a dedicated following from almost all social classes and outlooks – from the likes of Botticelli and Ficino to the *ciompi* and the destitute. His influence extended far beyond the restrictions of the voting class: the disfranchised majority now, for the most part, hung on his every word.

A year or so later, Savonarola would describe the new democracy as this 'government introduced by me'. Yet as things now stood, besides being favoured by most of those within the government, he also held sway over the majority who had no say in the government. His public forum was not the Great Council, but the pulpit, where none could debate with him or vote against him. Most agreed with the new system that Savonarola had, at the very least, played a major part in introducing, but it was not long before some began to have their misgivings about the extent of his power, both within the government and amongst the population at large, and about how he might choose to use this power. Savonarola himself had earlier warned how 'in Italy, and most of all in Florence, where there is both force and intelligence in abundance, where men have acute minds and restless natures, government by one man can only end in tyranny'. Yet Savonarola had also claimed that the voice of God spoke through him; and the voice of God to which he most frequently alluded was that of the Old Testament, that which unleashed 'the scourge of God', a voice that was willing to destroy all who did not enter his Ark, a voice that brooded no gainsaying. There was mounting unease at this situation, and as Landucci recorded, after listening to Savonarola's preaching many people began to express their superstitious apprehension, saying amongst themselves, 'This wretched priest will bring us bad luck.'

After Charles VIII left Florence, he led the French army south towards Rome. His march was unopposed, and when he reached the Eternal City, Alexander VI fled the Vatican, taking refuge in the ancient papal fortress of Castel Sant' Angelo. By this stage Charles VIII had been joined by Alexander VI's sworn enemy, Cardinal della Rovere. All had observed how the depravity, greed and megalomania of Alexander VI had become even more pronounced since ascending to the papal throne. With utter disregard for sacred or secular public opinion (and even for papal precedent), he had openly moved his children into the Vatican. These included the notorious Cesare Borgia and his sister Lucrezia, whose infamy would soon exceed even that of their father. Cardinal della Rovere did his utmost to persuade Charles VIII to depose Alexander VI, or at least make him submit to a council for the reform of the papacy – which would have amounted to the same thing, but would have involved considerable humiliation and taken longer.

Charles VIII lined up his artillery outside the Castel Sant' Angelo and ordered the pope to come out and meet him, but to no avail. However, after one shot from a powerful French cannon had caused a large section of the ancient medieval walls of the castle to collapse in a heap of rubble, Alexander VI agreed to a meeting. But Cardinal della Rovere had taken into account neither the naive Charles VIII's superstitious reverence for the pope, nor the wiliness of Alexander VI himself. When the pope emerged in all his glory, Charles VIII sank to his knees and attempted to kiss

Alexander VI's feet. With avuncular benevolence Alexander VI raised the overawed young French king to his feet and gave him his blessing. There was no question of the pope being deposed, or even called to order. Nonetheless, Charles VIII's commissioners saw to it that Alexander VI understood the full nature of the defeat that the French were inflicting upon him. The French army occupied Rome, and the Vatican was required to contribute to Charles VIII's needy campaign funds before he set out on the final leg of his journey to Naples.

When the French army left Rome it was accompanied by a 'gift' from Alexander VI consisting of no fewer than nineteen mules laden with boxes of jewels, gold plate and rich tapestries. (It had cost Alexander VI just six similarly laden mules to buy the papacy.) The French insisted that this mule-train should be accompanied by the pope's son, Cesare Borgia, who would join their campaign as a show of goodwill (and as a hostage). But the French were no match for the guile and treachery of the Borgia family. Within two days Cesare Borgia had eluded his captors, taking with him no less than half the train of mules. The boxes carried by the other mules were found to be empty.

Charles VIII was enraged, but was persuaded nonetheless to continue on to Naples. On hearing of the French approach, King Alfonso II immediately abdicated and entered the sanctuary of a monastery, whereupon the new king, his son Ferrante II, simply fled the country, allowing the French army to enter Naples unopposed in triumph. For the next few months Charles VIII indulged his gargantuan sexual appetites on the aristocratic ladies of Naples and their virgin daughters, whilst his soldiers indulged their similar appetites on the less virtuous women of the city, unaware that syphilis had just reached Naples by way of Spain from the New World.

The French king was eventually persuaded to abandon his ambitious scheme to liberate Constantinople from the Turks and then take Jerusalem. Instead, he would return with his army to France. However, Alexander VI was determined to avenge his humiliation; he set about persuading the other Italian powers that the French insult to the leader of the Christian flock, St Peter's representative on Earth, should not go unpunished. He even managed to persuade Ludovico 'il Moro' Sforza, who now regretted his original invitation to Charles VIII to invade Italy, to join an alliance with the papal forces and the powerful Venetian army, so that in March 1495 a Holy League against the French was signed in Venice. Only Florence refused to join: Savonarola insisted that the city could not resist Charles VIII, as he was the instrument of God's will.

In May 1495 Charles VIII duly led his vast French army out of Naples, leaving Ferrante II to be welcomed back by the relieved population. The French soldiers now began their 700-mile march north, followed by their long medieval train of hangers-on, their collection of pillaged holy relics and Charles VIII's precious Sword of Charlemagne, spreading syphilis through Italy in their wake. At their approach, Alexander VI fled from Rome; meanwhile Commines was despatched on a French diplomatic mission to Florence to determine whether the city would renege on its word and join the Holy League. Here he went straight to meet Savonarola:

because he had always preached strongly in favour of the King, and it was his word which had prevented the Florentines from turning against us, for never had any preacher ever had so much influence over the city.

The worldly Commines was once again impressed by Savonarola and began asking him about his prophecies:

He has preached that the present state of the Church will be reformed by force of arms. This has not yet happened, although it very nearly did [when Charles VIII was in Rome], and he still insists that it will happen . . . I also asked him if the king will be able to get back [to France] without danger to himself, in view of the great army which has been assembled by the Venetians, about which he seemed to know more than I did . . . He replied that the King would have to fight his way back, but his courage would see him through, though he might only have one hundred men with him, because God who had led him here would also lead him back.

In the event, Savonarola's prediction had more than an element of truth. A month later, on 6 July, the French army encountered the combined forces of the Holy League at Fornovo on the banks of a tributary of the Po, some seventy miles south-east of Milan. The French troops were heavily outnumbered – some say by as much as three to one, though they were supported by their fearsome artillery. The battle was fought in chaotic conditions amidst a thunderstorm, and even if technically it resulted in a French victory, there was a devastating loss of life on both sides. Charles VIII was able to proceed back to France with considerably more than 100 men, but he lost much of his army's booty, holy relics and his beloved Sword of Charlemagne.

Alexander VI was outraged at Charles VIII's escape. He blamed Florence for the defeat of the army of the Holy League, and more specifically the malign influence of Savonarola. Senior clergy in Rome were urging Alexander VI to use his prerogative and take direct action against Savonarola. Amongst the most enthusiastic of these was Fra Mariano da Genazzano, the one-time favourite preacher of Florence, whom Savonarola had humiliated to the point where he had left the city. Fra Mariano was now head of the Augustinian order and had the ear of Alexander VI.

Though Savonarola had for years now been preaching, in the strongest possible terms, against corruption in the Church, he had not yet made any direct reference to Alexander VI. In the light of this, Alexander VI chose to exercise guile, rather than any heavy-handed papal authority, in dealing with Savonarola. On 25 July he wrote a papal Brief addressed to Savonarola in Florence. Ridolfi accurately characterises this as 'a most peculiar document which might be figuratively compared to the famous poisoned sweets of Borgia'. Alexander VI's Brief was coached in the most friendly and disarming diplomatic terms, explaining:

We have heard you proclaim that what you have said concerning future events does not proceed from yourself but comes from God. We therefore desire, as it is the duty of our pastoral office, to discourse with you so that we may gain from you a greater understanding of what is agreeable to God, and put this into practice. Thus we exhort you, in the name of holy obedience, to come to Rome without further delay, where we will receive you with love and charity.

Savonarola may have been an idealist, but he was not naive. He well knew what would happen if he took up Alexander VI's invitation: trial, imprisonment or, more likely, assassination en route would be his fate. On 31 July he wrote to Alexander VI apologising for not being able to take up his invitation:

> firstly, because my body has been weakened by illness, and I am suffering from fever and dysentery. Secondly, my constant exertions on behalf of the welfare of the state of Florence have caused me to suffer from a constant agitation, in both my body and my mind . . . so bad is this that my physicians have ordered me to cease preaching and give up my studies, for unless I take proper remedies I will be bound for an early grave . . . It is God's will that I remain here for the time being, and I have been urged by prudent counsel not to leave . . . However, if Your Holiness wishes to learn what I have publicly preached concerning coming events such as the ruin of Italy and the renewal of the Church, I am in the process of printing a small book on these matters.* As soon as this is completed, I shall be most careful to send Your Holiness a copy.

This may seem on the surface like a blend of effrontery and defiance (to say nothing of sheer bravado), and there is little doubt this was how it was received by the Church authorities in Rome. In fact, as we have seen, Savonarola was a stickler for the truth. This illness was no manufactured excuse: his constant exertions both in the government and in the pulpit, to say nothing of his self-imposed regimen of vigils and fasting, seem to have led him to the verge of a severe mental and physical breakdown. Indeed, so serious was this debilitation that even he himself feared that he might not recover from it. On Wednesday 29 July, just two days before sending his letter to Alexander VI, Savonarola had preached a 'last sermon' in the cathedral. The Signoria and all the leading figures in the administration were amongst the packed and expectant congregation.

It is worth paying some attention to the details of this sermon, for at

---

* This was his *Compendium Revelationum* ('Compendium of Revelations').

the time Savonarola certainly viewed it as a specific, possibly even final, testament. Although he opened by proclaiming that his preaching that day was 'inspired by love', he soon returned to his constant theme, in his usual passionate manner, fulminating against the sinners whom he saw all around him in Florence — the gamblers, the loose women, the blasphemers, the sodomites and others whose sins were too vile to mention. Their very presence polluted the city, and despite his presence they persisted in their vices. How much worse would it be when he was no longer able to preach? An example must be made: any found to be guilty of such sins merited no less than the death penalty. 'I warn you, Almighty God desires justice . . . Renounce all dancing, gaming, and close down the taverns. This is a time for weeping, not for rejoicing . . . as punishment for just one sinner, God vented his wrath upon the entire tribe of Israel. God would only be appeased by the death of this sinner.'

Turning his attention to the Signoria and the rulers of the city, he insisted that they proceed at once with plans for building a new hall to house the Great Council, and that a law should be passed abolishing the *parlamento*, which had been used by previous unscrupulous rulers to bring in new measures to protect their rule.*

Finally, at the end of his sermon, Savonarola bade his flock farewell: 'O My People, when I stand here before you in this pulpit I am always strong, but when I descend from it down those stairs, I believe that my ailments will return. It will be some time before I see you once more. Then I will preach to you again, if I am still alive.' He mentioned that his absence might only be 'for a few months'. Yet then he exclaimed, 'I am content to be a martyr, indeed I pray for this each day.'

Some have seen this final remark as a presentiment of his death. He was now to take on directly the full might of the papacy, in the form of

---

* Here, contrary to appearances, Savonarola was being historically accurate. The Florentines may have been proud of their *parlamento*, but it was nonetheless open to abuse. The citizens who came to vote were unarmed, but the entrances to the Piazza della Signoria were manned by armed men, ostensibly to keep order. However, these had on occasion been used to turn away voters who were known to be anti-Medici, while those who were allowed to enter the square had then been intimidated into voting for the establishment of new councils whose sole purpose had been to preserve Medici power. Savonarola placed his political faith in the less pliable democracy of the Great Council.

the devious and vengeful Alexander VI, and he may well have felt that he was venturing out of his depth. Savonarola was not a man to be easily cowed, yet direct personal contact with the pope – even if only in the form of a papal Brief – must surely have made him aware of the full enormity of the task he had so blithely taken upon himself in his idealistic youth. Other commentators on this sermon have pointed to its lack of modesty and supreme ambition. For all his wish for rule by the people, and freedom from tyranny, Savonarola was in fact advocating a tyranny of his own. He preached freedom from evil, yet both his 'freedom' and his 'evil' were double-edged. The freedom, as well as the evil, fell into two categories: freedom from political evil (tyranny), and freedom from spiritual evil (vice). The people must be made free to rule themselves, but they must also be made free from rule by their vices. Both would require coercion – one by the people on their own behalf, the other exerted on the people themselves. Here we are brought face to face with the profound distinction between public life and private life. Reflecting on his own life, Savonarola saw little or no distinction between the two: one must reflect the other. Few would disagree that there is an overlap between the civic and the spiritual (or personal) realm; but Savonarola had chosen to see them as synonymous, even identical. Just as there was no room for personal vice, so there was no room for opposition to the rule of the people. Here was a testament that would resound through each ensuing century, right down to our own: fundamentalism seeing itself as freedom from all things that do not conform to its principles, with the necessity to purge society of these corrupting elements. Such missionary fundamentalism may begin in the monastery, yet it must by its very nature spread out into the world – and here it is contrary to its very being to coexist with any opposition.

Having delivered himself of his testament, Savonarola retired to his cell at San Marco to finish his letter replying to Alexander VI, and to make the final corrections to his 'Compendium of Revelations'. This short work of around a hundred pages, which appeared in Latin and Italian versions, is a key document in our understanding of Savonarola at this stage in his life. Significantly, it opens with a justification: he wishes to set down in his own words his most widely known prophecies and visions. Many of these had become exaggerated and distorted as they had been passed on by word of mouth, and he now wished people to understand their truth: to see them for what they were, in the very words that he had used to describe them. Where previously he had not always claimed to be a prophet, he now fully accepted the mantle, claiming: 'The Lord has placed me here, and said to me: "I have placed thee as a watchman in the centre of Italy ... that thou mayest hear My words and announce them."' He claimed that he was able to tell his visions came from God because 'they are infused with a certain supernatural light'. Modern psychological patients afflicted with hallucinations frequently speak of an 'ethereal light' that accompanies their visions, once again reinforcing Savonarola's claim that he almost certainly 'saw' what he characterised as his 'symbolical visions' and 'heard' the prophetic voices that he claimed were 'spoken by angels'.*

Revealingly, Savonarola also described how his supernatural gift evolved:

> To begin with I predicted the future by saying what was written in the Bible, using reason and parables, because people were not yet ready to hear me. After this I began to reveal what I knew of the future from a source other than the Bible. Until at last I confessed openly that what I was saying came directly from God.

It is not difficult to detect the growth of self-induced belief here, as it evolved from intense but reassuring readings of biblical events, through identification with those who featured in these events, to full-blown self-delusion – aided as it was by extreme fasting, vigils and a regime of the strictest self-denial. Alone in his cell, in a mental world of the Old Testament and the Book of Revelation – a world of prophets, the wrath of God being visited upon the errant tribe of Israel, and the vision of doom accompanying the end of time – it is not surprising that he began to see himself as inhabiting such an essentially pre-Christian world.†

The tongue-tied mumbler who had delivered his first feeble sermons in

---

* Many migraine sufferers experience scintillation or flickering brilliance during their hallucinations, whose content can be utterly convincing to those undergoing this condition. Hildegard of Bingen's descriptions of her religious visions, as well as the visionary paintings of William Blake and Van Gogh, all contain these characteristic features.
† The Book of Revelation is of course far from being pre-Christian, yet its tone and indeed many of its images hark back to the prophets of the Judaic era.

Florence had at last found release in his revelatory Lenten sermons at San Gimignano. Comforting himself that he had not been abandoned by God, he had read avidly of this apocalyptic world, and now he had taken his first steps into it. Even so, in his 'Compendium' Savonarola faced up to the question that he must, as a devout believer, have asked himself many times: 'Could these visions be the work of the Devil?' He decided, on his own empirical grounds, that these could not be the work of the Devil – his visions and prophecies had come true, and not once had they deceived him. However, such 'symbolical visions' are notoriously open to all manner of interpretation. Savonarola harked back to the visions he had seen of the sword of God poised ready to scourge the corrupt world, as well as the black cross rising out of the city of Rome. These visions had either come to pass (at least metaphorically) or were about to do so. We have already seen how Savonarola's prophecy that the 'scourge of God' would arrive from 'across the mountains' could just as well have applied to the Turks as to the French. Seward even mentions how in the 'Compendium' Savonarola made a revealing admission:

> Describing his embassy to Charles, he recalls explaining that God had appointed the King as His 'minister of justice'. He had told Charles that he knew the French were coming long before, but God would not let him speak the king's name.

At the time Savonarola had made his original prophecy (1492), Charles VIII had only just come of age and taken full possession of the French throne. Few had then known of the young king's dreams of glorious conquest, which had not materialised until two years later. Besides, Florence remained France's close ally and, as such, would have had nothing to fear from any French invasion. Up until this point Savonarola's prophecy had been vague and general (predicting only that 'the new Cyrus' would come from 'across the mountains'). It was not until Piero de' Medici had begun to vacillate in his loyalty to France that Florence had reason to fear Charles VIII. Only then, according to Savonarola, had God 'let him speak the king's name'. Probably it would be more exact to say that only then had Savonarola *realised* the new Cyrus was to be Charles VIII.

The next part of the 'Compendium' describes in some detail a pilgrimage that Savonarola claimed to have made to see the Virgin Mary in heaven, accompanied by four companions: Faith, Simplicity, Prayer and Patience. His inspiration here was undoubtedly Dante's *Divine Comedy*, though his description of his actual meeting with the Virgin has echoes of the early sixth-century Roman philosopher Boethius' description of his encounter with the female embodiment of Philosophy. This appears in Boethius' *The Consolation of Philosophy*, a book that widely influenced medieval and Renaissance Christianity and was certainly well known to Savonarola. Others have remarked upon the similarity between Savonarola's detailed description of the Virgin's bejewelled throne and that which appears in the Coronation of the Virgin, the last of the Mysteries of the Rosary, a subject that was not only popular with Dominican monks, but also inspired many artists. These borrowings would appear to have been unconscious, as is frequently the case in the poetic imagination. Savonarola's visions and prophecies may have been biblical in manner, yet they undeniably contained elements that were beyond purely biblical poetry. He may on occasion have referred to his visions as 'symbolical', yet at other times he undeniably stressed that he wished his visions to be taken literally.

Did Savonarola convince himself that he had actually visited the Virgin Mary in heaven? There can be no doubt that he persuaded many amongst his congregation that he had done so. This was not a sceptical age: in the previous century people would point out Dante in the street, believing that he had travelled through hell, purgatory and paradise, just as he had described in his *Divine Comedy*. Not for nothing was Savonarola accompanied on his divine pilgrimage by 'Simplicity': the 'little friar' always maintained that his sermons were primarily addressed to 'simple folk'. Others less simple, such as Ficino and Botticelli, were left to judge in their own minds the veracity – poetic or actual – of his visions. In the 'Compendium of Revelations', which would not have been available to illiterate 'simple folk', Savonarola answered his more sophisticated critics:

They know I do not mean to claim that my mortal body has visited Paradise, only that I experienced this in a mental vision. For certain, the trees, streams, doors and thrones that I describe do not exist in

Paradise. If these sceptical critics had not been so blinded by their own malice, they would understand how such scenes were placed before my mind's eye by the angels.

Such a defence is credible as a description of poetic inspiration, even for those who do not believe in angels. Yet Savonarola allowed no room for such open interpretation of the messages contained in his visions: here the word of God spoke through him. And his conversation with the Virgin Mary in heaven certainly fell into the latter category. She told him how:

The City of Florence shall become more glorious, more powerful and more wealthy than it has ever been. All the territory that it has lost shall be restored, and its borders will be extended further than ever before. With the guidance of the Holy Spirit, you have prophesied the conversion of the infidels, of the Turks and the Moors, and more, and this will all take place in good time, soon enough for it to be seen by many who are alive today ... But as you have said, the renovation of the Church cannot take place without the suffering of many tribulations. Therefore, let it not seem strange that Florence shall have her share of troubles, though she shall suffer less than the rest ... The good citizens will be less afflicted, according to their conduct, and in particular according to how severely they pass laws against the blasphemers, the gamblers, the sodomites and other evil doers ... And with these words I was dismissed from the company of the Holy Virgin.

In Savonarola's 'Compendium of Revelations' we see him as the potent blend of a medieval religious poet (the mystic visionary) and an Old Testament prophet.* Here lay the further strength of Savonarola's appeal to both intellectuals and the 'simple folk'. Yet whereas the religious mystic usually existed at the fringes of society, the Old Testament prophets placed themselves fair and square at its heart. They sought to lead the people of

---

* An interesting comparison can be made here with Joan of Arc, who was both a mystic visionary (hearing voices and seeing angels) and a prophet (who led France to the victories she had foreseen).

Israel, to castigate them in the name of God and rule over them. If Savonarola was to fulfil the role he had now created for himself, it was inevitable that he would have to intensify the political leadership he had assumed, on behalf of democracy and the poor, and take over a greater measure of secular power.

The publication of the 'Compendium of Revelations' in Florence on 18 August 1485 meant that Savonarola's influence, if not his actual power, began to reach a far wider audience. Such was its popularity that within three weeks four further editions had come out in Italian. A month later the first Latin edition appeared, translated by Savonarola himself. This was the edition that spread his name far and wide amongst the clergy and scholars; and just as he hoped, it was soon being read beyond the borders of Italy. During 1496 no fewer than four further Latin editions would be printed, including one in Paris and one in southern Germany. According to Burlamacchi, even Sultan Bejazit II in Constantinople ordered a copy, which was translated for him.

The widely perceived corruption of the Church, especially since Alexander VI had become the successor to St Peter and thus God's representative on Earth, had created a thirst for revelation which came directly from the divine source. Indeed, Savonarola's apocalyptic visions were so reminiscent of the Revelation of St John the Divine, the last book of the Bible, that some even wondered if these visions might not be a long-awaited continuation of the holy book. Likewise, Savonarola's prophecies of the renewal of the Church were seen as nothing less than a vision of a miraculous reformation,* and struck many throughout Christendom with the full force of a miracle that was long overdue.

---

*The actual Reformation, instigated by Martin Luther, would not begin until twenty-two years later, in 1517. This would not bring about the internal revolution Savanarola sought, but would become essentially external and resulted in a schism that he would have deplored.

15

The Voices of Florence

D ESPITE THE EVIDENT popularity of Savonarola's sermons, along with widespread satisfaction that Medici rule had been replaced by a more republican government, Florence was now a divided city. And the focus of this division was undeniably Savonarola. The most loyal supporters of the 'little friar' remained the *Frateschi* (the 'Friar's Men'), mainly drawn from amongst the monks of San Marco and their intellectual friends. However, Savonarola's largest support came from those referred to derisively as the *Piagnoni* – a word that covered a spectrum of meanings. Literally, it means 'snivellers', 'grumblers' or 'wailers' – that is the downtrodden who were always snivelling away or complaining, and wailing out their prayers. These were Savonarola's beloved 'simple folk', who despite his pleas for forgiveness and reconciliation still retained a deep-seated hatred for the Medici and their supporters, many of whom had of course fled the city. However, although those who remained behind had for the time being prudently adopted a low profile, they nonetheless represented a considerable force, who referred to themselves as the *Bigi* (the 'Greys'), and would soon begin plotting for the return of Piero de' Medici. As for Piero de' Medici himself, he too still represented a distinct threat to Florence. Along with his well-connected brother Cardinal Giovanni, he had begun to solicit support for the Medici cause amongst various states, as well as the upper echelons of the Church, especially Alexander VI. Savonarola's rejection of the Holy League had ensured that opinion in Rome, and indeed amongst leaders throughout Italy, was now swinging behind the reinstatement of the Medici.

However, the main opposition to Savonarola soon emerged from within

Florence itself, in the form of the *Arrabbiati* (the 'Enraged Ones'),* a widespread group who resented Savonarola's interference in the city's secular government, some of whom also favoured a return to the old Medici days. Then there were the secular liberals who called themselves the *Bianchi* (the 'Whites'), to distinguish themselves from the 'Greys'; though glad to see the back of the Medici, they retained a nostalgic affection for the easygoing times of Lorenzo the Magnificent, and also believed that priests had no place in a republican government. Another group on the same side of the divide as the *Arrabbiati*, though hardly as passionate in their views, were the *Tiepidi* (the 'Tepid Ones' – that is, lukewarm, or moderate in their opinions). The *Tiepidi* were opposed to Savonarolan reform and drew much of their support from the permissive priests who saw no reason why their vows should confine them to a life of puritan penury. Besides being popular amongst the wealthy families from which many of the *Tiepidi* originated, this faction also had important links with Rome.

Nonetheless, the two main opposing groups in Florence remained the *Arrabbiati* and the *Piagnoni*, with the others aligning themselves alongside either one of these, with more or less sympathy. Savonarola remained the essential divisive factor. Both of these leading factions had their fervent advocates in the Great Council, even though the disenfranchised *Piagnoni* were not directly represented. Savonarola made it his duty to see that *Piagnoni* interests were taken into account, and their sheer numbers amongst the population, who now felt a new confidence as a result of the city's liberation, ensured that their influence was felt.

The importance that Savonarola attached to the Great Council cannot be overestimated, at least at this early stage. He saw it as the safeguard of the citizens' recently gained freedom, and pressed the Signoria to start as soon as possible on the building of a large chamber in the Palazzo della Signoria where the working quorum of 500 members of the Great Council could conduct their daily business. This chamber would be a material and symbolic manifestation of the new government, and the site chosen was on the first floor above a courtyard on the north side of the building known as the *Dogana* (formerly used as a customs house). The Signoria

* Not for nothing does this word have connotations with 'rabid' and thus 'rabies'.

seems to have handed over the entire project to Savonarola from the outset, and he quickly appointed the local architect Simone del Pollaiuolo, a close friend and firm believer in his ideas. The building of this great chamber attracted widespread popular attention, and an indication of this interest (as well as the speed with which it was constructed) can be judged from entries in Landucci's diary. On 18 July 1495 he recorded: 'at the *Dogana* the foundations for the Great Hall were being laid; and the *Frate* was constantly encouraging this work'. Less than a month later, on 12 August, he noted: 'The vaulting of the roof of the Great Hall has been finished.' This must have been some feat for a hall of such a size. The present Salone dei Cinquecento (Chamber of the Five Hundred), as it is still known, is only a slight extension of the original hall, yet it measures 170 feet long, 75 feet wide and more than 25 feet high.

Some have seen this chamber, and the range of groups across the political spectrum that met within it, as the beginnings of modern political party politics as we know it. There is no doubting an embryonic resemblance here, but as the modern historian Lauro Martines argues: 'though we may use the word "party", we must [not confuse] the implied meaning with anything like the anatomy of a modern political machine'. Even in republican Florence, there was nothing approaching democratic politics in our modern Western sense, just as there was no idea of universal suffrage. Class, group and family interests held sway, whilst ideology remained for the most part incoherent, certainly not articulated in any explicit programme.

Hence, even comparatively democratic Florence was unable to sustain a political party system as such. Any notion of semi-permanent adherence was unlikely to survive in a constitution where the elected Signoria only lasted in office for two months, and where membership of the Great Council expired after six months. Under such circumstances alliances between leading figures were liable to switch, and any that reached beyond family ties were quick to revert to trusted kinship loyalty at the first signs of difficulty. At the same time, there remained the all-important matter of commercial partnerships so essential for business of any sort, and the power of patronage, without which no young man could fulfil his political, administrative, commercial or artistic ambitions. These too were mainly structures of extended family loyalties, cemented by marriages and so forth.

You did not send a man to represent your business or act as your manager in another city unless you could be absolutely sure of his loyalty and willingness to follow instructions. On top of this, as Martines makes clear, the political process was simply not capable of tolerating overt dissent, 'or even – as an acknowledged right – peaceful opposition to a governing clique'. The entire notion of a democratic opposition remained unacceptable. Those who spoke out publicly against government policy were liable to be arrested and thrown in prison. Even if a senior member of a leading family voiced his opposition publicly, he and his entire family could be sent into exile or silenced by punitive taxes which could reduce them to ruin.

Indeed, opposition remained a clandestine and dangerous business. Not for nothing were the ardent Medici supporters known as the *Bigi*, a bland colour tone that was intended to emphasise their low-profile invisibility – for their contacts with Piero de' Medici, as well as their suggestion that he launch an invasion that they would support, were undeniably treason, and as such punishable by death. Opposition thus manifested itself in subversive action, the opposite of loyalty to the state. Violence, such as assassination, was another political measure to which opposing factions were liable to resort. Savonarola was a particular target, and when he left San Marco to walk through the streets to another church where he was delivering a sermon, he was invariably accompanied by a bodyguard of loyal followers. As Landucci recorded: 'On 24 May some people attempted to attack Frate Girolamo in the Via del Cocomero after he had delivered a sermon.' Indeed, Savonarola himself in his letter to Alexander VI on 31 July included amongst the reasons for his inability to visit Rome:

There are many enemies here who are thirsting after my blood and have made several attempts upon my life, both by assassination and by poison. For this reason I am unable to venture out of doors in safety without endangering myself, unless I am accompanied by armed guards, even within the city, let alone abroad.

There had also been a serious downturn in trade, resulting largely from the continuing independence of Pisa, which had simply refused to resubmit to Florentine rule once the French garrison imposed by Charles VIII had withdrawn. The port of Pisa stood at the mouth of the River Arno and thus controlled much of Florence's overseas trade. In an attempt to remedy this stranglehold the Signoria in Florence had hired a mercenary army to retake Pisa, but so far this had proved both ineffective and costly. Even such wealthy merchants as Lorenzo di Pierfrancesco could no longer afford to support the art that had played such a leading role in the Renaissance in Florence. As a result, Florentine artists were beginning to seek employment in other cities, and the Renaissance was spreading throughout Italy with profound effect upon an age when, according to the great nineteenth-century Swiss historian Jacob Burckhardt:

> both sides of human consciousnesss — that which turned inwards as well as that which turned towards the outer world — lay obscured beneath a common veil, either dreaming or merely half awake. This veil was woven out of faith, childlike prejudices and illusion; and seen through it, the world and its history appeared tinted in strange hues. Man was conscious of himself only as a member of a race, a nation, a party, a corporation, a family, or in some other general category. It was in Italy that this veil first dissolved into thin air, allowing an *objective* perception and treatment of the state, as well as all things of this world in general. At the same time, the *subjective* side asserted itself with similar emphasis, allowing man to become a self-aware *individual* and to recognise himself as such.

Perceptive minds, such as those of Lorenzo di Pierfrancesco, understood that this profound transformation which was taking place within their culture was progressive in nature — despite its insistence upon harking back to the achievements of the classical era. Western European humanity was evolving — commercially expanding trade routes into new continents, and culturally expanding on a similar scale into territory previously unexplored by Europeans. The clock could not be turned back. Savonarola may have been a moving force for a more equitable society, yet ironically such political progressivism was yoked to a cultural and moralistic conservatism. As a patron of the arts, Lorenzo di Pierfrancesco was determined that, at least in its progressive sense, Lorenzo the Magnificent's legacy should be encouraged. When his favourite young artist Michelangelo returned to Florence a year after his flight to Bologna, Lorenzo di Pierfrancesco resolved to help him as best he could during these difficult times. According to Ascanio Condivi, to whom Michelangelo recounted his life during his last years:

> When Michelangelo returned to his homeland he began carving a marble statue of Eros, at the age of six or seven, lying as if asleep. When Lorenzo di Pierfrancesco de' Medici saw this work he could not but admire its classical beauty, and suggested a plan to Michelangelo, telling him, 'If you could treat the marble so that it looks as if it has been buried, I can send this to Rome and pass it off as a rare ancient work which has recently been unearthed, and you could get a far better price for it.' Michelangelo was such a genius that he knew even the most devious tricks of his trade, and when he heard Lorenzo di Pierfrancesco's words he immediately set to work as he had suggested.

But this scam did not go entirely according to plan. The man chosen by Lorenzo di Pierfrancesco to negotiate the sale in Rome of Michelangelo's statue to the wealthy Cardinal Raffaele Riario succeeded in persuading the cardinal of the authenticity of this 'rare ancient find', for which he then paid an undisclosed, but substantial, sum. The go-between then kept most of this for himself, cheating both Michelangelo and Lorenzo di Pierfrancesco. Meanwhile Cardinal Riario, who was a renowned connoisseur, soon discovered that his 'ancient' sculpture was in fact a contemporary fake. However, he was so impressed by the sheer skill of Michelangelo's work that he invited the artist to Rome to work for him — thus fulfilling what had probably been Lorenzo di Pierfrancesco's intention all along. Michelangelo would live in Rome for the next three years, producing some of his first masterpieces for a series of rich patrons. These included a magnificent larger than life-sized statue of a tipsy *Bacchus*, the Ancient Roman god of wine, which Vasari perceptively noted has 'all the slenderness of male youth somehow combined with the sensuality and roundness of the female form'. By contrast, this was also the period when Michelangelo produced his first transcendent religious masterpiece, the *Pietà*, depicting Mary grieving over the naked body of the dead Christ in her lap, a work that caused Michelangelo's contemporary Vasari to wonder at:

> the miracle of how such a formless block of stone could be trans-
> formed to such a perfection of the flesh as nature herself is scarce
> capable of producing.

Such depictions of the delights of wine and the perfection of naked flesh were hardly the kind of work that Michelangelo could have produced in Savonarola's 'City of God'. Michelangelo's profound belief in God may have been attuned to that of Savonarola, but only by escaping from his influence was Michelangelo capable of fulfilling the genius that had first been recognised in him by Lorenzo the Magnificent. Only amidst the corruption of Rome would this most religious of artists be able to carry forward the promise of the Renaissance and realise his own leading role in its promulgation.

Botticelli, on the other hand, remained behind in Florence. According to Vasari, who grew up in Florence just two decades later and must there-fore have heard at first hand from fellow citizens who had lived through these times:

> Botticelli became such an ardent follower of Savonarola's teachings
> that he was induced to give up painting altogether. As this meant he
> had no means of earning a living his life fell into the greatest disorder.
> Yet this only served to make him an even more fervent member of
> the Piagnoni and abandon all thought of following his vocation.

Vasari was almost certainly wrong about Botticelli abandoning painting during this period, for several canvases have been reliably dated from these years. However, there is no doubt that the market for paintings all but ceased in Savonarola's 'City of God', leaving many accomplished artists without any source of income. Possibly as a result of poverty, Botticelli is known to have transferred his studio and moved in with his brother Simone Filipepi, who lived in the Via Nuova. Simone was renowned as a strong

Piagnoni sympathiser, though his continuing love of secular literature would seem to go against his alleged belief in the imminent and absolute truth of Savonarola's apocalyptic predictions. Around this time, in the latter half of 1495, Botticelli was probably still involved in completing his drawings to illustrate Dante's *Divine Comedy* – a private task that may well have encouraged the rumours concerning his abandonment of his vocation.

Many experts believe that during this time Botticelli also painted his late masterpiece *Lamentation over the Dead Christ*, which depicts the traditional grieving figures around Christ's prostrate body. This is the work of a soul coming to terms with his new life. The Virgin Mary's expression is utterly blank with grief, the saints around her exhibiting their own range of sorrowful emotions. The face of the female figure to the right all but blends with that of the dead Christ; as she presses her cheek to his, one can almost sense the closeness of her breath against Christ's deathly palllid cheek. Yet if we look more closely we can see that this is unmistakably the face that Botticelli once depicted in *The Birth of Venus*, as she rose from the waves. Whilst the figure to the left tending to the wounds in the dead Christ's feet is recognisable as one of the dancing goddesses from *Primavera*. Botticelli's serene pagan beauties have succumbed to heart-rending grief over the figure who has succeeded them in Botticelli's heart.

In many ways this *Lamentation* reflected a similar transformation that was taking place amongst the people of Florence – or at least among the majority who now saw Savonarola as their leader, politically as well as spiritually. They would no longer just be his followers, they would *believe* in him. They would abandon their old way of life, their joys and their sadnesses, to dedicate themselves as the new citizens of the 'City of God'. There was no denying the strength of faith, amounting almost to a contained collective hysteria, that now began to infuse the downtrodden *Piagnoni* and their followers.

Yet as we have seen, not all of Savonarola's followers were *Piagnoni*. Even amongst those who fervently believed in him and his call for a return to the simplicity of the early Christian way of life, there still remained that intellectual element that had once included so many of Lorenzo the Magnificent's circle at the Palazzo Medici. Representative of these was Ficino, who wished Savonarola to reinforce his colleagues' blind faith with the strength of an earlier tradition. Where Savonarola harked back to the Old Testament prophets, Ficino still wished to persuade him to incorporate the philosophical tradition of Platonism into his faith. As well as inspiring humanism, Plato's ideas had also provided an intellectual backing for much Christian theology. Ficino regarded Plato much like a Christian saint whose ideas had prepared the ground prior to the arrival of Christ himself. Where St John the Baptist had come to be regarded as Christ's religious herald, Plato should be recognised as his intellectual forerunner.

Plato's inclusion in the Christian heritage would unite all who were attracted to Savonarola's beliefs, as well as giving this faith a philosophical foundation that few amongst the growing number of Renaissance intellectuals throughout Italy could have resisted. Here was a faith that would eliminate the growing pagan element amongst the humanists. If Savonarola was to establish Florence as the centre of a new Christendom, surely this was the way forward. Here lay the foundations of a religious Renaissance to match – indeed, surpass – the artistic and intellectual Renaissance that had been born in Florence. What the Bible promised for the *Piagnoni*, Plato could provide for intellectual believers and leaders all over Italy, who had become so disillusioned with the corrupt Church establishment in Rome.

Yet now, to Ficino's consternation, Savonarola continued to have his doubts about the orthodoxy of some of Plato's later thinking, and especially that of his followers. Such late Platonic thinking had led Ficino to believe in a number of hermetic ideas, some of which had originally struck a peculiar chord with a number of Savonarola's metaphysical notions. We know from Savonarola's record of his revelations that he believed in the existence of, and even saw, such things as angels and demons. He was also a profound believer in prophecy, most notably when this sprang from the visions he saw in his mind's eye. But such notions of prophecy derived directly from the prophets of the Old Testament. On the other, hand, Savonarola detested other more esoteric forms of prophecy such as astrology. Such beliefs were pure heresy.

16

'A bolt from the blue'

INITIALLY, IT SEEMED that little attention had been paid in the Vatican to Savonarola's impudent reply to Alexander VI, refusing his cordial invitation to visit Rome. The pope had other matters on his mind: after the humiliation inflicted on him by Charles VIII and the French army on their passage through Rome, he now had to re-establish his power in the Holy City, and at the same time plan his next political move on the Italian scene.

After Savonarola had delivered his 'last sermon' at the end of July 1495, overseen the first edition of his 'Compendium of Revelations' into print and despatched his letter replying to Alexander VI, he had retired to the summer countryside to recover from the mental and physical exhaustion brought on by his ascetic way of life and by his strenuous attempts to guide Florentine politics, all exacerbated by his dysentery. It seems most likely that he stayed at the hospice of Santa Maria del Sasso in the mountains at Casentino some thirty miles east of Florence. Two years previously this had become part of the independent Tuscan Congregation under the rule of Savonarola, and his stay thus coincided with his intention to visit all the institutions that had recently come under his rule. Away from the heat and stress of the city, along with the self-imposed intensity of his life at San Marco, Savonarola had gradually begun to recover his health and strength.

Then, some time during the second week in September, with all the force of 'a bolt from the blue', a papal Brief arrived in Florence from Rome. This was dated 8 September, was certainly not composed by Alexander VI, and was probably not even written on his direct orders. However, its composition and method of address betrayed all the skill of a highly accomplished political operator, to say nothing of a man well versed in the ways of the Church. It is now known that this so-called papal Brief was in fact penned by Bartolomeo Floridi, Bishop of Cosenza, a leading member of the papal secreteriat, almost certainly at the prompting of Piero de' Medici or his followers in Rome.*

All the better to serve his purpose, and possibly to cover his tracks, Floridi deviously chose not to send his Brief directly to Savonarola at San Marco, but instead to 'the prior and Monastery of Santa Croce'. This was the centre of the main clerical opposition to Savonarola in Florence, the home of the rival Franciscans. Consequently, as doubtless intended, the contents of this so-called papal Brief quickly spread through Florence, especially amongst the *Arrabbiati* and the Medici supporters, a week or so before the Brief was passed on to San Marco. Even then it did not pass immediately into Savonarola's hands, as the original receipt indicates that the prior was at the time *'gratia recuperandae valetudinis absens'* – in other words, he was still away recuperating, probably at Casentino.

The Brief itself was a chilling document. After opening with a few general observations about how dangerous matters, such as 'schisms within the Church' and 'heretical thinking', can result from 'adopting a false simplicity', it then passed on to name 'a certain Girolamo Savonarola', who had:

> become so deranged by recent upheavals in Italy that he has begun to proclaim that he has been sent by God and even speaks with God . . . claiming that anyone who does not accept his prophecies cannot hope for salvation . . . Despite our patience he refuses to repent and absolve his sins by submitting to our will. Consequently, we have decided to put an end to the scandalous secession of the Tuscan Congregation from that of Lombardy, to which we only consented because of the exhortations of certain deceitful friars. We have decided to re-unite these congregations under the rule of the Lombardy Vicar-General Sebastiano Maggi, who will lead an inquiry into the activities of Savonarola as well as into his writings. Until this inquiry is completed, Savonarola is suspended from all preaching

---

* Two years later Floridi would be arrested by Alexander VI on a charge of forging papal Briefs. As a result, he would be stripped of office and flung into the papal dungeons of Castel Sant' Angelo on a starvation diet of bread and water, which would soon bring about his death.

... Anyone who does not comply with the requirements of this brief will suffer instant excommunication.

Savonarola's immediate reaction to this document can only be imagined. Now he stood to lose the independence that he had gained at such cost – for which he had compromised the very integrity upon which all his spiritual aims were based, entering into his pact with the dying Lorenzo the Magnificent.

Savonarola may not actually have received the so-called papal Brief until he returned to Florence. His reply to it was certainly written in Florence, and is dated 29 September, probably no more than a day or so after he first read its contents. Savonarola realised that if he was to have any chance of retaining his independence and fulfilling the role that he felt God had given him, he would have to convince Rome of his cause. In this letter he would have to demonstrate, and redeem, the very nature of his faith. Painstakingly he justified himself, point by point, attempting to refute each of the accusations made against him. The difficulty of doing this, yet at the same time not contradicting the authority of the pope and the ortho-doxy of Church doctrine, proved a formidable task. As a result, a number of his arguments appear somewhat too clever for their own good. Having extolled the virtues of his pure and simple faith above all else, Savonarola now found himself relying upon his exceptional intellect to argue its case.

His meticulous reply extended over more than ten closely written pages. Later, he would famously maintain that the papal Brief contained 'no less than eighteen mistakes'; however, just a few of his arguments will suffice to give the flavour of this letter. Savonarola claimed that contrary to the allega-tions made in the Brief, he had always been submissive to the Church: he had committed no heresy, because all he had done was call for sinners to repent. When it came to his role as a prophet, his argument was particularly devious:

With regards to prophecy, I have absolutely never made any claim to be a prophet. However, it would not be heresy were I to do so, for I have foretold things that have already come to pass, and the other things I have foretold will be proven true when they come to pass in the future.

His most elaborate and pedantic arguments were reserved for his rebuttal of the papal Brief's claims concerning the separation of the Lombardy and Tuscan Congregations. Savonarola insisted that this separation had not been the result of 'the exhortations of certain deceitful friars', as it had come about through the intervention of Cardinal Caraffa, the Cardinal Protector of the Dominican order. (Cardinal Caraffa's subterfuge, and then slipping the ring from the pope's finger – which certainly involved deceit, and arguably extortion too – were not mentioned, although Savonarola would certainly have been informed of what had happened.) Furthermore, he went on to argue, although the move for separation may have been instigated by the Dominicans of San Marco, they could hardly be stigmatised as 'deceitful friars' when they were known far and wide for their exemplary piety. Not least, Savonarola contended that it was definitely unjust to appoint the Vicar General of the Lombardy Congregation to head an inquiry into his behaviour, for Vicar General Maggi was known to have become his sworn enemy as a result of the separation. Ridolfi summarises Savonarola's extraordinary conclusion:

> Thus the accusations made against him were exposed as nothing but low slander. And for this reason, he indicated that he would take no action in accord with these superior orders until His Holiness, recognising his innocence, absolved him from all blame in this matter.

This last 'indication' was certainly dangerous. However, Savonarola was playing on the fact that Alexander VI's unwarranted interference in the affairs of the Dominicans was liable to cause deep ructions within the Church hierarchy. In consequence, immediately after finishing his reply to the pope, he wrote to Cardinal Caraffa, as head of the order, pleading for his support in this matter and claiming:

> I am well aware of who is behind all these lies about me, and understand that they are the work of perverse citizens who wish to reestablish tyranny in Florence.

Savonarola was confident that his arguments would win the day. So much so, that he now took matters into his own hands. Regardless of his insistence in his letter that he had always been submissive to the wishes of the Church, he defied the order in the papal Brief banning him from preaching by delivering a sermon on Sunday 11 October. This was followed by another the next Sunday. Savonarola's motives for this action appear to have been to forestall his enemies. He had almost certainly heard from Rome (probably by way of Cardinal Caraffa) that Alexander VI had now covertly chosen to support the Medici cause and was backing a possible coup. The central messages of Savonarola's sermons were both specious and directly political. First, he claimed that he had written to the pope and that his position had been resolved. He then advised the citizens of Florence that it was necessary to take immediate measures against the *Arrabbiati*, who were plotting against him, and to defend themselves against an imminent Medici coup. Now, instead of urging Florentines to forgive their enemies, he deliberately incited them to violence: 'The time for mercy is past, it is time you took up your swords ... cut off the head of anyone who opposes the republic.' Later, he drove home his message with what was unmistakably a direct reference to Piero de' Medici: he urged the citizens of Florence to behave like the Ancient Romans when faced with the traitors who sought to overthrow the republic and restore Tarquin as their king: 'Cut off his head, even though he be head of his family, cut off his head!'

Yet by the time he came to preach a third sermon, on Sunday 25 October, his entire attitude had undergone a transformation. This time he bade his congregation farewell, adding cryptically: 'Pray to God that I will be inspired when the time comes for me to preach once more.' Savonarola had somehow received advance warning of what was about to take place. In a Brief from Alexander VI dated 16 October (which at the time of the sermon was still on its way from Rome to Florence), the pope had stated unequivocally:

We command you, by virtue of your vow of obedience, to cease preaching forthwith, both in public and in private, until such time as you are able to present yourself before us.

This time there was no mistaking the author, the authority or the authenticity of the papal Brief (though in accord with protocol, it was once again signed by Floridi, to whom it would have been dictated). Alexander VI was determined to silence Savonarola. Yet why did he not officially excommunicate him?

Alexander VI now found himself facing the possibility of a serious threat to his very papacy itself. It had become clear that Charles VIII was once again considering the possibility of leading the French army into Italy, and this time he would not hesitate to depose Alexander VI at the first opportunity. Savonarola had remained in contact with Charles VIII, and had in fact written to him during the summer, urging him to do just this. Savonarola remained convinced that Charles VIII represented the 'scourge of God' and, should he fail to act in his appointed capacity, or behave in a manner not worthy of this role, God would not fail to punish him, as he had pointed out to the king personally when he had prevented him from sacking Florence.

As a result of this new threat, Alexander VI had decided to pursue a different policy in Italy, one that was no longer so reliant upon the Holy League, which was already showing signs of falling apart. His long-term aim would be to try and lure France into an alliance. This would be a difficult task, but it seemed the best hope to enable him to realise his political ambitions – or, indeed, to remain in power. And for this he would need the goodwill of Savonarola. Any attempt to excommunicate the 'little friar' would have upset both the people of Florence and Charles VIII, who still looked upon Savonarola as his friend. However, by taking the minor step of forbidding him from preaching, for disobeying the order in the previous papal Brief, Alexander VI knew that he was well within his rights. In fact, such a response would have been expected of him, in order to maintain his authority as pope: neither the people of Florence nor Charles VIII could have expected less. By silencing Savonarola, Alexander VI knew that he would be rendering him virtually ineffective. Savonarola's power – over the people and his followers within the Church – lay above all else in his oratory.

During the ensuing months, Alexander VI found himself under considerable pressure to rescind his order silencing Savonarola, especially if he wished to gain the favour of Charles VIII. In consequence, when both the Florentine ambassador and Cardinal Caraffa once more pressed him to sign an order permitting Savonarola to start preaching again early in 1496, Alexander VI let it be known verbally that Savonarola could go ahead and preach the coming Lenten sermons. However, he refused to sign any document to this effect: Savonarola's licence was thus limited, and open to immediate denial.

Carnival time, in the run-up to Lent, was traditionally a period of boisterous celebration in Florence. This was when Lorenzo the Magnificent had laid on his most elaborate and excessive entertainments, such as the bawdy dramas for which he had composed rhymes like 'The Song of the Peasants' ('We've all got cucumbers, and big ones too . . .'). The activities of Carnival stemmed from the pre-Christian pagan festivals of Ancient Rome, and their true meaning had long since been lost in time. According to traditional custom, the citizens put on fancy dress and wore masks, roaming the streets and participating in wild revelries, often involving obscene ditties and lewd antics. Bonfires would be lit, around which men and women would perform bacchanalian dances. Barriers would be erected at the entrances to the different neighbourhoods, and any who wished to pass would be subjected to rude personal questions and coerced into paying 'customs' money. Things sometimes went too far during the ritual stone-throwing fights between gangs of boys from rival districts, when participants would frequently suffer ugly wounds, cracked skulls and even, on occasion, be killed. Many respectable citizens felt that these 'celebrations' were now getting dangerously out of control, and Savonarola latched onto this sentiment, organising a systematic campaign aimed at stamping out such 'unchristian' behaviour.

To do this, he made use of boys between the age of twelve and eighteen. In preparation for the traditional Christian rite of passage that confirmed full membership of the Church, allowing participants to take Holy Communion, the young men of Florence would be required to attend religious classes. Here they would learn their catechism, the questions and answers they would be expected to remember for the confirmation ceremony. Savonarola realised that these classes presented a unique opportunity to organise the youth of Florence into a strong religious force capable of combating the excesses of Carnival. He instructed the friars from San Marco who gave these classes to win over their charges to the simple faith that he preached in his sermons. Ideal candidates for such radicalising zeal, these impressionable adolescent boys soon became enthusiastic converts to Savonarola's brand of fundamentalism. They were then organised into groups, clad in white for purity, and sent out into the Carnival streets with the aim of preventing any excesses. Altars, complete with crucifix and candles, were set up at the main city crossroads, where the boys sang hymns, encouraging the passers-by to stop and join in with them. Stealing a march on the revellers, they also set up their own street barriers, where instead of ridiculing those who sought to pass and bullying them into giving money, they would humbly seek alms for the poor. And by contrast with the gangs who roamed the streets looking for stone-throwing fights with their neighbourhood rivals, 'Savonarola's boys' knocked on doors collecting items for charity.

Landucci, ever the upright citizen, recorded with pride that 'some of my sons were amongst those blessed and pure-minded troops of boys'. In his diary, he described an incident involving Savonarola's boys during Carnival and the reaction it provoked:

> Some boys took it upon themselves to confiscate the veil-holder of a girl walking down the Via de' Martegli, and her family created a great uproar about it. This all took place because Savonarola had encouraged the boys to oppose the wearing of unsuitable ornaments by women.

Savonarola also encouraged similar high-handed action towards the gamblers that he detested, 'so that whenever anyone said, "Here come Savonarola's boys!", all the gamblers fled, no matter how rough they were'. Likewise, the 'little friar' had it in for his favourite abomination, which remained so popular in Florence: 'The boys were so respected that everyone foreswore evil practices, and most of all the abominable vice. Such a thing was never mentioned by young or old during this holy time.' The 'abominable vice' to which Landucci here refers was sodomy, which was widely practised throughout the city at this time on both men and women – by young men because of the unavailability of young women, who were required to remain virgins until they were married, and by husbands who wished to prevent their wives from producing a ruinous number of children. At Savonarola's request, one of the first meetings of the Great Council in December 1494 had passed a new law imposing the death-penalty for sodomy. Yet despite Savonarola's strictures, the city refrained from any mass burning at the stake of sodomites: over the coming three years just one man would be condemned, and he 'was also said to be an infamous thief and bandit, for which the penalty was also death'. As Lauro Martines puts it: 'Even in the face of a strong commitment to the Friar, Florence had too much political wisdom to witch-hunt active homosexuals and sodomised women.' Yet this might be seen as the exception that proved the rule. In so many other spheres, Savonarola's coercion to religious fundamentalism was growing ever more effective.

Despite these puritanical constraints, Savonarola's repression was evidently felt by many to be nothing compared to the repression from which the more democratic 'City of God' had relieved its citizens. Instead of the subtly pervasive and corrupting repression of Lorenzo the Magnificent and the Medici party enforcers, the people were seemingly liberated by their new-found holiness. As Landucci put it: 'God be praised that I saw this short period of holiness. I pray that he may give us back that holy and pure life . . . what a blessed time it was.' Although there was definitely some reaction against 'Savonarola's boys' when they launched their campaign during the pre-Lenten Carnival of 1496, Landucci's pious sentiments were undoubtedly echoed by a large number of his fellow citizens.

He paints a vivid picture of what took place on Shrove Tuesday 1496, the day before the beginning of Lent, when in previous years the raucous behaviour had reached its traditional climax:

16 February. The Carnival. A few days earlier Savonarola had preached against such stupid Carnival traditions as gangs of boys throwing stones at each other and building camps out of twigs. Instead, he said that they should be out collecting alms for the *poveri vergognosi* [the destitute]. . . So instead of erecting barriers in the streets, the boys behaved like holy innocents, holding up crucifixes at street corners. As this was the last day of Carnival, after Vespers the bands of boys assembled in their four quarters of the city, each bearing its own special banner . . . They marched accompanied by drummers and pipers, accompanied by the official mace bearers and servants of the Palazzo della Signoria, singing praises to heaven, all bearing olive branches in their hands. This sight moved many good and respectable

citizens to tears . . . In all, some six thousand boys or more, all between the ages of five and sixteen, are said to have taken part.

These four processions came together at the Ospedale degli Innocenti.* This joint procession then wound its way through the entire city, singing hymns and collecting items for charity, stopping off at various major locations – including many of the city's best-known churches, such as Savonarola's San Marco, before crossing the river to the Oltrarno, returning across the Ponte Vecchio and proceeding to the cathedral. Indicatively absent from this itinerary was the Palazzo Medici, which would certainly have been a stopping-off point for any such city processions during the previous decades – an unsurprising omission, given the circumstances, yet one that would have been of profound and moving significance to all: the times had changed, and those days were over.

The lengthy hymn-singing procession must have taken well over an hour, possibly two, if it stopped at all the places dutifully listed by Landucci in his diary. Likewise, the long route must have been seen by a large percentage of the population of Florence – who either lined the routes or looked down from their windows – many of whom would, under normal circumstances, have spent the day revelling. Although not all the people of Florence were in favour of this new development, no serious incidents such as barricading the streets or stone-throwing were recorded by contemporary sources.

When the procession reached the cathedral:

the church was packed out with men and women, divided with the women on one side and the men on the other, and here the offering was made, with such faith and tears of holy emotion as ever witnessed. Around several hundred florins must have been collected. Many gold florins were put into the collecting bowls, but mostly it was in small copper coins and silver. Some women gave their veil-holders, some their silver spoons, handkerchiefs, towels, and all kinds of other things. It seemed as if everyone wanted to make an offering to Christ and

---

* The movingly named early-Renaissance building (literally 'Hospital for the Innocents') was in fact the city orphanage, where unwanted babies and abandoned children were taken in and taught a trade.

His Mother. I have set down these things because they are true, and I did see them with my own eyes, at the same time experiencing great emotion.

Although the last sentence has the feel of a subsequent addition, its message would only seem to confirm the extraordinariness of what Landucci felt he was experiencing on this day. Once more, the most civilised city in Europe was ahead of its time. This was a revolution, no less – the first in the dawn of the modern era. In this aspect, Savonarola can be seen as being the precursor of a tradition that would go on to produce such figures as Luther, Cromwell, Robespierre, even Lenin. And it is not difficult to see in Savonarola embryonic elements of all these figures – just as it is not difficult to see in Landucci's ecstatic words ('what a blessed time it was ...' etc.) a presentiment of Wordsworth's celebrated stanza on the French Revolution:

> Bliss was it in that dawn to be alive,
> But to be young was very heaven! ...

Next day, Ash Wednesday 1496, Savonarola delivered his first Lenten sermon in the cathedral before a congregation packed to overflowing:

steps for Savonarola's boys were set up along the walls, opposite the chancel behind the women ... and all the boys on the steps sang sweet praises to God before the sermon began. And then the clergy entered the chancel and began singing the Litanies, to which the boys responded. It was all so beautiful that everyone wept, even the most reserved men amongst them, saying: 'This is a thing of the Lord.'

Many have considered Savonarola's Lenten sermons for 1496 as the finest he delivered. There is less of the extreme apocalyptic imagery of his early sermons, and instead he put forward arguments outlining his aims. In his opening sermon he saw a specific future involving those who had recently done so much to promulgate his ideas:

In you, young men, I place my hope and that of the Lord. You will govern the city of Florence, for you are not prone to the evil ways of your fathers, who did not know how to get rid of their tyrannical rulers or appreciate God's gift of liberty to his people.

He also dealt with the unresolved matter of his relations with the Church, resorting once more to skilful intellectual argument:

I have written to Rome explaining that if by accident I have in some way written or preached anything which is heretical . . . I am prepared to apologise and unreservedly withdraw anything that I have said. I will always submit to the rule of the Church.

He even went so far as to argue that the Church was infallible with regard to dogma.

However, although the Church itself was infallible here, this did not mean that churchmen and the faithful were compelled to obey each and every order from clerical superiors, even if such a command came from the pope himself. Savonarola insisted: 'The pope cannot command me to do something which contradicts the teaching of the Gospels.' This was to be a continuing theme of his entire Lenten sermons. He insisted, 'We must obey God rather than man.' He reserved his particular contempt for 'the high priests of Rome . . . you whose lust, love of luxury and pride have been the ruin of the world, violating men and women alike with your lasciviousness, turning children to sodomy and prostitution . . . you who spend the night with your concubine and in the morning conduct the sacraments'.

Crucially, it seems that Savonarola had now realised that if he confined himself to the Tuscan Congregation over which he ruled, he would inevitably be isolated by the Church hierarchy, and then moves would begin to declare his teachings a heresy. Rome would summon Florence's enemies, the city would be attacked and defeated, whereupon all his reforms would come to nothing. Thus he was left with no alternative but to extend his ambitions and seek to reform the entire Church. As a consequence, his rhetoric hardened. Those who inhabited the city of Rome must be prepared to suffer the fates of hell: 'You will be clapped in irons, hacked to pieces with swords, burned with fire and eaten up by flames.' In a later Lenten sermon he would describe his apocalyptic visions comparing the fate of Rome to that of Babylon:

> The light will vanish and amidst the darkness the sky will rain fire and brimstone, while flames and great boulders will smite the earth ... because Rome has been polluted with an infernal mixture of scripture and all manner of vice.

The *Arrabbiati* and Savonarola's enemies within the Church in Florence were gleefully reporting his every word to Rome. His call to defy any pope who contradicted the gospel was bad enough, but his reference to 'you' who spend the night with a concubine and next morning conduct Mass was immediately recognisable to all who heard it, whether they were listening in the congregation or received reports of it amongst the hierarchy in Rome: this was an unmistakable allusion to the behaviour of Alexander VI.

With each ensuing sermon, the authorities in Florence became increasingly worried. The Signoria knew that they could not restrain Savonarola for fear of antagonising the *Piagnoni*, yet they were well aware that the growing anger amongst the *Arrabbiati* might boil over, and were fearful of what measures Alexander VI might take against the city. There is evidence that the authorities deputed Piero Capponi to speak with Savonarola, warning him of the dangers he was inviting. Surprisingly, this seems to have given Savonarola cause for thought, as can be seen from his last sermon of the series, delivered after Easter on 10 April. He opened with his customary defiance, insisting that he would never obey orders to do anything wrong, whether they came from his religious superiors or even the pope himself. Addressing any such an enemy, he insisted: 'It is you who are wrong. You are not the Church, you are simply a man and a sinner.' Yet something that Capponi had passed on to him must have had a chastening effect, for he then alluded to what lay ahead in his struggles. 'Do you wish to know how all this will end for me? I can tell you that it will end with my death, when I shall be cut to pieces.' As if attempting to forestall this fate, he now incongruously sought to argue his innocence of any transgression against Alexander VI:

> Information has been relayed to His Holiness, both by letter and by word of mouth, that I have been criticising him for sinful behaviour. This is not true. As it is written in the Bible: 'Thou shalt not curse thy ruler.' I have never done such a thing, and I have definitely never referred to anyone by name whilst preaching from this pulpit.

This was disingenuous to say the least. Savonarola had certainly taken the precaution of never mentioning Alexander VI by name, but all in the congregation had known to whom he was referring.

News of Savonarola's sermons had angered rulers throughout Italy. They would never have allowed a priest to preach such inflammatory sermons within their own states, and knew that the very airing of such views could only lead to trouble amongst their own citizens. This subversive priest had to be stopped. Just as Savonarola knew that he could only succeed if his message spread out into the world and succeeded in conquering Rome, so the rulers of Italy realised that their leadership was open to question as long as Savonarola continued to preach his fundamentalist religion, with its dangerous political connotations. He had to be silenced, once and for all, and the person who had to do this was the pope. Yet Alexander VI was still aware that if he made any serious attempt to punish Savonarola, he would only outrage the citizens of Florence, who would in turn call upon Charles VIII to hasten his plans to invade Italy and dethrone him. Playing for time, Alexander VI appointed an ecclesiastical committee of senior theologians to investigate Savonarola's behaviour, and his preaching, for evidence of heresy.

One of the reasons why people had been turning to Savonarola in such numbers was the persisting desperate situation that was now unfolding in Florence. The Pisans continued to resist all attempts by the Florentine mercenary army to retake their city, which meant that by now much trade in Florence had almost ground to a standstill. This situation had only been made worse by the exceptional weather, which had blighted much of Italy for almost a year now. According to Landucci on 4 May 1496, 'Throughout this time it never stopped raining, and the rainstorms had gone on for about eleven months, there never once being a whole week with no rain.' Things got so bad that on 18 May he reported, 'There came such a great flood that it washed away the young corn planted in the fields, even as far down in the plains as here; while at Rovizzano* it swept through two walls on the roadside.'

With the failure of the coming harvest inevitable, the peasants began streaming in from the countryside for the protection of the city, where entire families were soon camping out on the streets and begging for food. The prevailing air of Christian compassion amongst the citizenry meant that none starved, and Savonarola organised the monks of San Marco to distribute food and suitable clothing collected during Lent. Even so, these vermin-ridden families living on the pavements soon began to present a public health hazard. Worrying gossip spread, and as early as 14 May Landucci had heard that 'The plague has returned in several districts of Florence.' Two weeks later, he recorded, 'Many people began suffering from a certain complaint called "French boils". This looked like smallpox; but it went on increasing, and no one knew a cure for it.' This was almost certainly syphilis, rather than the buboes (boils) that are symptomatic of the bubonic plague†. After paying for the upkeep of the mercenary army fighting at Pisa, there was little left in the public coffers, leaving the Signoria powerless to deal with the growing number of refugeees from the country-side or the spread of disease.

Meanwhile in Rome the committee of theologians reported back to Alexander VI that they could find no evidence of heresy amongst Savonarola's teachings. This unexpected finding was almost certainly due

* A weavers' village two miles east of the city walls up the Arno valley. Landucci's 'corn' is, of course, wheat and other types of grain, rather than maize.
† The plague that recurred in many Italian and European cities several times during this period was not as virulent as the Black Death (or bubonic plague) that had swept through Europe around 150 years previously, killing as much as one-third of the entire population. These later plague outbreaks in Florence (and other cities) usually proved fatal for those who caught the disease, but seldom spread much beyond several cases in the immediate vicinity. After some months the disease was liable to vanish as suddenly and mysteriously as it had arrived. All this suggests that these later plagues may have been the less common septicaemic (blood infection) or pneumonic (attacking the lungs) variant of the disease. Significantly, as Landucci seems to indicate, the plague at that time in Florence, and the 'French boils', were widely regarded as two distinct diseases.

to the presence of Cardinal Caraffa on the committee. If anyone was to discipline a Dominican friar it should be the Vicar General of his order, not the pope. Leaders of other orders expressed similar sentiments. No one wished for any unwelcome precedent that extended the power of the pope at their expense. Besides, all were agreed that Savonarola could hardly be accused of heresy when all that he had preached was backed up by his exceptional biblical scholarship.

Alexander VI then decided upon a different tactic. Some time during the first weeks of August he summoned to audience Fra Ludovico da Ferrara, who was not only the Provost General of the Dominican order,* but also happened to come from Savonarola's home city. Ludovico da Ferrara was instructed to undertake a confidential mission to Savonarola at San Marco, to ask his advice on how to persuade the city of Florence to become the pope's ally.

Fra Ludovico duly travelled to Florence, where he conferred with Savonarola, revealing to him that if he cooperated with Alexander VI's plans, the pope promised that – to the great honour of Florence – he would make him a cardinal. Savonarola was unwilling to give any immediate response to Fra Ludovico, and merely told him, 'Come to my next sermon and you'll hear my reply.'

Savonarola had been invited by the Signoria to deliver a sermon the following Saturday 20 August in the recently completed hall of the Great Council.† This sermon was not expected to confine itself to religious matters, and was a semi-official means by which the Signoria and senior members of the administration were informed of his ideas on political matters and foreign policy. Unlike his passionate sermons in the cathedral, here Savonarola spoke in more sober terms, addressing a number of questions that he knew were uppermost in the minds of several senior officials. He explained why he had taken it upon himself to stay in correspondence with Charles VIII: this was to remind the king of his duty

---

* The titular head of the order. Cardinal Caraffa, as Vicar General, was the executive head in charge of the everyday running of the order.

† In some aspects, however, the hall would remain incomplete for some time, at least partly owing to economic reasons. Not until eight years later would Leonardo da Vinci and Michelangelo be commissioned to cover the two great side walls with murals depicting historic Florentine victories.

to fulfil his role as the 'scourge of God'. At the same time he denied the accusation that he opposed Alexander VI's Holy League. He had remained against Florence joining the League only because the city had given its word to Charles VIII that it would remain his ally. After dealing with various other matters, such as aid for those living in the streets, he turned to the rumour that was now sweeping Florence that he was about to be made a cardinal. At this point his manner changed abruptly. Once again, it was as if he was delivering a sermon with all the ire and conviction of an Old Testament prophet. He denied vehemently that he had any wish to receive a cardinal's crimson hat:

> If I coveted such a thing would I be standing before you in this threadbare habit? . . . On the contrary, the only gift I seek is the one God gives to his saints – death, a crimson hat of blood, that is all I wish for.

In his Lenten sermons Savonarola had foretold his own death ('I shall be cut to pieces'); now he more explicitly revealed his longing to become a martyr. He appeared to regard such an end as inevitable, and it is worth bearing this in mind during the ensuing events, for it must have informed his every decision.

Meanwhile the heavy rains continued, wreaking their effect across the countryside, leaving a desolate scene: 'In many places the corn had not yet been harvested. The entire season is late and neither the corn, nor the grapes, nor the figs have yet ripened.' Food stocks were now dangerously low in Florence, and the city faced the prospect of a possible famine.

At the same time, the war against Pisa continued to go badly. The besieged Pisans were being supported by ships from Venice and Milan. These would soon be aided by a number of troops sent by the Holy Roman Emperor Maximilian I, who had been called in by Ludovico 'il Moro' Sforza of Milan.* Florence could ill afford to pay the wages of its

---

* Maximilian I, who ruled over territories in Austria, Germany and Burgundy, was opposed to France. He was also keen to be seen supporting Alexander VI, and had joined the Holy League. His ambition was to be officially crowned as emperor by the pope, a tradition dating back to Charlemagne's time, which had fallen into abeyance.

mercenaries, and some simply decamped to the other side, where they felt they would be better paid.

Piero Capponi had been placed in charge of the Florentine forces and did his best to rally the unenthusiastic mercenaries nominally under his command. When the Pisan forces broke out and sought to cut the Florentine line of supply to the port of Livorno, on the coast fifteen miles to the south, Capponi moved to repulse them. A brave man, he led his men from the front, encouraging the mercenaries into effective action. However, in the course of leading an attack on the castle at Solana, in the hills above Livorno, he was struck by a shot from an arquebus (an early form of musket). His wound proved fatal, and he died on the field of battle.

News of Capponi's death caused great grief amongst the people of Florence, for he was still regarded as a hero for publicly standing up to Charles VIII. Capponi's body was transported back to his home city on a barge up the Arno, and on 27 September he was given a public funeral, which attracted large crowds.*

Just over a month later, Landucci recorded how news arrived from the Florentine allies in Livorno:

that twelve ships bearing cargoes of corn had arrived there, but this turned out to be a false report. Instead this was the fleet of the King of France, and the Livornese went out and routed the camp of the Emperor Maximilian I, slaying about forty men and capturing their artillery

The siege of Pisa was hardly ended by this 'rout', but at least the Florentines knew that they could now rely upon French aid, and that their dwindling supplies of corn would soon be replenished.

All such hopes were dashed when news came through that Charles VIII's son and heir, the dauphin, whose birth in September had been greeted with such great joy by the king, had died just twenty-five days later on 2 October. Charles VIII was overcome with grief, and put off his planned invasion of Italy. Savonarola had of course warned Charles VIII that God

---

* The lasting affection of Florence for Capponi can be seen in the fact that he still has a street named after him, north of the city centre near the former site of the Porta San Gallo.

would chastise him if he did not act as 'God's scourge' and invade Italy once more. Now another of his prophecies had come true, but no one in Florence rejoiced at this fulfilment of his word: Florence was left alone, facing enemies on all sides, and some of its citizens were beginning to tire of these 'prophecies'.

Savonarola's enemies amongst the *Arrabbiati* and the Medici supporters immediately seized upon this opportunity to try and stir up feeling against the 'little friar'. Had he not written just a year ago in his 'Compendium of Revelations' that the Virgin Mary had told him how 'The City of Florence shall become more glorious, more powerful and more wealthy than it has ever been. All the territory that it has lost shall be restored, and its borders will be extended further than ever before.' What of this prophecy? Florentine commerce was all but at a standstill, and the city could not even retake Pisa.

Savonarola replied to such criticisms in the sermon that he preached in the cathedral on 28 October. Far from being repentant about the lack of fulfilment of these prophecies, instead he berated his congregation. Florence was not worthy of such fortune until the city was purified. The citizens of Florence were being punished for their lack of repentance. There was still too much evil in the 'City of God'. The congregation listened, fearfully, but for how much longer would they be willing to place their faith in the Holy Spirit?

Alexander VI was overjoyed when he heard that the French reinvasion had been cancelled, and immediately ordered the papal troops to march north and take Florence. These troops were joined by a contingent from Siena. As this combined force moved towards Florence, the Florentine mercenaries abandoned the siege of Pisa and marched to cut them off. The two forces met at Cascina, in the Po valley east of Pisa. The Florentine mercenaries soon put the papal troops to flight, and then ran amok, raping and pillaging their way through a number of hillside villages before returning to besiege the city of Pisa. Yet this only brought temporary relief for the Florentines. The Venetian fleet now began a concerted blockade of Livorno, causing a French fleet bringing grain from Marseilles to turn back. At the same time the Holy Roman Emperor Maximilian I disembarked with further troops at Pisa.

Ranged up against Florence were the combined forces of Venice, Milan and the imperial troops of Maximilian I, with Alexander VI and Naples remaining in the background as declared aggressors. At the same time Piero de' Medici and his brother Cardinal Giovanni were making plans to raise a mercenary army to march on Florence. Ironically, it was the arrival of Maximilian I in Pisa that soon led to a division amongst the allies, when it became clear that he had in mind retaining Pisa for himself. This antagonised both the Venetians and the Milanese, who both had similar secret plans of their own; while Piero de' Medici was adamant that Pisa should remain a Florentine possession.

Even so, Florence now effectively had no allies, and internally the situation was no better. The administration had run up a huge public debt in continuing to finance its mercenary army; and regardless of the Savonarolan reforms, the government was becoming increasingly unpopular, especially amongst the moneyed classes, who were required to continue propping up the increasingly desperate military situation. Despite the victory at Cascina, the prospects looked grim.

17

The Bonfire of the Vanities

As feared, Florence underwent a winter of famine. The picture that Landucci painted of life in the city at this time makes for grim reading. On 25 January 1497 he recorded:

The price of corn was 3 *lire* 14 *soldi* a bushel.* And at this time a woman died amidst the crowd in the *Piazza del Grano* (The Corn Market), where government stores of bread and corn were being sold. We also heard that a poor peasant came into Florence to beg for bread, leaving his three small children starving at home. When he returned to find that they were dying, and he had no food for them, he took a rope and hanged himself.

On 6 February, despite an official decree lowering the price of corn by '12 or 15 *soldi* a bushel' just a week or so beforehand, Landucci recorded how the distribution of free grain to the destitute resulted in an even worse incident:

Several women were suffocated in the crowd in the *Piazza del Grano*, and some of them were brought out half-dead, which may seem incredible, but it is true, because I saw it myself.

---

* There were twenty soldi to one lire. In normal times a bushel of corn cost less than one lire. It is difficult to compare prices exactly, but informed estimates suggest that an unskilled labourer during these difficult times would only earn enough each day to feed his family (of around eight people) on a loaf of bread and a few vegetables. As well as distribution of free grain by the commune (that is, the city authorities), monasteries such as San Marco passed out bread to the starving as best they could.

Many incredible things were now taking place in Florence. Next day saw the culmination of that year's carnival weeks, when Carnival itself was 'celebrated' in Savonarola's new style. Again 'Savonarola's boys' had spent the preceding weeks setting up altars at street corners, parading through the streets dressed in white, singing hymns and knocking on doors seeking items for charity. These collections had by now taken on a more insistent tone, and the items that Savonarola's boys sought were more specifically characterised as 'vanities'. Activities extended far beyond taking girls' ornate veil holders, and included the collecting of all manner of luxuries and ornaments that might be regarded as distracting their owners from the fundamentalist Christian way of life preached by Savonarola. This certainly included the items that women used for adorning themselves – such as jewellery, scented 'dead hair' (wigs), mirrors, perfume ('lascivious odours') and colourfully dyed cloth for making dresses. Needless to say, items associated with gambling were also much sought out – including dice, packs of cards, gaming tables and even chess sets. Indeed, anything that brought pleasure was fair game for Savonarola's boys on their collecting rounds: secular Latin books (which were said to contain all manner of lewd stories), Boccaccio's scurrilous tales and Petrarch's famous love poems, even works by the Ancient Greek philosophers ('pagan heresies'), and books by poets ranging from Ovid to Poliziano. Just as sought-after were musical instruments of all kinds, as well as statues and paintings that did not depict religious scenes – such as popular figurine copies of Donatello's suggestive hermaphroditic statues, as well as paintings of the naked female form. Even paintings of religious subjects were not immune, in particular those 'which are painted in such a shameful fashion as to make the Virgin Mary look like a prostitute'.

It has been claimed that during this period Botticelli piously surrendered a number of his secular paintings from his studio; and though many historians continue to dispute this, it would certainly seem to have been characteristic of the artist's troubled frame of mind at this time.

Botticelli – now in his early fifties – was one of the few survivors from the charmed intellectual circle that had gathered around Lorenzo at the

Palazzo Medici. By this stage he had taken to painting a series of stark crucifixions. In these Christ's face hangs down, below his long matted dark hair, infused with a look of pain and resignation, showing all the signs of being realised with deep empathy by Botticelli. Although he believed in Savonarola, there was no doubt that, in his poverty and anguish, Florence had become a deeply painful place for him.

Meanwhile another survivor, the diminutive stuttering Ficino, had become an embittered old man. In the heyday of Lorenzo's time at the Palazzo Medici, Ficino had written celebrating the Ancient Greek tradition of platonic relationships between beautiful young men and their older mentors as the most exalted form of love. But now in the wake of Savonarola's condemnation of homosexuality, Ficino found himself lambasted as a sodomite. The man who had once been a revered philosopher, admired as a canon of Florence Cathedral, was now reduced to a scandalous figure. After Savonarola had scorned his attempt to introduce his beloved Plato into the Christian fold, Ficino had retired to the countryside at Careggi, but had recently been driven back into the city by the famine. Here he was shunned by his former friends. The Medici supporters distrusted him because of his former association with Savonarola, and yet figures like Botticelli would have nothing to do with him either, because Savonarola now regarded him as a heretic.

The bonfires in each neighbourhood around which people had traditionally danced in abandoned fashion during the pre-Savonarolan Carnival were now all amalgamated into one massive bonfire in the Piazza della Signoria, which was intended to accommodate all the vanities that Savonarola's boys had collected. An eight-sided wooden pyramid had been constructed, with seven tiers, one for each of the seven deadly sins. The vanities were placed on these tiers, and the inside of the pyramid was filled with sacks of straw, piles of kindling wood, and even small bags of dynamite (intended to spread the flames throughout the pyramid, as well as cause incendiary firework effects such as bangs and showers of sparks). In the end, this 'Bonfire of the Vanities' rose to sixty feet, and the circumference at its base was 240 feet. At its peak was placed a wooden effigy made to look like the traditional image of the Devil, complete with hairy cloven-hoofed goats' legs, pointed ears, horns and a little pointed beard.* Such was this wondrous collection of vanities that it is said a Venetian merchant who was passing through Florence offered 22,000 ducats if he could be allowed to take them with him rather than let them be wastefully burned. This was a colossal sum, especially in a time of famine – during these years one could have bought a modest palazzo for one-tenth of this amount. Nonetheless the merchant's offer was indignantly refused, and he soon left the city fearing for his own safety when he saw that the face on the figure atop the bonfire had been adapted to resemble his own.

On the day of Carnival, 7 February 1497, the 'Bonfire of the Vanities' was finally lit. Watching this destructive conflagration were the *gonfaloniere* and senior officials of the administration gazing down from the balcony of the Palazzo della Signoria, while the assembled choirs of Savonarola's boys dressed in white chanted hymns, as well as songs mocking worldly luxuries, which had been especially composed for the occasion. As the bonfire crackled into life, trumpets sounded from the palazzo, and the *Vacca* tolled. The large assembled crowd applauded the flames before joining the choir of Savonarola's boys in their hymn-singing. It seemed as if Florence was now truly the 'City of God'.

Next day, Savonarola preached the first of that year's Lenten sermons. These were on texts taken from Ezekiel, one of the more virulent of the Old Testament prophets, who is today perhaps best known for his pronouncement:

> Thus saith the Lord GOD, Behold, I will stretch out mine hand against [mine enemies] ... And I will execute great vengeance upon them with furious rebukes; and they shall know that I am the LORD, when I shall lay my vengeance upon them.

* This 'monstrous image' was also intended as the personification of the previous Carnival, where such effigies had often topped the bonfires around which people danced. Originally this would have been the figure of Pan, the Ancient Greek god associated with sexual licence, fertility and spring. The resemblance between the traditional image of the Devil and the Ancient Greek god Pan was not coincidental. The gods of one religion were habitually either incorporated into the religion that succeeded it (such as Athena, the Ancient Greek virgin goddess, becoming the Virgin Mary) or were co-opted to become its bogey figures (such as Pan becoming the Devil). Pico della Mirandola had recognised this trait, and made it part of his universal philosophy. Savonarola had gone to great pains to 'cure' him of such thinking, which undermined the uniqueness of Christianity.

This was hardly the sentiment likely to be adopted by one who would rest on his laurels now that he had succeeded in establishing the 'City of God' in Florence. Indeed, Savonarola had by this stage become fully aware that only one course lay open to him if he was to succeed, or even survive: he must challenge and overcome the full might of Rome, thereby banishing corruption from the very heart of the Church, so that it could be purified from within. Anything less, and he would be destroyed: the martyr's death that he had hinted might lie in wait for him would inevitably come about – unless he rallied the faithful against the evil of Rome. And this he proceeded to do in no uncertain fashion, gradually growing in both boldness and vehemence with each passing sermon. By 4 March he had roused himself to such a pitch that he was declaring:

> Friars have a proverb amongst themselves: 'He comes from Rome, do not trust him.' O hark unto my words, you wicked Church! At the Court of Rome men are losing their souls all the time, they are all lost. Wretched people! I do not claim that this is true of everyone there, but only a few remain good. If you meet people who enjoy being in Rome, you know they are cooked. He's cooked, all right. You understand me?

When Savonarola passed from the plural to the singular, his packed congregation would have recognised that he was referring to none other than the pope. As if sensing that perhaps he had gone too far, Savonarola immediately distanced himself, claiming: 'I am not speaking of anyone in particular.'

Yet, carried on the tide of his own emotion, he was soon throwing all caution to the winds once more:

> O harlot Church, once you were ashamed of your pride and lust, but now you acknowledge this without the least show of remorse. In former times, priests would refer to their sons as 'nephews', but now they quite openly call them 'sons' on every occasion.

There could be no mistaking the object of these remarks. What had previously been gossip amongst the more educated classes had now become common knowledge. All now knew that Alexander VI was the first pope openly to acknowledge his bastard offspring, dispensing with such euphemisms as 'nephew' or 'niece' — even going so far as to move his sons and daughter into the papal apartments at the Vatican. More pertinently still, the sixty-six-year-old Alexander VI's most recent mistress Giulia Farnese, a married Roman woman of good family who had begun her liaison with the pope when she was still a teenager, had recently given birth to his son — news of which would certainly have reached Savonarola at San Marco by way of the Dominican grapevine, and would have been known to the better-informed members of his congregation.

Likewise, news of Savonarola's sermons was eagerly relayed to Rome by his enemies, especially amongst the Franciscans and the Augustinians. This made life particularly difficult for the Florentine special envoy, Alessandro Bracci, when he arrived in Rome and presented himself before Alexander VI on 13 March. Political relations between Rome and Florence were at their lowest ebb over Pisa and the Holy League, and Bracci had been strictly instructed by the Florentine administration on the position that he was to adopt concerning the city's foreign policy. Bracci opened his speech to the pope with the customary diplomatic niceties, expressing Florence's deep respect and support for His Holiness, whilst at the same time taking care to avoid any specific commitments. He then proceeded with some trepidation to the more specific matters that he had been instructed to inform Alexander VI about. These included a demand for the return of Pisa, along with a reminder that Florence had the support of Charles VIII, to whom the city was committed by an unbreakable alliance, which thus unfortunately precluded any possibility of Florence joining Alexander VI's Holy League.

Alexander VI made it plain that he was unimpressed by this flim-flam, especially when it came from the man representing the city that allowed Savonarola to continue preaching such blasphemous and defamatory sermons against him. Dispensing with all but the most perfunctory of diplomatic pleasantries, Alexander VI addressed the unfortunate Bracci:

> My Lord secretary, you may be as fat as we are, but if you will pardon
> me saying so, your message is distinctly lean and skinny.* If you have

* Evidently not all classes in Florence were suffering from the scarcity of food and high price of corn.

nothing further to say, you might as well return home . . . We cannot understand how you have taken up such a stubborn and obstinate attitude. Presumably it has something to do with the faith you place in the prophecies of that soothsayer of yours. If we could be allowed to address your people directly, we are convinced that our true arguments would soon disillusion you and cure you of the blindness and error into which you have been led by this friar. However, what causes us even greater pain – and at the same time gives us just reason for our antagonism towards you – is that your Signoria and citizens give their support to him. And all this is done without any just cause whatsoever, as he vilifies us and makes mincemeat of our dignity – us the very occupiers of this most Holy See.

The pope could be secure in his angry reaction, for unbeknown to Bracci, to Florence, and even to Savonarola, the political situation in Italy had undergone a dramatic shift in Alexander VI's favour. He had entered into secret negotiations with Charles VIII. News now reached Florence, and was then carried by fast messenger down the road to Rome, that Alexander VI had succeeded in turning the tables on Florence: in France on 25 February Charles VIII had finally been persuaded to sign a treaty with the Holy League. This may have been unfortunate for Bracci in Rome, but for Savonarola in Florence it was nothing less than a political disaster. His 'scourge of God' had disappeared. Alexander VI and the Holy League may have been in some disarray, but one thing was clear: there was absolutely no prospect of anyone coming to the aid of Florence if one, or more, of her encircling enemies chose to invade her territory. And this state of affairs was unlikely to change in the foreseeable future. As a result of this news, disillusion with Savonarola's role as a prophet became more widespread throughout Florence. The *Arrabbiati* and the *Bigi* had adopted the slogan 'We are for the natural world' (as distinct from the supernatural world – that is, prophecies), and this now began to gain wider currency amongst the population.

When Savonarola heard of this, he was so stung that he determined to answer his critics in his next sermon. As if obsessed, he returned again and again to what they were saying about the 'natural world'. Similarly, according to the contemporary diarist Parenti he also attacked Charles

VIII, 'condemning him as stupid and idle', adding that just as he had truly predicted 'the death of his son, now he predicted his death'. Although Savonarola took care not to mention Charles VIII by name (a point confirmed by the printed text itself), Parenti was in no doubt to whom he was referring in this sermon.

If we view Savonarola's predictions from a modern rational scientific point of view, it is undeniable that here he was going out on a limb. Unlike the tyrants whose deaths he had previously prophesied, with such spectacular effect and such spectacular accuracy, Charles VIII was just twenty-six years old and in good health. The indications are that in this case Savonarola's self-belief got the better of him: he had become so encouraged by the success of his previous prophecies that he felt any convictions he held with sufficient strength and faith were now infallible. At the same time, he had evidently become so enraged by the success of his enemies that his emotions overrode any intellectual caution or prudence: he realised that his entire future was at stake. He was beginning to lose influence; and if this drift continued, his power in the city was liable to evaporate. His position was anomalous: he was a foreigner, and he held no elected role in the administration. His power depended upon his influence over the frequently changing members of the Signoria and on his ability to impose his will upon the populace through his sermons. 'Savonarola's boys' could not otherwise have been so effective in bringing about the huge propaganda coup represented by the 'Bonfire of the Vanities', which by now had all of Italy talking.

In Savonarola's eyes, Charles VIII had once and for all failed to fulfil the role that God had given him: the 'scourge of God' therefore had himself to be scourged. God had no alternative but to destroy Charles VIII for disobeying his commandment. Thus Savonarola certainly felt justified in prophesying this event. In modern psychological parlance this may be regarded as wish fulfilment or self-delusion; yet in the psycho-religious atmosphere prevalent in Florence at the time, as well as in Savonarola's mind, this prophecy was not disingenuous.

Savonarola continued preaching his 1497 Lenten sermons on the prophet Ezekiel, and the citizens of Florence continued to starve as a result of the famine. On 19 March Landucci recorded, 'More than one child has been found dead of hunger in Florence.' Just eight days later, he wrote:

Throughout this time, men, women, and children were collapsing from exhaustion and hunger, some them dying of it. At the hospital many were dying as a result of weakness from starvation.

Amidst such an atmosphere of doom and disaster, Savonarola's Lenten sermons in the cathedral attracted crowds as large as ever. Landucci records that 'fifteen thousand people attended his sermon every weekday', a figure that would probably have accounted for half the able-bodied population at the time. However, weakened by Charles VIII's pact with the pope, Savonarola now found his critics more vociferously confident. Landucci mentions in his entry for Good Friday:

A friar preached in Santo Spirito,* who spoke against Fra Girolamo, and all through Lent he had been saying that the *Frate* was deceiving us and that he was not a prophet.

The population of Florence was splitting into two aggressively divided camps. A despatch sent by the Ferrarese ambassador during March revealed:

The city is more divided than ever before, and all are apprehensive that there will soon be an outbreak of civil violence. If this does happen it will be very dangerous for the city. Savonarola is doing his best to forestall this, but his enemies have become widespread and determined, particularly after news of the blessed truce [between France and the Holy League].

The political situation within Florence had been subtly shifting against Savonarola for some months now. In January, Francesco Valori had been elected *gonfaloniere*. Valori was a member of a well-respected family, who had been a staunch political ally and trusted friend of Lorenzo the Magnificent, to such an extent that he had even married into the Medici family. In 1491 he had been selected by Lorenzo as one of the five-man delegation sent to

---

* This friar is generally identified as Fra Leonardo da Fivizzano; Santo Spirito was on the Oltrarno and a centre of the Augustinians, who had been Savonarola's enemies since he had humiliated Fra Mariano da Genazzano, the man who was now superior of their order in Rome.

have a quiet word with Savonarola, intimating that perhaps the new prior of San Marco should tone down his sermons. However, just three years later Valori had been filled with consternation when Piero de' Medici had taken it upon himself, without even consulting the Signoria, to set out on a personal mission to Charles VIII. When news reached Florence of what Piero de' Medici had surrendered at his meeting with the French king, Francesco Valori had been outraged, and after the flight of Piero from the city he had felt no qualms about becoming an enthusiastic supporter of the *Piagnoni*, as well as lending his support to Savonarola and his social reforms. By 1497 his election as *gonfaloniere* was long overdue: his popularity was widespread, he was known as a powerful but sympathetic character and had many qualities of leadership. Alas, he was not a man of great intelligence, and the few times when he came up with an original idea it was prone to become an obsession. In the words of Guicciardini, who would have known him, Valori 'imposed his views regardless of what other people thought, bullying and abusing anyone who disagreed'. One of his first ideas, at the start of his two-month term as *gonfaloniere*, was to extend the democratic scope of the Great Council by lowering the age of election to its membership from thirty to twenty-four. At first sight this seemed a highly commendable idea, and Valori was surprised and disappointed when Savonarola advised him against such an unprecedented move. He refused to listen to Savonarola's canny political advice and went ahead with his plan regardless.

Savonarola may have been fundamentalist, but he had long since learned that when it came to secular matters, pragmatism usually succeeded rather than idealism. Just as Savonarola had foreseen, Valori's idealistic move proved a disaster. This drastic lowering of the voting age caused an influx into the Great Council of headstrong, hedonistic young men of the merchant class, many of whom had come of age during the time of Lorenzo the Magnificent. They retained the self-confident arrogance of the privileged youth of this era, and detested all that Savonarola stood for. The liberal *Bianchi* and the pro-Medici *Bigi* gained control of the Great Council, and at the election for the next *gonfaloniere*, to take over in March and April, the winning candidate was Bernardo del Nero, the grand old man of the Medici faction. Now seventy-five years old, but still physically able, he was the leader of the *Bigi*, the party that remained fanatically opposed to Savonarola and all he stood for. Despite this, Bernardo del Nero in fact owed his life to Savonarola; in 1494, after the flight of Piero de' Medici, del Nero and his family had only been rescued from the fury of the mob as a result of Savonarola's passionate sermon forbidding any revenge against Medici supporters. Del Nero had not forgotten this, and as a result had always treated Savonarola himself with an air of respect, despite the fact that he abhorred the move towards a wider democracy and the puritan fundamentalism that had accompanied this. He had done his best to restrain the more hotheaded *Bigi* faction, which was all for the violent overthrow of the government. On the other hand, there would no longer be the usual quiet consultations between the *gonfaloniere* and the prior of San Marco over the best direction for public policy. Savonarola's influence over the government of Florence would remain in abeyance, at least for the next two months while del Nero was *gonfaloniere*. How much popular support the new *gonfaloniere* could muster during March and April remained to be seen.

Within just three weeks of Bernardo del Nero taking up office, rumours of all kinds began circulating amongst the citizens. On 21 March Landucci recorded:

We suspected a plot by Piero de' Medici, who was said to be intending to enter Firenzuola*, where he would give flour and corn to the people, making them cry *Palle*; but none of this turned out to be true.

The city gates were closed as a precaution, but there was no sign of Piero or any Medici forces outside the walls, or even reports of sightings of such forces passing through the countryside on their way to the city. Meanwhile inside Florence the situation continued to deteriorate. As Landucci recorded on 9 April: 'The price of corn went up to 4 *lire* 10 *soldi*.' Four days later, he reported: 'The price of corn went up to 5 *lire*.' With twenty soldi to the lire, this meant an increase of more than 10 per cent in just four days. However, Landucci adds on the same day (12 April): 'I sold a small quantity that I had over, at 4 *lire* 14 *soldi*. I regard myself on this account as ungrateful.'

* A northern gate in the city walls.

Those who could do so were evidently hoarding supplies, yet even the ones who reckoned they had sufficient to pass on small quantities to friends or neighbours, at prices below the going rates, felt some guilt at making a profit with such over-inflated prices. The citizens of Florence were becoming conflicted in all manner of ways: personal, political and spiritual.

Then on 25 April, Landucci recorded: 'We heard that Piero de' Medici was at Siena with a large number of troops, so that we had to set night guards at the gate and the walls.' Siena was just forty miles south of Florence, the capital city of the independent territory between Tuscany and Rome, and long regarded as a traditional enemy of Florence. Piero de' Medici, aided by the power, money and influence of his younger brother Cardinal Giovanni, had at last managed to put together an invasion force, which was evidently marching north from Rome and presumably picking up reinforcements on the way. Although Landucci's ensuing diary entries were unembellished with details, their very simplicity and haste give an indication of the trepidation that must have swept through Florence:

> 27th April. We heard that Piero de' Medici was at Staggia.* 28th April. We heard that he was at Castellina. In fact, before 24 hours had passed he had reached Fonti di San Gaggio, with 2,000 men on foot and on horseback†. Consequently, before the dinner hour the *Gonfaloniere* and all the leading citizens armed themselves and assembled at the *Porto di San Piero Gattolino*‡.

Yet things did not turn out quite as Piero de' Medici had expected. Bernardo del Nero had ordered that the Porto di San Piero be locked and guarded, and had also organised the city's few pieces of light artillery along the ramparts. In his capacity as *gonfaloniere*, del Nero was bound by oath

---

* Staggia was a small town thirty miles south of Florence.
† Castellina was a village in the mountains six miles north-east of Staggia. Fonti di San Gaggio was just south of the city walls of Oltrarno. These varied locations evidently came from rumours heard by those who were fleeing the immediate countryside for the comparative safety of the city walls.
‡ This was the main gate in the southern city walls of Oltrarno, now known as the Porta Romana, at the southern end of the Boboli Gardens (which of course did not exist at that time).

to defend the city, and was determined to go through the motions, even if only to avoid any charge of treason. However, elements within the *Bigi* had sent a message to Piero, assuring him that his very presence would provoke a popular uprising within Florence. This would be followed by an invitation to enter the city, whereupon the gates would then be thrown open and he would be greeted by welcoming crowds as he rode back to the Palazzo Medici and resumed power.

But no popular uprising took place. Precisely why nothing happened remains uncertain. There would undoubtedly have been much 'encouragement' to take to the streets, with rallying calls of '*Palle! Palle!*' by groups of *Bigi* organisers riding through their districts. Yet when the moment of truth arrived, even those who most opposed Savonarola appear to have been not quite so keen on a Medici return to power as they had led others to believe. Besides, by now certain relief supplies had begun reaching Florence from the port of Livorno, and the citizens were no longer willing to be bribed into submission by the offer of free corn from Piero de' Medici. Although there can be no doubt that the population was still deeply divided, it soon became clear that the city was not prepared to welcome Piero. Bernardo del Nero and his 'armed chief citizens' (who would have contained many staunch *Bigi* supporters) watched uncertainly from the walls while the streets of the city remained silent. The gates stayed closed, and Landucci recorded how, later that day:

at about 21 in the evening (5 p.m.) [Piero de' Medici] turned back and went away, seeing that he had no supporters in Florence. It was considered a most foolish thing for him to have put himself in such danger, for if we had wished, we could have captured him; if the alarm bell had rung outside, he would have been surrounded. As it was, he returned to Siena, not without fear.

Landucci's speculative optimism is certainly open to doubt, yet at the same time there is no doubting the proud Piero's loss of face, and news of his public humiliation quickly spread throughout Italy. The son of Lorenzo the Magnificent had become a laughing stock. On his return to Rome, Piero was a broken man and sought to obliterate the memory of his disgrace by launching into a bout of dissipation. This would later be recounted in some detail by his close friend Lamberto dell'Antella:

> He here abandoned himself to a licentious and most scandalous life. He would rise from his bed late in the afternoon for dinner, sending down to the kitchen to see if they had prepared any particular dish which took his fancy. If not, he would leave for the San Severino, where every day a sumptuous banquet was served, and he here spent most of his time. When he had finished his meal, it was his custom to retire to a private room with a courtesan until it was time for his evening meal. Or sometimes he would stay there even later, and then head straight out for the streets of Rome with a bunch of dim-witted loose-living companions. After carousing the night away he would return to his wife around dawn. In this way, he dissipated his time and energy in gluttony, gambling, lewdness and all kinds of unnatural vices.

By now Piero de' Medici was living off the last of Lorenzo the Magnificent's collection of jewels and plate, which his brother Cardinal Giovanni had managed to rescue before fleeing from Florence. Piero's dissipation led to a serious deterioration in his already headstrong and arrogant personality:

> He expected all with whom he came into contact to be subservient to him and obey his every bullying whim. He showed no gratitude or mercy for any who served him. No matter how faithful or devoted his companions, he was liable to turn on them at will in the most savage fashion.

He even turned against his close friend Francesco del Nero, ordering Lamberto dell'Antella 'to arrange for his assassination' – probably as an act of revenge against his relative, Gonfaloniere Bernardo del Nero, for not opening the gates of the city to him. Soon Piero would go so far as to turn against his own brother:

He was liable to treat the Cardinal with such extreme insolence, even when they were in public together, that his brother all but refused to see him. Even so, as soon as the Cardinal received any new income from his many benefices, Piero immediately turned up to claim a share. Within two or three days this would all have been squandered or gambled away.

So while the increasingly indolent and chubby Cardinal Giovanni often woke at sunrise, taking breakfast in bed and reading till the afternoon, his more athletic older brother seldom took to his bed until after sunrise, and well the worse for wear. Their father too had been capable of similar bouts (of both sorts), but his pride and ambition had enabled him to overcome such behaviour. For this reason, he had recognised early his own faults in both Piero and Giovanni, and had taken great pains to warn them against such lapses. Lorenzo the Magnificent had possessed qualities of greatness, and as we know he had been perspicacious enough to realise that at least one of his two sons might also possess such qualities ('One is foolish, one is clever'). He had an inkling that as long as they remained close, together they might prove a formidable force, in both Florence and the Church. Yet now Piero and Giovanni were becoming increasingly alienated.

Despite this, Cardinal Giovanni continued to scheme for his brother's return to power in Florence. To this end, he cultivated the friendship of the powerful Augustinian Mariano da Genazzano, who remained Savonarola's sworn enemy and continued to use all his considerable influence with Alexander VI, constantly urging him to take action against Savonarola. By now neither the pope nor anyone close to the Vatican needed much encouragement in this matter. As the permanent Florentine ambassador Ricciardo Becchi had reported: 'The outrage against Savonarola is increasing amongst all parties in Rome, to such an extent that it is no longer possible to speak in his defence.'

18

'On suspicion of heresy'

JUST SIX DAYS after the failure of Piero de' Medici's 'invasion', Savonarola was due to deliver the Ascension Day sermon on 4 May 1497 at the cathedral. But Landucci records how:

a number of Savonarola's sworn enemies set a vicious trap for him. On the night before he was due to deliver his sermon, they had forced their way into the church, breaking open the door beside the belfry, and entered the pulpit, which they covered with dirt.

Burlamacchi confirms this, rather more explicitly informing how the intruders smeared the pulpit with excrement and covered it with a putrefying donkey hide, together with its stinking innards. They also hammered nails up under the lectern, so that if Savonarola made one of his familiar gestures, emphasising his point by banging his fist down on the pulpit, these would stab through his skin. (This latter attempt at sabotage could well have backfired: the self-flagellating Savonarola would certainly not have been distracted from preaching on account of such minor pain, and the sight of his gesticulating hands dripping blood would doubtless have caused a sensation, prompting the more gullible members of the congregation to believe that they were witnessing a miracle – bleeding stigmata, or some such.)

However, the desecration was discovered next morning and cleared up. Savonarola was adamant that his sermon should go ahead, despite rumours that had begun circulating through the city that he would be assassinated. This was his last chance to preach in public, for the Signoria had issued a decree banning all sermons from 5 May. The increasingly precarious political situation, so easily inflamed, doubtless influenced this decision as much as any anti-Savonarolan members amongst the Signoria. The authorities also had another pressing reason for banning public gatherings. Further isolated cases of the plague had been reported in the slum quarters during the winter, an indication that a more serious epidemic might well break out with the coming of the hot months of summer.

Savonarola's Ascension Day sermon saw a packed cathedral, drawing his supporters from all over the city. The event was not to pass off without serious incident. Landucci described the scene that he witnessed:

> about two-thirds of the way through his sermon, there was a noise from over by the choir, like someone banging a stick on a box. We believe that it was done on purpose by those same men who had desecrated the pulpit. Immediately, there was a commotion with everyone crying: 'Jesu!' because the people were excited, and just waiting for these bad men to cause a disturbance. Not long after the people had settled down again, there was another cry of 'Jesu!' because of a disturbance near to the pulpit, where there were some secretly armed men ready to defend the *Frate*. They now caught sight of some of the men they suspected, and as these approached the pulpit a man by the name of Lando Sassolini struck another called Bartolomeo Guigni with the flat of his sword.

Whereupon a riot broke out amongst the congregation. The great doors of the cathedral were swung open and the terrified crowd ran out into the piazza. Some of Savonarola's supporters hurried to nearby houses, returning with arms, and joined the others gathered around the pulpit, determined to protect him against his armed enemies. Meanwhile Savonarola remained in the pulpit on his knees, praying. Eventually his would-be assassins retreated out of the cathedral, melting away through the streets. The throng of Savonarola's armed supporters then hurried him on the ten-minute journey up the Via del Cocomero back to the safety of San Marco.

This event would appear to indicate that a majority of the citizens of Florence still supported Savonarola, and that any attempt to 'displace' him would result in a violent civil war. As a result of the latest elections for the Signoria and the leading councils, at the beginning of May the more extreme *Arrabbiati* had replaced the *Bigi* as the most influential faction in the government. Even so, the leading *Arrabbiati* were determined at all costs to avoid civil conflict, an outbreak that might easily spell the end of Florence as an independent republic. Other hotheads amongst the *Bigi* and the *Arrabbiati* (who did not call themselves the 'Enraged Ones' for nothing) were still inclined to give vent to their feelings, and the situation remained tense, with a number of violent incidents taking place. On the feast of Corpus Christi, Savonarola's boys once again marched through the streets carrying red crosses in their hands, but as their procession passed over the Ponte Santa Trinità towards Oltrarno, someone ran out from the crowd, snatched the cross from the leader's hands, 'broke it and then threw it into the river, as if he was some kind of infidel'.

Just a week after the riot in Florence Cathedral, Alexander VI finally decided to act against Savonarola. Previously he had held back, expecting the entire situation to be resolved by Piero de' Medici's restoration, followed by Florence joining the Holy League. But now Piero had failed, and Savonarola continued to defy Alexander VI, to the point where things were getting out of hand and the pope saw no alternative but to assert his authority. At last he took the ultimate step of officially excommunicating Savonarola 'on suspicion of heresy'. This banned him from preaching, administering or taking Holy Communion, whilst at the same instructing that 'all people are forbidden to assist him in any way, either to speak to him or to approve of anything he does or says, or they too will be excommunicated'. However, in order to take effect, the pope's Brief of Excommunication had to be delivered from Rome to Florence, a task that Alexander VI was aware might involve some difficulty. Significantly, this was entrusted to the learned theological scholar Gianvittorio da Camerino, who just two months earlier had delivered a sermon in Florence vehemently attacking Savonarola. Despite the Signoria's *Arrabbiati* sympathies, they had viewed da Camerino's sermon as a flagrant incitement to civil disorder and had expelled him from the city, a sentence that put him in line for the death-penalty if he returned. The choice of da Camerino was almost certainly influenced by the pope's advisers, notably Genazzano, and was intended as a direct provocation with the aim of bringing matters to a head.

Da Camerino set out at once from Rome for Florence, but on entering

Tuscan territory he became mindful of the fact that, despite his position as the pope's emissary, this might not in fact grant him full diplomatic immunity from the Signoria's decree. In consequence, he quietly withdrew to the safety of Siena, where he sent a message ahead to the Signoria in Florence requesting a letter granting him safe conduct so that he could fulfil his papal mission. There was no immediate reply to this; indeed, after more than three weeks of waiting it became clear to da Camerino that his message was unlikely to receive acknowledgement of any kind. The Signoria was well aware of the purpose of da Camerino's mission, and the effect upon the city that its successful accomplishment was liable to cause. Meanwhile in Rome the pope was unable to ascertain the whereabouts of da Camerino: his Brief of Excommunication appeared to have vanished into thin air. After almost a month of waiting, da Camerino decided to entrust copies of the papal Brief to an anonymous courier, who was instructed to deliver these to the five centres of clerical opposition to Savonarola in Florence for whom they were intended – most notably the Franciscan Church of Santa Croce, the Church of Santa Maria Novella (whose Dominicans remained loyal to the pope), as well as the Augustinian Church of Santo Spirito. And it was at these five churches, on 18 June, before their gathered Sunday congregations, that Savonarola's excommunication by the pope was formally proclaimed with bell, book and candle. This time-honoured ritual involved the solemn tolling, as at a funeral (the bell), the closing of the Bible (the book) with the proclamation 'We judge him damned, with the Devil and his angels, to the eternal fires of Hell', and finally the snuffing out of the flame of a taper (the candle) to mark the exclusion of the excommunicated soul from the light of God. At Santo Spirito, this ritual was triumphantly performed by Savonarola's enemy Fra Leonardo da Fivizzano, who had preached against him throughout the previous Lent.

Savonarola's reply was soon in coming. The very next day he wrote, and had printed for distribution, a letter entitled *Contro la escomunicazione surrettizia* ('Against surreptitious excommunication'). Indicatively, this was written not in scholarly Church Latin, but in Italian, the language of the people, and was addressed 'To All Christians and those beloved of God'. In this letter, Savonarola defended himself against Rome, making it quite clear that he had no intention of accepting his excommunication and rallying his faithful flock around him, claiming: 'God will vouchsafe us from all danger and grant us a great victory.' Soon afterwards he would publish a second letter, in Latin, entitled *Contra sententiam excommunicationis* ('Against sententious excommunications'). This was intended for the eyes of the theologians, together with other academics and learned authorities, and in it he brought the full power of his intellect and learning to bear on the matter of his excommunication. He had only been accused of 'suspicion of heresy': there had been no proof or evidence given, no charge had been brought against him, there had been no trial, and he had not been found guilty. In this more scholarly defence he quoted precedents where members of the clergy had been urged to defy wrongful excommunications. He even went so far as to recall the advice issued earlier in the century by Martin V, the much-admired pope whose election had brought an end to the Great Schism.* Martin V had pronounced that Christians were under no obligation to ignore anyone who had been excommunicated, unless explicit papal instructions had been issued to do so. Despite Alexander VI having done precisely this, Savonarola felt himself to be under no obligation to cease preaching. On 19 June, the very day after his excommunication by Alexander VI had been publicly read from the pulpits of five of Florence's major churches, Savonarola preached a sermon at San Marco that attracted a large crowd of his admirers from throughout the city.

Yet by this time the atmosphere in Florence had undergone a transformation. The new *Arrabbiati* Signoria had begun relaxing many of the prohibitions put in place by earlier Signoria on the advice of Savonarola. On 11 June, Landucci recorded:

The *palio*† of Santa Barbara was held. This race has not been run for years in Florence, because of Savonarola's sermons. This *Signoria*

---

* The Great Schism lasted from 1378 until 1417, during most of which time there were two popes, one in Rome and another in Avignon, neither of whom recognised the other's authority.
† The traditional annual horse race, which had taken place over a mile-long course through the city streets, with the jockeys colourfully attired in the emblems of each of the city's districts. The crowds lined the streets, cheering on the horse representing their district, and the day on which the race was run always had a festival air. Such universal light-hearted public enjoyment, combined as it was with widespread gambling, would have been anathema to Savonarola. A remnant of such races can be seen today in the annual *palio* that is still held in the central piazza of Siena.

decided that it should be allowed to take place, ignoring Savonarola, saying: 'Let's cheer the people up a little; should we all behave like monks?'

A week later, news of Savonarola's excommunication had been greeted with outbreaks of public rejoicing – in part spontaneous, but certainly encouraged by the *Bigi* and the *Arrabbiati*. The less virulent *Tiepidi* and the secular liberal *Bianchi* also welcomed the apparent end of Savonarola's rule. People danced in the piazzas and prostitutes reappeared overnight in the streets where they had traditionally been permitted. Public ballads ridiculing Savonarola, his monks and the *Piagnoni* were circulated and sung in the revived taverns, whilst crowds gathered outside San Marco to jeer at Savonarola and his followers, singing their ballads and yelling obscenities.

Yet these revelries took place against a background of public alarm, which may well have played a part in inspiring the devil-may-care attitude of the revellers. As many had feared, after the reports of isolated cases of the plague in the slums during the winter, the advent of summer – with the usual putrid smells and increased vermin pervading the streets – brought a more serious outbreak of the disease. Landucci's diary makes grim reading, and what it recorded must have sent a chill through the heart of all Florentines, whether rejoicing or lamenting the rescinding of Savonarola's puritan laws:

28th June. They say there were 60 deaths a day from fever.
30th June. The plague has struck in several houses in the city, and in eight houses in the *Borgo di Ricorboli** . . .
3rd July. Yet more houses infected with plague have been discovered, making everyone think of fleeing.

In the midst of all this, the pro-Savonarolan Domenico Bartoli was elected *gonfaloniere* and took up office on 1 July, and this fortuitous appointment may well have saved Savonarola's life, preventing the *Arrabbiati* from taking things into their own hands.

*

* The suburb of poor fishermen's shacks upstream by the city walls on the south bank of the Arno.

Fresh supplies of corn were beginning to reach the city from the port of Livorno, and the new administration immediately took measures to alleviate the suffering of the *Piagnoni*. At one time the price of corn had risen to well over five lire (100 soldi). By 8 July the new administration had ensured sufficient reserves for Landucci to record: 'The officials of the *Abbondanza** fixed the price of corn at the corn market at 35 *soldi*.' Even so, this was still over double the normal price.

Throughout July the situation remained conflicted, but not violently so, largely because of the depleted population. Landucci recorded:

> 29th July. There was an eclipse of the sun, and many people were dying of plague and fever, which caused the city to empty itself of its inhabitants, everyone who could going into the country.

Many of the superstitious, especially amongst the poor who were unable to retire to the country, saw the eclipse as an evil omen, whilst amongst the others who stayed behind in the city were a number who remained secretly determined to overthrow the government.

Back in Rome, Piero de' Medici had finally fallen out with his close friend Lamberto dell'Antella, putting him in fear of his life. Although dell'Antella was exiled from Florence, he decided to travel to Siena, from where he wrote to various influential friends in Florence, imploring them to appeal to the Signoria on his behalf, begging for a pardon. If he was allowed to return, dell'Antella made it plain that he was willing to provide the Signoria with much vital information concerning the Medici and the activities of their supporters in Rome.

Following Piero de' Medici's abortive invasion, the Signoria had set up an elaborate spy network in the countryside surrounding the city, so that they could receive at once any information concerning the approach of travellers who might be reconnoitring for any future invasion. When dell'Antella became impatient with the lack of any reply from Florence, and decided to pay a clandestine visit to his family estate just four miles outside the city, the authorities were at once alerted of his movements. As he

---

* Florence's equivalent of a Ministry of Supply.

approached his estates he was arrested and taken to Florence under armed escort. Here he was immediately subjected to the usual treatment meted out to such prisoners: he was tortured by the traditional Florentine method known as the strappado. This involved the prisoner's hands being bound behind his back and then hooked to a pulley, which was raised, hauling the prisoner into the air suspended by his wrists. The pulley was then released so that his body dropped until he was suspended just above the ground, his fall broken by the rope tied around his wrists. The pain was excruciating, and the drop was liable to dislocate the shoulders (which would then be manipulated back into place by an attendant surgeon, so that the procedure could continue). Prisoners would be subjected to several strappados, usually in the presence of members of the policing committee and some of the Signoria, so that they could hear at first hand his confession.

Dell'Antella's motives for returning to Florence do not appear to have been entirely pure, for when he was arrested he was found to be carrying a number of secret messages. After several strappados dell'Antella produced the names of the people for whom these documents were intended, as well as confessing all that he knew about the activities of the Medici and their supporters in Rome.* Dell'Antella then named the leading citizens in Florence whom Piero de' Medici had sworn to put to death on his return to power, and he also confessed a whole list of traitors within the city who were actively plotting to overthrow the government in favour of the return of Piero de' Medici. Before fleeing into exile to join Piero de' Medici, dell'Antella had accumulated several enemies amongst the influential families of Florence and certainly had several old scores to settle. As a result, many contemporaries (including those present at his confession) had certain doubts about the extensive list of 'traitors' that eventually emerged.

The Signoria immediately began making plans for the arrest of those on the list. Amongst these were several eminent figures and members of the city's most distinguished families. They included Gino Capponi, Andrea de' Medici (a relative of Lorenzo di Pierfrancesco), Lorenzo Tornabuoni (from the family of Lorenzo the Magnificent's wife), the leading *Bigi* member

* It was this confession that produced the precise details of Piero de' Medici's daily round of debauchery (see p. 272).

Niccolò Ridolfi, and even former *gonfaloniere* Bernardo del Nero, who had refused to open the city gates for Piero. The last three were so unsuspecting of their predicament that when they were invited to the Palazzo della Signoria they attended voluntarily, assuming that they were to be consulted for advice concerning the difficult situation in which dell'Antella's confessions had placed the city. All three, including the seventy-two-year-old del Nero, were immediately arrested, marched off to the police headquarters at the Bargello and subjected to the strappado.

Just five days after dell'Antella's arrest, Landucci recorded:

10 August. Everyone in the city was talking about what should be done with the prisoners; some said they were not guilty, others insisted they were guilty.

These three, along with two others, were put on trial on 17 August. All five were quickly found guilty and sentenced to death, with their families banished into exile. In line with the reforms brought in at Savonarola's suggestion, their defence counsel Messer Guidantonio Vespucci lodged an appeal. The city was soon filled with wild, conflicting rumours as to their fate. Were they in fact innocent? Would the Signoria dare to put to death such important citizens? If they were put to death would this inflame the situation, causing an outbreak of civil war? News now spread that Piero de' Medici had bestirred himself from Rome and had travelled once more to Siena, hoping to recruit sufficient troops to march on Florence. This time his appearance at the city walls was bound to provoke an uprising of some sort. The appeal of the five men sentenced to death had to be dealt with as soon as possible.

A matter of such great importance could only be democratically decided by a meeting of the Great Council. Yet there was simply no time to summon sufficient members, as so many had left the city for their farms and villas in the countryside. This was very much the custom during the hot months of summer, but the outbreaks of the plague and fever had resulted in a particularly large exodus that year. Consequently, the idea of calling a meeting of the Great Council was dismissed, and instead on 21 August the pro-Savonarolan *gonfaloniere* Domenico Bartoli used his prerogative to summon the smaller council known as the Pratica. This consisted of around 200 men, including the Signoria, senior figures in the administration and others of experience in the city. They would debate the merits of the appeal by the five condemned men, which would then be decided by a vote of the Signoria. The condemned remained in their cells at the nearby Bargello and were not permitted to be present at their appeal, nor was their defence lawyer Messer Vespucci allowed to attend; Savonarola, who held no post in the administration, was of course also absent, though his views were certainly represented. From the outset, those present were bitterly divided. The meeting began in the morning, and would continue through the afternoon and on into the night. Soldiers patrolled the Piazza della Signoria outside, in order to prevent any public demonstrations, and at eleven o'clock that night they heard the raised voices of men shouting in anger, from the open windows of the palazzo above them where the meeting was taking place. The very nature of the republic, and its future course, was being argued out amidst the flames of the flickering candles. All five of the condemned were important citizens – members of ancient distinguished families, prosperous merchants, senior guild members, a former *gonfaloniere*. Despite their known pro-Medici sympathies, they were moderates. They were also respected, for the most part popular figures (even with many who favoured Savonarola), and few amongst the citizenry at large were convinced of their guilt. If such men could be summarily executed, their families stripped of their assets and despatched into exile, this would mark a serious transformation in the politics of the republic. Such a prospect stirred fierce passions, and by midnight the meeting to discuss the appeal had degenerated to the extent that:

> the Palace that night was like a forge, or rather, a cavern of fury, and all the men present driven by contempt and as if by a mad rage, with weapons in hand, wounding words, and full of quarrels ... so that a number of noblemen feared for their safety.

Still the situation remained in deadlock. For the appeal to be successful, six of the eight Signoria had to vote in favour, but by now only four or five had been convinced. At one point the nobleman Carlo Strozzi advanced

on the seated Signoria, seized Piero Guicciardini* and threatened to throw
him from the opened window into the square below if he did not reverse
his vote and come out against the appeal. This physical attack constituted
a serious crime, but by now matters had progressed far beyond legal niceties.
Indeed, the contemporary Cerretani goes so far as to claim that if the
defence lawyer Vespucci had been present, and had begun putting forward
arguments in favour of the defendants, he would certainly have been thrown
out of the window.

At two in the morning the meeting was finally brought to a climax by
Francesco Valori, the leader of the *Piagnoni*, who had also been appointed
to a senior post in the administration. According to the historian Guicciardini (who doubtless heard a first-hand account from his father):

> Francesco Valori at last leapt to his feet in a rage, seizing the ballot
> box in his hand and pounding loudly on the table before the Signoria,
> demanding that either justice be done or all hell would break loose.
> He then gave a fierce ultimatum, declaring that either he would die
> or the conspirators would die.†

This particular confrontation caused one member of the Signoria, an
artisan called Niccolò Zati, to fear for his own safety. As a result he decided
to change his vote, casting it against the appeal, thus making up the required
six votes. The death-penalty was confirmed. Immediately word was sent to
the public executioner, and with undue haste the five condemned men were
led out of their cells, one by one, barefoot and in chains, to the traditional
place of execution, the courtyard of the Bargello. The executioner's block
was surrounded by a layer of hay, and after each beheading a further layer
of hay was spread over this so as to prevent the condemned man from
seeing the splattered blood of his predecessor. By four in the morning it
was all over.

* Father of the renowned Renaissance historian Francesco Guicciardini.
† Some sources place the violent Strozzi incident immediately after this. Martines, drawing as
well on Cerretani and Parenti, makes a case for it happening 'in the hours leading up to the
final decision . . . in the midst of that furore', which seems more likely under the circumstances
described, despite the testimony of Guicciardini's father.

Despite this haste and secrecy, word quickly spread through the dark-ened city. Landucci recorded

Everyone was astonished that such a thing could be done; it was diffi-cult to understand. They were put to death the same night, and I could not restrain myself from weeping as I saw young Lorenzo Tornabuoni carried past the Canto de' Tornaquinci on a bier, shortly before dawn.

At that time of year dawn was between five and six, by which time Landucci, a mere apothecary, not only knew what had happened, but was waiting outside his corner shop at the Canto de' Tornaquinci for the cortège to pass on its way to the neighbouring Palazzo Tornabuoni. He would not have been alone: the darkened street would have been lined with silent figures, some doubtless as moved as Landucci.

Savonarola's behaviour during this period remains puzzling. As early as 9 July Landucci had recorded:

Plague broke out in *San Marco*, and many of the *Frati* left the monastery and went out into the country to the villas of their fathers and rela-tives and friends. Savonarola remained at *San Marco*, with only a few *Frati*. By now there were around thirty-four houses stricken with the plague in Florence, and there was also widespread fever.

Such action was characteristic of Savonarola – determined to remain at his post, even if this endangered his life. He may have been forbidden to preach by the Signoria on account of the plague, to say nothing of his excommunication, but he was still able to consult in private, especially with powerful figures like Francesco Valori and other influential *Piagnoni*. Indeed, the *Piagnoni* constantly looked to the 'little friar' for guidance. And when the Tornabuoni family begged Savonarola to intercede on behalf of the amiable and popular young Lorenzo, Savonarola is said to have asked the Signoria to show mercy – though seemingly in a manner which made it plain that he was only going through the motions. In fact, there is no record of his intervention, and some even doubt that he did anything at all. In direct contrast to his plea for forgiveness amongst opposing citizens after the flight of Piero de' Medici, Savonarola made no public appeal for clemency with regard to any of the condemned men. All we have is a letter he sent to Giovambattista Ridolfi, brother of the condemned Niccolò, on 19 August – that is, two days after the original trial had condemned him to death:

> Thus, my Giovambattista, in this time of your adversity revive the virtue of faith and the greatness of your spirit and consider that the honours of this world, as well as its riches, vanish like the wind, and our time upon earth forever grows shorter ... Perhaps God has ordained this penance for your brother's salvation. Suffering can often save those who might otherwise be damned on account of their prosperity.

Hardly consoling words for the brother of a man under sentence of death, and indicatively offering no hope of reprieve. Note too that Savonarola addressed him as 'my Giovambattista' (the original Italian, *Giovambattista mio*, gives the flavour more strongly). And so he should have done, for Giovambattista Ridolfi was one of his closest and most loyal followers – which makes this letter appear all the more inconsiderate, not to say heartless, although it was undeniably in accord with that unworldly facet of Savonarola's nature.

Precisely how much Savonarola was adhering to that facet, and practising what he preached, during this period is open to question. He may have remained in isolation – both spiritual and medical – at San Marco, along with his few closest disciples, but this was also a period when he (or at least his followers) sought to consolidate his political power against the backlash that inevitably followed the five executions. Surprisingly, despite widespread sorrow (such as that of Landucci), this appears to have worked to such an extent that the Milanese envoy reported on 10 September: 'For the time being it is undeniable that the Friar's party are in complete control of the government, without any opposition.' Bartoli's two-month term as *gonfaloniere* was followed in September by three further *Piagnoni* sympathisers in succession holding this office. Such was Savonarola's popularity that during November the diarist Parenti recorded:

So great was the esteem in which Fra Girolamo was now held in the city that medals containing his portrait were cast in bronze. One side showed his head surrounded with the inscription *Savonarola ordinis praedicatorum doctissimus* [Savonarola of the succession of the greatest prophets], and the other showed Rome with a dagger suspended above it and the encircling words *Gladius Domini super terram cito et velociter* [The sword of the Lord, striking and swift].

Savonarola spent his days and nights in seclusion in his cell writing what many consider to be his major literary legacy. From around July 1497 until early February 1498, he embarked upon a period of prodigious creative output, producing no fewer than two complete books in six months. One of these was virtually his spiritual testament, whilst the other was a summary of his political ideas. As if this were not enough, at the same time he also comprehensively revised and translated into Italian *Disputiones adversus astrologiam divinatricem*, the anti-astrological work that he had co-authored four years previously with Pico della Mirandola.

Triumphus Crucis (*The Triumph of the Cross*) contained a summation of Savonarola's spiritual beliefs. Surprisingly, the work begins from a sceptical point of view, using words that would not have been out of place in the works of Descartes, the rationalist thinker who was to initiate modern philosophy well over a century later. 'We will not rely upon any authority, and will proceed as if we reject the teachings of any man in the world, no matter how wise he might be. Instead, we will rely solely upon natural reason.' He then goes on to analyse this bold assertion. 'Reason proceeds from the seen to the unseen in the following manner. All our knowledge is derived from the senses, which perceive the outer world; the intellect, on the other hand, perceives the substance of things.' This remarkable piece of philosophising prefigures both the empiricism and the rationalism of early modern philosophy. However, the ensuing sentences make it clear that Savonarola did not accept such enquiries for their own sake (as would Descartes and his contemporary, the early empiricist John Locke). Instead, Savonarola assumes that the passage from outer knowledge (the senses) to inner knowledge (reason) is a progress towards a specific end: 'the knowledge of matter thus rises to the knowledge of the unseen and hence to God'. This is followed by the further assumption that 'philosophers seek to find God in the marvels of visible nature'. He then compares this to the similar process of how 'in the visible Church we seek and discover the invisible Church, whose supreme head is Jesus Christ'. All pretence to scepticism and rational argument are then replaced by Savonarola's familiar apocalyptic visions, combining the awesome grandeur of the Old Testament with the simple faith of the New Testament. The mystic chariot of old passes across the heavens, bearing Christ the conqueror with his crown of thorns, and his bloodied wounds, illuminated by the celestial light from on high, 'shining like a triple sun, representing the Blessed Trinity'.

The work continues in similar fashion through four books of fundamentalist argument, backed by the force of Savonarola's considerable intellectual reasoning, along with metaphysical pronouncements and compelling visions such as were found in his sermons – the very combination that achieved the astonishing feat of simultaneously convincing both the finest and the simplest minds in Florence. However, somehow this testament lacks the force of his presence, which is so much easier to envisage in passages from the transcriptions of his sermons. It is these latter that best enable us to imagine the cowled figure in the pulpit beneath the high nave of Florence Cathedral, his mesmeric voice ringing out over the sea of rapt faces below, carrying on his personal dialogue with them, questioning and answering himself, conjuring up before them the frightful visions that had come to him in his solitary cell during his long vigils of agonising deprivation, self-laceration (and possibly the incapacitating pain of migraine-induced hallucinations).

. Now, with Florence surrounded by her enemies, having been smitten by plague and fever, it was the memory of this charismatic figure that inspired the new *gonfaloniere* urgently to seek out Savonarola's political advice. The man elected *gonfaloniere* at the turn of 1498 was the *Piagnone* Giuliano Salviati, who along with his Signoria found himself at a loss when faced with the city's seemingly insurmountable internal divisions and external threats. It was as if the children of Israel were awaiting Moses' descent from the mountain with the Ten Commandments. Yet no such practical advice was forthcoming from Savonarola. This time there would be no suggestion of astute political reforms intended to unite the citizens in a patriotic political unit, nor did he elect to echo biblical tradition with thundering pronouncements as if writ in stone. It was as if Savonarola knew that the time had come for him to deliver himself of his entire testament, both sacred and secular – the accumulated wisdom of experience that he had gained with God's guidance during his forty-five years on Earth.

So instead of coming to the aid of Florence once more in her time of need, Savonarola chose to remain in seclusion and write his political testament, *Trattato circa il reggimento e il governo della città di Firenze* (*Treatise on the rule and government of the city of Florence*). In this he summarises in more general terms much of the political advice he had given out in his sermons at earlier times of crisis. In place of the Old Testament prophet was the voice of guidance, specifically aimed at 'the mutable, restless and ambitious character of the Florentine people which is best suited to a civil government, that is to say a republic'. Indeed, it is no idle claim to assert that Florentines, more than any other citizens of the time, were the most apt audience for such a work. Not since Ancient Greece had there been a city state in which the people (or at least a sizeable section of them) had become accustomed to having such a say in their government. Even when this freedom had been completely subverted by the Medici, Lorenzo the Magnificent had well understood the necessity of making it appear as if the democratic processes were being observed.

Unlike some previous classics in political philosophy (such as Plato's *Republic*) Savonarola's treatise was to be no prescription for a heavenly utopia. This was a work of Renaissance political philosophy, written some fifteen years before Machiavelli's *The Prince*, which is usually taken as the pioneering work in this field. (Indeed, *The Prince* contains credible evidence that Machiavelli had read Savonarola's treatise.) Savonarola points out that man is a free agent and, as such, must submit to government of some sort. He examines the flaws and evils of tyranny, and warns against its opposite, popular anarchy. Instead, he proposes the best safeguard to human freedom to be a Great Council, on the Florentine model, which helps to guarantee the democratic nature of a society.

Savonarola's *Trattato* was far in advance of its time, just as the republican government of Florence (which Savonarola had played such a large part in forming) was in many ways a forerunner of our modern Western political state. This is not to say that Florence was a popular liberal democracy such as we would recognise; nor that Savonarola's treatise was a consistent prescription for such rule. On the contrary: at the outset Savonarola does in fact state that the finest form of government would undoubtedly be absolutist rule by a righteous man. However, he was forced to concede that both reason and experience indicated that 'government of this sort is not practical for all types of people . . . especially Florentines'.

What is one to make of this? No one could possibly have coerced Savonarola into making such a statement. Yet it is precisely here that he pinpoints his own flaw. He believed in a free government for the Florentines, yet at the same time he insisted upon a strict morality being imposed upon these 'mutable, restless and ambitious' people. The man who sought to introduce a strong code of justice also sought to introduce a strong code of morality. Civil freedom should come at the expense of personal freedom. Such anomalous motives are frequently encountered in revolutionary leaders of all types (from Cromwell to Lenin). Yet justice and morality, by their very definition, are the concern not of one man but of the people, who for the most part do not see social justice and personal morality as identical matters. This particular political incongruity may remain unresolved to this day, but Savonarola was the first modern political philosopher to recognise it, even if it was at the expense of his own cherished beliefs.

19

Open Defiance

B Y EARLY 1498 Florence was in the grip of yet another unusually fierce winter. On 6 January Landucci recorded: 'At this time the cold was extreme, and the Arno froze over.' Later he would write of 'there having been frost for more than two months'. Such weather had driven the people from the countryside back into the city, yet by way of relief, 'There was not so much talk about the plague now, as it was only in one or two houses, but not more than that.' 6 January also marked the feast of the Epiphany, celebrating the visit by the three Magi to the infant Christ, which in the city was honoured by a traditional symbolic ceremony:

The *Signoria* of Florence went to the offering at *San Marco*, and approached Fra Girolamo to kiss his hand at the altar. Many thoughtful men were surprised by this, not just his enemies but also among his friends.

Rumours began to spread that Savonarola would soon emerge from San Marco and resume delivering his famous sermons, thus openly defying the papal authority of his excommunication. The ambassador from Ferrara, curious to discover whether there was any truth in these rumours, called on Savonarola and asked him directly if he intended to resume preaching. Savonarola replied that he would do this 'when he received the sign from those who were able to command him'. The ambassador asked if this meant that he was awaiting an order from the pope or the Signoria, but Savonarola replied that he would not act on orders from the Signoria, or from the pope, who had done nothing to reform his own wickedness and persisted in refusing to annul Savonarola's wrongful excommunication. Instead, Savonarola claimed, 'he awaited the command of One who was superior to the pope and to all other living creatures'.

The Signoria was left in a predicament. Florence was desperate for the pope to intervene in the matter of Pisa, and return the port to Florentine rule in order to relieve the continuing food shortages in the city. At the same time the Signoria also recognised the need to maintain its popularity amongst Savonarola's supporters by attempting to persuade Alexander VI to rescind the excommunication. An indication of the importance the Signoria and the citizens of Florence attached to the matter of Savonarola's excommunication can be seen in the fact that the lawyer Domenico Bonsi was despatched as a second ambassador to Rome specifically to negotiate with Alexander VI on this matter, in the hope of obtaining for Savonarola a 'total and free absolution'. But Alexander VI was adamant. Florence had now become integral to his wider political ambition of domination in Italy, and in order to achieve this he needed the city to join the Holy League that he now commanded. Only if Florence joined the league would he even consider the matter.

The 'One who was superior to the Pope and to all other living creatures' soon spoke to Savonarola, and he immediately announced that he intended to resume preaching the pre-Lenten sermons. On 11 February the cowled figure with his hooked nose and piercing eyes left San Marco, surrounded by his bodyguard of loyal acolytes, proceeding down the Via del Cocomero to Florence Cathedral. This year the theme of his sermons was to be taken from Exodus, the second book of the Old Testament, which told how Moses had led the tribe of Israel out of slavery in Egypt to the Promised Land. 'As soon as Savonarola stepped up into the pulpit, the people were so overjoyed at his return that they immediately burst into song with the words of the popular hymn "*Te deum laudamus*" (We praise thee, O God).' Not in any way mollified by this reception, Savonarola began in all austerity, echoing the words spoken by Abraham: 'Lord, I who am but dust and ashes, wish first of all this morning to speak to Thy Majesty . . .' After presuming to address God, he turned to his congregation, determined not to mince his words with regards to his excommunication and his attitude towards the power of Alexander VI:

A governor of the Church is a tool of God . . . but if he is not used like a tool of God he is like a broken tool, all of which are alike . . . he is no greater than any man . . . You may say to him, 'You do not do good, because you do not let yourself be guided by the supreme Lord'. And if he says, 'I have the power', you may say to him, 'That is not true, because there is no hand guiding you, and you are a broken tool.'

As if this were not bad enough, he then launched into an unmistakable personal attack on Alexander VI and his supporters in Rome:

What was the purpose of those who lied in order that I should be excommunicated? . . . Once my excommunication was announced they once more abandoned themselves to excessive eating and drinking, to greed of all kinds, to consorting with concubines, to the sale of benefices, and to all manner of lies and wickedness. On whose side will thou be, O Christ? On the side of the truth or lies? Christ says, 'I am the truth . . .'

Savonarola was making his position unequivocally clear. He now even more explicitly linked his excommunication to the immoral behaviour of the pope and those around him, at the same time openly declaring that he had no intention of obeying such a man, or of accepting his pronouncements. Savonarola was making a direct and public challenge to Alexander VI. There could be no going back now, on either side.

Savonarola's sermon was greeted with some awe, and not a little trepidation, by the citizens of Florence. Landucci for one recorded:

Many people went to hear him, and it was much discussed, because of his excommunication; however, a lot of people did not go for fear of being excommunicated, saying: *giusta vel ingiusta, temenda est* [just or unjust, it is to be feared]. I was one of those who did not go.

Landucci may have supported Savonarola, but he remained cautious where the authority of the Church was concerned, as indeed did many other *Piagnoni*. Just six days after Savonarola's first sermon, Landucci wrote: '17th February. Fra Girolamo preached in *Santa Maria del Fiore* [Florence Cathedral], and fewer people went.'

It was around this time that an extremist group amongst the anti-Savonarolans, consisting largely of brash upper-class young hedonists known as the *Compagnacci*,* decided to take matters into their own hands. They hatched a plot to assassinate Savonarola by blowing him up while he was delivering one of his sermons in the cathedral. A local munitions expert called Baia was hired to conceal the gunpowder beneath the pulpit, but the plot was called off at the last minute because the *Compagnacci* realised that during such an explosion people sitting in the front rows of the congregation, some of whom would be relatives of their own families, were liable to 'be maimed or killed'. Martines suggests that this would have been 'the first "terrorist" bomb in the history of Europe'. Significantly, this incident also illustrates how deeply the sympathies and antipathies towards Savonarola still ran through the city, even dividing several upper-class families.†

On the very same day that Savonarola was delivering his second public sermon in Florence Cathedral, one of the two Florentine ambassadors in Rome, Domenico Bonsi, sent a despatch complaining to the Signoria.‡

> I am being attacked on every side by cardinals and prelates, who come to complain in the strongest possible fashion about the behaviour of Your Excellencies [in allowing Savonarola to preach]. They all tell me of the Pope's great anger over this matter. You have enemies all over Rome, who are doing their best to whip up feelings against you.

---

* The Rude or Ugly Companions; a modern, more colloquial equivalent would be the 'Bully Boys'.

† Some sources, such as Villari, place this plot almost a year earlier, intended for Savonarola's Ascension Day sermon in May 1497, with the pulpit being smeared with excrement only after the explosive idea had been abandoned. Villari cites Burlamacchi amongst others as his source. Martines, the modern expert, prefers the reliability of the contemporary journal of Lorenzo Violi.

‡ In fact, according to protocol, this was addressed to the Council of Ten, who were responsible for the foreign affairs of the republic, but there can be no doubt that it was intended for the *gonfaloniere* and the Signoria, as its wording makes clear.

Alexander VI had realised that the Florentines were unwilling to bargain over Savonarola and their entry into his Holy League – a realisation that filled him with anger. Moreover he was being passed daily communiqués from the outraged Augustinians in Florence containing detailed descriptions of Savonarola's actions and pronouncements. On 25 February, Alexander VI summoned both Bracci and Bonsi to appear before him at his papal court, where he began remonstrating to them about Savonarola, 'expressing himself in the strongest possible terms and with great passion'. Bonsi was commanded to send an immediate despatch to the Signoria in Florence, informing them that if they did not silence Savonarola 'either by restraint or by some other method [His Holiness would impose] a universal interdiction upon the entire city'. This was the equivalent of a collective excommunication: certain sacraments were banned, no divine services could be held and, perhaps most intimidating of all, no Christian burials were permitted. Alexander VI went on to announce that he had made this pronouncement publicly, in formal court session in front of his cardinals, prelates and the ambassadors to the Holy See, 'in order to make clear that there could be no question of him countermanding this order'. Working himself up into an even more passionate state, the pope then ordered to be read out certain scurrilous sonnets circulating in Florence that had come to his notice (doubtless through the agency of the Augustinians). These made a mockery of the pope, in the most vulgar fashion, holding him and his authority up to ridicule before the common citizens. Each time that the Florentine ambassadors attempted to reply to Alexander VI they were immediately silenced. They would obey his orders forthwith and without question.

That very day, a chastened Bonsi hurriedly sent his despatch to Florence. Yet in order that there should be no mistaking the pope's intentions, on the same day Alexander VI himself dictated two Briefs, expressing his views in the strongest possible manner, and had these sent to Florence forthwith. This time there could be no excuses, no pretences that messages had gone astray, no quibbles over the legality of his orders. Either Savonarola was silenced, or the Florentine republic stood in the gravest possible danger – and it would be evident to all that such danger extended beyond the realms of the spiritual. Behind Alexander VI loomed the combined power of the Holy League.

Yet on 27 February, even as the diplomatic couriers were galloping north along the ancient Via Cassia on the last stages of the 150-mile journey to Florence, Savonarola was mounting the steps of the pulpit in San Marco to deliver his Carnival-day sermon. This was followed by the usual procession of Savonarola's boys bearing candles and singing hymns as they passed through the streets, banging at doors requesting the donation of luxurious items for the annual Burning of the Vanities. Amazingly, a considerable number of such items remained in certain houses, but their collection was not wholly welcomed and Savonarola's boys found themselves receiving a mixed reception:

> A big stack of things was piled up on the *Piazza de' Signori*. These vain objects consisted of nude statues and gaming boards, heretical books, Morganti*, mirrors and many other vanities, adding up to a great value, estimated at thousands of florins . . . although some lukewarm people† gave trouble, throwing dead cats and all kinds of filth upon it.

Other reports speak of hymn-singing processions being stoned, barricades being erected to prevent them from entering certain districts, and in some cases Savonarola's boys even being physically attacked with sticks and having their white robes torn from their backs. The poor were still enduring meagre grain handouts and resented the destruction of such valuable items, which could have been sold to buy in provisions; many moderate citizens were growing tired of the killjoy puritan atmosphere that prevailed and that was becoming more and more invasive of their personal lives; while the *Arrabbiati* continued to stir up as much trouble as they could. When the papal Briefs demanding Savonarola's silence finally arrived in Florence, according to Guicciardini: 'A great council was held on this subject and there were much argument and controversy.' Despite the inevitable clash

---

* A satirical anti-religious epic poem, which had been much admired during the time of Lorenzo the Magnificent and had remained popular after his death.
† A referennce to the *Tiepidi* moderate anti-Savonarolan faction, who were becoming increasingly exasperated at his behaviour, especially his defiance of papal authority and the possibility that Alexander VI might retaliate by issuing an interdiction, thus endangering their souls in the eyes of God.

between the pro-*Arrabiatti* and pro-*Piagnoni* factions, many on all sides felt sympathetic with the view expressed by Giovanni Combi:

> As for this Brief, there was no point in sending it to us, any more than to Perugia.* It would dishonour us to obey ... It would be a mark of our ingratitude [to Savonarola] if we obeyed. We are deeply obliged for all that he has done for us ... In him we have a treasure that anyone might envy.

According to Guicciardini, Savonarola's opponents:

> whose influence with the people was constantly growing, objected to his disobedience and protested that his arrogance would only annoy the Pope at the very time when the return of Pisa was under discussion with him and the league. This was the very moment when they should be attempting to encourage the Pope. However, Savonarola's supporters defended him, insisting that the work of God should not be interfered with by worldly matters and that they should not permit the Pope to meddle in the Republic's affairs on such grounds.

After several days of more or less heated discusssion, a final vote was taken:

> At last a great majority advised that [Savonarola] should not be allowed to preach. And so the Signoria commanded him and he obeyed, leaving Fra Domenico da Pescia to preach instead of him in San Marco and others of his friars in other churches.

This was a distinct fudge, as all would have been well aware. Domenico da Pescia was Savonarola's most fervent supporter in San Marco, and all knew that he, as well as the others amongst his friars, would simply deliver Savonarola's sermons word for word regardless of any directives from Rome.

The population was possessed by an increasingly volatile mix of

---

* Formerly a papal possession, which had rejected papal rule the previous century.

conflicting patriotic beliefs, class and political divisions and religious affiliations. These mixed feelings were reflected in the views of the newly elected *gonfaloniere* and his Signoria, which replaced the pro-Savonarolan rulers on 1 March 1498. The *gonfaloniere* himself, Piero Popoleschi, was a known opponent of Savonarola, though he was not an extremist. His eight-man Signoria was divided: four were known *Arrabbiati* supporters, while three were pro-*Piagnoni*. The eighth member of the Signoria, Piero Fedini, felt unable to commit himself. However, as seen with the recent appeal against the death-sentence of the five plotters, according to the Florentine constitution six votes from amongst the *gonfaloniere* and his Signoria were required to pass any important motion. Thus, Fedini's dithering left the Signoria powerless to take any decisive action against Savonarola, at least for the time being.

All the indications were that the city was shaping up for a fateful contest, which would have a decisive outcome. And when that day arrived, no one wanted to be on the losing side – Florence being notorious for its violent and vengeful behaviour following the settlement of major political disputes. There was a general air of foreboding about the city, as many sensed what might be in store. Some prepared for the day, while others took precautions:

> The leaders of the opposing faction, seeing that many high-spirited young men of quality bearing arms were enemies of the friar, had gathered them together in a band called the *compagnacci*: their leader was Doffo Spini, and they often met and dined together. As they were men of good family and bore arms, they kept everyone in fear of them; so much so that Paolantonio Soderini, who was passionately for the friar, had his son Tommaso enter their company in order to have a stake on their side in case of misfortune.

Others continued to be steadfast, as a matter of principle, for reasons of their own or simply because there was no going back. The universally despised sixty-five-year-old Ficino had for some time now regarded himself amongst the last group. Living the life of a frightened man, he no longer felt safe for more than brief periods at his villa in Careggi. Conversely, whilst in the city he could only stay for limited periods at the houses of the few who were prepared to offer him hospitality and were willing to tolerate his acid-tongued personality for the sake of his former renown. Just a few months previously Ficino had complained in a letter to one of his few remaining friends, the leading Venetian publisher Aldus Manutius, that his prized collection of manuscripts and books – editions of Plato and other ancient philosophers in the original Greek, as well as a wealth of classical literature – was now scattered in houses in various parts of the city 'because of three furies that antagonise the already constantly miserable Florence: the plague, famine and political turmoil – and, what is worse, the other human dissembling of that plague in disguise'. The last comment was a barely concealed reference to Savonarola. When, in the following month, Savonarola had failed to intervene on behalf of the death-sentence of his close lifelong friend Bernardo del Nero, Ficino's bitterness and fury knew no bounds.

Ficino vented his spleen by writing a diatribe against Savonarola, which would be published three months later. The original manuscript was contained on four sides of closely written Latin manuscript and was headed: 'Apology of Marsilio Ficino on behalf of the many Florentine people, who have been deceived by the antichrist Hieronymus of Ferrara, greatest of all hypocrites . . .' Summoning the full extent of his biblical scholarship, which approached that of Savonarola himself, Ficino vilified the prior of San Marco, frequently quoting St Paul:

> For such boasters are false prophets, deceitful workers, disguising themselves as apostles of Christ. And no wonder! Even Satan disguises himself as an angel of light. Thus, it is not strange if his ministers also disguise themselves as ministers of righteousness. Their end will match their deeds.

Meanwhile his former friend Botticelli continued living in the house of his brother Simone, whose increasingly vehement *Piagnoni* views had led him to host regular meetings with his group of friends. It is said that these took place in Botticelli's studio, which would certainly have been the most likely room in the house to be of an appropriate size to accommodate such meetings, which would surely have been attended by the artist himself.

We can imagine this small earnest group gathered about the candlelight, whilst lying against the shadowy walls must have been propped Botticelli's latest unfinished paintings, which according to his biographer Ronald Lightbown expressed 'the profound sense of disturbance, of living in apocalyptic times, in the latter days of the world, that was felt by many Florentines during the later 1490s'.

The Signoria now received an ultimatum from the Vatican: unless Savonarola was taken into custody and despatched to Rome at once, Florence would be placed under an interdict and the collective excommunication that all its citizens feared would come into force. At the same time, the goods belonging to every Florentine merchant living in Rome would be seized and the merchants themselves would be cast into the dungeons of the notorious Castel Sant' Angelo. It looked as if Florence was on the brink of war with Rome, which would inevitably summon the overwhelming forces of the Holy League in its support. But the Signoria's dilemma persisted: if Savonarola was arrested, this would inevitably provoke a civil war within the city.

It was now that Savonarola played his masterstroke. He was well aware that powerful rulers throughout Europe had become outraged by Alexander VI. His personal behaviour, to say nothing of his devious and treacherous political scheming, had brought many to the point where they would be only too pleased to be rid of him. As a result, Savonarola decided to write a circular letter to these rulers, suggesting that they should summon a Council of the Church with the purpose of deposing Alexander VI and replacing him with a more fitting candidate for St Peter's throne. Savonarola chose to address his letter to the Holy Roman Emperor, as well as the kings of Hungary, Spain, England and France. He had particular confidence in Charles VIII, despite his pact with Alexander VI. Savonarola had received intelligence that the French king's grief over the loss of his son had led him to reform his ways. The prodigious sexual feats such as he had displayed during his occupation of Naples were a thing of the past, and he now 'turned his thoughts to living according to God's commandments', leading him also to look with disapproval on the behaviour of Alexander VI. In consequence, Charles VIII himself had already given thought to summoning a Council of the Church, and had even begun discussing this matter with his cardinals.

Savonarola's letter to the European leaders was direct and to the point:

The time to avenge our disgrace is at hand and the Lord commands me to expose new secrets, revealing to all the world the perilous waters into which the ship of St Peter has sailed. Such circumstances are due to your lengthy neglect of these matters. The Church is filled with abominations, from the crown of her head to the soles of her feet, yet not only do you neglect to cure her of her ailments, but instead you pay homage to the very source of the evils which pollute her. Wherefore, the Lord is greatly angered and has for long left the Church without a shepherd . . . I now hereby testify, *in verbo Domini* [in the word of the Lord], that Alexander is no pope, nor can he be regarded as one. Aside from the mortal sin of simony by means of which he purchased the Papal Throne, and daily sells Church benefices to the highest bidder, as well as ignoring all the other vices which he so publicly flaunts – I declare that he is not a Christian, and does not believe in the existence of God, and thus far exceeds the limits of infidelity.

Yet these were merely Savonarola's opening remarks. Only now did he come to the heart of the matter, the true purpose of his letter. As Villari put it: 'Savonarola then proceeded to invite all the princes of Christendom to summon a council as soon as possible, designating a location which is both appropriate and free from outside influence.'

Savonarola added personal messages addressed to each of the rulers. The Holy Roman Emperor, Maximilian I, was informed that his dignity would be at stake if he did not perform the worthy act of rescuing the Church from its present disgrace. And, overlooking his own prophecy of Charles VIII's death, Savonarola addressed to the French king his most personal plea:

You surely cannot have forgotten the sacred role which the Lord has bestowed upon you, which means that should you fail to join this holy enterprise the punishment inflicted upon you will be far in excess of that meted out to the others. Be mindful that God has already given you the first sign of his wrath.* You who bear the title of Most Christian King,† you whom the Lord has chosen and armed with the sword of his vengeance, are you prepared to stand aside and witness the ruin of the Church? Are you willing to ignore the grave dangers that imperil her?

Here was the 'little friar' in his role as the saviour of Christendom. This was an open declaration of war against Alexander VI. There could be no compromise. It could only end in a victory for the papacy of Alexander VI or a victory for the man who wished to lead the Church out of the corrupt and tyrannical rule of its oppressors. It could only be a fight to the death. Now it became clear why Savonarola had chosen Exodus for the theme of his Lenten sermons before he had been silenced. He would be the Moses who led the tribe of Israel out of tyranny to the Promised Land.

An important distinction must be reiterated here. As can be seen from Savonarola's letters, he had no intention of splitting the Church. He wished to reform it from within, with the installation of a truly worthy pope who would put an end to corruption. Savonarola's reformation sought to leave the Church intact.

Florence, the most culturally advanced city in Europe, which had given birth to the Renaissance, was now the focus of a new breakthrough, this time in the religious field: a vision of a progressively egalitarian Church, founded on the ideas of early Christianity. These republican ideas harked back to the similar democratic ideas of the ancient classical world – that touchstone of the Renaissance. Yet they were also accompanied by a regression to the authoritarian fundamentalism of the Old Testament. The paradox inherent in this cannot be overstressed: the democracy Savonarola sought offered a freedom that he could not accept.

---

* A reference to the death of Charles VIII's infant son.
† The title *Rex Christianissimus* (Most Christian King) had been bestowed by the Church upon Clovis, the first King of the Franks, at the turn of the fifth century, and had since become a hereditary title of the kings of France.

20

The Tables Are Turned

WORD QUICKLY REACHED Rome about Savonarola's drastic intention to send a circular letter to the rulers of Europe. This was the most serious threat yet to Alexander VI's papacy, and he knew that it must be stopped at once, no matter the cost. Making use of all his many loyal contacts both within Florence and throughout Italy, Alexander VI would do his best to intercept Savonarola's letters. In Florence the Augustinians and other religious orders, as well as the *Arrabbiati* sympathisers and even the moderate *Tiepidi*, were all utterly opposed to the summoning of a council. Such a revolutionary move would do nothing but throw the Church into disarray, pitting leaders and national interests against each other, possibly even resulting in a split such as the disastrous Great Schism, which had only with great difficulty been healed just over eighty years previously.

Throughout March 1498, *Arrabbiati* spies watched all gates in the city walls from their opening at dawn until their closing at dusk, apprehending any Dominicans who might be messengers carrying copies of Savonarola's letter. Savonarola had been prepared for this and made astute use of several sympathisers amongst the secular population. His close friend, the merchant and former *gonfaloniere* Domenico Mazzinghi, was instructed to write a personal letter to his friend Giovanni Guasconi, the Florentine ambassador at the French court, who would then discreetly pass this on to Charles VIII. In the event, Mazzinghi wrote two such letters, in the hope that at least one of them would reach its destination. Simone del Nero, who had remained loyal to Savonarola despite the recent execution of his brother Bernardo, sent a letter to his brother Niccolò, who was the Florentine ambassador in Spain, with orders to make a discreet approach to the joint rulers, King Ferdinand II of Aragon and Queen Isabella of Castile. At the same time, Giovanni Combi, an ardent champion of the city's new independence, was induced to write to Maximilian I in Germany. Each of these letters was conveyed by courier, sealed and addressed as if it were a personal or commercial communication, yet each also contained Savonarola's circular letter, together with his appended private communication to each individual ruler.

The precise fate of these letters remains something of a mystery. The King of Spain was away in Portugal and never received his copy. The letters to England and Hungary vanished without trace, as it seems did the letter to Germany. Mazzinghi's precautions proved fully justified, as only one of his letters was received by Charles VIII. Disastrously, the courier carrying the other letter to France was waylaid and robbed by a group of brigands as he crossed Milanese territory. The brigands realised the value of the letter in their possession and sold it to Ludovico 'il Moro', Duke of Milan, who in turn passed it on to the pope. Alexander VI now had in his possession concrete evidence of Savonarola's treachery to the papacy.

Yet ironically the chief threat to Savonarola at this point would arise from an incident that took place within Florentine territory. The incident itself had obscure beginnings, being instigated by one of Savonarola's most bitter enemies, Francesco da Puglia, a monk from the opposing Franciscan order whose Florentine headquarters was Santa Croce, in the east of the city. A year or so previously, during early 1497, Francesco da Puglia had delivered a sermon at Prato, some ten miles north of Florence, during which he forcibly expressed his objections to Savonarola and all that he stood for – challenging anyone who believed in his doctrines, and accepted the invalidity of his excommunication by Alexander VI, to undertake with him an ordeal by fire. This ancient medieval practice involved the contestants walking through fire, sometimes barefoot over a lengthy bed of red-hot coals, at others times passing along a passageway through a large bonfire. The winner was the contestant who managed to complete the ordeal unharmed – this being taken as a sign from God that his cause was the true one. All the evidence indicates that Fra Francesco was in fact being rhetorical here, indicating the strength of his abhorrence for Savonarola; he did not seriously expect anyone to accept his challenge to such an outmoded ritual.

Yet it so happened that on this very day Savonarola's closest and most loyal supporter, Domenico da Pescia, had also been in Prato, and his ingenuous enthusiasm had led him to take up Fra Francesco's challenge. When the Franciscans in Florence got wind of what had happened, Fra Francesco was at once ordered to return to Santa Croce and the matter was quietly forgotten.

However, during the 1498 Lenten sermons that Savonarola was having delivered for him by Domenico da Pescia, he again emphasised that God spoke through him. On this occasion he was particularly insistent. His claims culminated in the exhortation:

> I entreat each one of you to pray earnestly to God that if my doctrine does not come from Him, He will send down a fire upon me, which shall consume my soul in Hell.

Although it was not intended as such, this was seen by Fra Francesco as a direct provocation, and during the sermon that he preached on 25 March at Santa Croce he returned to the theme of ordeal by fire, this time directly challenging Savonarola himself, on account of the claim he had made to his congregation.

Savonarola simply ignored this challenge. At the time he was not only composing the written texts of the forthcoming Lenten sermons that he was to have delivered for him, but was also preoccupied with making arrangements for his all-important circular letter to be delivered to the rulers of Europe, as well as formulating his additional personal messages to each of these rulers. Besides, he had long considered medieval practices such as ordeal by fire to belong to the superstitions of the past. On the other hand, he did not dismiss such medieval practices as self-flagellation and extreme fasting, as well as other self-imposed ordeals and penances – these he accepted as bringing the soul of man closer to God and an understanding of the truth. Even the gift of prophecy, his visions, his dreams, and his conviction that he spoke with God, he accepted: these he felt to

be part of his actual experience.* Other medieval practices, such as ordeal
by one of the elements,† divination, hermetic practices, alchemy and
astrology, he dismissed with contempt. He could also muster strong biblical
and intellectual arguments against belief in such practices, as he had shown
in his debates with his friend Pico della Mirandola, in which he had eventually triumphed over his brilliant adversary's every objection. Ordeal by
fire fell into the category of superstition, and thus a challenge such as that
issued by Fra Francesco was not worthy of consideration.

Yet Savonarola had not reckoned on the naïve, unthinking fervour of
his disciple Domenico da Pescia. Savonarola had delegated Fra Domenico
as one of the loyal Dominicans to deliver sermons on his behalf, and as
a consequence Fra Domenico not only saw himself as the public face of
Savonarola, but also chose to see himself as the object of Fra Francesco's
challenge. As before, he was not willing to shirk what he saw as his responsibility. On 28 March Landucci recorded:

'Fra Domenico preached in *San Marco*, saying that he was willing to
pass through fire ... On the same day Fra Francesco preached at
Santa Croce declaring that he too was willing to pass through fire,
declaring, 'I believe that I shall burn, but I am willing to do so for
the sake of liberating the people of this city. If *he* does not burn,
then you may believe that he is a prophet'.

This makes it clear that there was little doubt about Fra Francesco's
expectations concerning the ordeal: he was now willing to die, in order to
rid Florence of Savonarola. But as soon as he heard that Savonarola was
not going to take part, and that instead Fra Domenico would take
Savonarola's place, he insisted that 'his quarrel was with Savonarola alone,
and although he himself expected to be consumed by the flames he was
quite ready to enter the fire in order to ensure the destruction of that

* There would appear to be no hypocrisy or misuse of reason in Savonarola's argument here.
Even modern psychology does not deny that such experiences may indeed seem all too real to
those who undergo them.
† As well as ordeal by fire, during the medieval era there had been in various parts of Europe
ordeals by the other three elements: ordeal by water (which could result in drowning), earth
(that is, burial) and air (being cast from a high tower or cliff).

disseminator of scandal and false doctrine. On the other hand, he would have nothing to do with Fra Domenico.'

This should have been the end of the matter. Savonarola had already admonished Fra Domenico in the strongest possible terms, and Fra Francesco was only too relieved to be freed from his obligation to undergo what he had come to believe would be certain death. But by now other parties had become involved, and were determined that the matter should go ahead. If such a trial was to take place, it would first require the permission of the Signoria, which meant that this was no longer just a matter for the appropriate Church authorities, but was a political matter. By now Gonfaloniere Popoleschi had browbeaten his Signoria into a more reliably pro-*Arrabbiati* stance, and as such they were all in favour of proceeding with the ordeal. The *Arrabbiati*, who may well have been behind the entire challenge in the first place, now became the driving force: pressure was exerted upon the Franciscans to persuade Fra Francesco to insist upon Savonarola personally accepting his challenge. Rumours were spread that if Savonarola refused the challenge, he would be revealed as a charlatan and a heretic, unwilling to put his doctrine to God's test. These rumours were said to emanate from Fra Francesco, whilst at the same time the *Arrabbiati* disingenuously assured him that he would never have to enter the fire, as no ordeal would be permitted to take place.

Yet the more extreme members of the pro-*Arrabbiati* faction would tolerate no such thing. When the hot-headed, gilded youth of the *Compagnacci* gathered at their regular banquet, they decided:

If Savonarola enters the fire, he will certainly be burned; if he does not enter the fire, he will lose all credit with his followers. We will then be able to raise a riot, during which we will be able to seize him in person.

There can be no doubt that some amongst them were intent upon murdering Savonarola. It was now that Fra Domenico's enthusiasm once again got the better of him, and he played into their hands. The day after this banquet, ignoring Savonarola's instructions and without his consent, Fra Domenico published a document entitled *Conclusiones*:

The Church of God needs to be reformed, it must be scourged and renovated. Likewise Florence too must be scourged before it can be renovated and return to prosperity. The infidels must be converted to Christianity. All these things will come to pass in our time. The excommunication issued against the reverend father our brother Hieronymo is invalid. Those who choose to ignore this excommunication are not sinners.

In fact, these *Conclusiones* said no more than Savonarola had been preaching in his sermons for some time now. However, this was precisely the opportunity for which the *Compagnacci* and the *Arrabbiati* had been waiting. Here, in writing, was confirmation of Savonarola's defiance of the Church; here was the acceptance of Fra Francesco's challenge. On 28 March the Signoria insisted upon their notary examining the document, and then summoned Fra Domenico to the Palazzo della Signoria, requiring him to authenticate it with his signature. Soon after this Fra Francesco was persuaded to acknowledge this challenge with his signature, which he eventually did with extreme reluctance. To complicate matters, another of Savonarola's acolytes, called Fra Mariano Ughi, now also put himself forward, saying that he was willing to accompany his fellow Dominican, Fra Domenico, into the fire if the Franciscans were also willing to produce a second candidate.

Versions of what was happening at the Palazzo della Signoria swept through the city, with rumour followed by counter-rumour. Things appeared to be getting out of hand, and a general atmosphere of hysteria was beginning to spread through the streets. Barbaric and superstitious medieval practices like ordeal by fire had long since lapsed in such a cultured and sophisticated city as Florence. Indeed, it was well over a hundred years since such a thing had taken place here. Many were horrified, while others amongst the population were only too keen to witness such a gruesome spectacle: few talked of anything else. Meanwhile Savonarola remained alone in his cell at San Marco, praying for God's guidance. At this stage he appears to have concluded that he was being politically outmanoeuvred, and that there was nothing he could do about this.

On Friday 30 March a Pratica council was held at the Palazzo della Signoria to decide upon the matter, and whether such a thing should be permitted to take place within a civilised city. As usual the meeting was attended by 200 or so of the ruling citizens, who would debate the matter before it was finally voted upon by the Signoria. This would be a repeat of the recent debate over the appeal against the death-sentence for the five 'traitors', though all present were aware that the outcome of this Pratica was liable to be of even graver importance for the republic. No sooner had the meeting begun than Savonarola's supporter, former *gonfaloniere* Domenico Mazzinghi, unexpectedly declared that he was in favour of the trial taking place, 'for this will surely result in such a miracle that it will reflect upon the glory of God, as well as bringing peace to our city'. The moderate Girolamo Rucellai took a more commonsensical approach, though ultimately he too came to the same conclusion:

All this uproar about a trial by fire is so much nonsense. The most important thing we should be discussing here is how we can get rid of the friars and the non-friars, the Arrabbiati and the non-Arrabbiati, so that we can bring peace to our people. As far as I am concerned, if this trial restores harmony amongst our citizens, then let it go ahead ... We should be worried about the city, not about a few friars getting burned.

At this point, the worldly Filippo Guigni tried to defuse the increasingly fraught situation with an attempt at levity, remarking:

To me, this idea of passing through fire seems all very odd, and I for one am against it. Why don't we instead use a trial by water? This would be much less dangerous. If Fra Girolamo could pass through water without getting wet, then I would certainly join in asking for his pardon.

But by now passions had run too high to appreciate such attempts at wit. At one point, Giovanni Canacci, one of Savonarola's most bitter enemies, became so enraged that he leapt to his feet to interrupt the proceedings;

yet it was this very anger that caused him to make practically the only contribution which reflected well upon those present:

> When I hear you all saying such things, I wonder whether I would be better off dead than alive. If our forefathers who founded this city could but hear that we were even discussing such a matter, making ourselves such a disgrace that we will become the laughing stock of the world, they would have refused to have anything whatsoever to do with us. Our glorious city has sunk to its lowest ebb for many a long year, and all about us there is nothing but confusion.

Yet in the end even Canacci could see no other way out of their predicament: 'I implore your Excellencies [the Signoria] to deliver our people from this wretchedness no matter the cost, either by fire, air, water or any other method you want.'

So low had the city of Lorenzo the Magnificent now sunk — in its own eyes, as well as the eyes of all Italy. The city that had given birth to the Renaissance had fallen into division and disgrace, its commerce all but stagnant and its 'vanities' consigned to the flames, its embittered people faced with the prospect of anarchy, its weak rulers reduced to abject collusion. Barely any of those present at the Pratica, even amongst Savonarola's most enthusiastic secular supporters, believed that the ordeal by fire would result in a miracle. Anyone who took part in it would undoubtedly be burned. Yet the decision of the Signoria, overwhelmingly backed by the Pratica, was that the ordeal should go ahead, with the two Franciscans taking part against the two Dominicans. The Pratica also solemnly decided what action should be taken when the result of the ordeal was known. If one of the Dominicans was burned to death, then Savonarola would be exiled. If one of the Franciscans was burned to death, then Fra Francesco would be exiled. (By now one of his fellow Franciscans had offered to take his place in the ordeal, as by this stage he had become too terrified to do so.) Furthermore, the Pratica decided, if either side refused to submit to the ordeal, then their leader would automatically be exiled. However, if both sides suffered deaths, then the Dominicans would be declared the losers (in which case Savonarola would be exiled). The reasoning of the

Pratica was as transparent as it was unjust: they were determined to get rid of Savonarola.

Yet this could not be the final dispensation. Although the ordeal itself fell under the jurisdiction of the Signoria of Florence, those taking part in it were members of the Church, which meant that it would also require the permission of Alexander VI. The Signoria sent a despatch to the Florentine ambassador in Rome; but when Bonsi was granted an audience with Alexander VI, His Holiness informed the ambassador that he could not possibly give his official consent to such an ordeal. On the other hand, it soon became clear that the pope was going to issue no Brief condemning it. However, a covert message now reached the Signoria, probably by way of Fra Mariano da Genazzano in Rome to the Augustinians in Florence, that Alexander VI was in fact in favour of the ordeal taking place. This would be the end of Savonarola, and as soon as he was exiled from Florence, Alexander VI would have him arrested and brought to Rome.

Ironically, Savonarola himself reacted to the prospect of the ordeal with a remarkably similar ambiguity. Initially, he had abhorred the entire idea of an ordeal by fire. But as he fasted alone in his cell at San Marco the secret belief had grown within him that this event might indeed produce the miracle that would justify him and all his actions. This would be akin to the fulfilment of his prophecies, just as when Charles VIII had arrived as the 'scourge of God'. Several contemporary sources confirm this change of heart in Savonarola, alluding to a series of events that brought it about.

One of Savonarola's closest followers amongst the monks at San Marco was Fra Silvestro Maruffi, a man of deep spirituality who was prone to ill-health, hypochondria and insomnia, a condition that rendered him susceptible to having visions similar to those of his prior. Savonarola had formed the most profound respect for Fra Silvestro, to the point where he now placed as much faith in the other monk's visions as he did in his own. At this time, Fra Silvestro described to Savonarola a vision he had experienced in which the guardian angels of both Fra Domenico and Savonarola himself had promised him that Fra Domenico would pass through the flames unscathed. This, combined with Fra Domenico's unwavering faith and enthusiasm for taking part in the ordeal, had finally convinced Savonarola that he should give it his blessing. Savonarola then sent word to the Signoria confirming that he did so, saying that it should take place a week later, on Friday 6 April. Several contemporary sources corroborate this, as well as what happened next, differing only in detail. Guicciardini gives the general picture:

> The day having been decided, Fra Girolamo was given permission by the Signoria to preach; and preaching in San Marco he showed the great importance of miracles and said that they should not be used except in necessity when reason and experience proved inadequate. Because the Christian faith had been proved in infinite ways and the truth of the things predicted by him had been shown with such efficacy and reason that anyone who was not obstinate in evil living could understand them, he had not made great use of his ability to perform miracles so as not to tempt God. Nevertheless, because they had now been challenged, they willingly accepted this challenge, and all could be sure that on entering the fire the result would be that their friar would emerge alive and unharmed while the other would be burned. If the opposite took place, they might boldly state that all he had preached was false. He went on to say that not only his friars but anyone who entered the fire in defence of this truth would emerge in a similar fashion. And then he asked them whether, if necessary, in the cause of so great a work ordained by God, they too would be willing to go through the fire. With a great shout almost all present answered that they would: this was the most amazing thing, for without any doubt, if Fra Girolamo had told them to, very many would indeed have entered the fire.

This sermon was delivered before a packed congregation consisting of friars and nuns, as well as lay *Piagnoni*, women and children. Savonarola's preaching must have inspired a collective hysteria that went far beyond those who had taken holy orders.

The ordeal was to be held in the Piazza della Signoria so that the miracle, or the sight of the victims burning alive, could be witnessed by as many of the population as possible. In the midst of the piazza a raised walkway consisting of brick and rubble covered with earth was constructed.

This was seven feet high, ninety feet long and sixteen feet wide.* On either side of the walkway were heaped two lines of logs, covered with brushwood and boughs, and 'all the wood was soaked with oil, spirit and resin to make it burn better'. For the ordeal, these two incendiary lines were to be set alight along their entire length until they blazed like an inferno. Between the two lines was a pathway just five feet in width, and the contestants in the ordeal were each to start simultaneously at opposite ends of this ninety-foot-long path, walking through the inferno until they emerged at the other end unscathed, or were consumed by the flames.

News of this coming event was by now spreading to all the major cities of Italy and even beyond the Alps. The courts, the monasteries and the merchant classes all had their own information networks by way of ambassadors, travelling friars, commerce routes, couriers and so forth. Such had been the interest generated by Savonarola and his previous activities, especially his sermons and his prophecies, that news of this latest development quickly filtered down to the public at large. The coming ordeal by fire was a topic of speculation, from the taverns and market places to the palazzi and the priories. Was Savonarola really capable of performing a miracle? This time there could be no question of fakery or mass delusion, or even prophetic coincidence: this ordeal would take place for all to see.

It could hardly be claimed that this would represent a turning point in the evolution of human consciousness, yet there can be no doubt that the result of such a sensational event, which had so taken hold of the public imagination, might be seen as a contributory factor to the lengthy process of transformation that was taking place during this era, which we now refer to as the Renaissance. Concrete physical confirmation, or a single practical disproof, of the belief in miracles would at this point doubtless spread ripples of speculation far and wide amongst those of an enquiring disposition. Here, at the earliest dawning of the new scientific understanding, the truth was to be judged by an experiment whose result was verifiable. ('The ordeal by fire' was called in Italian L'esperimento del fuoco. A

---

* The details of this construction can be found in Landucci, *Diario*, p.135, where he gives the proportions in the contemporary measurements of *braccia*. *Braccio* means 'arm', and this was effectively a length of just under two feet. Thus Landucci gives the height of the walkway as four *braccia*, its length as fifty.

century later, Galileo and his contemporaries, the true pioneers of scientific experimental method, would start using the word *esperimento* to describe the tests, or ordeals, to which they subjected their practical ideas.)

During the days leading up to the ordeal, Savonarola himself wrote and published a short document entitled *Riposta*, in which he attempted to justify himself and his attitude towards the coming event. This ends:

> Those who know themselves to be genuinely inspired by the Lord will certainly come through the flames unharmed, if the ordeal actually takes place, which is by no means certain. As for me, I am keeping myself for a greater cause, for which I shall always be prepared to lay down my life. The time is at hand when the Lord will manifest himself in supernatural signs and omens, but these will not come about as a result of the beseeching or the will of men. For the time being, let it be sufficient that, by sending some of our brethren, we will be equally exposed to the wrath of the people if the Lord does not allow them to pass unscathed through the fire.

During the final days leading up to the ordeal, Savonarola ordered the gates of the monastery of San Marco to be locked: no one was permitted to enter or leave. Sealed off from the outside world, the community of friars embarked upon a vigil of continuous prayer on behalf of their two brethren who were about to take part in the ordeal.

Then, on Thursday 5 April, the very eve of the ordeal, the Signoria suddenly announced that it would be postponed for a day. The Signoria evidently had reason to believe that a message from Alexander VI forbidding the ordeal was on its way from Rome. Yet within twenty-four hours the Signoria mysteriously appear to have convinced themselves that no message forbidding the ordeal would be forthcoming, and decreed that it should go ahead the next day, Saturday 7 April. At the same time they issued an unpexpected new decree, modifying their previous one, and specifically stating: 'In the event that Fra Domenico is burned, Fra Girolamo is to leave Florentine territory within three hours.'

The combination of the Signoria's certainty that no papal Brief would arrive, and the issuing of the new decree immediately banning Savonarola from Florentine territory (under the circumstances, the border would almost certainly have taken longer than three hours to reach) further indicates that the Signoria must have received covert instructions, perhaps by way of Genazzano and the Augustinians, from Alexander VI. The specific details of Savonarola's speedy banishment would have meant that in just three hours from the moment the result became clear at the event itself, at which he was certainly expected to be present amidst the packed Piazza della Signoria, he would have had to flee through the angry throng (in some danger of his life even then) and make his way to a fast horse that had been kept waiting in preparation. Not only did Savonarola abhor this privileged form of transport, but it would have been unthinkable to him to make prior arrangements for what he would have seen as a cowardly flight in the event of his loyal friend's excruciating death. Even so, he would certainly have been apprehended after three hours, by which time he would no longer have been deemed under Florentine protection, even if he was still travelling through Florentine territory. This would have meant that he could have been intercepted and arrested on behalf of the pope within hours of leaving the city gates, by whichever band of armed *Arrabbiati* or *Compagnacci* was lying in wait for him, having already been commandeered for this very task. In a matter of days he would have been delivered to Rome, into the hands of Alexander VI. Here the 'little friar' who had had the temerity to send letters to the rulers of Europe, encouraging them to call a Council of the Church intended to depose the pope, could have expected little mercy from a man such as Alexander VI.

21

Ordeal by Fire

B Y DAWN ON 7 April 1498 people were already filing into the Piazza della Signoria. Only three entrances were left open, and these were heavily guarded by armed men. No spectator was permitted to carry arms, and on specific orders of the Signoria no women or children were permitted to enter the square, on the grounds that their expressions of emotion might stir the crowd beyond control. By ten o'clock in the morning the piazza was crammed with spectators, a large portion of whom were *Piagnoni* and their supporters; but it was equally evident that other large sections of the crowd were openly anti-Savonarolan. Anticipating this tense situation, the Signoria had commandeered a thousand men to take up various strategic positions throughout the piazza, with the aim of maintaining order and quickly thwarting any disturbances that might occur. These armed men too consisted of representatives of both sides of the divided population, making no effort to hide their sympathies. With a show of characteristic arrogance, Doffo Spini, the head of the *Compagnacci*, led in a group of several hundred of his supporters, all resplendent in full armour. Warned by the Dominicans that the *Compagnacci* might well make a move to seize Savonarola, the *Piagnoni* sympathiser Marcuccio Salviati had raised a corps of 300 armed men who also reported for guard duty in the piazza that day. All troops present were nominally under the command of Giovanni della Vecchia, the Signoria's Captain of the Square, who in addition commanded 500 armed men of his own. Most of the men of this detachment were ordered to guard the Palazzo della Signoria, containing Gonfaloniere Popoleschi and his Signoria, in case any attempt was made to storm the building by *Piagnoni*, who were now under no illusions concerning the Signoria's anti-Savonarolan sympathies.

By noon all three public entrances to the piazza had been sealed to prevent any further spectators cramming into the already overcrowded space. Despite the colourful appearance of the multitude and the soldiery beneath the April sky, the atmosphere was far from festive, with tension mounting as the time passed. The contesting parties had been ordered to present themselves in the piazza at 1 p.m., and at the appointed hour 200 Franciscans duly arrived. Dressed in their plain brown robes tied with knotted white ropes, they filed silently between the cleared crowds across the piazza, their heads bowed. Without any outward display or show of emotion, they took up their allotted position in the open Loggia dei Signori, beside the Palazzo della Signoria, which had been divided in two by a wooden barrier to separate the opposing parties. The Franciscan side of the barrier, on the eastern side closest to the Palazzo, was protected by breastplated *Compagnacci*, whilst Salviati had deputed a squad of his pro-Savonarolan troops to guard the western side. Before the Loggia, stretching from the edge of the raised pavement in front of the Palazzo della Signoria towards the western side of the piazza, stood the long raised-earth walkway ready for the ordeal, its sides piled with incendiary-soaked logs and brushwood.

Around noon Savonarola had celebrated High Mass at San Marco, before delivering a brief sermon to a large audience of fellow friars and supporters. Curiously, even at this late stage, he told them: 'I cannot be sure whether the ordeal will take place, because this does not depend upon us.' Yet he went on to assure his audience, 'if it does take place, victory will certainly be ours'.

Savonarola and his Dominican delegation then set out from San Marco, reaching the Piazza della Signoria half an hour after the arrival of the Franciscans. Landucci watched their entrance:

And then came the Dominicans, with the greatest show of devotion. There was a great number of *Frati*, about 250, walking in pairs, followed by Fra Domenico bearing a crucifix, and then Fra Girolamo holding aloft the Host; whilst behind them was a great multitude with torches and candles, devoutly singing hymns. After they had taken their place in the Loggia and prepared an altar, they sang a mass; and the people awaited the great spectacle.

Yet the expectant crowds were in for a disappointment if they expected the ordeal to get under way at once. It soon became clear that the Franciscans were determined to raise certain procedural objections. According to the eyewitness Parenti, Fra Domenico had taken it upon himself to don for the occasion a full-length cloak 'of fiery red velvet'. It was evident to many present that he was playing up to the full his central role in this potentially miraculous occasion, although the ironic symbolism of his flame-coloured attire seems to have escaped him. As Martines has observed, it was as if he was 'engaged in an extraordinary and contradictory pantomime of the martyrdom that he believed would not overtake him'. Chief amongst the Franciscan objections were these very robes that Fra Domenico had decided to wear ('The Franciscans were afraid they might be bewitched') in order to protect him from the flames. When his red cloak was removed, the Franciscans further protested that the Dominican robes he was wearing underneath the cloak might also be 'bewitched', and Fra Domenico was taken into the Palazzo della Signoria, where these too were removed and he was stripped naked. According to word that later circulated amongst the *Piagnoni*, the Franciscans even insisted upon scrutinising his genitals for any untoward supernatural signs.

Fra Domenico was made to don the robes of another Dominican friar before he returned to the Loggia. Even then, the Franciscans insisted that Savonarola or one of his fellow Dominicans might attempt to bewitch him before the ordeal, so he was made to wait amongst the Franciscans, where he stood clutching the crucifix that he firmly believed would protect him from the flames.

Next the Franciscans insisted that Fra Domenico should not be permitted to enter the flames carrying his crucifix, in case this too was somehow 'enchanted'. Savonarola proved willing to concede this point, on Fra Domenico's behalf, and suggested that instead he should enter the flames bearing a piece of the consecrated Host* that Savonarola himself had borne into the piazza. Once again there was an objection, and representatives of

---

* Holy Mass during this period usually involved the taking of a piece of bread torn from an unleavened loaf, known as the Host, as well as a sip of wine, after they had both been consecrated by the priest, a ritual that transformed them into the body and blood of Jesus Christ. This was no mere symbolic act, and the Host was regarded as the actual body of Christ.

the Dominicans and the Franciscans were invited into the Palazzo della Signoria for a theological discussion of this matter, while Fra Domenico and Savonarola waited outside. The Franciscans were determined not to let the Host enter the flames, on the grounds that this 'was most wicked' and 'against the Church', whilst the Dominicans insisted that even if the appearance of Christ's body (the bread) was consumed by the flames, its essence (Christ's body itself) could not possibly be affected.

Outside, the mood of the vast confined crowd was beginning to change. All had come expecting a spectacle – some in the belief that they would witness a miracle, no less; others stirred by anticipation of the gruesome sight of people being burned to death. In expectation of such a wonder, one way or the other, both factions had been willing to remain patient for a considerable time, but by now their patience was beginning to wear thin, as the disputations went on and on behind the closed doors of the palazzo. Savonarola, becoming increasingly worried about this developing state of affairs, sent an urgent message into the palazzo, insisting that both sides settle their differences as soon as possible so that the ordeal could go ahead. The reply from the palazzo made it clear to Savonarola that if this was his attitude, the Dominicans were quite free to proceed with the ordeal on their own. Savonarola naturally turned down this request. Villari, summarising the many detailed eyewitness reports, described what happened next:

> The patience of the multitude was now running out. All of these people had been assembled in the piazza for many hours: most had been without food or water since dawn, and were becoming impatient at the boredom and futility of waiting in vain for something to happen. Grumbling murmurs were beginning to arise from all parts of the crowd, interspersed with the occasional seditious cry. The *Arrabbiati*, who had been eagerly awaiting just such an opportunity, tried to turn it to their advantage. A lackey employed by Giovanni Manetti was encouraged to incite a disturbance, and all of a sudden the piazza was in a tumult. Many of the exits from the piazza were closed, so that the people found themselves hemmed in and confined on all sides. Consequently they began to rush forward towards the

palazzo. This had evidently been the moment when the *Arrabbiati* had planned to grab Savonarola and put an end to him with their bare hands. Indeed, they attempted to do just this, but Salviati lined up his men in front of the Loggia, and then drew a line on the ground with his sword, exclaiming: 'Whoever steps over this line will find himself run through by the sword of Marcuccio Salviati!' And such was the determined manner in which he said these words that no one dared step forward.

Meanwhile the troop of soldiers employed by the Signoria to guard the palazzo, seeing the crowd surging forward, advanced into their path and began forcefully driving them back. 'By now the Signoria was completely at a loss as to what to do.' Fortunately the situation was transformed by the outbreak of a sudden violent storm, with thunder, lightning and a deluge of rain. This might have put an end to the entire proceedings, but the crowd was by now so determined that they refused to budge, continuing to stand there despite the continuing downpour. Even so, some could not help seeing this as an omen of God's displeasure at the ordeal taking place. Then the storm ceased as suddenly as it had begun. The city mace-bearers, the official heralds of the Signoria, emerged from the palazzo to announce that the ordeal had been cancelled. This was greeted with consternation amongst the crowd.

By now it was becoming dark, and the *Arrabbiati* did their best once again to take advantage of the situation. Rumours were spread that the ordeal had been cancelled because Savonarola had not permitted Fra Domenico to take part in it. There was some truth in this, as Savonarola had refused the Dominican pair permission to undertake the ordeal on their own, and the crowd had witnessed this refusal. Those at the front who had been able to hear and understand what was going on had quickly relayed the information to those behind them. Even the *Piagnoni* were now becoming persuaded that Savonarola ought to have taken up the challenge himself. Here had been his chance to reveal his miraculous powers before all who believed in him, and at the last moment he had been revealed as a charlatan. The mood of the crowd began to change. The Franciscans soon departed the square, and some time afterwards the Dominicans were hustled out through the angry crowd under cover of darkness, making their way quickly back to San Marco.

With hindsight, it is possible to see that Savonarola was tricked into this ordeal. Indeed, judging from his words, it seems that he himself may well have had increasing misgivings about the entire affair for some days beforehand. The aim of the Signoria, in league with the *Arrabbiati* and the *Compagnacci*, had been to turn the crowd against Savonarola, and in this they certainly succeeded. Savonarola was now seen as the one who had deprived the people of Florence of their spectacle: he was a charlatan and a cheat, who was incapable of miracles and had never intended his friars to be put to the test. The remaining crowd in the piazza began giving vent to their anger, before they were eventually dispersed and sent home into the night by the attendant armed troops.

This was in many ways the significant event, the pivotal moment. Prior to the planned ordeal the city had been divided. As a result of this fiasco, even the *Piagnoni* turned against Savonarola – in significant numbers, if not totally. From now on the *Arrabbiati* had the upper hand and were determined to exploit this.

22

The Siege of San Marco

NEXT DAY, 8 April 1498, was Palm Sunday. At first the streets were ominously quiet. In the afternoon, as people left their houses, it soon became clear that the entire atmosphere of the city had been transformed. It began with minor incidents. As citizens of the better classes decked in their Sunday finery strolling through the Old Market encountered passing pro-Savonarola adherents (identifiable by their plain dress) and other evident *Piagnoni*, they began reacting aggressively towards them, calling them names, spitting at them, later even jostling them and pulling at their clothes. In the main streets and squares makeshift posters began appearing on the walls denouncing leading citizens who were known supporters of Savonarola, such as Mazzinghi, Valori and Soderini. Groups of bully-boy *Compagnacci* chased after any *Piagnoni* they encountered, beating up those they managed to catch.

Later Savonarola's close disciple Fra Mariano Ughi was due to deliver the Palm Sunday sermon in Florence Cathedral, and well before Evensong the benches had begun to fill. Those who remained loyal to Savonarola saw this as an opportunity to rally together and show their continuing support. At the appointed hour Fra Mariano left San Marco and proceeded down the Via del Cocomero, surrounded by the usual company of monastic followers-cum-protectors, who now habitually accompanied any friar from San Marco on his way to deliver a sermon outside the safe confines of his own monastery church. Yet no sooner had Fra Mariano and his group emerged than they were greeted by a hail of stones hurled by street urchins who had been hired by the *Compagnacci*.

By the time Fra Mariano had managed to make his way to the cathedral, 'the benches were already full'. Yet not all of those present were supporters of Savonarola: amongst them were groups of *Compagnacci* hell-bent on disruption, who:

> began to strike the backs of the seats where the women were sitting, using coarse language and saying: *Adante con Dio, piagnonacci* (Get out of here, you snivelling psalm-singers). As a result, many amongst the congregation rose to their feet, and there began a great tumult in the church, with anyone who could make it to a door being lucky. When some of the other men protested, the *Compagnacci* tried to cuff them contemptuously and begin a dispute. Some even used their weapons against several of the partisans of the *Frate* as they were fleeing towards the Via del Cocomero. A number of these were struck and wounded, so that in a few hours the whole city was up in arms.

Chaotic scenes developed outside the cathedral, with the *Compagnacci* encouraging their supporters with cries of 'Let's get the Friar! On to San Marco! On to San Marco!'

Meanwhile other supporters of Savonarola had gone to San Marco to attend Vespers, but Landucci described how the piazza in front of the church was soon filled with a ranting anti-Savonarola mob:

> making it impossible for many men and women who were in San Marco to come out. I chanced to be there; and if I had not managed to get out through the cloister, and go away towards the *Porta di San Gallo*, I might have been killed. Everyone was arming himself, in fact; and a proclamation from the *Palagio* [Palazzo della Signoria] offered 1000 ducats to anyone who should capture Fra Girolamo and deliver him up to the authorities. All Florence was in commotion . . .

The friars had quickly locked and bolted the front doors of the church. They then ensured that the terrified women caught up in the church, together with others amongst the congregation who had no stomach for violence, managed to follow the prudent Landucci and make their escape by the back way out of the monastery.

[323]

Many of the friars began making preparations to defend San Marco, which seemed to be under imminent threat of attack by the baying mob, which continued to swell outside, and had been so incited by the *Compagnacci* that by this stage they were evidently beyond control. Together with the friars gathered inside the monastery were some thirty of so *Piagnoni* and leading secular Savonarola supporters. Amongst them was Francesco Valori, who had initially counselled the friars against any violence, telling them that in keeping with their monastic vows it was better they should leave the city, returning to take over San Marco when the Signoria had restored order and things were back to normal. But the friars had refused to contemplate deserting their home and made it clear that they were determined to defend the house of God. In fact, a few of the friars had for some time now been making preparations for just such an eventuality. An old unoccupied cell beneath the cloister had been converted into a secret armoury by two junior friars named Fra Silvestro and (ironically) Fra Francesco de' Medici, and here they had already assembled a formidable array of weapons. These included:

Twelve breastplates and a similar number of helmets; eighteen halberds, five or six crossbows, various shields, four or five arquebuses, a barrel of gunpowder and a crate of leaden bullets, as well as a couple of small primitive mortars.*

These weapons had been smuggled into the monastery by the leading *Piagnoni* Francesco Davanzati and his henchman Baldo Inghirami, who now took it upon themselves to draw up plans for the defence of the monastery, handing out arms, posting guards at strategic points along the walls and lookouts at high windows. Sixteen of the friars had volunteered their willingness to take up arms under the command of Inghirami, who was to direct the defence of the monastery. Once the strong doors separating the church

---

* A halberd was a pike-like weapon with a long wooden shaft tipped by a metal capping consisting of a spike, an axe-blade and a sharpened point. An arquebus was the earliest form of rifle: a long-barrelled musket operated by a matchlock, generally using gunpowder and firing round lead bullets. It came into use earlier in the century, was effective only at short range and liable to explode, making it often more dangerous to the user than the target. The early mortars were a form of short-barrelled wide-bore cannon, which used gunpowder to fire into the air cannonballs or stones and were equally dangerous for all concerned.

from the inner monastery had been locked, the high walls with narrow windows that encompassed the monastery itself gave it a formidable defence.

Amazingly, all these preparations had been made without the knowledge of Savonarola, who would certainly have forbidden such activity. Indeed, he remained until a late stage largely ignorant of what was taking place within his own monastery – though he quickly became aware of what was happening outside, as the yelling mob surrounded San Marco and began throwing stones, together with other missiles and refuse, over the walls. And as prior it must have been his order to begin sounding the great San Marco bell, known as *La Piagnona* (in part because of its wailing toll, as well as the more obvious reason that it summoned the *Piagnoni* to church services). On this occasion, the tolling of the bell was intended to sound the alarm, signalling for the civil militia to be sent to restore order. But the Signoria appeared to be in no mood to allow such necessary action to be taken, and instead sent their official mace-bearing heralds to proclaim outside San Marco that all within were to lay down their arms. At the same time, Savonarola was ordered into exile, the proclamation specifically stating that he had to be beyond the borders of Florentine territory within twelve hours. This latter, more realistic, stipulation was presumably intended to reinforce the authenticity of the Signoria's order, as well as its feasibility, in the hope that Savonarola might take this opportunity to escape with his life. However, the proclamation had precisely the opposite effect. The friars inside San Marco who heard it refused to believe that it was anything other than a trick by the *Compagnacci* to get them to open the doors, so that their armed men could burst in and attack them.

When it became evident that the proclamation had produced no effect, the Signoria began to argue amongst themselves over what action they should take in order to maintain their authority, with some suggesting that an order be issued for the removal of all arms from the immediate region of San Marco, simply to avoid bloodshed. During the discussion of this, and alternative measures, tempers flared to such an extent that at one stage two of the Signoria made to draw their arms as they confronted one another. But the anti-Savonarolan majority soon prevailed over the voices of the moderates, who were mainly concerned to avoid a riot, as civil division was now spreading throughout the city. With similar intention, the pro-Savonarolan Domenico Mazzinghi, who held a senior post in the administration, expressly went to the Palazzo della Signoria and reminded the members of the ruling body, and others gathered in the palace, of their sovereign duty to maintain order. But according to one of those present, he was 'rebuffed with every villainy in the world, and had it not been for several noblemen, I think he would have been killed'.

Meanwhile in San Marco, Savonarola was determined to prevent any serious violence. Donning his official sacred vestments and taking up a crucifix, he declared that he intended to leave San Marco and surrender himself in the piazza outside, justifying his actions: 'Let me go forth, since this storm has only arisen because of me.' But the friars and their secular supporters who were with him refused to let him do this, begging: 'Do not leave us! You will only be torn limb from limb; and what would become of us once you are gone?'

As darkness descended, Francesco Valori made good his escape from the besieged monastery, with the intention of gathering together as many loyal *Piagnoni* as he could muster, so that they could come and defend San Marco. Landucci described how Valori:

> got out of *San Marco* secretly, into the garden at the back and along the walls, but here he was seized by two villainous men and taken to his house. Later in the evening he was fetched by the mace-bearers of the *Signori*, who promised that his life would be spared, and marched him off to the *Palagio*. But on the way . . . a man came up behind him and struck him on the head with a bill-hook two or three times, so that he died on the spot. And when they ransacked his house, they wounded his wife so that she died, and they also wounded the children and their nurses, stripping the house of everything.

By now the mob had begun to break into the houses of several leading *Piagnoni* supporters, pillaging them, and other murders took place.* Landucci went on:

---

* Understandably, amidst the darkness and general chaos pervading the city, the order of events that took place that night varies slightly in the different contemporary accounts. I have not adhered precisely to Landucci's account, but have chosen what appears to have been the most likely sequence.

At the same time, there was fighting around San Marco, where the crowd was constantly increasing; and they brought three stone-throwing machines into the Via Larga and the Via del Cocomero. By now several people had been wounded and killed. It was said that between fifteen and twenty people were killed in all, and about a hundred were wounded.

At about six in the night [i.e. 2 a.m.] they set fire to the doors of the church and the cloister of *San Marco*, and bursting into the church began to fight.

The friars were determined to hold out, confident that Valori would soon return to save the day, having rounded up a crowd of armed and enthusiastic *Piagnoni* supporters from all over the city. Accounts vary, but it seems that more than a dozen armed friars, along with their supporters, now gave battle to hold back the incited rabble invading the church:

It was an extraordinary sight to see these men with helmets on their heads, breastplates donned over their Dominican robes, brandishing halberds as they charged through the cloister yelling 'Long live Christ!' and calling their comrades to arms.

Brandishing drawn swords, friars chased back the invaders. Meanwhile the besiegers had got hold of ladders and began trying to scale the walls into the monastery. They were repulsed by monks hurling down tiles stripped from the roof of the building. Yet by all accounts the hero of the day was a German friar by the name of Fra Enrico, a tall muscular fellow who, according to at least one account, literally flung himself into the fray and seized an arquebus from one of the invaders, before using it to repulse the attackers. A more likely version has him stationing himself in the pulpit with one of the arquebuses from the monastery arsenal, and firing down into the fray that was erupting in the nave of the church. Here he would have had the time and the means to reload with ammunition and reprime his weapon with gunpowder. Amidst the explosions from his own and other arquebuses, the resultant clouds of acrid smoke, the general confusion, yells and shrieks of the battling crowd below, Fra Enrico is said to have killed several invaders, using the pulpit to steady his aim and select his target. It was as if the apocalyptic visions that Savonarola had described from this selfsame pulpit were now materialising in the very place once occupied by his rapt congregation.

All sources concur that heavy fighting persisted in and around San Marco for a number of hours that night. Despite being unable to restrain several of his friars from taking violent action, Savonarola is said at one stage to have taken up a position in the choir of the church, which was illuminated by burning torches. Here, surrounded by the majority of his faithful brethren, he led prayers, until the approaching mayhem became too threatening, whereupon a number of the friars seized the burning torches and advanced on the crowd. According to some contemporary sources, this sight caused consternation amongst many of the invaders, who superstitiously believed that a band of angels had descended from heaven to defend San Marco. But the panic and flight of the invaders from the church were not comprehensive, nor did they last for long. When the mayhem re-erupted and once more the situation became too dangerous, Savonarola led his acolytes in procession out of the church and into the monastery, where they reassembled in the Greek Library. Here, against the background of the crowd outside rioting and shouting, marked by occasional explosions from arquebuses, Savonarola addressed his assembled faithful:

Every word that I have said came to me from God, and as He is my witness in heaven I do not lie . . . I am departing from you with deep sorrow and anguish, so that I can surrender myself into the hands of my enemies. I do not know whether they intend to kill me. However, you can be certain that if I die I shall be able the better to aid you from heaven than I have been able to do here on earth.

Even at this late hour it was suggested to Savonarola that he could still escape by way of the garden, using the same route as Valori. According to some sources, Savonarola considered this. Yet it was now that the Judas amongst his disciples chose to act. Within the community of San Marco, one monk had traitorously vowed his secret allegiance to the *Arrabbiati*: this was Fra Malatesta Sacramoro, who now approached Savonarola and suggested: 'Should not the shepherd lay down his life for the sake of his flock?'

Fra Malatesta evidently had a good insight into the way Savonarola's mind worked, for the 'little friar' at once ceased all hesitation, silenced any debate and declared his irreversible decision to give himself up to the authorities. After receiving communion he took his leave of his fellow friars, kissing each one of them. Many of his closest followers begged to be allowed to go with him, but in the end Savonarola allowed only one friar to accompany him: Fra Domenico da Pescia, whose unswerving faith at the prospect of the ordeal by fire had so impressed him.

By now the Signoria had at last despatched a contingent of armed troops under the command of Giovanni della Vecchia, who had imposed an element of order amongst the rioters, as well as managing to force his way through to the cloister inside the monastery. Savonarola sent two of his friars into the cloister to parley his surrender to della Vecchia's men-at-arms. The friars informed the men: 'We agree to hand over the Frate if you promise to take him safely to the Palagio.' Having received this assurance, Savonarola and Fra Domenico proceeded out into the cloister, where della Vecchia's men had just been joined by the official mace-bearers from the Signoria, who immediately took charge of the two friars.

It was now probably around 3 a.m. or maybe even later.* The mace-bearers barely had time to manacle Savonarola and Fra Domenico before the angry mob surged around them, attempting to break through the men-at-arms and lay hands on the prisoners. As they were led away between the soldiers into the Piazza San Marco, the crowd, illuminated in the darkness by flickering torches, jeered, yelled insults and spat into their faces. At one stage someone attempted to burst through the line of soldiers and thrust his flaming brand into Savonarola's face, yelling sarcastically, 'Behold

---

* The times given by contemporary sources vary considerably. For instance, the events that Landucci described as taking place at '6 in the night' – that is 2 a.m. (see p.327) – probably took place somewhat earlier, while Burlamacchi gave the time of Savonarola's arrest as 'the sixth hour of the night' (1937 edn, p.161). Ridolfi stated 'It was now after the seventh hour of the night' (Vol. I, p.368) and in a note (n.27) he discusses Burlamacchi and this problem of timing. All that can safely be stated is that the arrest and the ensuing events took place in the darkness of what we would call the early hours – that is, some time before first light, which began just before 5 a.m. in Florence at that time of year.

the true light!' Just as the two prisoners were being ushered through the side door of the Palazzo della Signoria someone managed to land a kick on Savonarola's backside, shouting, 'Look, that's where his prophecies come from!'

Once inside, Savonarola and Fra Domenico were led before Gonfaloniere Popoleschi, supported by his Signoria and numerous dignitaries. Popoleschi could not refrain from gloating over the victory that he had engineered with his fellow *Arrabbiati*. His voice heavy with sarcasm, he asked the two hapless and humiliated prisoners whether they still persisted in believing that their words came from God. Both replied that they did indeed. Whereupon they were led off to separate places of imprisonment within the palazzo. Savonarola was marched up the stone stairway to the top of the tall turreted tower, where he was locked in the tiny stone cell known as the *Alberghettino* (little inn), whose narrow window looked down over the Piazza della Signoria. Ironically, this was the very cell where Cosimo de' Medici had been imprisoned in 1433, when the Albizzi family had temporarily succeeded in ousting the Medici from power. The canny Cosimo de' Medici had used his network of contacts and managed to save his life by bribing his way out of the *Alberghettino*; meanwhile his friend Pope Eugene IV and other Italian heads of state had protested on his behalf, to ensure that his death-sentence was rescinded and he was allowed to travel with his family into exile, where he had access to sufficient funds to help contrive the Medici's return to rule. But Savonarola had no such network, no such means, no access to such sympathetic powers. The pope and heads of state throughout Italy all rejoiced at his downfall, and the population of Florence had turned overwhelmingly against him. Only the remaining downtrodden *Piagnoni* still supported him, sullenly and in secret.

23

Trial and Torture

L ANDUCCI DESCRIBED THE atmosphere in Florence after day duly dawned on Monday 9 April 1498:

> People laid down their weapons, but everyone continued talking about what had happened. It was as if hell had opened beneath our feet: everyone kept saying *ladro e traditore* (wretch and traitor), no one dared to say a word in support of Savonarola, or they would have been killed, and everyone jeered at the citizens, calling them *Piagnoni* and hypocrites.

The *Compagnacci* roamed the streets in triumph, displaying the weapons that had been discovered in San Marco, claiming them as evidence that Savonarola had intended to lead an armed insurrection against the government. He was not only a charlatan, but also a traitor. Middle-class *Piagnoni* sympathisers fled for the countryside; others, secretly taking their families and any portable valuables, simply went into exile in fear of their lives.

Savonarola was brought down from the *Alberghettino* late on Monday morning, when he was probably subjected to some informal questioning by the Signoria. Having been taken into custody, he would now be subject to the due process of law. This would involve him being interrogated and tortured before a judicial commission set up to discover whichever laws he might have broken, and whether his claims to be a prophet and to have spoken with God were true.

Next day things began in earnest:

At the ninth hour in the evening [i.e. 5 p.m.] Savonarola was carried to the *Bargello* by two men on their crossed hands because his feet and hands were clapped in irons. Fra Domenico was brought there in a similar fashion. On arrival they were both seized: Fra Girolamo was put to the rack three times* and Fra Domenico four times; and Fra Girolamo said: 'Take me down and I will write you my whole life.' As you can imagine, when right-minded men who had faith in him heard that he had been tortured many were reduced to tears.

By now the two accused had been joined by a third friar. Savonarola's closest adviser, the ailing Fra Silvestro Maruffi, whom Savonarola had valued so much on account of his visions, had initially hidden himself when San Marco was overrun, but his presence had been betrayed by the turncoat Fra Malatesta, with the result that he too had been taken into the custody of the Signoria.

The man appointed to be Savonarola's chief interrogator on the judicial commission was the notary Francesco de Ser Barone, usually known by his nickname 'Ser Ceccone'. An unsavoury character, Ser Ceccone had been a close supporter of Piero de' Medici, responsible for carrying out a number of his underhand deeds. Ironically, when Piero and his brother Cardinal Giovanni had fled the city, Ser Ceccone had sought sanctuary in San Marco, emerging only after Savonarola had guaranteed his safety by issuing from the pulpit the strongest warning against the taking of reprisals by either side. From then on Ser Ceccone had adopted the guise of a firm *Piagnoni* supporter, but had in fact been an informer, passing on his information directly to Doffo Spini at the *Compagnacci* dinners, which he continued to attend, whilst at the same time regularly attending all of Savonarola's sermons at the cathedral.

Anomalously, as a mere notary he was not legally permitted to conduct any official investigation, but the Signoria had decided to overlook such niceties. Ser Ceccone could be relied upon to deliver a verdict that would ensure Savonarola's conviction.

* The original Italian refers to *tratti di fune* (pulls on the rope) — in other words, they were subjected to the traditional Florentine strappado, rather than the customary conception of the rack.

The judicial commisssion appointed by the Signoria consisted of seventeen citizens, fervently anti-Savonarola to a man. They included Doffo Spini, as well as a number of leading *Compagnacci*; another member was the diarist Piero Parenti, whose feelings were clear from his chronicle of day-to-day events; also present was Giovanni Manetti, the man who had been responsible for stirring up the crowd against Savonarola as they waited for the ordeal by fire. Manetti was recorded as asking for permission to conduct a public inspection of Savonarola's genitals: rumours were circulating concerning an astrologer's prediction that a hermaphrodite prophet would arrive in Italy, and Manetti wished to set his mind at rest that Savonarola was not the man fulfilling this role. Manetti was duly permitted his request, which was completed to the satisfaction of his fellow commissioners; such humiliation of the prior of San Marco was to be just the beginning.*

Meanwhile the Signoria had set about dismantling any possible official opposition to their actions. Elections for the Great Council were called, with no *Piagnoni* supporters permitted to stand as candidates, and any even suspected of *Piagnone* sympathies were soon weeded out of the administration.

Savonarola's interrogation would continue over the ensuing week until 17 April. (An indication of the seriousness and urgency of these proceedings can be judged from the fact that they were not even adjourned for Good Friday, 13 April, or Easter Sunday two days later, the holiest events in the Christian calendar.) The interrogation proceeded by means of the habitual Florentine method used in criminal investigations. Savonarola would first have been invited to confess to the charge of treason. If his subsequent confession was not considered adequate, he would have been reminded that further evidence could be extracted by means of the strappado. If, even after this warning, his confession still did not satisfy the commissioners, then his hands would be tied behind his back and he would be subjected to one drop after another of the strappado until he did 'confess'.

The effect of all this on Savonarola, his body rendered frail from constant

---

* Rumours of the arrival of such a prophet may also well have prompted the Franciscans' insistence upon inspecting Fra Domenico's genitals for any 'supernatural signs' before the ordeal by fire.

fasting, self-denial and frequent self-flagellation, can barely be imagined. The ingenious advantage of the strappado was that it was not fatal if judiciously administered. Moreover, the method did not numb the body, rendering it equally painful each time it was administered. Such interrogation was legal in Florence, as indeed 'trial by ordeal' of one sort or another remained an integral part of the judicial process throughout most of Europe, much as it had done during the medieval era. However, in this case, Savonarola's entire trial was in fact illegal. Priests did not fall under the jurisdiction of the civil authorities and could only be tried by the Church courts.

This hardly mattered where Savonarola was concerned. By 12 April, within forty-eight hours of Savonarola having been carried in irons into the Bargello, news had reached Alexander VI of what had happened. That very day His Holiness conveyed his feelings to the Signoria in Florence:

> It gave us the greatest pleasure when your ambassador informed us of the timely measures you have taken in order to crush the mad vindictiveness of that son of iniquity Fra Hieronymo Savonarola, who has not only inspired such heresies amongst the people with his deluded and empty prophecies, but has also disobeyed both your commands and our orders by force of arms. At last he is safely imprisoned, which causes us to give praise to our beloved Saviour, whose divine light sheds such truth upon our earthly state that He could not possibly have permitted your faithful city to have remained any longer in darkness.

The Signoria was explicitly given permisssion to examine Savonarola under torture; however, Alexander VI made it quite plain that he should then be despatched to Rome, where he would be tried before the appropriate ecclesiastical tribunal. This would have involved more traditional methods of interrogation, such as the rack, branding irons and other devices of the Inquisition, which traditionally tried its victims on charges of heresy. Ironically, the Inquisition remained the preserve of Savonarola's own order, the Dominicans. Such gruesome methods, in the hands of expert practitioners, were guaranteed to extract the last morsels of information from the hapless victim.*

The Signoria were heartened by Alexander VI's Brief, which not only allowed them to torture Savonarola with impunity, but also lifted from the city the threat of general excommunication. It even went so far as to give dispensation for those who had been guilty of attacking and desecrating Church property during the siege at San Marco. However, the Signoria were reluctant to comply with Alexander VI's crucial request: Savonarola would not be despatched to Rome. This was more than just a matter of the city of Florence asserting its independence. Over the years during which Savonarola had been consulted by the Signoria, he had inevitably gained an intimate knowledge of the workings of the city government, its secret policies, as well as its methods of gathering intelligence. These would certainly have included sympathetic informants providing confidential intelligence from Rome, possibly even spies within the Vatican itself. Alexander VI would make sure that he extracted as much of this vital information as he could from Savonarola, which he would then use to pursue his own political ends: informants would be eliminated, Florentine strategy anticipated and thwarted, the city's weaknesses exploited. For the good of the republic, Savonarola had to be kept in Florence, even if this displeased His Holiness — which it certainly did. This was one of the reasons why Savonarola's trial was conducted with the maximum secrecy. None beyond the seventeen members of the inquisitorial commission, the surgeon and members of the Signoria were permitted to attend. Savonarola was not even allowed a defence counsel, on the grounds that as a priest he would not have been permitted one in the ecclesiastical court before which he should have been tried. The logic of this argument was to be typical of the conduct of Savonarola's case.

On 13 April, probably the very day that Alexander VI's Brief arrived in Florence, important news reached the city from another source. It was learned that on 7 April (that is, the very day on which the ordeal by fire

---

* Where the Inquisition was concerned, torture was in practice frequently inflicted for its own sake. Then, as now, the 'truth' extracted by such extreme methods was always liable to conform with what the victim thought the torturer required of him, and this method was thus not always reliable as a method of extracting trustworthy information.

was to have taken place), Charles VIII had cracked his head on the stone lintel of a doorway, rendering him unconscious, and despite all the efforts of his physicians the twenty-seven-year-old King had died within a matter of hours. The prophecy that Savonarola had solemnly pronounced just over a year previously had now been fulfilled. This news seems to have given many in Florence cause for thought, especially when it filtered down to those amongst the silent, sullen *Piagnoni* who remained Savonarola's secret supporters. Yet it would have no effect upon Savonarola's fate. The wheels had by now been set in motion: it would take more than the 'miraculous' fulfilment of his prophecy to stop them.

Sources differ as to how many 'drops' of the strappado Savonarola suffered. As we have seen, the gossip reaching Landucci claimed that he suffered three times. At the other extreme, Botticelli's brother, the ardent *Piagnone* Simone Filipepi, claimed that Savonarola suffered fourteen drops in one day, which would definitely have rendered him incapable of confession of any sort and would almost certainly have proved fatal. Others go so far as to claim that burning coals were pressed to the soles of Savonarola's bare feet as he hung suspended after the drop, though many dispute this as a hagiographic overelaboration of his suffering. With feelings so polarised, and the events taking place in secret, the truth is difficult to assess. At any rate, the modern judgement is that Savonarola's frail body probably took at the most four drops before he broke and told his torturers: 'Take me down and I will write you my whole life.' But this was far from being enough. What the Signoria required was a number of specific admissions that would have proved Savonarola guilty of treason, thus allowing them to execute him. Ser Ceccone duly began interrogating Savonarola and taking down his answers.

The evidence suggests that Ser Ceccone's record of these events was deliberately slanted to achieve the intended result. No original transcript exists, and all we have are the unsubstantiated printed texts that were released later in the year. Admittedly, in his broken state Savonarola would have confessed to many things, but it is highly unlikely that he did so as recorded in the printed version of Ser Ceccone's transcript. Even so, the printed text is still worth examining for the simple reason that it was probably a biased *version* of the events that took place, as distinct from being a complete fabrication. Internal evidence supports this assessment: the problem lies in discerning where the truth tails off and falsehood takes over, and here the text provides us with a number of plausible clues. The picture it paints is hardly that of a skilled interrogation, yet it is this very muddle that hints at a basic underlying reality.

First of all, Savonarola was asked to confess that his prophecies were not the result of divine revelations, and that his claim that God spoke to him was false. According to Ser Ceccone's record, Savonarola denied that he was a prophet. This was a serious confession, which he must have known would have profound consequences amongst his *Piagnoni* supporters – yet there is good reason to believe that he did make it. Admittedly, Savonarola had on a number of earlier occasions denied that he was a prophet – though equally incontestably, he had on many later occasions accepted the mantle of a prophet, both in name and in the manner in which he preached. His contemporary apologists such as Burlamacchi, Fra Benedetto Luschino and Gianfrancesco Pico della Mirandola (the biographer and nephew of the philosopher) accepted that Savonarola made this confession, yet at the same time defended his thinking on this point. And there is no doubt that they were close enough to Savonarola to have been conversant with his method of thought. Savonarola would have been well aware that prophets such as Amos and Zachariah had on occasion denied that they were prophets, as indeed had John the Baptist. According to the Gospel of St John, even Jesus himself had given an evasive answer on this question.*

However, there is no denying that Savonarola did believe he was a prophet, and did indeed see many of his prophecies fulfilled. Some of them were ambiguous and open to wide interpretation (such as the arrival of the 'scourge of God'), while others predicted highly probable events (the deaths of the tyrants, for instance); yet his wish-fulfilment-cum-prophecy concerning the death of Charles VIII, which was neither ambiguous nor probable, not only came true, but had no effect on the interrogators who had forced him to confess that he was not a prophet.

Savonarola's confession was followed by a justification of his motives, which appears totally antithetical to his personality:

* 'Art thou that prophet? And he saith, I am not.' John, Ch. 1, v.21.

Regarding my aim, I say, truly, that it lay in the glory of the world, in having credit and reputation; and to attain this end, I sought to keep myself in credit and good standing in the city of Florence, for the said city seemed to me a good instrument for increasing this glory, and also for giving me name and reputation abroad.

Even so, such cooked-up motives hardly constituted treason. Under further brutal interrogation, Savonarola went on to admit that he had always agreed with the formation of the new republic, from its very inception after the flight of Piero de' Medici. However, the reasons he gave for this appear equally implausible, showing no evidence of the belief in social justice that had so inspired his sermons in favour of the new republic and the establishment of the more democratic Great Council. Instead, he had supported such things:

because it seemed to me to go best with my aims. I sought to shape it accordingly ... I intended that those who called themselves my friends should rule more than the others, and this is why I favoured them as best I could.

Such a forced admission was edging him closer to dangerous ground. Yet once again, seeking political influence could hardly be labelled a capital offence, especially in Florence. Still Ser Ceccone pressed on, accusing Savonarola of fixing elections for the Signoria and the Great Council. But even in his broken state, Savonarola refused to confess to this. And according to the record, when he was asked if he had an alliance with Piero de' Medici he replied, 'I strongly opposed him.' This also has the ring of truth, further revealing the haphazard nature of Ser Ceccone's doctored text: such a patriotic claim was unlikely to have been included in any complete fabrication intended to convict Savonarola of treason. When Ser Ceccone demanded to know if Savonarola had written to Charles VIII, he willingly admitted having done so. He had done this for the benefit of Florence, as was evident. Consequently, he also admitted that he had called for a Council of the Church, with the aim of ridding it of corruption – again, hardly a treasonable motive, at least where Florence was concerned. And besides, the attitude towards the behaviour of Alexander VI was all but universal. Yet when Savonarola was asked if he sought to become pope himself, he replied: 'No, I did not wish to become pope – for if I had succeeded in my purpose I would have deemed myself above any cardinal or pope.' In other words, he had in mind higher spiritual aims, rather than Church office, although when pressed (probably after further torture), he allegedly went back on his earlier claim and did admit that if he had been elected, he would not have refused the office of pope.

It seems probable that Ser Ceccone was adhering to a list of questions that had previously been drawn up by the Signoria and the others in attendance, and that he was simply proceeding in consecutive order, with no real adversarial strategy in mind, other than discovering evidence of Savonarola's treason. Yet no matter how inept such a method may have been, it was still capable of springing surprises to catch the fatigued and all-but-broken accused off-guard. How did Savonarola receive his excellent intelligence concerning what was going on in the city and beyond? Did he demand that his friars break the secret of the confessional by passing on to him certain vital information thus gleaned? Savonarola denied such charges.

Occasionally Savonarola was outwitted. When Ser Ceccone asked him whether he had been in favour of the ordeal by fire, Savonarola denied this; but he did consequently admit to allowing it to go ahead 'for the sake of his reputation'. And here, for once, this may have been the truth. Savonarola had been manoeuvred into a situation where he felt bound to accept the challenge of the Franciscans. This may be the single occasion in Ser Ceccone's report where Savonarola's claim that he acted on account of his reputation was true. All the other claims – 'I intended to rule . . .', 'my aim was . . . the glory of the world', 'to increase . . . my name and reputation abroad . . . my pride . . . my hypocrisy', and so forth – which are repeated to the extent that they become a constant refrain, are unmistakably insertions by Ser Ceccone or others. This was not the language used by Savonarola: their very repetition after so many of Savonarola's answers, as well as their uncharacteristic sentiments, is simply unbelievable.

Finally, on 18 April, after a week of interrogation (or *processi* – that is, trials, as they were officially designated), Ser Ceccone retired to 'formalise and set in order' his transcription. When later that day this was read out to Savonarola, he objected to its obvious falsifications, promising Ser Ceccone: 'If you publish this, you will die within six months'.* Early next day, Savonarola was ordered to put his name to this document. Initially he refused, but after the threat of further strappado and other 'encouragement' he eventually signed.

Later that same day, Landucci recorded: 'The protocol of Fra Girolamo, written in his own hand, was read out to the Council in the Great Hall.' Although the deposition was doubtless announced as such, it cannot have been in Savonarola's own hand. Only his signature would have been authentic. The printed version in Vallori's biography, Document XXVI, extends over twenty-seven closely printed pages up to this point; the 'protocol' would have been a shorter summary. After undergoing the strappado, Savonarola's ability to write would have been severely impaired, to say the least, to the extent that even if he had only written the protocol, it would still have taken him an unconscionable amount of time and effort to do so. With Alexander VI demanding Savonarola's presence in Rome, and Florence remaining in a state of disarray, the Signoria would have been in too much of a hurry to allow for such a time-wasting procedure. It is necessary to emphasise these points owing to the utter lack of material evidence, in order to build up the case for what necessarily remain suppositions concerning the original document. Savonarola was fighting for his life, whilst amongst themselves the authorities of the new republic abandoned all pretence at the justice whose restoration had been the justification for the overthrow of the Medici.

Landucci went on to record the devastating effect that Savonarola's protocol had on him:

> This very man whom we had regarded as a true prophet had now confessed that he was not a prophet at all, and that he had not received from God the things which he had preached. He confessed that many of the things which had taken place during the years when

---

* This improbable prophecy, which almost certainly fell into the same psychological category as that concerning Charles VIII, would also be fulfilled. However, the only source for this prophecy is the fervently pro-Savonarolan Burlamacchi.

he had preached had not happened because he had prophesied them. I was present when this protocol was read out, and I was astonished, being utterly dumfounded with surprise. My heart was grieved to witness such a marvel collapse in ruins because it had been founded upon a lie. Florence had lived in the expectation of a new Jerusalem, where the laws would be just and the city would be such an example of righteous life that it would be a splendour upon this earth, and lead to the renovation of the Church, the conversion of unbelievers and the consolation of the righteous.

Landucci would not have been alone amongst the *Piagnoni* supporters who believed Savonarola to be a prophet, and he was certainly not the only one to be similarly devastated by the public reading of the protocol. The *Piagnoni* dream of a new Jerusalem where social justice prevailed was shattered: Florence was to be no 'City of God' after all.

However, the Signoria quickly came to the conclusion that Savonarola's confession, even in its present corrupted state, was simply not enough. All this was hardly treason: he had confessed to no capital offence, and Alexander VI would soon be insisting once more that he be conveyed to Rome. Consequently, it was decided that Savonarola should undergo a second 'trial', which commenced under the same conditions of secrecy just two days after the public reading of the protocol from the first trial. Once again, the leading interrogator and recorder of evidence was Ser Ceccone, but this time – according to his printed report – the trial took place 'without torture or any harm to the body'. This was contradicted by rumours reaching Landucci, who just two days into the second trial recorded, 'The *Frate* was tortured.' He also noted on the same day that several leading *Piagnoni* supporters were arrested, including former *gonfaloniere* Domenico Mazzinghi.

The following day, 24 April, the trial approached its final stage, and Savonarola was asked to sign his 'confession'. This time he appears to have written at least part of the document himself; however, there were also lines written and added by Ser Ceccone. This we know because Savonarola wrote, or was forced to write, that 'in some places there are notes in the margin written by Ser Francesco di Ser Barone [Ser Ceccone]'. This gave

Ser Ceccone carte blanche to add, at a later time, whatever he (or the Signoria and the others attending the trial) so wished. Evidence of such post-facto insertions can be seen in the astonishing admisssion allegedly made by Savonarola that, although as prior of San Marco he 'consecrated the bread and wine every day for mass, and gave holy communion', he 'never went to confession'. He revealed:

> my reason for not going to confesssion was that I did not wish to disclose my secret intentions to anyone, and because I could not have been absolved from these sins as I did not intend to give up my intentions. Yet I did not care about this, on account of the great end I had in mind. When a man has lost his faith and his soul, he can do whatever he wants and pursue every great thing. I hereby indeed confess to being a great sinner, and I want very much to do this correctly and for this I am willing to do a great penance.

It is extremely difficult to believe that Savonarola lost his faith in God whilst in pursuance of 'the great end' he had in mind – especially when this end was to establish Florence as the 'City of God'. A master of logic like Savonarola, who had debated with a philosopher such as Pico della Mirandola, was hardly likely to contradict himself in such a manner. Indeed, despite Ser Ceccone's ham-fisted methods, it is surprising that the Signoria or the dignitaries present, amongst whom were men of some intelligence, permitted such a blunder to pass. Presumably by this stage they were beyond caring, having the speedy despatch of their own 'great end' in mind.

Some parts of the printed document of Savonarola's second trial do have a certain ring of truth. As we have seen, Savonarola had over the years developed considerable political acumen, and the printed version of his second trial would seem to confirm this. In it, he indicated that he well understood the only way for democracy to work in the Florentine republic:

> My intention, as I have said in reply to other questions, was that the citizens who I had decided were good, should hold all positions of power, or at least govern with a majority of four to three, and that

the others, who are known as the *Arrabbiati* – although in order to preserve my honour I did not call them by this name – should be kept out of government as much as possible.

So far so good: but he knew that any workable democracy – especially under the conditions prevailing in Florence at the time – required an opposition of some sort, for even his supporters were not above political suspicion:

It was not my intention totally to exclude and drive out [all opposition], for I was very much in favour of having an obstacle against the leaders of our faction, having suspected that these same leading citizens would in the end become so predominant and hold such power that they would fashion a narrower form of government of their own and wreck the Great Council.

Savonarola's belief in the workings of the Great Council took into account the frailties of human nature. If such passages were not authentic, then it remains difficult to see any reason for Ser Ceccone or the Signoria to have made them up. And once again, such ideas were hardly a capital offence.

At the same time, Savonarola's closest allies were also being subjected to interrogation. The fervently loyal Fra Domenico da Pescia, whose belief in his master had even extended to his willingness to undergo ordeal by fire, was to suffer horribly at the hands of the authorities. His inquisitors tried to persuade him that Savonarola had in fact confessed to all manner of sins, from being a false prophet to heresy, but Fra Domenico continued to insist, 'In the certainty of my mind, I have always believed, and in the absence of any proof to the contrary, still firmly believe in the prophecies of Savonarola'. As well as being subjected to the strappado, Fra Domenico was also forced to endure the *stanghetta*.*

* More widely known as the Spanish Boot or Iron Boot, this was a widespread instrument of torture in medieval Europe. It usually consisted of iron plates, which would be strapped to encase the foot so that iron wedges could be hammered between the casing into the flesh. Sometimes the 'boot' would consist of two casings with inner iron spikes, which could be strapped tighter and tighter. Or it could be larger and sealed, so that water could be poured over the foot inside, which could then be held over a fire until it gradually boiled.

After further agonies, Fra Domenica informed his inquisitors:

> I have tried to be as precise to you as I would be at the hour of my
> death, and indeed I may well die if you torture me any further, for
> I am utterly broken, my arms have been destroyed, especially my left
> one, which your tortures have now dislocated for a second time.

Yet still they continued, and still he could not bring himself to lie,
declaring, 'I have always thought him an altogether upright and extraordinary man.' As with Savonarola's trials, there is a question here over documentary sources. At the back of Villari's biography, as Document XXVII,
he includes the two different 'original' versions of the transcript that have
come down to us. These are printed side by side for comparison. According
to Villari, the version in the left column is 'the true document written in
his own hand', whilst the other is 'the false document'. In the light of Fra
Domenico's claim that 'my arms have been destroyed' (*ho guaste le braccia*), it
is difficult to see how he could actually have *written* this 'true' document.
More likely, he dictated it, read it through and appended some sort of
signature. Villari himself gives an eloquent defence of his conclusions:

> When they read Fra Domenico's confession, the authorities felt obliged
> to insert various alterations [in order to] efface the tone of heroism
> which was notable in every word ... When I put together the two
> copies of these depositions, which I myself discovered, I found that
> the one which was altered by the Signoria was better assembled, more
> grammatical and had a better style than the true and genuine confes-
> sion. This real version contains evidence of a sincere and natural
> eloquence that does not come from art, but is the spontaneous expres-
> sion of an open soul. It is not possible to read this examination
> without being profoundly moved, it is as if we are transported into
> the very torture chamber itself, witnessing the pitiless wrenching of
> the limbs, hearing the grating of the bones, aware of the frail exhausted
> voice, so sublime and pure, of this heroic monk who welcomes death
> with the angelic smile of a martyr.

Such sentiments may appear rather overblown in our secular age, yet something similar must certainly have taken place. Fra Domenico's belief was indestructible; and, miraculously, he survived his tortures.

By contrast, the third member of the trio of monks arrested at San Marco, the sickly otherworldly Fra Silvestro Maruffi, whose visions had so inspired Savonarola, proved all too human. Having unsuccessfully tried to hide in San Marco, he now faced his inquisitors filled with terror. Once again Ser Ceccone conducted the proceedings. Fra Silvestro soon denounced Savonarola, as well as all the claims he had made, before giving a complete list of all the citizens who regularly visited Savonarola at San Marco. Even so, when questioned about Savonarola's interference in affairs of state, he could offer no evidence. He also unwittingly contradicted the 'admission' that Savonarola had made in his signed legal document that he 'never went to confession'. Fra Silvestro explained how:

> on twenty or twenty-five occasions, when he was about to deliver a sermon, he would come to my cell and tell me, 'I do not know what to preach. Pray to God for me, because I fear that he has abandoned me because of my sins.' And he would then say that he wished to unburden himself of his sins, and would make confession to me. Afterwards he would go away and preach a beautiful sermon. The last time that he did this was when he preached in San Marco on the Saturday before the last Sunday of Lent. Finally I say that he has deceived us.

Again, the abrupt break in style and tone suggests that this last sentence was inserted by Ser Ceccone. Yet even Fra Silvestro's abject confession was not sufficient to condemn Savonarola to death.

The friars of San Marco proved to be of similar frailty to Fra Silvestro. As a result of their violent resistance during the siege of San Marco they had been excommunicated by Alexander VI. In an attempt to redeem themselves and have this sentence annulled, on 21 April they composed a collective letter to the pope, which was signed by almost all the friars in the community. This letter has been vilified as an abject surrender to the pope, as well as a grovelling betrayal of their beloved prior, and indeed it is both of these. However, it is possible to read this document as a letter addressed to the pope, in his office as ruler of the Church and as the occupant of St Peter's throne, rather than to Alexander VI himself, whom Savonarola had so passionately castigated. The distinction is subtle, but real in this case: they were not prostrating themselves before the degenerate monster who sat on St Peter's throne, but before God's representative on Earth. This distinction becomes clear and significant when the letter describes how the friars themselves felt with regard to Savonarola:

> Not only ourselves, but men of much greater wisdom, were persuaded by Fra Girolamo's cunning. The sheer power and quality of his preaching, his exemplary life, the holiness of his behaviour, what appeared to us as his devotion, and the effect it had in purging the city of its immorality, usury and all manner of vices, as well as the events which appeared to confirm his prophecies in a way beyond any human power or imagining, and were so numerous and of such a nature that if he had not retracted his claims, and confessed that his words were not the words of God, we would never have been able to renounce our belief in him. For so great was our faith in him that all of us were ready to go through fire in order to support his doctrine.

This revelatory admission would seem to be an accurate and succinct summary of the entire Savonarola 'phenomenon' and its effect upon those who came into contact with him. It certainly accords with the way many modern commentators view what took place in Florence during these years: a collective delusion, which was almost certainly shared by Savonarola himself. The impressionable friars, many of whom were young, educated, of good families, and were genuinely appalled at the humanism that had been adopted by so many of the city's intellectuals, as well as by what they saw as the lax morals that accompanied this renaissance of classical values, had quickly fallen under the spell cast by the charismatic 'little friar'. His influence had proved both intellectually radical and powerfully inspirational, whilst its prophetic religious manner included a heady mix of fundamentalism and passion bordering on fanatic hysteria.

The bewildered young friars of San Marco believed in Savonarola; amidst a world of profound change, they longed for the certainty of which he preached. This was the truth, and it would be realised if only the people could be induced to adopt the virtue and purity necessary for Florence to become the 'City of God'. The evidence given in the letter by the monks of San Marco is the most concise and clear insight we have into the faith that Savonarola infused in his believers – which, as we have seen, ranged through all classes. At some point this may even have touched Lorenzo the Magnificent himself – after all, it was he who had invited Savonarola back to Florence, and he who had called for the prior of San Marco to visit him on his deathbed. Others, from Pico della Mirandola, through the monks of San Marco, to the lowest *Piagnoni*, eventually embraced his ideas. This was the faith that had inspired Fra Domenico under torture, to the verge of martyrdom.

The *Arrabbiati* now decided to take matters into their own hands. They knew that many *Piagnoni*, more obdurate than Landucci, had not been convinced by the public reading of Savonarola's confession, and that for as long as Savonarola lived they would have a figurehead to rally around. He needed to be discredited, once and for all, and it was clear that forged evidence would never do this. Only genuine and utterly convincing evidence would now suffice. So on 27 April the *Arrabbiati* launched a round-up of people known, or suspected, of remaining *Piagnoni* sympathisers. Their intentions were twofold: first, they wished to uncover convincing incriminating evidence of a plot which would ensure that Savonarola was executed for treason; and second, they wished to launch a lightning reign of terror, which would permanently destroy the *Piagnoni* movement. Landucci recorded the events of that day: 'All the citizens arrested for this cause were scourged, so that from 15 in the morning [11 a.m.] till the evening there were unending howls of agony coming from the *Bargello*.' Yet despite all the cries of terror and abject confessions, still no convincing evidence against Savonarola emerged, and on 1 May, 'All citizens were sent back home; and only the three poor *Frati* remained.'

By this stage the *Arrabbiati* were becoming desperate, and on 5 May the new *gonfaloniere* and the Signoria, now exclusively composed of *Arrabbiati*, called a Pratica to decided what to do. Alexander VI was still insisting that all three friars should be transported to Rome to be tried by the Church courts, as was their due. It was suggested that the only way to prevent this was for the friars to be tried yet again in Florence, in the hope that this time genuine incriminating evidence would be obtained from at least one of them. Summoning all his authority as the former *gonfaloniere*, Popoleschi protested against this:

> both on account of the way in which the previous examinations were conducted, and for the sake of peace and public order in the city. If we proceed to examine them in the same way as before this will only give rise to a scandal, as we have already been informed by the diplomatic representatives of every state in Italy.

The 'examinations' may have been held in the privacy of the Bargello, but word of the way in which they had been conducted had by now spread throughout Italy, where it provoked widespread public revulsion. That a civilised republic like Florence could behave in such a manner towards men of the cloth was nothing less than a disgrace to the entire country. On top of this, the French ambassador Giovanni Guasconi, who was known to be a close friend of the new king Louis XII, had made plain his sympathy for Savonarola and the *Piagnoni*. The support of Florence's ally was at stake.

In the end, the Pratica decide to send a despatch to ambassador Bonsi in Rome. He was instructed to inform Alexander VI that the Signoria wished to make an example of Savonarola and his two friars in Florence, where the execution would be witnessed by his remaining supporters, who would realise once and for all that their cause was now futile. On the other hand, if Alexander VI insisted upon further examination of the friars concerning religious matters, he was welcome to despatch a Papal Commission to Florence for this purpose.

24

Judgement

To the surprise of the Signoria, Alexander VI agreed to their proposal. In fact, he now wished to see Savonarola eliminated as quickly as possible. This would not only destroy a dangerous source of public defiance to his authority, but would put an end to Savonarola's call for a Council of the Church, with the aim of deposing him. As ever, Alexander VI also had a further, more devious motive. The execution of Savonarola in Florence was liable to result in public disturbances, making the city ungovernable. This would provide an ideal opportunity for the reimposition of Medici rule. In a stroke, the city would be returned to stability, and would be ruled by an ally in the form of Piero de' Medici, who would regard him with gratitude.

Alexander VI selected his two-man Papal Commission with some care. His first choice was the aged theologian Giovacchino Torriani, general of the Dominican order, who would lend the commission indisputable dignity and authority. Although just five years previously, in 1493, Torriani had in fact supported Savonarola's wish to form a breakaway Tuscan Congregation, more recent events in Florence had deeply disturbed him. However, the leading figure in the delegation was undoubtedly Alexander VI's second choice: his thirty-six-year-old protégé, Bishop Francesco Remolino,* an ambitious forceful character, whose legal expertise as a judge in Rome had proved his great worth to the pope in eliminating several of his enemies. Like the pope, Remolino was of Spanish descent and had become a close friend of the pope's notorious son, Cesare Borgia. His loyalty had already seen him rewarded with no fewer than four bishoprics.

* Sometimes referred to as Remolines or Remolins; in Florence, possibly because he had been sent from Rome, he was often called Romolino.

Meanwhile Savonarola languished in gaol. Much mythology has grown up around this period, and it features heavily in various forms in the contemporary biographies, which at this point tend heavily towards hagiography. Even so, certain facts seem evident. Savonarola's cell was bare and he was forced to sleep on the stone floor. During the day it was dim, at night pitch-black, and he was allowed few visitors. His gaoler, a man of evil repute, was very much in favour of the *Arrabbiati* and treated his prisoner accordingly. However, close contact with the 'little friar' and observation of his saintly fortitude are said to have convinced this uncouth fellow of Savonarola's cause. In response, Savonarola is said to have written for him a small tract entitled 'A Rule for Leading the Good Life'. Given Savonarola's pitiful physical and spiritual state, this seems unlikely, yet just such a tract would be published later in the year. The hagiographies also speak of Savonarola writing pious scraps for his gaoler to deliver to his daughter, and even of miraculously curing him of syphilis.

However, there is a second, more profound tract that shows many signs of having been written by Savonarola himself, and as such could not have been written at any other time in his life. Given his bodily condition, this was probably dictated to one of the loyal friars who were permitted to visit him. Entitled 'An Exposition and Meditation on the Psalm '*Miserere*', it begins:

> Unfortunate am I, abandoned by all, I who have offended heaven and earth, where am I to go? With whom can I seek refuge? Who will have pity on me? I dare not raise my eyes to heaven because I have sinned against heaven. On earth I can find no refuge, because here I have created a scandalous state of affairs ... Thus to Thee, most merciful God, I return filled with melancholy and grief, for Thou alone art my hope, Thou alone my refuge.

Savonarola then quoted the celebrated opening lines of Psalm 51, '*Miserere mei, Deus: secundum magnam misericordiam tuam*' ('Have mercy upon me, O God, according to thy loving kindness'). Later, he compared himself with Christ's favourite disciple, St Peter, whom Christ had told on the night before his crucifixion: 'Verily I say unto thee, That this day, even in this night, before the cock crow twice, thou shalt deny me thrice.' And so it had come about. Yet St Peter had only denied Christ when he was asked whether he knew him:

> But these questions were just words; what would he have done if the Jews had come and threatened to beat him . . . He would have denied once more if he had seen them getting out whips . . . If St Peter, to whom Thou granted so many gifts and so many favours, failed so miserably in his test, what was I capable of, O Lord? What could I do?

This would appear to prove that Savonarola did indeed break down under torture and made certain untrue confessions concerning his faith. Possibly he agreed that he gave up going to confession (which we know was untrue); maybe he even went so far as to agree that his words did not come from God (despite his conviction that they did); possibly he even denied that he saw visions (his description in the 'Compendium of Revelations' of how he had these visions is utterly in accord with the modern psychological findings). However, it is still difficult to believe, as Ser Ceccone's document claimed, that he confessed his 'aim was . . . the glory of the world' and that he 'lost his faith and his soul'. It is worth considering a seemingly pedantic distinction here. St Peter denied that he knew Christ; he certainly did not deny his faith. Savonarola may well have denied that he knew God's words; yet, like St Peter, he seems not to have denied his faith. The similarity would appear to have been intentionally exact – a comparison that would have been all too evident to an exceptional theologian such as Savonarola. He may have been cowed into signing a document that denied his faith, but he had not actually done so.

It is difficult to doubt the authenticity of the words in this last document attributed to Savonarola, now usually known simply as 'Exposition'. Over the coming years they would profoundly move the many who eventually read them. Indeed, Savonarola's 'Exposition' would have an 'extraordinary fortune': over the course of the following two years no fewer than fourteen editions of this tract would be published – in Latin, 'vulgar Italian', and even 'vulgar German'. Here was an almost saintly expression of spiritual despair: a document of rare profundity and passion, which was appreciated by scholars, clergy and laymen throughout Italy, Germany and beyond. Here was a document whose popularity would prove a dangerous focus, as dissatisfaction with the corrupt behaviour of the Church and its clergy on all levels grew ever more widespread.*

Judging from the intensity and bleakness of emotion expressed by Savonarola in 'Exposition', by this stage he felt certain that he would soon be executed. In which case he was aware that this would probably involve him being burned at the stake as a heretic. Events were soon to confirm this likelihood. On 19 May 1498 the Papal Commission reached Florence, and by now the public mood was evident, for as the commission members rode through the city, the crowd of onlookers lining the streets shouted, 'Death to the friar!' Remolino replied, 'Indeed he will die.' The *Arrabbiati* were overjoyed at the attitude of the ambitious young bishop from Rome, and in gratitude despatched to his residence a beautiful young prostitute dressed as a pageboy. The grateful Remolino assured his hosts that there could be no doubt about the outcome of the coming trial: 'We shall have a good bonfire. I have reached the verdict already in my heart.'

Savonarola's trial before the Papal Commissioners began the next day, with Bishop Remolino as the sole interrogator and just five Florentine dignitaries present as observers for the secular government. During the course of the preliminary questioning it became clear that Savonarola had recovered some of his composure during the month since his previous trial, which he had put to such good use composing his 'Exposition'. This work may reveal an author amidst the most profound spiritual turmoil, yet he depicts the travails of this crisis with the clarity of a man who has regained

---

* Latin editions would certainly have reached England long before any English version appeared. The first known English edition, which came out in 1543, was entitled 'An exposicyon after the maner of a coteplacyo vpon .lj. Psalme called Miserere me De'. Such was the demand for this work that it was soon followed by other translations, suggesting that it proved popular amongst upper-class women who were educated to read, but had not been taught Latin, as well as amongst literate, less-educated men, such as merchants, certain guild members and officials. These translations appeared despite England's separation from the Church of Rome in 1531 – a further indication, if such was needed, of the regard in which this work came to be held by all Christians.

his previous intellectual perspicacity. When Remolino began questioning Savonarola about his previous confessions, he 'observed how [Savonarola] would pretend to answer a question, first by telling some of the truth and then obscuring it, but always without lying'.

His interrogator's patience soon snapped in the face of such apparent deviousness:

> Remolino ordered that he be stripped of his robes so that he could be given the rope [strappado]. In absolute terror, he fell to his knees and said: 'Now hear me. God, Thou hast caught me. I confess that I have denied Christ, I have told lies. O you Florentine Lords, be my witness here: I have denied Him from fear of being tortured. If I have to suffer, I wish to suffer for the truth: what I said, I heard from God. O God, Thou art making me do penance for having denied Thee under fear of torture. I deserve it.

The transcript continued: 'It was now that Savonarola was undressed, whereupon he sank to his knees once more, showing his left arm, saying that it was completely useless.' Evidently it had been permanently dislocated during his previous subjection to the strappado, and must have remained dangling uselessly at his side during the previous month. As Savonarola had his hands bound behind his back, in preparation for them to be yanked into the air, he was clearly raving with terror, repeating: 'I have denied you, I have denied you, God, for fear of torture.' While he was being hauled into the air, he kept repeating frantically, 'Jesus help me. This time you have caught me.'

Savonarola was by now reduced to the limits of endurance. One can but imagine the actual incoherence, raving and screaming which must have punctuated the more coherent words that appeared in the transcript. As Ridolfi observed, this included 'such things as Ser Ceccone would never have recorded in his collection of lies'. There is no denying that this document of Savonarola's third trial has a chilling ring of truth, evoking all manner of terror, its narrative and tone uninterrupted by any out-of-context insertions.

Remolino was an expert judicial examiner, having refined his technique in the interrogation chambers of Rome, where there were far fewer restraints upon procedure than in republican Florence. By this stage Savonarola was all but out of his mind, pleading 'Don't tear me apart!' and 'Jesus help me!'

Sadistically playing with his victim, Remolino asked, 'Why do you call upon Jesus?'

Savonarola managed to reply, 'So I seem like a good man.'

But when Remolino persisted with the question, Savonarola could only reply, 'Because I am mad.' Soon he was begging, 'Do not torture me any further. I will tell you the truth, I will tell you the truth.'

Amidst the goading questions, Remolino suddenly asked, 'Why did you deny what you had already confessed?'

Savonarola could only reply, 'Because I am a fool.'

What was Remolino doing here? Savonarola had already revealed quite plainly why he had confessed to Ceccone. He had denied that he spoke with God, and that he saw visions of the future, only through his terror of torture. Yet this time he had told Remolino that he wished to suffer for the truth, that what he had said he had indeed heard from God. It was as if Remolino was determined to force Savonarola to admit that his earlier confession to Ceccone was true. For all his ruthless ambition, Remolino was still a man of God. Did he wish to make utterly sure that he was not an instrument in the interrogation (and possible martyrdom) of a prophet? This is certainly one of the interpretations that can be put on the bare outline that has come down to us through the various versions of this transcript – an interpretation that is reinforced by the later questions, where Remolino subtly sought to discredit the orthodoxy, and thus the validity, of Savonarola's faith.

When Savonarola was finally lowered to the ground, he once again confessed, 'When I am faced with torture, I lose all mastery over myself.' He then added, with some relief, 'When I am in a room with men who treat me properly, then I can express myself with reason.'

Yet it was now that Remolino's masterly cunning came into play. He knew that Savonarola was in such a state that he was beyond reason. Sensing this, he began firing at him an inconsequential series of loaded questions, in the hope of forcing Savonarola inadvertently to condemn himself. At one point Remolino asked him, 'Have you ever preached that Jesus Christ was just a man?'

Savonarola replied, 'Only a fool would ever think such a thing.' Had he given the wrong answer to this, or even a muddled reply, he could have been charged with heresy.*

Other dangerous questions followed. Remolino asked, 'Do you believe in magic charms?'

Savanorola was just able to reply, 'I have always derided such nonsense.' And somehow he managed to hold his ground.

On the second day of questioning, when Savonarola was seemingly capable of giving more coherent replies, Remolino turned in more detail to a matter that he had touched upon during the first day – a matter whose facts were of most interest to his master Alexander VI. Under the threat of further administration of the strappado, Remolino probed Savonarola with questions about the Council of the Church, which he had unsuccessfully attempted to summon in order to depose the pope. But Remolino soon realised that Savonarola could only tell him what he already knew. All the Italian leaders remained against Florence, and none had dared to commit to any move against Alexander VI. Remolino demanded to know which cardinals had been in favour of the council, but once again Savonarola's answers accorded with Alexander VI's intelligence. All had been wary of any such move. Yet Alexander VI evidently retained his suspicions, for Remolino pressed Savonarola again and again about Cardinal Caraffa of Naples, who had played such a crucial role in obtaining for Savonarola the establishment of an independent Tuscan Congregation. However, even after further application of the strappado, Savonarola continued to insist, 'I did not make any contact with the Cardinal of Naples concerning the Council.'

Remolino reluctantly concluded that he would be able to collect no further information on this matter and soon ended the day's interrogation, indicating that he would deliver his verdict the following day.

Even while Savonarola was still being examined by the Papal Commission, the Signoria summoned a Pratica to discuss Savonarola's sentence. Despite the overwhelming *Arrabbiati* majority at this Pratica, the venerable legal expert Agnolo Niccolini, formerly a supporter of Piero de' Medici,

* Believers in the Arian heresy, which caused the most serious split in the ancient Church less than three centuries after the death of Christ, basically declared that Christ was 'begotten' – in other words, that he was a man, and not divine.

gave his opinion that it would be a crime to execute Savonarola, 'for history rarely produces such a man as this'. Niccolini went on:

This man would not only succeed in restoring faith to the world, should it ever die out, but he would disseminate the vast learning with which he is so richly endowed. For this reason, I advise that he be kept in prison, if you so choose; but spare his life, and grant him the use of writing materials, so that the world may not be deprived of his great works to the glory of God.

But the majority were all for Savonarola's execution:

because no one can rely upon any future Signoria, as they change every two months. The Friar would almost certainly be released at some stage and once again cause disturbance to the city. A dead man cannot continue to fight for his cause.

In truth, the authorities remained seriously afraid of Savonarola and his remaining followers. Savonarola's modern biographer Desmond Seward has produced intriguing evidence of such fears from the contemporary journal written by Sandro Botticelli's brother Simone Filipepi. This records how, some eighteen months later, Doffo Spini, the notorious leader of the *Compagnacci*, happened to call late one winter's night at Botticelli's studio. As they sat before the fire, Botticelli began questioning Spini about Savonarola's trials, which he knew Spini had attended. Spini confided to him, 'Sandro, do you want me to tell you the truth? We never found anything that he had done wrong, neither mortal sin, nor venial.' According to Spini, if they had spared Savonarola and his two fellow friars, and allowed them to return to San Marco, 'the people would have turned on us, stuffing all of us into sacks and tearing us to pieces. The whole thing had gone too far – we had to do it just to save our own skins.'

On 22 May, Remolino conducted a further brief examination of Savonarola, without even bothering to include his fellow commissioner Torriani. After this, an official message was despatched to Savonarola ordering him to appear the following day, 'when his trial would be concluded and he would receive his sentence'. Savonarola could only reply to the papal messenger, 'I am in prison; if I am able, I will come.' Prior to Remolino sending his report to Alexander VI, the Papal Commissioners then met the Florentine authorities to ratify the fate of Savonarola, along with that of Fra Domenico and Fra Francesco, neither of whom the commissioners had even bothered to question. In an attempt to display a modicum of Christian compassion, which all present must surely have recognised as breathtaking hypocrisy, Bishop Remolino suggested that the life of the obdurate but saintly Fra Domenico should be spared. But one of the Florentines reminded Remolino, 'If this friar is allowed to live, all Savonarola's doctrines will be preserved.' Whereupon Remolino reverted to his true character and replied, 'One little friar more or less hardly matters; let him die too.'

Bishop Remolino then retired to compile his report to Alexander VI. This incorporated Savonarola's confessions from Ser Ceccone's transcript without any regard for consistency, including all its farcically inaccurate details, obvious forgeries, insertions, lies and exaggerations. 'He confesses to inciting citizens to revolt, to deliberately causing shortages of food which caused many of the poor to starve to death, and to murdering important citizens . . .', and so forth. Not surprisingly, Remolino reported in the strongest possible terms Savonarola's confession concerning his attempt to summon a Council of the Church, and how:

> He sent letters and communications to many Christian princes, urging them to defy your Holiness and to create a schism in the Church. Such was the depth of iniquity and evil in this dissimulating monster that all his outward appearance of goodness was nothing more than a charade.

At this, Remolino's imagination appeared to fail him, and he chose instead to protect the sensibilities of his Borgia master from the truth of Savonarola's wickedness: 'Of such a horrendous nature were his vile crimes that I cannot even bring myself to write them down, let alone pollute my mind with the thought of them.'

The three monks were finally condemned 'as heretics and schismatics and for having preached new things etc'. On the morrow all three of them were to be 'degraded' (that is, stripped of their priesthood), whereupon they would be handed over to the appropriate secular authorities for due punishment.

It soon became plain to all that this punishment had already been decided. Landucci wrote of Savonarola's fate (which was to be shared with his two fellow friars):

> 22 May. It was decided that he should be condemned to death, and that he should be burnt alive. That evening a scaffold was put up at the end of a walkway which reached into the middle of the Piazza della Signoria . . . and here was erected a solid piece of wood many *braccia* high, with a large circular platform around its base. A piece of wood was nailed horizontally near the top of the vertical piece of wood making it look like a cross. But people noticed this, and said: 'They are going to crucify him.' And when word of this reached the ears of the authorities, orders were given to saw off part of the wood, so that it would not resemble a cross.

This was the very spot where, six weeks previously, the ordeal by fire had been due to take place.

25

Hanged and Burned

SAVONAROLA WAS KNEELING in his cell, lost in prayer, when the officials from the Signoria, led by Ser Ceccone, burst through the door on 22 May 1498 to inform him that he had been condemned to death. The condemned man offered no reply and simply returned to his devotions – without even asking what form his execution was to take.

The two who had been condemned to die with him reacted very differently. Both had been aware that they faced death, yet only the saintly Fra Domenico had already taken anticipatory steps. He had written a letter to the Dominican monks at the monastery of Fiesole, of which he was prior, bidding his community a heartfelt farewell. Yet despite his utter reliance upon faith, he also knew when and how to take practical action. In his letter, he instructed his monks to:

> Collect up from my cell all the writings of Fra Girolamo that are to be found there, have them bound into a book, and place a copy of this in our library. Also place another copy in the refectory, chained to the table, where it can be read aloud at mealtimes, and so that the lay brethren who serve can also read it amongst themselves.

This letter must have been smuggled out by one of the few allowed to visit the condemned men in their cells, for surprisingly it reached its intended recipients. Even though Fra Domenico's life had not been spared, 'Savonarola's doctrine [would be] preserved', just as the Pratica had feared and wished to prevent.

Fra Silvestro, on the other hand, was overcome with terror when the verdict was read out to him. Inconsolably, he begged to be allowed to put his case before the citizens of Florence, who he felt sure would grant him mercy on account of his reputation for living a life of blameless spirituality.

The three condemned monks, in their separate cells, were now each joined by a member of the Compagni de' Neri, the black-robed, black-cowled brotherhood who traditionally spent the final hours with those who had been condemned to death. Jacopo Niccolini was the brother who had been assigned to Savonarola by the Signoria, because of his well-known lack of sympathy with the *Piagnoni*. Despite this, Niccolini seems to have been deeply impressed by Savonarola from the moment they met, finding his composure under such circumstances nothing less than a spiritual inspiration. When Savonarola asked Niccolini if he could use his influence to secure a final meeting between the three condemned monks, so that he could pass on to them words of advice to help them face their ordeal, Niccolini readily agreed. Surprisingly, he even managed to persuade the Signoria to allow such a meeting to take place, under suitable supervision. Ironically, the three were brought together in the hall of the Great Council, which Savonarola had done so much to establish as the democratic heart of the government of the Florentine republic.

The three monks had not set eyes on each other since the night of the siege of San Marco on 8 April. During the ensuing six weeks they had each been separately interrogated and tortured — an ordeal that had broken Savonarola temporarily, Fra Silvestro permanently, but had not succeeded on Fra Domenico. Even so, they had each been informed by their interrogators that the other two had confessed to heresy, charlatanism, false prophecy and misleading the people. Savonarola was said to have confessed that he was not a prophet, had never seen any visions and had not spoken with the voice of God. His companions had certainly not been informed that he had later recanted these confessions, claiming that they had only been induced by the prospect of unbearable torture.

The three of them cannot have known what to believe of each other. Understanding that their meeting would necessarily be brief, Savonarola immediately took charge of the proceedings. Turning to the faithful Fra Domenico, he said:

I hear that you have requested to be cast into the fire alive. This is wrong, for it is not for us to choose the manner of our death. We must accept willingly the fate which God has assigned for us.

He then turned to the pitiful Fra Silvestro, telling him sternly:

In your case, I know that you wish to proclaim your innocence before the people. But I order you to put away all thought of this idea, and instead to follow the example of Our Lord Jesus Christ, who refrained from protesting his innocence, even when he was on the cross. We must do likewise, because his is the example which we must follow.

The two friars then knelt before their superior, Savonarola, and he gave them his blessing. Savonarola was assisted back to his cell – being in leg irons, with his body in such a broken state, he was barely able to walk on his own.

Describing Savonarola in his cell during the time that followed, Ridolfi wrote, 'The account of his last hours is like a page from the lives of the Church Fathers.'* The pro-Savonarolan Burlamacchi recounts an incident that became part of the Savonarola legend.† Villari paraphrases this:

It was already well into the early hours by the time he returned to his prison cell. By this stage he was so beset with drowsiness and exhaustion that in a gesture of affection and gratitude he rested his head on Niccolini's lap, lapsing almost immediately into a light sleep, and such was the serenity of his spirit that he seemed to smile as if seeing pleasant visions in his dreams.

* The Church Fathers were the spiritual leaders of the Christian Church during the first five centuries or so after the death of Christ, many of whom lived exemplary lives, some enduring martydom with great spiritual fortitude.
† The main contemporary source for the ensuing events remains the pro-Savonarolan Burlamacchi, whose descriptions, perhaps inevitably, stray at times into hagiography. Yet there were others who left a record of these times. Landucci describes the later events as he saw them. Sources such as Parenti, Nardi and Cerretani also gave descriptions that for the most part tally with the main outline of the facts. Guicciardini, regarded by many as the father of modern history, who grew up in Florence and was fifteen years old at the time, would begin his considered description of these events just ten years later. I have at points made use of all these sources.

When Savonarola awoke, he appears to have been surprised that he had fallen asleep. In a gesture of gratitude towards his compassionate companion, he is said to have vouchsafed him a prophecy that there would come a time in the future when Florence would find itself overwhelmed with a disastrous calamity. 'Remember this carefully,' he told Niccolini. 'These things will come to pass when there is a pope by the name of Clement.' Just such events would occur in 1529, when Florence would be subjected to the prolonged privations of a ten-month siege, before capitulating; all this would take place during the reign of Pope Clement VII. Even one of Savonarola's most informed and sympathetic biographers, Pasquale Villari, is driven to suggest that the details of this prophecy 'do not seem credible', adding: 'We must assume that unless the name Clement was inserted at a later date by devout believers in the friar, this can only be regarded as a fortuitous coincidence.'

At daybreak on 23 May the three condemned men were led from their cells and assembled together once more. Their wrists were manacled, but they were no longer in leg irons, enabling them to stumble down the steps inside the Palazzo della Signoria and out into the piazza. According to Guicciardini:

> A multitude of people came to witness Savonarola's degradation and execution, every bit as as large as the one that had congregated in the same place on the day set for the ordeal by fire, hoping to witness the miracle they had been promised.

On the raised stone terrace outside the palazzo were formally assembled three separate tribunals, each of which would play its part in the ensuing protracted solemn rituals — according to one contemporary 'the ceremonies lasted for the space of two long hours', beginning at eight and continuing until around ten in the morning.

The first tribunal was led by Benedetto Pagagnotti, Bishop of Vasona, a former friar of San Marco and ironically once a firm believer in Savonarola. Pagagnotti had been commissioned by Alexander VI to read out the papal Brief formally degrading the three friars, publicly stripping them of the priesthood. This Brief had in fact been despatched to Pagagnotti before the two Papal Commissioners had even left Rome – an unmistakable indication of precisely what Alexander VI had in mind for Savonarola and his two fellow friars. Pagagnotti was so discomfited when he faced Savonarola that he felt unable to look him in the face and stumbled over the words of the formal declaration, declaring at one point: 'I separate you from the Church militant and from the Church triumphant.'* Ever the theologian, Savonarola corrected him at this point: 'Only from the Church militant; the other is not within your jurisdiction.' Pagagnotti hurriedly corrected himself. Landucci recorded how 'They were robed in all their vestments, and each of these was taken off them one by one, with the appropriate words for the degradation.'

The second tribunal was led by Bishop Remolino, who then performed a ceremony exposing still further the duplicity of Alexander VI. Prior to the Papal Commissioners arriving at their judgement, and probably even prior to them setting out from Rome, His Holiness had issued Remolino with a Brief bestowing upon the three friars the pope's plenary indulgence. This granted them a formal pardon for all sins committed in this world, absolving them from punishment in purgatory in the next world. With this act of supreme papal hypocrisy completed, Remolino then formally handed over the three defrocked friars to the secular authorities within whose jurisdiction they now fell. This was the third tribunal, consisting of the Signoria, 'who immediately made the decision that they should be hanged and burnt ... then their faces and hands were shaved, as is customary in this ceremony.'†

The three condemned men, barefoot and clad only in their thin white undershifts, were then led from the terrace in front of the palazzo by two black-robed Compagni de' Neri, who accompanied them along the lengthy raised walkway that extended out into the piazza. At the end of this walkway was the circular platform with the gibbet, beneath which were heaped bundles of faggots and kindling wood in preparation for the bonfire.

---

* That is, the Church in heaven
† The two earliest printed Italian versions of Landucci (1865 and 1883, both Florence) refer to 'radendo loro el capo e mano' – that is, shaving the head and hands – thus specifically including their priestly tonsures.

From the sea of faces beneath them on either side of the walkway arose angry jeers, and some mockingly called out, 'Savonarola, now is the time to perform a miracle.' Evidence suggests that others, especially amongst the *Piagnoni*, were silently praying that he would do just this and would survive his execution.

The first to be led to the scaffold was Fra Silvestro. The hangman hurriedly ushered the condemned man up the steps to the top of the ladder leaning against the gibbet, placed the rope around his neck and then shoved him off the ladder so that he swung freely from the gibbet. The rope was too short, the noose not drawn tightly enough around his neck, and the iron chains wound around the condemned man's waist to weigh him down were insufficiently heavy, so that the hanging man remained choking. Landucci, who witnessed these events, described Fra Silvestro's fate: 'there not being much of a drop, he suffered for some time, repeating "Jesu" again and again while he was hanging there, for the rope was not drawn tight enough to kill him'. All this was intentional, so that the other two could be hanged beside him, and all three would still be alive when the fire was lit beneath them. Part of their punishment was that they would be able to feel the pain of the flames burning their flesh before they died.

The second to be hanged was Fra Domenico, who is said to have literally scampered up the ladder with a joyous expression on his face, ready to meet his maker. According to Landucci, he 'also kept saying "Jesu"' as he endured his similarly lengthy strangulation. Finally:

> the third was Savonarola, named as a heretic, who did not speak aloud, but to himself, and thus he was hanged. This all took place without final words being declaimed by any one of them. This was considered extraordinary, especially by good and thoughtful people, who were greatly disappointed, for everyone had been expecting some signs, and desired the glory of God, the beginning of the righteous life, the renovation of the Church, and the conversion of unbelievers. Yet not one of the condemned made any justification of their acts. As a result, many lost their faith.

Despite this disappointment, Guicciardini's description makes it plain that some people still had misgivings. He recorded that Savonarola's death:

which he suffered with unyielding fortitude without uttering a word either claiming his innocence or confessing his guilt. None of this altered anyone's opinion – either for or against him, or the strength of their feelings on this matter. Many viewed him as a charlatan; whilst on the other hand many were of the opinion that his public confession was simply a forgery . . . or that it had been falsely extracted from him after his frail body had been broken by the extremities of torture.

The execution did not end entirely without unexpected incident. Mention was made of the hangman sadistically jerking the rope around Savonarola's neck, causing his body to dance in the air and attempting to make a mockery of him before the crowd. Presumably it was this buffoonery which meant that the hangman was personally unable to complete the gruesome ceremony as intended. On the evidence of the paintings of this scene, the ladder leading to the top of the gibbet must have reached up well over twenty feet; however, before the executioner could descend the ladder to complete his task, a spectator had beaten him to it. A man with a lighted torch burst forward out of the surrounding crowd and set fire to the brushwood, yelling, 'Now at last I can burn the Friar who would have liked to burn me!'

As the fire quickly spread through the dried kindling on the circular platform around the cross, others in the front of the crowd began tossing little packets of gunpowder into the conflagration, causing small explosions and cascades of sparks. Just as the flames began to leap up into the air towards the hanging figures, a sudden wind blew up, forcing the flames away from their bodies. The crowd immediately began to back away from the fire exclaiming, 'A miracle! A miracle!' Yet the wind eventually dropped as suddenly as it had begun, and the crowd surged forward once more as the flames began to lick up around the bodies, sheathing them in fire. Burlamacchi, who certainly witnessed these events from a close vantage point, then goes on to describe how the fire burned through the rope securing Savonarola's hands behind his back, letting his arms fall free. The upward current of the fire then caught his right arm, raising it into the air, his hand opening dramatically, as if from amidst the flames he was blessing those who stood gazing up at him. This caused consternation amongst the many who witnessed it: women began sobbing hysterically, some fell to their knees, believing that they were being blessed by the man whom many had secretly believed to be a saint. Others simply fled from the piazza in fright and panic.

Yet not all were so overcome. The *Arrabbiati* had been determined to avoid any devotional scenes, and had hired groups of urchins to jeer and dance about the leaping flames. Some flung stones, which hit the dangling bodies being consumed by the flames, causing bits to fall from them down into the roaring heart of the fire. On orders from the Signoria, armed guards now formed a ring around the bonfire, forcing back the crowd, preventing spectators from gathering up any relics that might be removed. They were determined that Savonarola's execution should not be the beginning of a cult perpetuating his name and religious ideas. At the same time, further bundles of sticks were tossed into the fire, increasing its size and intensity.

The chains wrapped around the bodies were secured to the gibbet and kept them suspended, even as the fire burned through the ropes around their necks. While the flames consumed the bodies and organs of the condemned men, their limbs began to fall into the central inferno, leaving only glimpses of the blackened remains of their ragged torsos visible amidst the increasing conflagration. To make doubly sure that no relics could be obtained, Remolino took it upon himself to order the gibbet itself to be pushed over so that it fell into the fire, crashing down and carrying the blackened bodies with it. Remolino was in this instance acting beyond his jurisdiction: having passed on responsibility for the death-penalty to the civil authorities, these matters were now under the command of the Signoria. However, it seems that all in power were equally determined that Savonarola's death should put an end to both the man and all he stood for.

By this time the piazza had been cleared, and after the fire had cooled down the ashes were shovelled up into carts. When these had been filled, they were pushed down the street some 200 yards to the nearby Ponte

Vecchio, with the official mace-bearers lining either side of the carts to prevent any further attempts to secure relics. Here the cartloads of ashes were unceremoniously dumped into the waters of the Arno, their remnant dust-clouds gradually settling onto the surface, where they were carried off downstream by the current, over the weir and beyond the city walls, through the green Tuscan countryside towards the river mouth, where the waters dispersed into the sea.

Aftermath

SAVONAROLA'S PASSING was greeted with widespread relief, which soon gave way to hectic celebrations. The following month Landucci recorded how:

> everyone had begun indulging in degenerate behaviour, and at night-time one saw halberds or naked swords all over the city, with men gambling by candlelight in the *Mercato Nuovo* [New Market] and else-where without any shame. Hell seemed to have opened; and woe betide anyone who had the temerity to rebuke vice!

At the same time, the authorities launched a concerted attempt to extirpate Savonarola's teachings. Immediately after his execution, Bishop Remolino announced that anyone in possession of writings by Savonarola was to surrender them within four days or face excommunication. He then returned to Rome to deliver his official papal report, taking with him the beautiful young prostitute he had been given. The grateful Alexander VI would later reward Remolino by making him a cardinal.

The secular administration of Florence was purged of any remnant *Piagnoni* sympathisers. A number of other leading Savonarola supporters fled the city, though at least one remained. As much as any, Botticelli had found himself plunged into psychological turmoil by the struggle that had originated between Lorenzo the Magnificent and Savonarola. Vasari gave a last glimpse of the effect this had wreaked upon the genius whose radiant philosophical works had so enlightened the early Renaissance:

> As an old man, he became so poor that ... but for the support of friends he might have died of hunger ... Finally, having become old and useless, hobbling about supported by two sticks because he could no longer stand upright, he died infirm and decrepit.

Although the *Piagnoni* may have been humiliated, the citizens of Florence had no wish for a return to Medici rule. The more democratic Great Council, which Savonarola had done so much to instigate, had become a popular and respected element of the republican government, and Medici supporters too now found themselves out of favour. Such a clear-out of the old guard on both sides made way for a generation of talented new administrators. This included the young Machiavelli, who was voted into a senior post and proved so able that he was soon being sent abroad as a Florentine envoy.

Florence would remain militarily weak, under threat from Alexander VI and especially the army of his ruthless son, Cesare Borgia. In an attempt to remedy the situation, Machiavelli was hurriedly despatched as an envoy to the French court. Here he played a role in skilfully re-establishing Florence's close ties with the powerful new French king, Louis XII, thus continuing the policy advocated by Savonarola. This protected the city from invasion until the death of Alexander VI in 1503. Piero de' Medici died in the same year, but Cardinal Giovanni de' Medici had long cultivated the friendship of Alexander VI's rival, Cardinal della Rovere, who soon afterwards became the new pope, Julius II, and allowed Cardinal Giovanni to use the papal forces to retake Florence. However, within a few years the reinstated Medici rule proved so corrupt and unpopular that in 1527 it was overthrown in favour of a republic, which soon saw a re-emergence of Savonarolan fundamentalism, declaring itself the 'Republic of Christ'. This was eventually overthrown after a lengthy siege of the city by forces loyal to the Medici pope, Clement VII, which began in the fateful year of 1529, just as Savonarola is said to have predicted.

Lorenzo the Magnificent may have made the mistake of inviting Savonarola to return to Florence, yet the outcome of this invitation would not disrupt his secret long-term plans for extending Medici power far beyond the limits of the city state – plans that would see their fruition in later generations, when the Medici would become popes, and even rulers of France. The behaviour of two Medici popes – Leo X (the former Cardinal Giovanni) and Clement VII – would lead directly to the Reformation, which tore Christendom in two and changed the face of Europe

for ever. The controversial policies of the two Medici queens of France —
Catherine and Marie de Médicis — would be instrumental in preserving
the French nation as the single sovereign entity that consequently flourished as the most powerful country in Europe under the 'Sun King', Louis
XIV. If it had not been for Lorenzo the Magnificent and his ambitious
plans for his descendants, none of this might have happened. Indeed, the
history of Europe might well have taken an entirely different course.

In less than forty years the opposition between a quasi-benign but
corrupt capitalist system run by the leader of a family of powerful bankers
and an opposing fundamentalist who fulfilled a public longing for the
moral certainties of an earlier age, as well as for a more democratic egalitarian society, had moved far beyond the struggle between the Medici and
Savonarola within the city of Florence. By the time of Pope Clement VII
(1523–34) the Reformation was already well under way, and the reforms
that Savonarola advocated had split the unity of Christendom. Whilst
leading the Reformation, Martin Luther marked his admiration for
Savonarola by writing an introduction to his final 'Exposition', clearly
regarding him as a forerunner. Yet there were profound differences between
Savonarola and Luther. Savonarola believed in reforming the Church from
within, and would have viewed Luther as the worst form of heretical priest,
especially in the light of his marriage to a nun.

Following the Reformation, the dichotomy between a progressive materialism and the rule of spirituality would continue to underlie a number
of major revolutionary upheavals. In this, Savonarola had been ahead of
his time. Politically, his emphasis on democracy was undeniably modern.
Yet he was also arguably the first in modern Europe to face the problems
of leading a revolution where the euphoria of liberty was followed by
repression — in the name of maintaining the purity of the revolution, as
well as protecting it against its enemies. In the centuries following Savonarola,
this would become a virtually inevitable historical process, visible in one
form or another from the beheading of Charles I by the Puritans in England,
through to the French Revolution and Robespierre. This trend was still
recognisable in the twentieth century, from Lenin and the Bolsheviks in
Russia to the Ayatollahs in Iran. In the early years of the present century,
just as the struggle had spread beyond late fifteenth-century Florence to

embrace the whole of Europe, the modern variant of this clash between fundamentalism and materialism has spread beyond the nation state to become a worldwide phenomenon.

There was death in Florence – of Lorenzo the Magnificent, of citizens (from plotters to plague victims), of Savonarola. At the same time an entire era was dying, that of the Middle Ages. And as this old order died in Florence, it gave birth to the new: the full flourishing of the Renaissance and the modern political state.

Notes

Prologue: 'The needle of the Italian compass'

p.1 **'a fever [that] gradually ...'** *et seq.*: see Angelo Poliziano, *Letters* (in the original Latin and facing English), trans. & ed. Shane Butler (London, 2006), Book IV, Letter 2, p.231, 5. I have not adhered to Shane Butler's translation.

p.2 **Lazaro da Ticino**: appears in some sources as Lazzaro of Pavia, leading some people to confuse him with the renowned physiologist Lazzaro Spallanzani of Pavia, who lived in the eighteenth century.

p.3 **'museum of mummies'**: see Jacob Burckhardt, *The Civilization of Renaissance Italy*, trans. Middlemore (London, 1990), p.41

p.3 **'begat eight boys ...'**: epigram by the contemporary poet Marullus, cited in Latin in F. Ludwig von Pastor, *The History of the Popes*, ed. & trans. F. I. Antrobus, 40 vols (London, 1950 edn), Vol. V, p.240n.

p.3 **'Lorenzo was loved ...'**: Machiavelli, *Istorie fiorentine*, Book VIII, Sec. 36

p.4 **'so gentle it ...'**: cited in Christopher Hibbert, *The Rise and Fall of the House of Medici* (London, 1985), p.172

p.4 **'His great virtues ...'** *et seq.*: Machiavelli, *Istorie fiorentine*, Book VIII, Sec. 36

p.4 **'the needle of ...'**: this celebrated phrase is quoted in a wide number of sources. The actual Italian phrase is *ago di balancia*, which literally translates as 'the needle of the balancing scales', but the more poetic version referring to a compass has become the popularly accepted English translation, presumably because it is so apt. See, for instance, the entry on the Medici family in the celebrated 1911 edition of the *Encyclopaedia Britannica*, Vol. XVIII p.33, by the renowned Italian Renaissance scholar Pasquale Villari.

p.7 'the little friar': most sources mention Savonarola using this phrase; see, for instance, his latest biographer Lauro Martines, *Scourge and Fire: Savonarola and Renaissance Italy* (London, 2006), p.2

p.7 'using these very words . . .' *et seq.*: Fra Silvestro, the close adherent of Savonarola, is believed to have heard them from Savonarola himself; see *Lives of the Early Medici: As told in their correspondence*, trans. & ed. Janet Ross (London, 1910), p.340

p.8 'and restore . . .' *et seq.*: this meeting between Savonarola and the dying Lorenzo is discussed in varying detail by many authorities. See in particular William Roscoe, *The Life of Lorenzo de' Medici* (London, 1865), pp. 354–5, and Pasquale Villari, *La Storia di Girolamo Savonarola e de' suoi tempi*, 2 vols (Florence, 1887), Vol. I, pp.157–60, 182–6, who both refer to the original contemporary sources, as well as discussing their reliability.

p.9 'Lightning flies . . .': cited in Latin and English in Roscoe, *Lorenzo*, pp.368–9. I have not used Roscoe's translation.

1: A Prince in All but Name

p.11 In contemporary reports the year of Lorenzo's birth is given as 1448; this is because the Florentine New Year did not begin until the Feast of the Annunciation on 25 March. In this matter I have adhered to modern usage throughout.

p.12 'give way . . .': letter from Lucrezia to her husband, Piero de' Medici, dated 17 May 1446. See Ross, *Early Medici (correspondence)*, p.50

p.13 'theatrical performances . . .': see *History of the Popes*, ed. Antrobus, Vol. III, p.56, citing as his source the contemporary Giovanni de Pedrino, *Cronica di Forli*

p.13 'Lorenzo is learning . . .': letter from Lucrezia de' Medici to her husband Piero, 28 February 1458. See Ross, *Early Medici*, p.60

p.14 'by imitating . . .': letter from Marsilio Ficino to Lorenzo de' Medici, undated. See Ross, *Early Medici*, p.76

p.15 'to see him . . .': Machiavelli, *Istorie Fiorentine*, Book VIII, Sec. 36

p.15 'act as a man . . .' *et seq.*: letters from Piero de' Medici to Lorenzo in Milan, May 1465. See Ross, *Early Medici*, pp.93–5

p.15 Figures for the alum trade as a whole and the papal revenues of this period vary considerably. Mine are, in the main, extrapolated from Jean

Delameau, *L'Alun de Rome XVe–XIXe siècle* (Paris, 1962), as well as Raymond de Roover, *The Rise and Decline of the Medici Bank 1397–1494* (Harvard, 1963), who concentrates on the trading with Bruges and London. Two reliable facts indicate the overall size of the alum trade. In 1462, prior to the papal monopoly, the alum trade throughout Europe was in the order of 300,000 florins (Delameau p.19), while three years later the trade to Bruges and Venice combined amounted to 4,500 tons (Delameau, p.25).

p.16 'Put an end …': letter from Piero de' Medici to Lorenzo in Rome, March 1466. See Ross, *Early Medici*, pp.102–3

p.18 'I know nothing …': see de Roover, *Medici Bank*, p.365, citing as the original source the Report of Angelo Tani in the collection *Mediceo avanti il Principato* (in the State Archives of Florence), Filza 82, No.163

p.18 'I know the fickle …': this quotation appears in varying forms in many works; see, for instance, Hibbert, *Medici*, p.73. The original source is Cosimo's friend, the contemporary Florentine humanist Vespasiano di Bisticci.

p.19 'Messer Dietisalvi …' *et seq.*: Machiavelli, *Istorie fiorentine*, Book VII, Sec. 10

p.23 'When I see …': Lorenzo de' Medici, Sonnet V, opening '*Lasso a me! …*' see *The Autobiography of Lorenzo de' Medici The Magnificent*, trans. James Wyatt Cook (New York, 1995), pp.80–2. This has the Italian and English versions on facing pages: I have not adhered to Cook's translation.

p.24 'Lucretia [*sic*] was the mistress …': see Roscoe, *Lorenzo*, p.74

p.24 'Although neither …': cited in Cecilia M. Ady, *Lorenzo dei Medici and Renaissance Italy* (London, 1960), p.29. A copy of the few remaining pages of Lorenzo's *Ricordi* can be seen in the Florentine archives (*Publica Liberia Magliabechiana*). An Italian version, which differs slightly from this, can be found in Roscoe, *Lorenzo*, Appendix XI pp.464–7. Roscoe claims that he copied this from a version in Lorenzo's hand, which is now lost. For an English version, see Ross; *Early Medici*, pp.150–6. The *Ricordi* breaks off on 1 March 1485 (in fact, 1484 in the manuscript, which adhered to the ancient Florentine year that ended on 25 March).

p.25 'good height' *et seq.*: letter from Lucrezia de' Medici to her husband Piero, dated 'Rome 27 March 1467'. See Ross, *Early Medici*, p.108

p.25 'he who does not . . .': Machiavelli, *Istorie fiorentine*, Book VII, Sec. 11

p.26 'On the second day . . .': Lorenzo, *Ricordi*. See Roscoe, *Lorenzo*, Appendix XI, p.466

p.26 'I would like . . .': collation of letters written 1–4 December 1469 by Lorenzo de' Medici in Florence to Galeazzo Sforza, Duke of Milan – cited in Miles J. Unger, *Magnifico: Life of Lorenzo de' Medici* (New York, 2008), pp.168–9

p.27 'was greatly mourned . . .': Lorenzo, *Ricordi*. See Roscoe, *Lorenzo*, Appendix XI, p.466

p.27 'in as civil . . .': cited in Tim Parks, *Medici Money: Banking, Metaphysics and Art in Fifteenth-Century Florence* (London, 2006), p.199

p.28 'LAU.R.MED': cited in F.W. Kent, *Lorenzo de' Medici and the Art of Magnificence* (Baltimore, 2004), p.146

p.31 'because none could . . .': Angelo Poliziano, *Stanze Cominciate per la Giostra di Giuliano de' Medici* (Turin, 1954)

p.33 'Lorenzo, heady with youth . . .': Machiavelli, *Istorie Fiorentine*, Book VIII, Sec. 3

p.33 'With regard to this . . .': ibid., Book VIII, Sec. 2

p.35 'Therefore, with the blessing . . .': see Ross, *Early Medici*, p.229

p.35 'embittered and darkened . . .' *et seq.*: Jacob Burckhardt, *The Civilization of Renaissance Italy*, trans. S. Middlemore (London, 1990), pp.40–1

p.35 'without the sanction of . . .': document found amongst the Strozzi papers (Carte Strozziane Series I, No. 10, fols 190–1), cited in de Roover, *Medici Bank*, p.367

p.36 'It is likely . . .': ibid.

p.38 'We've all got cucumbers . . .': Lorenzo de' Medici, *Opere*, ed. A. Simioni (Bari, 1914), Vol. II, *Canti Carnascialeschi*, p.247

2: 'Blind wickedness'

p.39 'certain of the minor . . .': see Roberto Ridolfi, Vita di Girolamo Savonarola, 2 vols. (Florence, 1974), Vol. 1, p.14.

p.40 'a *cortège* of . . .': Villari, *La Storia . . . Savonarola* Vol. I, p.9–10, drawing on descriptions by contemporary chroniclers. Although the citation is from the original Italian version, I have here, and in some following instances, made use of the English translation undertaken with the author's supervision by his daughter Linda Villari. See Pasquale Villari, trans. Linda Villari (London, 1888), 2 vols.

p.40 'Borso was a . . .': Pius II, *Memoirs of a Renaissance Pope*, trans. F. Gragg (New York, 1959), p.114

p.41 'the giving of robes . . .': Michele Savonarola, *De Nuptiis Battibecco et Serrabocca*, cited in Edmund Gardner, *Dukes and Poets in Ferrara* (London, 1904), p.81

p.41 'subterranean dungeons . . .': Villari, *La Storia . . . Savonarola*, Vol. I, p.14

p.41 'That which God . . .': cited in Ridolfi, *Vita . . . Savonarola*, Vol. I, pp.5–6

p.42 'he was in the habit . . .': see Pacifico Burlamacchi, *La Vita del Beato Geronimo Savonarola* (Florence, 1937 edn), p.7. This comes from the anonymous sixteenth-century biography said to have been written by Fra Pacifico Burlamacchi (often called 'Pseudo-Burlamacchi', as many claim this was not his true identity). The author, whoever he was, knew Savonarola and his intimate circle, and probably either witnessed or heard much of his information at first hand. However, this short biography is not entirely reliable as it also includes several evident exaggerations and myths concerning its subject. Burlamacchi is one of the contemporary sources referred to in note to p.8.

p.43 'In the sadness . . .': the original version of this poem is cited in Ridolfi, *Vita . . . Savonarola*, Vol. I, p.10

p.44 Fra Benedetto of Florence: see *Vulnera diligentis* in Alessandro Gherardi, *Nuovi documenti e studi intorno a Girolamo Savonarola* (Florence, 1887), pp.7–8

p.44 'not had desire for . . .': Savonarola, *Prediche sopra Aggeo*, ed. L. Firpo (Rome, 1965), p.325

p.44 'lustfulness [and the] . . .': Savonarola's works abound in such sentiments: this particular instance is cited in Stanley Meltzoff, *Botticelli, Signorelli and Savonarola* (Florence, 1987), p.51

p.44 'the bloody . . .': Savonarola cited in Pierre Van Passen, *A Crown of Fire: The Life and Times of Girolamo Savonarola* (New York, 1960), p.29

p.44 'the partisans . . .': ibid., drawing on descriptions by contemporary chroniclers

p.45 'Caleffini reports . . .': ibid.

p.45 'Now those who live . . .': *et seq.*: Girolamo Savonarola, *A Guide to Right-eous Living and Other Works*, trans. Konrad Eisenbichler (Toronto, 2003), pp.62, 3

p.46 'Get thee out of . . .': Genesis, Ch.12, v.1 (King James version). Savonarola refers to this in a number of his sermons; see for instance *Predica XIX sopra Aggeo*, delivered on 19 December 1494. For the most part I have used the King James version of the Bible when translating Savonarola's references. This is of course anachronistic, as the King James translation would not be published in England until more than a century later; however, this version would seem best suited to convey the language and tone of Savonarola's words.

p.46 'truly this would have . . .': *et seq.*: Savonarola's letter to his father Niccolò, 25 April 1475. See Savonarola, *Le Lettere*, ed. Roberto Ridolfi (Florence, 1933), pp.1–3. There is an English version in Savonarola, *A Guide to Righteous Living . . .*, pp.35–7. Only the latter includes the address to his father.

p.47 'rejoice that God . . .': Savonarola, *Lettere*, p.4

p.47 'a strong man . . .': letter of 25 April 1475, ibid., p.1

p.48 'My son . . .': see Ridolfi, *Vita . . . Savonarola*, Vol. I, p.12, citing as his original source Fra Benedetto, *Vulnera Diligentis*, ms. nella Biblioteca Nazionale di Firenze, Magl. XXXIV. 7 (che si completa col Riccar-diano 2985), c. 13 t

p.48 'the silence which enveloped . . .': ibid., p.15

p.48 'where I found liberty . . .': ibid., p.16, citing several sources, including Burlamacchi and Giovanni Pico della Mirandola's *Vita*

p.49 'The sceptre has . . .': Ridolfi, Vita . . . Savonarola, Vol. I, p.9

p.50 'If the rapid . . .': Burckhardt, *Renaissance in Italy*, p.48

p.50 'long silent streets . . .': Charles Dickens, *American Notes and Pictures from Italy* (London, 1908), p.321

3: Lorenzo's Florence

p.59 'He uses the . . .': despatch of 29 July 1484 from Buonfrancesco Arlotti to Duke Ercole of Ferrara, cited in Gardner, *Dukes . . . in Ferrara*, p.207

p.59 'With great expense . . .': despatch of 12 August 1484 from Arlotti, cited ibid., p.208

p.60 'That same night ...': ibid., p.208

p.60 'Thus at last ...': Machiavelli, *Istorie Fiorentine*, Book VIII, Sec. 28

p.60 'Jesus, highest good ...': *et seq.*: Girolamo Savonarola, *Poesie, tratte dall' autographo*, ed C. Guasti (Florence, 1862), p.41

p.62 'mind and the radiance ...': Marsilio Ficino, *Opera*, ed. A. H. Petri (Basle, 1576), Vol. I, pp.834–5

p.62 'neither gravity ...': see Ronald Lightbown, *Sandro Botticelli* (London, 1978), Vol. I, p.72, citing A. Politian [Poliziano], *Prose volgari ineditedi e poesie ...*, ed. I. Del Lungo (Florence, 1867), pp.253–5

p.63 'thirteen leather bags': many sources mention these bags; see, for instance, Tim Parks, *Medici Money* (London, 2005), p.220, and Lauro Martines, *April Blood* (London, 2003), p.203

p.63 'Between May and September ...': de Roover, *Medici Bank*, p.366

p.64 'The city was in perfect ...': Francesco Guicciardini, *Storie fiorentine dal 1378 al 1509*, ed. Roberto Palmarocchi (Bari, 1931), p.72

p.68 'He was a man ...': cited in Roscoe, *Lorenzo de' Medici*, p.265

p.68 'fisher of men': cited in James Hankins, 'Marsilio Ficino', *Routledge Encyclopedia of Philosophy*, ed E. J. Craig, Vol. III, p.655

p.69 'not as a deserter' *et seq.*: cited in James Hankins, 'Pico della Mirandola', *Routledge Encyclopedia of Philosophy*, ed. E. J. Craig, Vol. VII, p.387

p.69 'piously philosophising': cited in Ridolfi, *Vita ... Savonarola*, Vol. I, p.69

p.70 One of his fellow ... *et seq.*: the following information on Savonarola's teaching and preaching, by his fellow monks and contemporaries, is taken from three contemporary sources: Savonarola's fellow monk, Placido Cinozzi, *Epistola*, p.10 *et seq.*, the contemporary historian of San Marco, Roberto Ubaldini, *Annalia* (Cronaco dell Convento di San Marco), p.153 *et seq.*, which was written in 1505; and Burlamacchi, *Savonarola* (1937 edn), p.16. Much of this information is more easily accessible in the English editions of the Villari and Ridolfi biographies. See Pasquale Villari, *Savonarola*, trans. Linda Villari (London, 1888), Vol. I, pp.71–3, and Roberto Ridolfi, *Savonarola*, trans. Cecil Grayson (London, 1959), pp.14–15, whose translations I have not followed precisely.

p.71 'I had neither ...' *et seq.*: Savonarola, *Prediche sopra l'Esodo*, ed. P. G. Ricci, Vol. I, p.50, and *Prediche sopra Ruth e Michea*, ed V. Romano, cited in Ridolfi, *Vita ... Savonarola*, Vol. I, p.26

p.72 'many reasons . . .': see the fifteenth-century document re the trial of Savonarola in the documents reprinted in Villari, *La storia . . . di Savonarola*, Vol. II, p.cxlix *et seq.*

p.72 'You should consider . . .': see letter 5 December 1485 in Savonarola, *Le Lettere*, ed. Ridolfi, pp.5–11

p.73 'Most honourable . . .' *et seq.*: ibid, pp.5–11

p.73 For the reasons Savonarola gave for the imminent scourge of the Church, as well as quotes from Savonarola's Latin notes for his 1486 sermons, which were discovered by Ridolfi, see Roberto Ridolfi, *Studi Savonaroliani* (Florence, 1935), pp.44–52. More readily available English accounts can be found in Ridolfi, *Savonarola* (trans. Grayson), pp.24–5, and Desmond Seward, *Savonarola and the Borgia Pope* (Stroud, 2006), p.45

p.74 'When I . . .' *et seq.*: Savonarola, *A Guide to Righteous Living . . .*, p.65

4: Securing the Medici Dynasty

p.76 'Be careful not . . .' *et seq.*: Letter from Lorenzo de' Medici to Piero de' Medici, 26 November 1484. See Ross, *Early Medici*, pp.260–5

p.78 'Not much is . . .': de Roover, *Medici Bank*, p.349

p.81 'He was wont . . .' *et seq.*: see Savonarola's sermon, cited in *Giovanni Pico della Mirandola: His life by his nephew Giovanni Francesco Pico translated from the Latin by Sir Thomas More* (London, 1890 edn), pp.26–7. Here I have modified More's sixteenth-century English for greater clarity.

p.82 'As a desyrous . . .': ibid., p.9, with the same qualification as above

p.83 'pleasant enough . . .': cited ibid., p.85

p.84 Slightly differing reports of this Arezzo incident appear in a number of biographies. See, for instance Eugenio Garin, *Giovanni Pico della Mirandola: Vita e Dottrina* (Florence, 1936), p.25, and Giovanni Semprini, *Giovanni Pico della Mirandola* (Todi, 1921), p.55 *et seq.* Both these sources cite the article by D. Berti in the journal *Rivista Contemporanea*, Vols. XVI–XVII (Turin, 1859), pp.49–51, docs I–III (one of which is *Antonimo Magliabechiano*). In English, see Seward, *Savonarola*, p.27

5: Pico's Challenge

p.86 A complete reprinted text of Pico's theses can be found in Giovanni Pico della Mirandola, *Conclusiones sive Theses DCCCC* (Geneva, 1973), pp.27–90

p.88 'maintain nothing . . .': see Pastor, *History of the Popes*, Vol. V, p.342

p.88 'on public . . .': Pico letter of 12 November 1486. See Chanoine Pierre-Marie Cordier, *Jean Pic de la Mirandole* (Paris, 1957), p.30

p.89 'heretical, rash, and . . .': see Pastor, *History of the Popes*, Vol. V, p.343

p.89 'in twenty nights': cited ibid.

p.89 'We have given . . .': G. Pico della Mirandola, *De hominis dignitate . . .*, ed E. Garin (Florence, 1942), Vol. I, pp.104, 6

p.91 'Pain in my feet . . .': cited in Hugh Ross Williamson, *Lorenzo the Magnificent* (London, 1974), p.262

p.91 'When the spirit escapes . . .': Roscoe, *Lorenzo*, p.308, n.41, gives the Italian version, though I have not adhered to Roscoe's translation

p.93 'This is the greatest . . .': letter from Lorenzo de' Medici to the Florentine ambassador in Rome, 14 March 1489. See Ross, *Early Medici*, p.303

p.93 'The Count della Mirandola . . .': letter from Lorenzo de' Medici to the Florentine ambassador in Rome, 19 June 1489. See Ross, *Early Medici*, p.310

p.94 'I much wish to . . .': letter from Lorenzo to the Florentine ambassador in Rome, 14 March 1489. See Ross, *Early Medici*, p.303

p.94 'So that you . . .': see Ridolfi, *Savonarola*, trans. Grayson, p.29. In this latest English translation (and the Italian original) the last-but-one word of the quotation reads 'your' (*vostra*): other sources relating this incident make it plain that Lorenzo must have been referring to 'our' seal – that is, the seal of the Medici. Pico's seal would have carried no authority with the Church at this time; indeed, it would certainly have undermined the request made in the letter. The original source of this quotation is an early version of Burlamacchi, *Vita del P.F. Girolamo Savonarola* (Lucca, 1764) – for full details of this, see Villari, *La Storia . . . Savonarola*, Vol. I, p.91 n.1. Except where indicated otherwise, from now on I have cited the Lucca 1764 edition of Burlamacchi, which is available in the British Library.

p.95 – 'that a scourge . . .' *et seq.*: see notes to pp. 72, 73 p.95 'to various cities . . .': letter dated 25 January 1490, Girolamo Savonarola, *Le Lettere*, ed. R. Ridolfi (Florence, 1933), pp.11–14

p.95 'In this way . . .': Savonarola, *Lettere*, p.12 *et seq.*

p.95 'when it is time . . .': ibid., pp.11–14

p.96 'he spoke with a voice . . .' *et seq.*: see Villari, *La Storia . . . Savonarola*, Vol. I, p.86, paraphrasing Burlamacchi, *Savonarola*, p.15

p.96 The four and twenty elders are described in Revelation, Ch. 4, v.4

p.96 'You must not be . . .': Savonarola, *Lettere*, pp.11–14

p.98 'Go and do the task . . .': see Burlamacchi, *Savonarola*, p.18

6: The Return of Savonarola

p.99 'for this delaye . . .': cited in Giovanni Francesco Pico della Mirandola, *Vita. . .* (trans. More), p.27

p.100 'Division of all the Sciences': see Villari, *La Storia . . . Savonarola*, Vol. I, p.108

p.101 'a man in whom God . . .': cited in Giovanni Francesco Pico della Mirandola, *Vita. . .* (trans. More), p.26

p.102 'I am the hailstorm . . .': Savonarola, *Prediche sopra Ruth e Michea*, ed. V. Romano (Rome, 1962), Vol. II, p.91. These and other collections of Savonarola's sermons are part of the Collected Works (*Edizione nazionale*), but as they are separate volumes and were issued at different dates, often with different editors, I have referred to them by their individual titles.

p.102 'he did not speak . . .': Francesco Guicciardini, *Storie fiorentine*, ed. R. Palmarocchi (Bari, 1931), p.108

p.102 'by all kinds of people': see Ridolfi, *Vita . . . Savonarola*, Vol. I, p.57, citing Girolamo Savonarola, *Compendio di rivelazioni*, ed A. Crucitti (Florence, 1933)

p.102 'I was unable . . .': ibid., p.58

p.102 'You fool . . .': ibid.

p.103 'a terrifying . . .': ibid.

p.103 'a time such as . . .' *et seq.*: see Seward, *Savonarola*, p.53, and Villari, *La Storia . . . Savonarola*, Vol. I, p.133 *et seq.*, both of whom cite their source as the autograph document by Savonarola known as *Compendium Revelationum* (for details of this, see Villari, *La Storia . . . Savonarola*, Vol. I, p.135 n.1)

p.103 'the preacher for . . .': see Ridolfi, *Vita . . . Savonarola*, Vol. I, p.56, citing

Savonarola, *Compendio di rivelazioni*, an Italian translation from the original Latin of some of the sheets contained in the above *Compendium*

p.103 'as a result ...': ibid. p.55

p.103 'which forces me ...': *et seq*.: Villari, *La Storia ... Savonarola*, Vol. I, pp.136–7, citing Documento VIII, p.xxxiii, which includes the entire sermon and is at the end of Vol. I

p.104 'I believe that Christ ...': cited in Martines, *Savonarola*, p.27

p.104 'a certain respect ...': Guicciardini, *Storie*, p.108

p.106 'a man eminent ...': see Poliziano *Letters* [Latin and English], Book IV, Letter 2, p.237

p.106 'The ultimate aim ...': see Villari, *La Storia ... Savonarola*, Vol. I, p.106, citing Girolamo Savonarola, *Compendium totius philosopiae tam ... moralis* (Venice, 1542), Book I, p.25

p.107 'I have met ...': Poliziano, cited in Ross Williamson, *Lorenzo*, pp.238–9

p.108 'musical voice ...': Poliziano, letter to Tristano Calco, cited in Villari, *La Storia ... Savonarola*, Vol. I, p.80

p.108 'Father, there is ...' *et seq*.: in a letter by his brother, the poet Girolamo Benivieni, to Clement VII, cited in Ridolfi, *Vita ... Savonarola*, Vol. I, pp.51–2

p.109 'I shall wax ...': cited in Latin in several sources: see Ridolfi, *Vita ... Savonarola*, Vol. I, p.65, citing as one of his sources Roberto Ubaldini, 'the future chronicler of San Marco'

p.109 'It is not for you ...': Acts, Ch. 1, vv.7–8

p.109 For the details and circumstances of Fra Mariano's sermon I have drawn on a variety of sources, including Villari, *La Storia ... Savonarola*, Vol. I, p.79 *et seq*., Ridolfi, *Vita ... Savonarola*, Vol. I, pp.64–5, and Seward, *Savonarola*, pp.55–6, as well as the two original sources from which they draw – namely, Burlamacchi, *Savonarola*, p.23 *et seq*., and Placido Cinozzi, *Epistola de vita et moribus Ieronimo Savonarola*, which can be found in P. Villari and E. Casanova, *Scelta di prediche e scritti di fra Girolamo Savonarola* etc. (Florence, 1887).

p.110 'You will not ...': see Ridolfi, *Vita ... Savonarola*, Vol. I, p.50, who cites the original Latin document reproduced in Villari, *La Storia ... Savonarola*, Vol. I, p. xxxiii, which pertains to 'after Easter 1491'. I have chosen a broad interpretation of this dating, which seems appropriate.

7: Cat and Mouse

p.111 'Who made me . . .' *et seq.*: Burlamacchi, *Savonarola*, p.24 *et seq.*

p.111 'A foreign monk . . .': ibid.

p.112 'Is he asking . . .': see Ridolfi, *Vita . . . Savonarola*, Vol. I, p.67, where he is paraphrasing Burlamacchi, *Savonarola*, p.24 *et seq.*

p.112 'This is . . .': my loose translation of the idiomatic Italian. See Ridolfi, *Vita . . . Savonarola*, Vol. I, p.68, citing Burlamacchi op. cit., p.25, and Cinozzi op. cit., p.13

p.113 'all his enemies met . . .': Machiavelli, *Istorie Fiorentine*, Book VIII, Sec. 36

p.113 'I know that you have . . .' *et seq*: this meeting is reported in the main biographies: see, for instance, Ridolfi, *Vita . . . Savonarola*, Vol. I, p.59, and especially Villari, *La Storia . . . Savonarola*, Vol. I, p.139, where note 3 gives a list of the many contemporary sources, which include Burlamacchi, Cinozzi and Benivieni op. cit.

p.114 'So great was the persecution . . .': see *The Autobiography of Lorenzo de' Medici: A commentary on my sonnets*, ed. & trans. James Wyatt Cook (Binghampton, 1995), Sonnet X, p.104. This has the Italian and English versions on facing pages; I have not adhered to Cook's translation.

p.115 'To prevent the . . .': see Ross, *Early Medici*, p.302

p.115 According to some sources . . . : see Parks, *Medici Money*, p.240. There is no doubt that Giovanni's education involved Lorenzo in considerable debts; however, there remains a suspicion that the particular sum mentioned here may in fact be Giovanni's debt of 7,500 florins with the Medici bank, referred to in de Roover, *Medici Bank*, p.370, which was outstanding two years later in 1494.

p.118 'accusing Lorenzo of . . .': see Ross Williamson, *Lorenzo*, p.261

p.118 'These great men . . .': see Roberto Ridolfi, *Studi Savonaroliani* (Florence, 1935), p.100; a note identifies this sermon as having been preached on the Saturday after the second Sunday in Lent.

p.119 'the whole city . . .': cited in Ross Williamson, *Lorenzo*, p.209

p.119 '30 loads of gifts . . .': Luca Landucci, *Diario Fiorentino dal 1450 al 1516*, ed. I del Badia (Florence, 1883), p.63

p.120 'to have changed . . .': ibid. p.209

p.120 'I recommend that . . .' *et seq.*: letter from Lorenzo de' Medici, March

1493, in *Laurentii Medicis Magnifici Vita (Adnotationes et Monumento)*, 2 vols (Pisa, 1784), Vol. II, p.308 *et seq.* A more readily available complete English version can be found in Ross, *Early Medici*, pp.332–5.

p.121 'one is foolish . . .': cited in de Roover, *Medici Bank*, p.370

p.123 '5th April . . .': Landucci, *Diario*, p.63

p.123 'That night Savonarola . . .': Ridolfi, *Vita . . . Savonarola*, Vol. I, pp.73–4

p.123 'on the night . . .' and following footnote: see Girolamo Savonarola, *Compendium Revelationum*, in Giovanni Francesco Pico della Mirandola, *Vita R.P.Fr. Hieronimi Savonarolae Ferrarensis Ord. Predicatorum*, ed. J. Quétif (Paris, 1674), Vol. I, p.231, and Girolamo Savonarola, *Compendio di rivelazioni*, ed. F. Buzzi (Casale Monferrato, 1996), p.47. For Villari's argument, see his *La Storia . . . Savonarola*, Vol. I, pp.154–6; for his vision date, see ibid., p.165.

p.124 'Pico arrived to see . . .' *et seq.*: Poliziano, *Letters*, pp.236–8

p.125 'and restore what has . . .' *et seq.*: see note to p.8

8: The End of an Era

p.128 'On the night . . .': Poliziano, *Letters*, p.248

p.128 'people heard wolves . . .': Guicciardini, *Opere* (Milan, 1998), p.190

p.128 'there were many . . .': Machiavelli, *Istorie fiorentine*, Book VIII, Sec. 36

p.128 'Besides these incidents . . .': Roscoe, *Lorenzo*, pp.359–60

p.130 'In the eyes of the world . . .': Landucci, *Diario*, p.54

p.131 'the people of Florence . . .': Machiavelli, *Istorie fiorentine*, Book VIII, Ch. 36

p.131 'It is now generally . . .': de Roover, *Medici Bank*, pp.372–3

p.132 'a sermon is preached . . .': Landucci, *Diario*, p.53

p.132 'Each morning in . . .': written by Niccolò Guicciardini, 13 April 1492. See Ridolfi, *Studi Savonaroliani*, p.264

p.132 'a black cross . . .' *et seq.*: this is a brief paraphrase, which is collated by Villari from Savonarola's own Latin and Italian versions; see Villari, *La Storia . . . Savonarola*, Vol. I, p.167. The Latin version can be found in Savonarola, *Compendium Revelationum*, which is included in Gianfrancesco Pico della Mirandola, *Vita R. P. F. Hieronimi* p.231 *et seq.* and an Italian version can be found in Savonarola, *Compendio di rivelazioni*, ed. Buzzi (Rome, 1996), pp.244–5

p.133 'All of Florence . . .': letter written by Bernardo Vettori, 7 May 1492, see Ridolfi, *Studi Savonaroliani*, p.107

p.135 'he could still . . .': Ascanio Condivi, *Vita di Michelangelo* (Milan, 1928), p.192

p.135 **become an exceptional preacher** *et seq*.: many contemporary sources, from Machiavelli and Poliziano to Condivi, comment upon Savonarola's sermons and his manner of preaching. Concerning his change of accent, as well as the development of his preaching style, see for instance Martines, *Savonarola*, pp.95–6, as well as a host of references in the standard biographies by Villari and Ridolfi.

p.140 **the dismissal of Soderini and Rucellai**: this is mentioned in Meltzoff, *Botticelli . . . Savonarola*, p.256. For the most part, precise details can only be gleaned obliquely; see, for instance, Donald Weinstein, *Savonarola and Florence* (Princeton, 1970), p.121

9: Noah's Ark

p.142 'is so ill-assembled . . .': see Villari, *La Storia . . . Savonarola*, Vol, I, p. 200. The offending Latin text was published more than forty years later in Girolamo Savonarola, *Reverendi P. Fra Hieronymi Savonarole in primam D. Joannis epistolam . . .* [Bernardini Stagni edition] (Venice, 1536)

p.142 '**Savonarola spoke in . . .**': this apparent paraphrase from Savonarola's sermons appears in Villari, *La Storia . . . Savonarola*, Vol. I, p.200

p.142 '**The length of the ark . . .**': Genesis, Ch. 6, v.15

p.143 '**each day he . . .**': Villari, *La Storia . . . Savonarola*, Vol. I, p.201

p.143 '*Gladius Domini . . .*' *et seq*.: Savonarola, *Compendium Revelationum*, pp.229–31

p.144 'he shall take . . .': cited in Seward, *Savonarola*, p.67

p.144 'I will go . . .': Isaiah, Ch. 45, v.2

p.145 'O Lord, we . . .': see Villari, *La Storia . . . Savonarola*, Vol. I, p.199. This is a paraphrase from Savonarola, '*Prediche sul Salmo* Quam bonus' (Prato, 1846), sermon XXIII, 562–79. The latter is a reprint of the original summaries made in Latin by Savonarola himself after delivering these sermons. According to Villari, ibid. p.188n., 'These sermons were later translated and published in an amended form by Girolamo Gianotti during the sixteenth century.' Interestingly, the Ottoman threat and the possibility of God making use of the Turks as his scourge was not 'amended' by Gianotti in the light of the later French invasion, which appeared to so many to fulfil Savonarola's prophecy.

p.147 'he gave up . . .': Giorgio Vasari, *Lives of the Artists*, trans. George Bull (Harmondsworth, 1965), Vol. I, p.227

p.147 'in mind alone . . .': cited in Ridolfi, *Vita . . . Savonarola*, Vol. I, p.146. There are many similar expressions of Savonarola's intellectual admiration for Pico.

p.148 'a previously undiscovered . . .': see Ridolfi, *Vita . . . Savonarola*, Vol. I, p.147

p.148 'From this we learn . . .': ibid. For Ridolfi's unimpeachable sources, see Vol. II, p.549 n.11, where he goes into considerable detail concerning Sinibaldi's notes, which appear in the margins of a copy of Domenico Benivieni, *Defensione* [of Savonarola] (Florence, 1496), which is conserved in the *Collezione Guicciardiniana* 3.7.91, at the Biblioteca Nazionale di Firenze.

p.149 'According to . . . the future chronicler . . .': see Ridolfi, *Vita . . . Savonarola*, Vol. I, p.147, 65

p.149 'advice and judgement': cited in Ridolfi, *Vita . . . Savonarola*, Vol. I, p.148. For further information on Savonarola's participation, see ibid., Vol. II, pp.349–50 n.13.

10: A Bid for Independence

p.152 'a life of sanctity . . .': Savonarola, *Le Lettere* (ed. Ridolfi), p.33

p.152 'He intended . . .': this is taken from Ridolfi, *Vita . . . Savonarola*, Vol. I, pp.101–2, who cites as his sources Alessandro Gherardi, *Nuovi documenti e studi intorno a Girolamo Savonarola* (Florence, 1887), p.61 *et seq.*, and Burlamacchi, *Savonarola* (1937 edn), p.51 *et seq.*

p.153 'When we have completed . . .': ibid.

p.154 'it is my intention . . .': Savonarola, *Le Lettere* (ed. Ridolfi) p.30

p.157 'At all times . . .': letter from Lorenzo de' Medici, March 1493, in *Laurentii Medicis Magnifici Vita (Adnotationes et Monumento)*, 2 vols (Pisa, 1784), Vol. II, p.308 *et seq.* A more readily available complete English version can be found in Ross, *Early Medici*, pp.332–5.

p.157 '[Cardinal] Rodrigo Borgia . . .': see Pastor, *History of the Popes*, Vol. V, p.385b, citing as 'the annalist' the contemporary historian Piero Parenti, *Storie fiorentine*, a work that was later edited and published. Pastor consulted the original document, which can be found in the Codex Magliabecchi, XXV, 2, 519, f.133b in the National Library, Florence.

p.158 'Now we are in . . .': this remark is cited in various forms in numerous sources. See, for instance, Seward, *Savonarola*, p.64; James Reston Jr, *Dogs of God* (New York, 2005), p.287; and the authoritative and respected late Michael Mallett, *The Borgias* (London, 1969), p.128 (where an unfortunate editorial error has resulted in a misleading compression).

p.159 For confirmation of the unlikely scene between Cardinal Caraffa and Alexander VI, see, for instance, Ridolfi, *Vita . . . Savonarola*, Vol. I, p.95, who cites several contemporary accounts (see Vol. II, p.526 n.24), including Cinozzi, *Epistola . . .*, p.12; Burlamacchi, *Savonarola* (1937 edn), p.56; and Ubaldini, whose history of San Marco cites Cardinal Caraffa himself.

p.160 'If you had arrived . . .': cited in Burlamacchi, *Savonarola* (1937 edn), p.56

p.160 'Have charity . . .': these traditional last words are cited in Villari, *La Storia . . . Savonarola*, Vol. I, p.177 n.1, where he gives several biographical and documentary sources

p.161 For general financial details of this period, see de Roover, *Medici Bank*; Parks, *Medici Money*; and Niall Ferguson, *The Ascent of Money* (London, 2008)

p.162 '*vivae vocis* . . .': cited in Ridolfi, *Vita . . . Savonarola*, Vol. I, p.102, giving his sources as Gheraradi, *Nuovi documenti . . .*, p.61 *et seq.*, and Burlamacchi, *Savonarola* (1937 edn), p.51 *et seq.*

p.163 'Hebrew, Greek . . .': cited in Villari, *La Storia . . . Savonarola*, Vol. I, p.178 n.2, where he gives Burlamacchi, *Vita del P. F. Girolamo Savonarola* (Lucca, 1764), p.44 *et seq.*, as his source

p.165 'A rumour quickly spread . . .' *et seq.*: see Ridolfi, *Vita . . . Savonarola*, Vol. I, p.113, citing as his source the contemporary eyewitness Alessandro Bracci, in a letter dated 23 June 1493. For further details, see Vol. II, p.232 n.32. I have used Bracci's sentences in a different order purely to preserve the time sequence.

p.166 'They contain ...': see the English edition, Roberto Ridolfi, *The Life of Girolamo Savonarola*, trans. C. Grayson (London, 1959), p.70

11: 'Italy faced hard times ...'

p.167 'Italy faced hard ...': Machiavelli, *Decennale Primo*, lines 1–3

p.167 There are many contemporary references to the general situation and historic developments in Italy, and especially in Florence, during the vital period 1493–4. See, for instance, the works of Guicciardini, Machiavelli, Landucci and Cerretani. I have made use of these, as well as the many more general descriptions written since: see, for instance, Paul Strathern, *The Medici*.

p.168 'boasted that the Pope ...': this remark was recorded by the contemporary Venetian historian Domenico Malipiero, *Annali Veneti* (Florence, 1843 edn), p.482

p.168 'For they sow ...': Hosea, Ch. 8, v.7

p.169 '20th January ...': Landucci, *Diario*, pp.66–7.

p.170 The incident of the snow carvings is mentioned by Vasari and Condivi, both of whom were contemporaries of Michelangelo and knew him personally. For an easily accessible English reference, see for instance Michael Holroyd, *Michael Angelo Buonarotti* (which contains in translation *The Life of Michelangelo* by Ascanio Condivi, London, 1911), pp.12–13 (Ch. 1, Sec. 11)

p.171 'a horde of ...' *et seq.*: Dante, *Inferno*, Canto XV

p.171 'perverse vices ...': Dante Aligheri, *Hell*, trans. Dorothy L. Sayers (Harmondsworth, 2001 edn), Canto XV, commentary p.97

p.171 'We heard that ...': Landucci, *Diario*, p.67

p.173 'the least deranged ...': cited in Jean Cluzel, *Anne de France* (Paris, 2002), p.31, giving as his source the early French historian Pierre de Brantôme, who was born some twenty years after the death of Anne of France.

p.175 'Lorenzo and Giovanni ...': Landucci, *Diario*, pp.67–8.

p.175 'a delegation of form ...': this is a paraphrase compiled from both sources. See eq. Landucci, *Diario*, p.68–9

p.177 'the fleet of the King ...' *et seq.*: Landucci, *Diario*, pp.69–70

p.178 'the prime mover of ...': Machiavelli, *Decennale Primo*, line 51 p.178 'Italy faced hard times . . .': Machiavelli, *Decennale Primo*, lines 1–3, 4–6, 16

12: 'I will destroy all flesh'

p.179 'I will destroy all flesh': Genesis, Ch. 6, v.17 (Revised Standard version)

p.180 'For Behold . . .': ibid.

p.180 'Lo, the sword . . .': see Bartolomeo Cerretani, *Storie Fiorentine*, p.12, which appears in J. Schnitzer, *Zur Geschichte Savonarolas* (Munich, 1904), Vol. III

p.180 'Everyone walked . . .': Cerretani, *Storie Fiorentine* (Schnitzer), p.12

p.183 'This small picture . . .': see Vasari, *Lives of the Artists* (trans. Bull), Vol. I, p.231, for a readily available original Latin version. I have not adhered to Bull's translation.

p.183 'Although he was . . .': Guicciardini, *Opere* (Bari, 1931), Vol. VI, p.63

p.184 'a young man of . . .': *Mémories de Philippe de Commynes*, ed. Mlle Dupont (Paris, 1843), Vol. II, p.336

p.184 'behind his hand . . .': ibid. p.340

p.184 'A rumour was . . .': Guicciardini, *Opere*, p.444

p.185 'with regard to . . .': see *Mémoires de Philippe de Commynes*, ed. Dupont, Vol. II, pp.348, 352, and Philippe de Commynes, *Mémoires*, ed J. Calmette & C. Durville (Paris, 1925), Vol. III, pp.52, 56–7

p.185 'that Lorenzo de' Medici . . .' *et seq.*: Condivi, *Vita di Michelangelo* (Milan, 1928), pp.50, 54

p.186 'if the place had . . .' Commynes, *Mémoires*, ed. Calmette, Vol. III, p.53

p.186 'those who . . .': ibid. p.56

p.186 'He told [Piero] that . . .' *et seq.*: ibid. pp.55–6

p.187 'All the girls . . .': Mantuan envoy to Florence, cited in Hibbert, *Medici*, p.185

p.187 'Before there was . . .' *et seq.*: Savonarola, *Prediche sopra Aggeo*, ed. Luigi Firpo (Rome, 1965), p.12

p.189 'During the course . . .': see Ridolfi, *Vita . . . Savonarola*, Vol. I, pp.121–2, where he paraphrases Savonarola, *Compendio di rivelazioni*, c.6

p.189 'A Dominican friar . . .': Mantuan envoy to Florence, cited in Hibbert, *Medici*, p.185

p.189 'that it is time . . .': Cerretani, *Storie fiorentine*, p.11

p.190 'a man of holy . . .': ibid.

p.193 'We're finished!': cited in Martines *Savonarola*, p.38

p.193 'forbidding anyone . . .' *et seq.*: Landucci *Diario*, pp.75–6

p.196 'Another proclamation . . .': Landucci, *Diario*, p.75

13: Humiliation

p.197 'seigneur de Balsac': see Commynes, *Mémoires* (ed. Calmette) Vol. III, p.66

p.197 'began pillaging . . .': ibid., p.67

p.197 'it was believed . . .': ibid., p.67 n.1

p.197 'others were behaving . . .': *et seq.*: ibid., p.67

p.198 'Black scorch marks . . .': Niall Ferguson, *The Ascent of Money* (London, 2008), p.27

p.199 'the Medici bank brought . . .' *et seq.*: de Roover, *Medici Bank*, p.370

p.200 'small in stature . . .': *et seq.*: Guicciardini, *Opere*, Vol. I, p.68

p.200 'At last you have arrived, O King! . . .' *et seq.*: see Commynes, *Mémoires* (ed. Calmette), Vol. III, p.145; also Ridolfi, *Vita . . . Savonarola*, Vol. I, Ch. 10, opening pages; Guicciardini, *History of Florence*; Savonarola, *Compendium Revelationum* et al. The words I have used are a compilation from these sources.

p.201 'the boat of true . . .' *et seq.*: see Martines, *Savonarola*, pp.55–6, paraphrasing and then citing Savonarola, *Prediche sopra Aggeo* (ed Firpo), pp.80–2. The reference to 'Camaldoli' is on Martines, p.43, from Cerretani.

p.202 'Girolamo Tornabuoni . . .': see Landucci, *Diario*, p.76

p.203 'There was great cause . . .': Villari, *La Storia . . . Savonarola*, Vol. I, pp.242–3

p.203 '*Viva Francia!* . . .' *et seq.*: all the main histories of the period describe the French entry into Florence. The best eyewitness reports, which mostly concur, are Cerretani, Landucci and Parenti, who are cited by historians ranging from Villari and Martines to Hibbert and myself (here and in *The Medici*). For the French point of view, see also John S. C. Bridge, *A History of France from the Death of Louis XI*, Vol. II, *The Reign of Charles VIII*, p.149 *et seq.*

p.204 'My brother . . .': *Lettres de Charles VIII*, ed. P. Pélicier (Paris, 1930), Vol. IV, pp.111–12

p.205 'A gang of . . .': see Villari, *La Storia . . . Savonarola*, Vol. I, pp.250–1, who has collated various contemporary sources, in particular Parenti and Cerretani

p.206 'only divine providence ...': Piero Parenti, *Storie fiorentine*, Vol. I, 1476–8, 1492–6 (Florence, 1994), p.142

p.206 'and all the while ...': Landucci, *Diario*, p.82

p.206 'We will have to sound ...' *et seq*.: the same applies to this famous incident as to the French entry into Florence. Contemporary sources such as Landucci, Cerretani, Guicciardini et al. allude to the treaty and the circumstances surrounding its signing, differing only in detail. Subsequent histories carry the same story, with much the same words, which have become fixed in legend.

p.208 'It is not me ...': This speech is paraphrased in Landucci, *Diario*, pp.87–8, and mentioned in several other contemporary accounts, though its original source is Savonarola, *Prediche XXVI sopra Ruth e Michea*.

p.208 'beneath the pious ...': see Ridolfi, *Vita ... Savonarola*, Vol. I, p.42

p.209 'if he had lived ...': cited in Ridolfi, *Vita ... Savonarola*, Vol. I, p.149; see also *Pico: His life ...* (trans. More), p.26

p.210 'the object of as much ...': see Villari, *La Storia ... Savonarola*, Vol. I, p.257, citing Parenti, *Storie Fiorentine*

p.210 'The scientists used ...' *et seq*.: *Daily Telegraph*, 7 February 2008

14: A New Government

p.211 'Florence was stripped ...': Guicciardini, *Opere*, ed. F. Palamanocchi (Bari, 1931), Vol. VI, p.105

p.211 'When Charles VIII ...': Guicciardini, *Opere* (Milan, 1998), p.208

p.212 'an election ...': Landucci, *Diario*, p.89

p.212 'Anyone who had ...': Guicciardini, *Opere*, ed. F. Palmanocchi (Bari, 1931), Vol. VI, p.101

p.212 'although they had ...': ibid., p.25

p.213 '12th December (Friday) ...': Landucci, *Diario*, p.91

p.213 'They decided that ...': Guicciardini, *Opere*, (Milan, 1998), p.209

p.213 'there were always ...' *et seq*.: Landucci, *Diario*, pp.94, 90, 92

p.214 '*Jesus Christus* ...' *et seq*.: see Seward, *Savonarola*, pp.94, 96, citing Savonarola, *Predica XIII sopra Aggeo* p.214 'the people no longer . . .' *et seq.*: Villari, *La Storia . . . Savonarola*, Vol. I, pp.265–6

p.215 For details of the Great Council, see Villari, *La Storia . . . Savonarola*, Vol. I, pp.285–7

p.215 'one-fifth of the male population . . .': Gene Brucker, *Renaissance Florence* (New York, 1968), p.268

p.215 'to encourage . . .': Guicciardini, cited in Villari, *La Storia . . . Savonarola*, Vol. I, p.287

p.216 'it so broadened . . .': see Lightbown, *Botticelli*, Vol. I, p.133

p.216 'went on discoursing . . .' *et seq.*: Landucci, *Diario*, p.93

p.217 'The new Signoria . . .': ibid., p.78

p.217 'government introduced . . .': letter from Savonarola, written 1495–6, cited in Seward, *Savonarola*, p.95

p.218 'in Italy . . .': see Savonarola, *Predica XIII sopra Aggeo* (12 December 1494)

p.218 'This wretched priest . . .': Landucci, *Diario*, p.97

p.220 'because he had . . .': *et seq.*: Commynes, *Mémoires*, ed. Calmette, Vol. III, pp.144–5

p.221 'a most peculiar . . .': Ridolfi, *Vita . . . Savonarola*, Vol. I, p.197

p.221 'We have heard you . . .': for the text of this letter, see Villari, *La Storia . . . Savonarola*, Vol. I, Documento XXIII

p.222 'firstly, because . . .': for the full text of this letter, see Savonarola, *Le Lettere* (Ridolfi), pp.55–8, also Villari, *La Storia . . . Savonarola*, Vol. I, Documento XXIV

p.222 'last sermon' *et seq.*: see Savonarola, *Prediche XXVI sopra i Salmi*, ed. Vincenzo Romano, 2 vols (Rome, 1969–74)

p.225 'The Lord has placed me . . .': *et seq.*: for the Latin version, see Girolamo Savonarola, *Compendium Revelationum*, in Giovanni Francesco Pico della Mirandola, *Vita R.P.Fr. Hieronimi* (ed. Quétif). For a modern Italian version, see Girolamo Savonarola, *Tratto sul governo della Città di Firenze (Casale Monferrato, 1996)*, which includes the *Compendio di rivelazione* (ed. Fausto Sbaffoni), pp.37–161. For English citations, see Herbert Lucas, *Fra Girolamo Savonarola* (London, 1906), pp.49–73; E. L. S. Horsborough, *Girolamo Savonarola* (London, 1911), pp.88–91; David Weinstein, *Savonarola and Florence* (Princeton, 1970), pp.116–8; and Seward, *Savonarola*, pp.140–5

15: The Voices of Florence

p.232 'at the *Dogana* ...' *et seq.*: Landucci, *Diario*, pp.112, 114

p.232 'though we may use ...' *et seq.*: Martines, *Savonarola*, p.149

p.233 'On 24 May ...': Landucci, *Diario* (1883 edn), p.106

p.233 'There are many enemies ...': see Savonarola's letter of 31 July 1495, cited in full in Villari, *La Storia ... Savonarola* (1887), Vol. I, Doc. XXIV, pp. cv–cvii

p.234 'both sides of human ...' Jakob Burckhardt, *Die Kultur der Renaissance in Italien* (1926 Leipzig edn), p.119

p.235 'When Michelangelo returned ...': Condivi, *Vita di Michelangelo* (1928), pp. 59–60

p.235 'all the slenderness ...': Giorgio Vasari, *Le Vite dei piu eccelenti pittori, scultori e architetti*, 4 vols, ed. Carlo L. Ragghianti (Milan, 1943–7), Vol. III, p.410

p.236 'the miracle of how ...': ibid., Vol. III, p.411

p.236 'Botticelli became such an ...': ibid., Vol. I, p.869

16: 'A bolt from the blue'

p.239 'a bolt from ...': see Ridolfi, *Vita ... Savonarola*, Vol. I, p.202

p.240 'the prior and Monastery ...': and further citations from this Brief, see Savonarola, *Le Lettere* (ed. Ridolfi), pp.231–3

p.240 '*gratia recuperandae* ...': see Ridolfi, *Vita ... Savonarola*, Vol. I, p.204, citing his source as *Codice Magliabechiano*, XXXV, 190. This receipt was not dated.

p.241 'no less than ...': from a sermon preached on 18 February 1498. See Savonarola, *Prediche sopra l'Esodo*, 2 vols, ed. Pier Giorgio Ricci (Rome, 1955–6), Vol. I, p.47

p.241 'With regards to prophecy ...' *et seq.*: see Savonarola, *Le Lettere*, pp.61–73

p.242 'Thus the accusations ...': see Ridolfi, *Vita ... Savonarola*, Vol. I, p.207

p.242 'I am well aware ...': cited in Villari, *La Storia ... Savonarola*, Vol. I, p.404

p.243 'The time for mercy ...' *et seq.*: from sermons delivered on 11 and 18 October 1495, cited in Savonarola, *Prediche spora i Salmi*, Vol. II, p.191 *et seq.*, p.218 *et seq.*

p.243 'Pray to God ...': ibid., Vol. II, p.241

p.243 'We command you . . .': for the full text of this papal Brief, see *Nuovi Documenti e Studi intorno a Girolamo Savonarola*, ed. Alessandro Gherhardi (Florence, 1887), pp.390–1

p.246 'some of my sons . . .': Landucci, *Diario*, p.125

p.246 'Some boys took . . .' *et seq.*: ibid, pp.123–4

p.247 'was also said . . .': cited in Martines, *Savonarola*, p.285.

p.247 'Even in the face . . .': ibid.

p.247 '16 February . . .': *et seq.* Landucci, *Diario*, pp.124–5

p.249 'Bliss was it . . .': William Wordsworth, *The Prelude* (London, 1926), Book XI, lines 108–9, p.401

p.249 'steps for Savonarola's boys . . .': Landucci, *Diario*, pp.125–6

p.250 'In you, young men . . .' *et seq.*: sermon delivered on 17 February 1496, see Savonarola, *Prediche sopra Amos a Zaccaria*, ed. P. Ghigglieri, 3 vols (Rome, 1971–2)

p.250 'the high priests of Rome . . .': *et seq.*: ibid., sermon 24 February

p.251 'The light will vanish . . .': ibid., sermon 23 March

p.251 'It is you who are . . .' *et seq.*: ibid., sermon 10 April

p.252 'Throughout this time . . .' *et seq.*: Landucci, *Diario*, pp.131–3

p.254 'Come to my next . . .': cited in Seward, *Savonarola*, p.158

p.255 'If I coveted . . .': sermon delivered on 20 August 1496. See Savonarola, *Prediche sopra Ruth e Michea*

p.255 'In many places . . .': Landucci, *Diario*, p.138

p.256 'that twelve ships . . .': ibid., p.139

17: The Bonfire of the Vanities

p.259 'The price of corn . . .' *et seq.*: Landucci, *Diario*, pp.143–4

p.260 'vanities', 'dead hair', etc.: such terms recurred frequently in Savonarola's Lenten sermons, which in 1497 were on Ezekiel (see note to p.262 below)

p.260 'which are painted . . .': see Savonarola, *Prediche sopra Amos*, sermon XIII, delivered on 6 March 1496

p.262 'monstrous image': see Villari, *La Storia . . . Savonarola*, Vol. I, p.505

p.262 'Thus saith the Lord . . .': Ezekiel, Ch. 25, vv.16–17

p.263 'Friars have a proverb . . .' *et seq.*: Savonarola, *Prediche sopra Ezechiele*, ed. Roberto Ridolfi, 2 vols (Rome, 1955), Vol. II, p.59

p.264 'My Lord secretary . . .': see Gherardi, *Nuovi documenti . . .*, p.151 *et seq.*

p.266 'condemning him as . . .': Parenti, cited in Ridolfi, *Vita . . . Savonarola*, Vol. I, p.277

p.266 'the death of his son . . .': see Savonarola, *Prediche sopra Ezechiele*, Vol. I, p.286

p.266 'More than one . . .' *et seq.*: Landucci, *Diario*, p. 145

p.267 'The city is more . . .': cited in Ridolfi, *Vita . . . Savonarola*, Vol. I, p.278, who gives as his original source Antonio Capelli, *Fra Girolamo Savonarola e notizie intorno al suo tempo*, in *Atti della Deputatzione di Storia Patri per le provincie Modensi e Parmensi*, Vol. IV (1868), pp.301–406

p.268 'imposed his views . . .': see Seward, *Savonarola*, citing Guicciardini, *Storie Fiorentine*, p.152

p.269 'We suspected a plot . . .': *et seq.*: Landucci, *Diario*, p.145.

p.269 'The price of corn . . .' *et seq.*: Landucci, *Diario*, p.146.

p.270 '27th April. We heard that . . .': *et seq.*: ibid., p.147

p.272 'He here abandoned . . .': *et seq*: see Villari, *La Storia . . . Savonarola*, Vol. II, pp.9–11, where Villari paraphrases the evidence given by Lamberto dell'Antella in *Documenti I*, which can be found at the back of Vol. II

p.273 'The outrage against . . .': cited in Villari, *La Storia . . . Savonarola*, naming as his source Gherardi, *Nuovi Documenti*, pp.84–6

18: 'On suspicion of heresy'

p.274 'a number of . . .' *et seq.*: Landucci, *Diario*, pp.147–8

p.276 'broke it and . . .': ibid., p.151

p.276 'on suspicion of heresy . . .' *et seq.*: see Alexander VI's papal Brief of Excommunication, Villari, *La Storia . . . Savonarola*, Vol. II, Documento V, pp.xxxix–xl

p.277 excommunication . . . bell, book and candle: literally the exclusion from the right to take Holy Communion. The Christian rite derives from the earlier Old Testament exclusion from the synagogue (see Ezra, Ch. 10, v.8). Examples in the New Testament appear, for instance, in Matthew, Ch. 18, v.17, and several times in the writings of St Paul (e.g. 1 Corinthians, Ch. 5, v.5 and 1 Timothy, Ch. 1, v.20). The ritual evolved through the centuries, but retained the same essentials.

p.277 'To All Christians . . .' *et seq.*: Savonarola, *Le Lettere*, pp.141–5 p.278 'The *palio* of Santa Barbara . . .': *et seq.*.: see Landucci, *Diario*, pp.152–5, which cover the entries for June and July 1497

p.282 '10 August . . .': ibid., p.156

p.283 'the Palace that night . . .': cited in Martines, *Savonarola*, p.194, giving Cerretani as his source.

p.284 'Franceso Valori at last . . .': see Guicciardini, *Opere* (Bari, 1931), Vol. VI, p.142, also cited from a different original edition by Martines, *Savonarola*, pp.195–6. I have collated these translations.

p.284 'in the hours leading . . .': see Martines, *Savonarola*, p.195

p.285 'Everyone was astonished that . . .': Landucci, *Diario*, pp.156–7

p.285 'Plague broke out . . .': ibid., p.154

p.286 'Thus, my Giovambattista . . .': Savonarola, *Le Lettere* (Ridolfi), p.178 *et seq*

p.286 'For the time being . . .': see Villari, *La Storia . . . Savonarola*, Vol. II, p.xxxv, where this letter from Paolo Somenzi to the Duke of Milan is reprinted amongst the documents

p.287 'So great was the esteem . . .': see Ridolfi, *Vita . . . Savonarola*, Vol. II, p.315, citing Parenti, *Storie fiorentine*, who in turn attributes these words to the contemporary priest and sculptor Ambogio della Robbia

p.287 'We will not rely . . .': *et seq.*: Girolamo Savonarola, *Trionfo della Croce* (Siena, 1899). This includes the Latin and Italian versions on facing pages, in very short chapters that are frequently only a page or two long. My quotes are taken from the last lines of the Prologue, the beginning of Chapter 1, and Chapter 2.

p.289 'the mutable, restless . . .' *et seq.*: cited in Villari, *La Storia . . . Savonarola*, Vol. II, p.99, giving as his source Savonarola, *Trattato circa il regimente il governo della città di Firenze*, Part 1

19: Open Defiance

p.291 'At this time . . .' *et seq.*: Landucci, *Diario*, p.161

p.291 'when he received . . .' *et seq.*: letter from Manfredo Manfredi to the Duke of Ferrara, dated 1 February [1498]; see Ridolfi, *Vita . . . Savonarola*, Vol. I, pp.319–20

p.292 'total and free . . .': see Gherardi, *Nuovi Documenti*, p.175

p.292 'As soon as Savonarola . . .': Savonarola, *Prediche sopra l'Esodo*, ed. P. G.

Ricci, 2 vols, (Rome, 1955), Vol. I, p.3, preamble to first sermon (Predica 1)

p.292 'Lord, I who am but ...' *et seq.*: ibid., Vol. I, pp.3, 18

p.293 'Many people went ...' *et seq.*: Landucci, *Diario*, pp.161–2

p.294 'be maimed ...': cited in Martines, *Savonarola*, p.1, giving as his source Lorenzo Violi, *Le giornate*, ed. G. C. Carfagnini (Florence, 1986), pp.73–4. Later direct Martines quote also from p.1

p.294 'I am being attacked ...' despatch from Bonsi to Florence dated 17 February [1498]. See Gherardi, *Nuovi Documenti* ... , p.178

p.295 'expressing himself ...' *et seq.*: despatch from Bonsi to Florence dated 25 February [1498]. See Gherardi, *Nuovi Documenti* ... p.180

p.296 'A big stack ...': Landucci, *Diario*, pp.130–1

p.296 'A great council ...': Guicciardini, *Opere* (Bari, 1923), Vol. VI, p.146

p.297 'As for this Brief ...': cited in Ridolfi, *Vita ... Savonarola*, Vol. I, p.332 giving his source as Clementi Lupi, *Nuovi Documenti inorno a fra Girolamo Savonarola*, Archivo Storico Italiano (Florence, 1842), Third Series, Vol. III (1866), Part 1, pp.3–77

p.297 'whose influence with ...': Guicciardini, *Opere* (Bari, 1929), Vol. I, pp.295–6

p.297 'At last a great ...' *et seq.*: Guicciardini, *Opere* (Bari, 1931), Vol. VI, p.146

p.299 'because of three furies ...': cited in Marsilio Ficino, *The Antichrist Girolamo of Ferrara ...*, ed. & intro. by Volkhard Wels (Texas, 2006), Introduction p.11, citing as the original source Marsilio Ficino, 'Letter to Aldus Manutius', dated 1 July 1497

p.299 'Apology of Marsilio ...' *et seq.*: see Ficino, *The Antichrist*, p.26

p.299 'For such boasters ...': ibid., p.27; Corinthians, Ch. 2, vv.13–15

p.300 'the profound sense ...' *et seq*: Lightbown, *Botticelli*, Vol. I, p.130

p.301 'The time to avenge our disgrace ...': cited in Villari, *La Storia ... Savonarola*, Vol. II, pp.132–3, where p.132 n.1 discusses the many sources for this letter, of which he considers the most authentic to be Riccardi, Codex 2,053

p.301 'Savonarola then proceeded ...' *et seq.*: Villari, *La Storia ... Savonarola*, Vol. II, p.133

20: The Tables Are Turned

p.305 'I entreat each one ...': Savonarola, *Prediche sopra l'Esodo*, cited in Pastor, *History of the Popes*, Vol. VI, p.41

p.306 'Fra Domenico preached ...' *et seq.*: Landucci, *Diario*, p.167

p.306 'his quarrel was with ...': cited in Villari, *La Storia ... Savonarola*, Vol. II, pp.138–9; p.139 n.1 gives an elaboration of the contemporary sources.

p.307 'If Savonarola enters ...': ibid., p.139, citing the contemporary diarists Burlamacchi and Cerretani as his sources

p.308 'The Church of God ...': ibid., p.140 n.2 for Latin text

p.309 'for this will surely result ...': *et seq.*: highly similar, but not always identical, accounts of the meeting of the Pratica on 30 March 1498, as well as the attributed quotes, appear in all the main biographies. See, for instance, Villari, *La Storia ... Savonarola*, Vol. II, p.142 *et seq.*; p.144 n.1 discusses the contemporary sources and their reliability. I have also been guided by Ridolfi and Martines (who cites *Consulte e pratiche della republica fiorentina, 1498–1505*, ed. Denis Fachard, 2 vols (Geneva, 1993), Vol. I, pp.64–5).

p.312 'The day having ...': Francesco Guicciardini, *Opere*, Vol. VI, *Storie fiorentine* (Bari, 1931), p.149

p.313 'all the wood ...': Landucci, *Diario*, p.135

p.314 'Those who know themselves ...': see Villari, *La Storia ... Savonarola*, Vol. II, pp.147–8, which cites the entire document. The autograph draft is in the codex of San Marco, sheet 168. This original manuscript is undated, but internal evidence confirms it as being written during the early days of the week preceding the date set for the ordeal.

p.314 'In the event that ...': cited in Villari, *La Storia ... Savonarola*, Vol. II, p.150, where n.2 gives full details of the original source in the Florentine archives.

21: Ordeal by Fire

p.317 'I cannot be sure whether ...': cited in Villari, *La Storia ... Savonarola*, Vol. II, pp.152–3. See *Esortazione fatta al popolo in San Marco il di 7 Aprile 1498*, which is included at the end of his *Prediche sopra l'Esodo (Sermons on Exodus)*

p.317 'And then came the Dominicans ...': Landucci, *Diario*, p.169

p.318 'of fiery red velvet': cited in Martines, *Savonarola*, p.226, giving as his original source Parenti, *Storie fiorentine* (Schnitzer), p.257

p.318 'engaged in an extraordinary . . .': ibid.

p.318 'The Franciscans were afraid . . .': Guicciardini, *Opere*, Vol. I, p.150

p.319 'was most wicked' *et seq.*: cited in Martines, *Savonarola*, p.228

p.319 'The patience of the multitude . . .' *et seq.*: see Villari, *La Storia . . . Savonarola*, Vol. II, pp.157–8. This account makes use of the detailed descriptions in Lorenzo Violi, *Le giornate*, ed. G. C. Carfagnini (Florence, 1986) and Fra Benedetto [of Florence] Luschino, *Vulnera diligentis*, ed. S. dall'Aglio (Florence, 2002), as well as Burlamacchi, *Savonarola*, while others such as Landucci also confirm these events. Fra Benedetto and Violi confirm Salviati's threatening words. These several descriptions vary in minor details, especially with regard to the order of some events, but Villari's would seem to be the most considered and vivid summary.

22: The Siege of San Marco

p.323 'the benches were already . . .': cited in Martines, *Savonarola*, p.232, giving Cerretani as his source

p.323 'began to strike the backs . . .': Landucci, *Diario*, p.170

p.323 'Let's get the Friar . . .': many contemporary sources record variations of these cries: see, for instance, Landucci, *Diario*, p.170; Burlamacchi, *Savonarola*, p.156

p.323 'making it impossible . . .' *et seq.*: Landucci, *Diario*, p.170

p.324 'Twelve breastplates . . .': see Villari, *La Storia . . . Savonarola*, Vol. II, p.ccxxxiii

p.326 'rebuffed with every villainy . . .': cited in Martines, *Savonarola*, p.234, giving as his source Parenti, *Savonarola* (Schnitzer), p.265

p.326 'Let me go forth . . .' *et seq.*: cited in Villari, *La Storia . . . Savonarola*, Vol. II, pp.166–7, using as his sources the original documents printed at the end of Vol. II, in this case *Documento* XXVIII, especially those sections relating to Fra Silvestre on p.ccxx *et seq.* and Alessandro Pucci on p.cclxxiij [*sic*] *et seq.* These are largely confirmed by Burlamacchi and other contemporaries.

p.326 'got out of *San Marco* secretly . . .' *et seq.*: Landucci, *Diario*, pp.170–1

p.327 'It was an extraordinary sight . . .' *et seq.*: see Villari, *La Storia . . .*

Savonarola, Vol. II, p.166. Here, and in the following description, Villari has conflated a number of contemporary reports, relying heavily upon that of Fra Benedetto, who was one of the armed monks.

p.328 'Every word that I have ...': Fra Benedetto Luschino, *Cedrus Libani*, ed. P. V. Marchese, *Archivo Storico Italiano*, App. VII (Florence, 1849), pp.82–6

p.329 'Should not the shepherd ...': cited in Villari, *La Storia ... Savonarola*, Vol. II, p.175, giving his contemporary sources as Burlamacchi, Violi and Fra Benedetto (who was present at the time)

p.329 'We agree to hand over ...': cited in Seward, *Savonarola*, p.245, giving as his source Burlamacchi, *Savonarola* (Lucca, 1764), p.144

p.329 'Behold the true ...' *et seq.*: ibid.

23: Trial and Torture

p.331 'People laid down ...' *et seq.*: Landucci, *Diario*, pp.171–2

p.332 'At the ninth hour ...': Landucci, *Diario*, p.172

p.334 'It gave us the greatest pleasure ...': Gherardi, *Nuovi documenti*, p.231

p.338 'Regarding my aim ...' *et seq.*: cited in Martines, *Savonarola*, p.250. One of the corrupted versions of Ser Ceccone's transcript was printed as *I processi di Girolamo Savonarola* (Florence, 1498). This was republished in Florence in 2001 under the editorship of Ida G. Rao *et al.*

p.338 'I strongly ...': cited in Seward, *Savonarola*, p.250

p.339 'No, I did not ...': cited in Villari, *La Storia ... Savonarola*, Vol. II, pp.195–6, giving as his source Document XXVI of the end of the same volume, which contains what purported to be an entire printed version of Savonarola's interrogations, now and later.

p.339 'for the sake ...': see Seward, *Savonarola*, p.251, paraphrasing the original text

p.339 'I intended to ...' *et seq.*: see above, and other sources such as Martines, etc.

p.339 'formalise and set ...': cited in Savonarola, *Vita ... Savonarola*, Vol. I, p.374

p.340 'If you publish ...' *et seq.*: cited in Ridolfi, *Vita ... Savonarola*, Vol. 1, p.374, giving as his source Burlamacchi, *Savonarola* (1937 edn), p.171. See n.47 in Vol.2, p.645 for Ridolfi's comments.

p.340 'The protocol of ...' *et seq.*: Landucci, *Diario*, p.173

p.341 'without torture or ...': *I processi* ... (ed. Rao), p.25

p.341 'The *frate* was ...': Landucci, *Diario*, p.174

p.341 'in some places there ...': cited in Ridolfi, *Vita* ... *Savonarola*, Vol. I, p.378, giving as his orginal source his own edition of the trials: *I processi del Savonarola*, ed. R. Ridolfi, in La Bibliofilia Vol. XLVI (1944), p.30

p.342 'consecrated the bread ...' *et seq.*: *I processi* ... (ed. Rao), p.25

p.342 'My intention, as I have said ...': ibid., p.27

p.343 'It was not my intention ...': ibid., pp.28–9

p.343 'In the certainty ...' *et seq.*: cited in Villari, *La Storia* ... *Savonarola*, Vol. II, p.207. The complete deposition of Fra Domenico's trial can be found at the end of Vol. II as Document XXVII.

p.344 'I have always thought ...': cited in Seward, *Savonarola*, p.252

p.344 'the true document ...': Villari in *La Storia* ... *Savonarola*, Vol. II, p.cxcix. Villari gives the sources of these documents in note 1 for each of them.

p.344 'When they read ...': ibid., pp.205–6

p.345 'on twenty or twenty-five ...': ibid., p.210, giving as his source the deposition of Fra Silvestro's trial which is printed at the back of this volume as Document XXVIII

p.346 'Not only ourselves ...': ibid., p.213. The Latin original of this letter can be found in F.-T. Perrens, *Jérome Savonarole d'après les documents originaux et avec des pièces justificatives en grande partie inédites* (Paris, 1856), Document XVII

p.347 'All the citizens arrested ...' *et seq.*: Landucci, *Diario*, p.174

p.348 'both on account of the way ...': cited in Villari, *Savonarola* (trans. L. Villari), Vol. II, p.399–400, giving as his original source Florentine Archives, Register, Sheet 86 t. This also appears in Lupi, *Nuovi Documenti*.

24: Judgement

p.350 'Unfortunate am I ...': cited in Ridolfi, *Vita* ... *Savonarola*, Vol. I, pp.385–6

p.350 'Miserere mei ...': Psalm 51, v.1

p.351 'Verily I say ...': Mark, Ch. 14, v.30

p.351 'But these questions ...': cited in Ridolfi, *Vita ... Savonarola*, Vol. I, pp.385–6

p.351 'extraordinary fortune' *et seq.*: Ridolfi, *Vita ... Savonarola*, Vol. II, p. 650 n.8

p.352 'An exposicyon after ...': see British Library, catalogue no. c.52, f.16.(2.)

p.352 'Death to the friar!' *et seq.*: these words appear in varying forms in the main biographies, such as Villari and Ridolfi, citing as their original source Burlamacchi, *Savonarola*, p.154

p.353 'observed how [Savonarola] would ...': see Seward, *Savonarola*, p.251

p.353 'Remolino ordered that ...' *et seq.*: see Villari, *La Storia ... Savonarola*, Vol. II, p. clxxxvij *et seq.* Amongst the documents printed at the back of Vol. II is the complete transcript of Savonarola's third trial, which runs from p.clxxxiv to p.cxcviij. Slightly differing versions of this transcript appear in *I processi ...* (ed. Ridolfi) pp.3–41, and the modern version in *I processi ...* (ed. Rao), of which I have also made use

p.353 'such things as Ser Ceccone ...': Ridolfi, *Vita ... Savonarola*, Vol. I, p.391

p.356 'for history rarely produces ...' *et seq.*: see Burlamacchi, *Savonarola*, pp.151–2. Indicatively there is no remaining original document of this meeting in the Florentine archives.

p.356 'Sandro, do you want ...': see Doc. 13 (b) in Lightbown, *Botticelli*, Vol. I, pp.169–70: original source *Estratto della Cronaca di Simone Filipepei*, which is in the Archivo Segreto Vaticano, Politicorum, XLVII, fol. 338 *et seq.*

p.356 'when his trial ...' *et seq.*: *I processi ...* (ed. Rao), p.43

p.357 'If this friar ...' *et seq.*: cited in Villari, *La Storia ... Savonarola*, Vol. II, p.234, giving as his original source Burlamacchi, *Savonarola*, p.154

p.357 'He confesses to inciting citizens ...' *et seq.*: this report was signed by both Torriani and Remolino, but is generally accepted as being written, at least for the most part, by Remolino. Versions of this entire report to Alexander VI, which differ in medieval Latin spelling and details of text, can be found in A. G. Rudelbach, *Savonarola und seine Zeit* (Hamburg, 1835), pp.494–7, and Fra Karl Meier, *Girolamo Savonarola aus grossen Theils handschriftlichen Quellen* (Berlin, 1836), pp.389–91. My citations are selected from the beginning of the latter.

p.357 'as heretics and schismatics ...': cited in Ridolfi, *Vita ... Savonarola*, Vol. I, p.293, giving as his original source the document appended to the end of the third trial: see Villari, *La Storia ... Savonarola*, Vol. II, p.cxcviij

p.358 '22 May. It was decided ...': Landucci, *Diario*, p.176

25: Hanged and Burned

p.359 'Collect up from my cell ...': Burlamacchi, *Savonarola*, p.155

p.361 'I hear that you have ...' *et seq.*: ibid., pp.156–7

p.361 'The account of his last ...': Roberto Ridolfi, 'Savonarola' entry, *Encyclopaedia Britannica* (2002 edn), Vol. X, p.485

p.361 'It was already well ...' *et seq.*: Villari, *La Storia ... Savonarola*, Vol. II, pp.238–9. The source of the story and the quote are Burlamacchi, *Savonarola*, pp.157 and 193.

p.362 'do not seem credible ...': ibid., p.239 n.1

p.362 'A multitude of people ...': Guicciardini, *Opere* (Bari, 1929), Vol. I, p.298

p.362 'the ceremonies lasted ...': cited in Martines, *Savonarola*, p.274, giving as his contemporary source Piero Vaglienti, *Storia dei sui tempi 1492–1514* ed. G. Berti *et al.* (Pisa, 1982), p.48

p.363 'I separate you from ...' *et seq.*: cited in Ridolfi, *Vita ... Savonarola*, Vol. 1, p.400. The initial incident is recorded in slightly differing forms by several contemporary sources, such as Iacopo Nardi, *Istorie di Firenze*, 2 vols, ed. A. Gelli (Florence, 1848), Vol. I, p.136, and Simone Filipepi, *Estratto della Cronaca*, in P. Villari and E. Casanova, *Scelta di prediche e scritti di fra Girolamo Savonarola* (Florence, 1898), p.504 *et seq.*

p.363 'They were robed in all ...': *et seq.*: Landucci, *Diario*, p.177

p.364 'Savonarola, now is ...': cited in Ridolfi, *Vita ... Savonarola*, Vol. I, p.402

p.364 'there not being ...' *et seq.*: Landucci, *Diario*, pp.177–8

p.365 'which he suffered ...': Guicciardini, *Opere* (Bari, 1929), Vol. I, p.298

p.365 'Now at last ...': Burlamacchi, *Savonarola*, pp.161–2

p.365 'A miracle ...': Burlamacchi, *Savonarola*, p.162

Aftermath

p.368 'everyone had began ...': Landucci, *Diario*, p.181

p.368 'As an old man ...': Vasari, *Le Vite*, Vol. I, pp.869, 871

Bibliography

Cecilia M. Ady, *Lorenzo dei Meici and Renaissance Italy* (London, 1960)

Archivo Segreto Vaticano, Politicorum

Ascanio Condivi, *Vita di Michelangelo* (Milan, 1928)

Domenico Benivieni, *Tratto . . . in defensione . . . Ieronimo da Ferrara* (Florence, 1496)

John S. C. Bridge, *A History of France from the Death of Louis XI, Vol. II, 'The Reign of Charles VIII*

Gene Brucker, *Renaissance Florence* (New York, 1968)

Jacob Burckhardt, *The Civilization of Renaissance Italy*, trans. Middlemore (London, 1990)

Jakob Burckhardt, *Die Kultur der Renaissance in Italien* (1926 Leipzig edn)

Burlamacchi, *Vita del P. F. Girolamo Savonarola* (Lucca, 1764)

Pacifico Burlamacchi, *La Vita del Beato Geronimo Savonarola* (Florence, 1937 edn)

Antonio Capelli, *Fra Girolamo Savonarola e notizie intorno al suo tempo*, in *Atti della Deputatzione di Storia Patri per le provincie Modensi e Parmensi*, Vol. IV (1868)

Giovanni Cavalcanti, *Istorie Fiorentine* (Florence, 1838)

Lettres de Charles VIII, ed. P. Pélicier (Paris, 1930)

Jean Cluzel, *Anne de France* (Paris, 2002)

Codice Magliabechiano (Florentine Archives)

Philippe de Commynes, *Mémoires*, ed. J. Calmette & C. Durville (Paris, 1925)

Mémoires de Philippe de Commynes, ed. Mlle Dupont (Paris, 1843)

Chanoine Pierre-Marie Cordier, *Jean Pic de la Mirandole* (Paris, 1957)

Dante Aligheri, *Hell*, trans. Dorothy L. Sayers (Harmondsworth, 2001 edn)

Jean Delameau, *L'Alun de Rome XVe–XIXe siècle* (Paris, 1962),

Charles Dickens, *American Notes and Pictures from Italy* (London, 1908)

Niall Ferguson, *The Ascent of Money* (London, 2008)

Marsilio Ficino *The Antichrist Girolamo of Ferrara . . . ed. & intro. Volkhard Wels (Texas, 2006)

Marsilio Ficino, *Opera*, ed. A. H. Petri (Basle, 1576)

Consulte e pratiche della republica fiorentina, 1498–1505, ed. Denis Fachard, 2 vols (Geneva, 1993)

Edmund Gardner, *Dukes and Poets in Ferrara* (London, 1904)

Eugenio Garin, *Giovanni Pico della Mirandola: Vita e Dottrina* (Florence, 1936)

Alessandro Gherardi, *Nuovi documenti e studi intorno a Girolamo Savonarola* (Florence, 1887)

Francesco Guicciardini, *Opere* (Milan, 1998)

Francesco Guicciardini, *Storie fiorentine*, ed. Roberto Palmarocchi (Bari, 1931)

John S. Harford, *The Life of Michael Angelo Buonarotti* (London, 1857)

Christopher Hibbert, *The Rise and Fall of the House of Medici* (London, 1985)

Michael Holroyd, *Michael Angelo Buonarotti* (which contains in translation *The Life of Michelangelo* by Ascanio Condivi) (London, 1911)

E. L. S. Horsborough, *Girolamo Savonarola* (London, 1911)

Domenico Malipiero, *Annali Veneti* (Florence, 1843 edn)

F. W. Kent, *Lorenzo de' Medici and the Art of Magnificence* (Baltimore, 2004)

Luca Landucci, *Diario fiorentino dal 1450 al 1516* (Florence, 1883)

Luca Landucci, *A Florentine Diary from 1450 to 1516*, trans. Alice Jervis (London, 1927)

Ronald Lightbown, *Sandro Botticelli*, 2 vols. (London, 1978)

Herbert Lucas, *Fra Girolamo Savonarola* (London, 1906)

Lucian, *Works*: Loeb edition in 8 vols., Greek with facing-page translation into English by A. M. Harmon (London, 1913)

Clementi Lupi, *Nuovi Documenti inorno a fra Girolamo Savonarola*, Archivo Storico Italiano (Florence, 1842)

Fra Benedetto Luschino, *Cedrus Libani*, ed. P. V. Marchese, *Archivo Storico Italiano*, App. VII (Florence, 1849)

Fra Benedetto [of Florence] Luschino, *Vulnera diligentis*, ed. S. dall'Aglio (Florence, 2002)

Niccolò Machiavelli, *Istorie fiorentine* (Florence, 1971)

Niccolò Machiavelli, *Discorsi* (Florence, 1971)

Niccolò Machiavelli, *Opere*, ed. F. Flora (Rome, 1949–50)

Michael Mallett, *The Borgias* (London, 1969)

Domenico Malipiero, *Annali Veneti* (Florence, 1843 edn)

Lauro Martines *April Blood* (London, 2003)

Lauro Martines, *Scourge and Fire: Savonarola and Renaissance Italy* (London, 2006)

Laurentii Medicis Magnifici Vita (Adnotationes et Monumento), 2 vols. (Pisa, 1784)

The Autobiography of Lorenzo de' Medici: A commentary on my sonnets, ed. and trans. James Wyatt Cook (Binghampton, 1995)

BIBLIOGRAPHY

Lorenzo de' Medici, *Opere*, ed. A. Simioni (Bari, 1914), Vol II, *Canti Carnascialeschi*

Lives of the Early Medici: As told in their correspondence, trans. & ed. Janet Ross (London, 1910)

Fra Karl Meier, *Girolamo Savonarola aus grossen Theils handschriftlichen Quellen* (Berlin, 1836)

Stanley Meltzoff, *Botticelli, Signorelli and Savonarola* (Florence, 1987)

Iacopo Nardi, *Istorie di Firenze*, 2 vols. ed. A. Gelli (Florence, 1848)

Piero Parenti, *Storie fiorentine*, ed. A. Matucci (Florence, 1994)

Tim Parks, *Medici Money: Banking, Metaphysics and Art in Fifteenth-Century Florence* (London, 2006)

F.-T. Perrens *Jérome Savonarole d'après les documents originaux et avec des pièces justificatives en grande partie inédites* (Paris, 1856)

Gianfrancesco Pico della Mirandola, *Vita R. P. Fr Hieronimi Savonarolae Ferrarensis Ord. Praedicatorum*, ed. J. Quétif (Paris, 1674)

Giovanni Pico della Miradola, *Conclusiones sive Theses DCCCC* (Geneva, 1973)

Giovanni Pico della Mirandola: His life by his nephew Giovanni Francesco Pico translated from the Latin by Sir Thomas More (London, 1890 edn)

Pius II, *Memoirs of a Renaissance Pope*, trans. F. Gragg (New York, 1959)

A. Politian [Poliziano], *Prose volgari inedite e poesie . . .*, ed. I. Del Lungo (Florence, 1867)

Angelo Poliziano, *Letters*, ed. & trans. by Shane Butler (London, 2006)

Angelo Poliziano, *Stanze Cominciate per la Giostra di Giuliano de' Medici* (Turin, 1954)

James Reston Jnr., *Dogs of God* (New York, 2005)

Roberto Ridolfi, *Studi Savonaroliani* (Florence, 1935)

Roberto Ridolfi, *Vita di Girolamo Savonarola*, 2 vols. (Florence, 1974)

Rivista Contemporanea Vols. XVI–XVII (Turin, 1859)

Raymond de Roover, *The Rise and Decline of the Medici Bank, 1397–1494* (Harvard, 1963)

William Roscoe, *The Life of Lorenzo de' Medici* (London, 1865)

Hugh Ross Williamson, *Lorenzo the Magnificent* (London, 1974)

Routledge Encyclopedia of Philosophy, ed. E. J. Craig Vols. 3 & 7

A. G. Rudelbach, *Savonarola und seine Zeit* (Hamburg, 1835)

Girolamo Savonarola, *A Guide to Righteous Living and Other Works*, trans. Eisenbichler (Toronto, 2003)

Girolamo Savonarola, *Compendio di rivelazioni*, ed. A. Crucitti (Florence, 1933)

Girolama Savonarola, *Compendium totius philosopiae tam . . . moralis* (Venice, 1542)

Girolamo Savonarola, *Le Lettere*, ed. Roberto Ridolfi (Florence, 1933)

Girolamo Savonarola, *Poesie, tratte dall'autographo*, ed. C. Guasti (Florence, 1862)

Girolamo Savonarola, *Prediche sopra Aggeo*, ed. L. Firpo (Rome, 1965)

Girolamo Savonarola, *Prediche sopra Amos a Zaccaria*, 3 vols., ed. P. Ghigglieri (Rome, 1971–2)

Girolamo Savonarola, *Prediche sopra l'Esodo*, ed. P. G.Ricci (Rome, 1962 *et seq.*)

Girolamo Savonarola, *Prediche sopra l'Esodo*, 2 vols., ed. Pier Giòrgio Ricci (Rome, 1955–6)

Girolamo Savonarola, *Prediche sopra Ezechiele*, 2 vols., ed. Roberto Ridolfi, (Rome, 1955)

Girolamo Savonarola, *Prediche sopra Ruth e Michea*, ed. V. Romano (Rome, 1962)

Girolamo Savonarola, *Prediche sul Salmo Quam bonus* (Prato, 1846)

Girolamo Savonarola, *Reverendi P. Fra Hieronymi Savonarole in primam D. Joannis epistolam . . .* [Bernardini Stagni edition] (Venice, 1536)

Girolamo Savonarola, *Tratto sul governo della Città di Firenze* (Casale Monferrato, 1996)

Girolama Savonarola, *Trionfo della Croce* (Siena, 1899)

Giovanni Semprini, *Giovanni Pico della Mirandola* (Todi, 1921)

Francesco de Ser Barone, *I processi di Girolamo Savonarola* (Florence, 1498)

Desmond Seward, *Savonarola and the Borgia Pope* (Stroud, England, 2006)

Paul Strathern, *The Medici: Godfathers of the Renaissance* (London, 2003)

Miles J. Unger, *Magnifico: Life of Lorenzo de' Medici* (New York, 2008)

Piero Vaglienti, *Storia dei sui tempi 1492–1514*, ed. G. Berti et al (Pisa, 1982)

Pierre Van Passen, *A Crown of Fire: The Life and Times of Girolamo Savonarola* (New York, 1960)

Giorgio Vasari, *Le Vite dei piu eccelenti pittori, scultori e architetti*, 4 vols., ed. Carlo L. Ragghianti (Milan, 1943–7)

Giorgio Vasari, *Lives of the Artists*, trans. George Bull (Harmondsworth, 1965)

Pasquale Villari, *La Storia di Girolamo Savonarola e de' suoi tempi*, 2 vols. (Florence, 1887)

Pasquale Villari, *Savonarola*, 2 vols., trans. Linda Villari (London, 1888)

P. Villari and E. Casanova, *Scelta di prediche e scritti di fra Girolamo Savonarola*, etc. (Florence, 1887)

Lorenzo Violi, *Le giornate*, ed. G. C. Carfagnini (Florence, 1986)

F. Ludwig von Pastor, *The History of the Popes*, 40 vols., ed. & trans. F. I. Antrobus (London, 1950 edn)

Donald Weinstein, *Savonarola and Florence* (Princeton, 1970)

William Wordsworth, *The Prelude* (London, 1926)

Index

INDEX

INDEX

Ovid, 260

Padua, 82
Pagagnotti, Benedetto, 362–3
Palazzo del Bargello *see* Bargello, Florence
Palazzo della Signoria, Florence
  seat of government, 4, 12
  Salviati attempts to seize, 33
  renovation of, 54
  lions kept in cage behind, 66
  Savonarola delivers private sermon at, 103–4
  and Giovanni de' Medici's ceremonial procession, 119
  French detachment goes to, 190
  Piero de' Medici makes his way to, 191
  Piero denied entry to, 192
  French army passes, 203
  discussion about new constitution at, 215
  Great Hall in, 231–2, 254 and n, 340, 360
  officials watch Bonfire of the Vanities from, 262
  alleged traitors arrested at, 282
  and ordeal by fire episode, 308, 309, 316, 317, 318, 319
  proclamation offering reward for capture of Savonarola, 323
  Mazzinghi goes to, 325–6
  Savonarola and Fra Domenico taken to, 330
  the three friars brought for execution from, 362
Palazzo Medici, Florence
  and government of Florence, 12
  designed by Michelozzi, 12
  Lorenzo the Magnificent born at, 11
  intellectual and artistic circle at, 13–14, 24, 30, 61, 64, 68–9, 83, 170
  Palazzo Pitti is intended to dwarf, 20
  during conspiracy against Piero the Gouty, 21, 22
  and Lorenzo and Giovanni di Pierfrancesco de' Medici, 31, 66
  Lorenzo makes speech from, during Pazzi conspiracy, 34
  Savonarola refuses to pay courtesy visit to, 111
  Savonarola returns gifts to, 112
  ceremonial banquet for Giovanni's installation as cardinal, 120
  emotional atmosphere during rule of Piero the Unfortunate, 182
  Charles VIII is offered the use of, 187
  Piero returns from French camp to, 191
  Piero and Giovanni barricade themselves inside, 193
  Piero escapes from, 193
  Giovanni remains for short time at, 194
  Giovanni rescues valuables from, 194–5, 199
  Balsac at, 197
  protected from pillagers, 198
  fire at, 198, 199
  Charles VIII takes up residence at, 204
  Savonarola goes to Charles VIII at, 207–8
  omitted from itinerary of processions of Savonarola's boys, 248
  brief references, 81, 82, 85, 91, 94, 119, 161, 172, 181

Palazzo Pitti, Florence, 20, 22
Palazzo Tornabuoni, Florence, 285
palio of Santa Barbara, 278n, 278–9
Papal Commission, 348, 349, 352–5, 356–7, 363
Parenti, Piero, 206, 265–6, 286–7, 318, 333
Paris, 82, 299
parlamento, 4, 211, 223 and n
Party of the Hill, 20–1, 27, 29
Party of the Plain, 20
Pastor, F. Ludwig von, 59–60
Paul II, Pope, 15, 16, 27, 28
Pavia, 167, 183, 184
Pazzi bank, 32, 34
Pazzi conspiracy, 6, 33–4, 49, 50, 63, 77
Pazzi family, 32–3, 34, 49 *see also* Pazzi conspiracy
Peter, St, 350–1
Petrarch, 136, 260
Piacenza, 95
Piagnoni
  as main group of Savonarola's supporters, 231
  and Botticelli and his brother, 236–7, 299–300
  and Valori, 268, 284, 324, 326, 327
  ridiculed, 279
  measures taken to alleviate suffering of, 280
  sympathisers in post as *gonfaloniere*, 286
  sympathisers in Signoria, 298
  and ordeal by fire episode, 316, 318, 320
  aggression towards, 322
  and siege of San Marco, 324, 326, 327
  continue to support Savonarola after his arrest, 330
  sympathisers flee from the city, 331
  and Ser Ceccone, 332
  sympathisers eliminated from administration, 333, 368
  and news of Charles VIII's death, 336
  and Savonarola's confession, 337
  and public reading of Savonarola's protocol, 341
  leading supporters arrested, 341
  sympathisers rounded up and scourged, 347
  and Savonarola's execution, 364
  brief references, 238, 251, 285, 294, 297, 312, 348, 360, 369
Pianoro, 97
Piazza della Signoria, Florence
  Piero de' Medici forced to leave, 192–3
  Giovanni de' Medici and supporters forced to retreat from, 193
  parlamento in, 211–12
  citizens gather to welcome new Signoria in, 217
  Bonfire of the Vanities in, 261–2, 296
  patrolled by soldiers to prevent public demonstration, 283
  ordeal by fire, 312–13, 315, 316–21
  execution of Savonarola and two friars, 358, 362–6
Pico della Mirandola, Gianfrancesco, 82, 100, 337
Pico della Mirandola, Giovanni
  aristocratic descent, 52
  appearance, 52

[421]